Heaven on Earth

Heaven on Earth

Edited by
T. DESMOND ALEXANDER
and
SIMON GATHERCOLE

PATERNOSTER

First published in 2004 by Paternoster

09 08 07 06 05 04   7 6 5 4 3 2 1

Paternoster is an imprint of Authentic Media,
PO Box 300, Carlisle, Cumbria CA3 0QS, UK
and PO Box 1047, Waynesboro, GA 30830–2047, USA
www.paternoster-publishing.com

British Library Cataloguing in Publication Data
A catalogue record for this book is available from the British Library

ISBN 1–84227–272–1

Cover Design by FourNineZero
Typeset by Waverley Typesetters, Galashiels
Print Management by Adare Carwin
Printed and bound by J. H. Haynes & Co., Ltd.

CONTENTS

PREFACE

Heaven on Earth is a collection of essays exploring the concept of Temple in the Christian Bible. Although the term 'temple' is likely, first and foremost, to evoke images of an ancient building, the concept has for Christians a much more vital connotation: within the New Testament, the church is presented as God's Temple. Here the apostles are presented as those who lay the foundation, while others are given the responsibility for continuing the building process so that the church may be, in Paul's words, 'filled with all the fullness of God' (Eph. 3:19).

Although we are convinced of the importance of this concept within Holy Scripture, considering it to be a central theme in the field of biblical theology, we have shied away from describing this volume as 'a biblical theology of the Temple'. Rather, we have adopted a more modest subtitle, 'The Temple in Biblical Theology', for we recognize that, while the present essays go some way towards being a biblical theology of the Temple, that objective remains partially unfulfilled. The reason for this rests in the very nature of this book, essays penned by experts on various parts of the Bible. While each essay contributes something of significance to the overall enterprise, universal agreement does not exist. Here and there differing interpretations of Scripture are reflected in the opinions expressed. While some might have hoped that as editors we would have striven to produce a completely uniformed outlook, to do so would have denied the opportunity for alternative viewpoints to be expressed with conviction, allowing the readers, and not just the editors, to evaluate their respective strengths and weaknesses. Where differences occur they reflect a need for further research to be undertaken in the hope that a better synthesis of the evidence may yet be achieved. In the light of this, the opinions expressed in this volume are not always those of the editors, nor should it be assumed that the contributors stand shoulder to shoulder in support of everything that each other has said.

Much of the present volume was originally presented as papers at the July 2001 meeting of the Biblical Theology Study Group of the Tyndale Fellowship for Biblical and Theological Research in

Cambridge. Almost all of the papers have been substantially reworked for publication and additional essays have been included. To each of the contributors, for giving of their time and expertise, we are deeply indebted. Finally, we are thankful to Paternoster for their support in accepting and preparing this volume for publication. We offer it with the prayer that its contents may enable others to understand better the place of the Temple in both Scripture and God's redemptive activity.

The Editors

ABBREVIATIONS

AGJU	Arbeiten zur Geschichte des antiken Judentums und des Urchristentums
ANET	*Ancient Near Eastern Texts Relating to the Old Testament*, edited by J. B. Pritchard
AOAT	Alter Orient und Altes Testament
ArBib	The Aramaic Bible
BAGD	Bauer, W., W. F. Arndt, F. W. Gingrich and F. w. Danker, *Greek-English Lexicon of the New Testament and other Early Christian Literature*
BETL	Bibliotheca ephemeridum theologicarum lovaniensium
BNTC	Black's New Testament Commenatries
BTB	*Biblical Theology Bulletin*
CBQ	*Catholic Biblical Quarterly*
CBQMS	Catholic Biblical Quarterly Monograph Series
EBC	Expositors' Bible Commentary
EQ	*Evangelical Quarterly*
ET	*Evangelische Theologie*
HTR	*Harvard Theological Review*
ICC	International Critical Commentary
JBL	*Journal of Biblical Literature*
JCS	*Journal of Cruciform Studies*
JJS	*Journal of Jewish Studies*
JSJSup	Journal for the Study of Judaism Supplement
JSNT	*Journal for the Study of the New Testament*
JSNTSS	Journal for the Study of the New Testament: Supplement Series
JSOT	*Journal for the Study of the Old Testament*
JSOTSS	Journal for the Study of the Old Testament: Supplement Series
NIBC	New International Bible Commentary
NICNT	New International Commentary on the New Testament

NICOT   New International Commentary on the Old Testament
NovT   *Novum Testamentum*
NovTSupp   Novum Testamentum Supplements
NTS   *New Testament Studies*
SBLDS   Society of Biblical Literature Dissertation Series
SBLSP   *Society of Biblical Literature Seminar Papers*
SNTSMS   Society for New Testament Studies Monograph Series
SSEJC   *Studies in Early Judaism and Christianity*
TDNT   *Theological Dictionary of the New Testament*, edited by
           G. Kittel and G. Friedrich
THKNT   Theologischer Handkommentar zum Neuen Testament
VT   *Vetus Testamentum*
WBC   Word Biblical Commentary
WTJ   *Westminster Theological Journal*
WUNT   Wissenschaftliche Untersuchungen zum Neuen
           Testament
ZAW   *Zeitscrift für de alttestamentliche Wissenschaft*

LIST OF CONTRIBUTORS

PETER WALKER is Lecturer in New Testament at Wycliffe Hall, Oxford.

JAMES PALMER is a Doctoral Candidate at Selwyn College, University of Cambridge.

PEKKA PITKÄNEN is Course Co-ordinator for the Open Theological College, University of Gloucestershire.

CARL ARMERDING is a Fellow of the Oxford Centre for Mission Studies and formerly principal of Regent College, Vancouver.

BOB FYALL is Director of Rutherford House, Edinburgh and formerly a tutor in Biblical Studies at Cranmer Hall, St John's College, Durham.

JOHN TAYLOR, formerly Bishop of St Albans, is Chairman of the Tyndale House Council.

ROGER BECKWITH was, until his retirement, the Warden of Latimer House, Oxford.

CRISPIN FLETCHER-LOUIS is Lecturer in New Testament at the Department of Theology, Nottingham University.

PETER HEAD is Research Fellow at Tyndale House, Cambridge, and Lecturer in New Testament in the Faculty of Divinity, University of Cambridge.

BILL SALIER is Lecturer in New Testament at Moore College, Sydney, Australia.

STEVE WALTON is Lecturer in New Testament at London School of Theology.

MARK BONNINGTON is Lecturer in New Testament at Cranmer Hall, University of Durham.

DAVID PETERSON is Principal of Oak Hill College, London.

STEVE MOTYER is Lecturer in New Testament at London School of Theology.

GREG BEALE is Professor of New Testament at Wheaton College, Illinois.

DANIEL STRANGE is Staff Worker for the Religious and Theological Studies Fellowship.

JONATHAN NORGATE is a Doctoral Candidate in Systematic Theology at the University of Aberdeen.

STEPHEN SIZER is Rector of Christ Church, Virginia Water.

SIMON GATHERCOLE is Lecturer in New Testament at the University of Aberdeen.

DESMOND ALEXANDER is Director of the Magee Institute at Union Theological College, Belfast.

INTRODUCTION

PETER WALKER

It has been described as the most 'contested and strategic piece of real estate in the world'. If true, then this book is vitally important. For its subject matter is a site on the east side of the Old City of Jerusalem, some thirty-five acres in extent, which has been the cause of violent disputes and which could yet unsettle further the already volatile Middle East. We are focusing in these essays on none other than what the Bible calls the 'mountain of the LORD' (Isa. 2:2).

We live in unsettling times, and at least one of these essays makes for very disturbing reading. This introduction was first drafted exactly one week after the horror of the attack on the World Trade Center in New York. The world is still coming to terms with a new world order and the frightening clash of worldviews between the modern West and (what might be called) the ancient East. Who knows where it will end? Some suggest Jerusalem.

I was there recently. Few visitors are travelling to Jerusalem these days in the wake of the continued violence between the Israelis and Palestinians. Christian institutions, dependent on pilgrim visitors, are struggling to make ends meet and the local church feels cut off from the rest of the world. What does it mean to uphold the name of Jesus Christ in the land of his birth, surrounded by those who dismiss his claims and who, because of their alternative religious commitments, fiercely dispute the ownership of that same land?

1. THE SITE OF CONTENTION

Near to the heart of that dispute is the issue of the Temple Mount – or, in Arabic, Haram Al Sharif (the 'noble sanctuary'). For over 1,300 years it has been the site of the golden-roofed Dome of the Rock and the El-Aksa Mosque, the third-holiest site in Islam (after Mecca and Medina). Ten days after the Israeli conquest of Jerusalem in 1967 it was given back into Muslim control. The Jewish authorities instead cleared the area below and to the west, which lies in front of one of the vast Herodian supporting walls. Here is the 'Western Wall', one of the most holy places in Judaism. The two religious groups are literally side by side; both committed to the significance of this one, hard-to-share place.

The reason the Jewish people pray at the Western Wall is, of course, because this is the western wall of the enormous platform on which was located the Jewish Temple. Or was it?

That may seem a startling question. Surely everyone is agreed that the area now covered by the Dome of the Rock was where Solomon built the First Temple and Herod rebuilt the 'Second' Temple? Well, almost everyone – but not quite! Recently Ernest Martin (see below) has launched his theory that the biblical Temple was further to the south, along the Ophel Ridge. More worrying are some of the statements emanating from the Muslim guardians of the site, contending that there is not the 'slightest evidence for the existence of a Jewish Temple on this place in the past'.[1] In the light of such comments archaeologists and others may be justified in wondering if the Muslims' removal in November 1999 of 12,000 tons of ancient archaeological fill (when constructing an entrance to a new underground mosque) was partly motivated by a desire to destroy precisely that kind of evidence. So people on all sides of this debate can rewrite the annals of history, precisely because that history may affect their present claims. Once we can be sure where the Temple actually stood, then the battle is on for its rightful ownership.

2. THE SITE WITH A FUTURE?

But for some people this is not just a matter of contemporary territorial disputes rooted in the past. It is also about future destiny. For such people (and they can be Jewish, Muslim or Christian) this small patch of land is going to play a vital role in God's future for the world. (For a full exposition of this way of thinking within each of the three mono-theistic religions, see Gorenberg's *The End of Days*.)[2] In this present volume of essays, the piece by Stephen Sizer focuses on the thought of Christian Zionists. Many Christian Zionists (who ought, by the way, to be distinguished clearly on this issue from most Jewish Christians or 'messianic believers') are convinced that a new Jewish Temple must be built on this site and that this will be the scene of the Antichrist in an end-times scenario. Some then go on to support the work of such Jewish organizations as the 'Temple Mount Faithful', who are making

---

[1] Sheikh Ikrima Sabri, the Mufti of Jerusalem, as quoted in an interview in *Die Welt*, 17 January 2001.
[2] G. Gorenberg, *The End of Days: Fundamentalism and the Struggle for the Temple Mount* (New York: Simon & Schuster, 2000).

elaborate preparations for the building of just such a Temple and have occasionally tried to lay a new foundation stone for this 'Third' Temple.

There is no denying, then, that this one site has the power to trigger passion and violence. Since 1998 each of Israel's Prime Ministers (Netanyahu, Barak and Sharon) has been caught up in powerful political clashes associated with these disputes concerning the Temple Mount. It is certainly a 'contested site'. Yet there remains the question as to whether it is also, biblically, going to be a 'strategic' site in the future.

3. THE VITAL ROLE OF BIBLICAL THEOLOGY

So our current, urgent political context (both locally within Israel/ Palestine and internationally between East and West) makes it imperative that Christians examine again the biblical material relating to the Temple.

There turn out to be a host of questions in this area. Yes, those concerned with future events in Jerusalem need to be asking questions, for example, about Ezekiel's visions of a new Temple (Ezek. 40–48), and whether these still await fulfilment or have already been fulfilled in Christ. They need too to understand Jesus' teaching in the Apocalyptic Discourse and the dramatic imagery throughout the book of Revelation. But there are other questions too. For example, what was God's purpose in establishing the Tabernacle and then the Temple within Israel's worship? How did the Temple connect up to Israel's vision of God's creation? What was the precise status of the Temple as restored after the exile in the sixth century BC? How did Jesus view the Temple and how would it be changed as a result of his coming? How could the first Christians start claiming that *they* were now the true Temple?

The Bible is an open book – long may it be so! Yet it needs careful interpretation if we are to answer these questions appropriately. In this situation what is urgently needed is the science of 'biblical theology' – that is, some ground rules not only for noting the biblical material on the Temple but also for *assessing what is a valid synthesis of that material*.

This is necessary because for evangelical Christians the Bible functions not only as history, but also as revelation. It is not just *de*scriptive, but also functions *pre*scriptively, revealing to us the will of God in the present. But getting from the past text to the present meaning is not as straightforward as it might first appear, and not just because of our very different cultures. For the Bible tells a story which is not static but which is moving forward. We are forced, in other words, to locate biblical passages appropriately within the context of the developing biblical story.

Most notably, Christians speak of the *Old* Testament and the *New*. They indicate thereby an awareness of major new instalments (or episodes) within the biblical storyline. Once this is recognized, then it soon becomes clear that, for example, the 'biblical' material found in the texts of the 'Old Covenant' will need to be interpreted through the lens of the New Covenant before we can claim to have found the 'biblical' teaching appropriate for today. This means, then, that there may be many things in the Bible which are there as matters of historical record, but discerning what is 'biblical' (in the more important sense of what is *directly applicable to today*) is not the same thing.

Our task, then, is not just to read the Bible, nor even indeed to interpret a particular passage of the Bible, but rather to do biblical theology – that which processes the whole and makes sense of it for the present.

4. THE ESSAYS AND THEIR ORIGIN

These essays enable us to do just that. They both give us the relevant material and also provide instructive models for how the biblical material can be processed and applied to today. Written by experts in their specialist field, each committed to the authority of Scripture, the different essays map out some of the key points in this debate. Most essays are concerned with particular books of the Bible, but all are concerned also to locate that material within the broader sweep of the Bible's message as a whole.

All of them recognize too that the Temple is a key and major theme in biblical thought, which we neglect to our impoverishment and at our peril. An appropriate focus on this Temple theme in the Bible, they concur, will not just have some repercussions in the Middle East, but can also vastly enrich *other key themes* within biblical thought. Our understandings, for example, of ethics, anthropology, creation, God's presence and the church will be so much poorer (so much 'flatter' and less biblical) if we do not take seriously what God has to teach us through the Temple.

This is seen, above all, with our Christology – our understanding of Christ himself. Probably all the writers in this volume would find themselves in agreement with Barth's emphasis (at least, as summarized by Norgate below) that 'any attempt to investigate the meaning and significant of the Temple without primary reference to Jesus Christ would be pointless. Thus we turn to the question of the Temple with Jesus Christ as our light source'. Several of the essays (including those focused primarily on the Old Testament) make explicit this essential link between the Temple and Christ. 'Significantly, however', Norgate continues, 'in the process of turning we also will see more clearly the light source.' In other words we gain a far deeper appreciation of the Christ who is presented to us in the whole of biblical revelation – for example, as himself the 'proper presence' of God, as the place of atoning sacrifice, or as the true high priest who is the 'image of God in man' (as outlined in Fletcher-Louis's essay).

Similarly our vision of creation and God's ultimate purposes of establishing a 'new creation' are immensely enriched by noting the way the Temple almost certainly functioned in Old Testament thought as a microcosm of creation, as a recapitulation of Eden and as a foretaste of creation restored. Such ideas (developed here by both Fletcher-Louis and Beale) throw a whole new light on numerous biblical passages, which previously might have seemed obscure, and clarify so well the final vision in Revelation of the new creation (depicted as a city without a Temple because it is *all* a Temple).

Bonnington's essay takes us into another important area, that of ethics. It forcefully reminds us that the application of Temple imagery to the church is not merely an interesting 'academic' idea. Yes, as Peterson highlights, this imagery affirms that the local congregation is a manifestation of the divine sanctuary, but it also demands a transformation in our lives. The Christian church embraces both the privileges and the responsibilities of being likened to God's Temple.

Meanwhile, the essays by Strange and Norgate helpfully tease out for us some of the conundrums that are brought to the surface as soon as we reflect on the Bible's presentation of the Temple as a manifestation of God's 'special' presence. How exactly can the God who *is everywhere* (immense and omnipresent) be said also to *be somewhere* (in the Temple, in Jesus Christ, at work today by his Spirit)? It is good to have the systematicians helping us to answer those profound questions so often asked by four year olds!

Finally, as is to be expected, the essays also cover a wealth of important historical details. In the Old Testament section there are significant discussions concerning the origins of the Tabernacle in Exodus, its final location in Jerusalem, some of the ambiguities associated with the building of a permanent Temple, the varied perspectives of Chronicles and Kings, and post-exilic hopes for its rebuilding and restoration. In the New Testament section there is detailed discussion about the gospels (noting, for example, John's consistent presentation of Jesus himself as the 'gracious replacement' of the Temple) and of the book of Acts (noting how this replacement is something which was discovered gradually). Personally, I found Motyer's piece on Hebrews particularly compelling for the way it articulated so well what I am sure is correct: namely that the book of Hebrews is a sustained and conscious critique of the Jerusalem Temple, but instead talks only of the Mosaic 'Tabernacle' precisely because the writer must tread carefully in bringing his audience round to this radical point of view.[3]

---

[3] I adumbrated something similar in 'Jerusalem in Hebrews 13:9–14 and the Dating of the Epistle', *Tyndale Bulletin* 45.1 (1994), pp 39–73 (esp. pp. 60–2). This was later developed in *Jesus and the Holy City: New Testament Perspectives on Jerusalem* (Cambridge/Grand Rapids: Eerdmans, 1996), ch. 6. This book attempted a thorough investigation of the New Testament teaching on both the Temple and the city of Jerusalem. Readers will sense

So this volume is vital reading for a wide range of reasons – not just those outlined at the beginning concerning modern Jerusalem. It is in fact the third to appear in the last decade on similar themes. Within the biblical worldview the Temple lay at the heart of two further realities: the city (of Jerusalem) and the land (of Israel). Some find it helpful to think of them in terms of concentric circles. Each of these three (Temple, city and land) has now been covered in collections of essays associated with Tyndale House (the biblical research library in Cambridge, UK). *Jerusalem Past and Present in the Purposes of God* (1992) focused on the city of Jerusalem; *The Land of Promise* (2000) focused on the land.[4] It is good to see this tripartite series now coming to completion with *Heaven on Earth*. Essentially this gathers together the papers that were delivered at a meeting in Cambridge in July 2001 of the Biblical Theology Study Group within the Tyndale Fellowship.

5. LEARNING FROM EARLIER CHRISTIAN APPROACHES

Yet, as ever, there is still work to be done. For example, if there had been more time and space, it would have been fascinating to note how Christians throughout the last 2,000 years have tried to process the biblical material about the Temple. After all (despite what we may sometimes think!), we are not the first generation to face the challenge of interpreting the Bible for our own day. Strictly, of course, this is not so much 'biblical theology' as 'historical theology'. Yet as we do our own 'biblical theology' there is great merit in considering how others have gone about it before. Ever since the formation of the biblical 'canon' there has been the urgent task of 'correctly handling the word of truth' (2 Tim. 2:15) and there is much that we can learn.

If we look, briefly, at the period of the early church, for example, we can note this issue of the Temple was a live one throughout the first 600 years.[5] Until the coming of Constantine (AD 324) Christians in Palestine were content simply to look over the ruins of the Temple (destroyed

---

my substantial agreement with all the New Testament papers in this present volume, but some differences of detail between my approach and that of Head and Bonnington. I regret that only after its publication did I begin to interact with the fruitful ideas of Fletcher-Louis and Beale.

[4] P. W. L. Walker (ed.), *Jerusalem Past and Present in the Purposes of God* (Cambridge: Tyndale House, 1992; reprinted Grand Rapids/Carlisle: Baker Book House/Paternoster Press, 1994); P. Johnston and P. W. L. Walker (eds), *The Land of Promise: Biblical, Theological and Contemporary Perspectives* (Leicester/Downers Grove: Apollos/IVP, 2000).

[5] For a full discussion of Christian approaches to the Temple in the patristic period, see my *Holy City, Holy Places? Christian Attitudes to Jerusalem and the Holy Land in the Fourth Century* (Oxford: Clarendon Press, 1989), especially ch. 11, and R. L. Wilken, *The Land Called Holy: Palestine in Christian History and Thought* (New Haven: Yale University Press, 1992).

by Titus and the Roman legions in AD 70). But after that date they effectively had responsibility for thinking what should now be done with the site. Should this large area within the city be repopulated, or should at least a church be built over the ancient holy of holies? No, they decided, the whole site should be left as a vast piece of desolate waste. After all, Jesus had predicted its destruction. It was not for his followers to rebuild that which he had dismissed.

So this pile of rubble was left as a valuable visual aid, confirming Jesus' prophetic teaching and divine foreknowledge. The pioneer of this patristic biblical theology regarding the Temple was Origen (*c*.180–*c*.255), followed two generations later by Eusebius (*c*.260–*c*.339). Both these Christian scholars were residents of Caesarea on the coast of Palestine, who also made visits to Jerusalem on several occasions. Eusebius' role was particularly important as he lived to see the reign of Constantine and indeed was the Bishop of Caesarea in Palestine. So, for example, he could write:

> Believers in Christ congregate from all parts of the world, not as of old time because of the glory of Jerusalem, nor that they might worship in the ancient Temple, but that they might learn about the city being taken and devastated ...

> The greatest miracle of all is the Divine word, the foreknowledge of our Saviour ... and, just as the prediction was, so are the results in fact remaining: the whole Temple and its walls ... have suffered desolation from that time to this.[6]

For Christians in this era, the deserted Temple site confirmed Jesus' predictions that 'not one stone would be left upon another' (Mark 13:2 and parallels). Yet it also proclaimed by its eloquent silence the radical shift between the days of the Old Covenant and the New: the time of the old order, with its repeated cultic sacrifices, had become obsolete; the 'time of the new order' had arrived to stay (Heb. 8:13; 9:10). Instead Christ had 'done away with sin by the sacrifice of himself' (Heb. 9:26). He himself was also the true Temple (John 2:21), and those who believed in him and were filled with his Spirit constituted the new Temple on earth (1 Cor. 3:16). The focus of Christian

---

[6] Eusebius, *Demonstration of the Gospel* 6:18:23; *Theophany* 4:18. In the first passage (written *c*.315) Eusebius is describing Christian visitors to Jerusalem in the third century; the second passage, however, was probably written *c*.327 (that is, after the arrival of Constantine's builders) and hence functioned as Eusebius' proactive vision for how the site should be kept in ruins for the future. Both Origen and Eusebius in their major Old Testament commentaries (on Isaiah and the Psalms respectively) refer regularly to the deserted Temple site, either as a fulfilment of prophecy or (more frequently) as a pointed contrast which reveals that the ultimate referent of the biblical text is now the worldwide church or the heavenly Jerusalem. See for example Eusebius's words on Psalm 88 (*Patrologia Graeca*, J. P. Migne [ed.], vol. 23, p. 1064b).

devotion was now on the 'Jerusalem above' or the 'heavenly Jerusalem', not on the 'present city of Jerusalem' (Gal. 4:25–26; Heb. 12:22).

6. THE AREA LEFT VACANT

In the succeeding generations after AD 325 there would be many Christians (such as Cyril, the Bishop of Jerusalem from 348–384) who would begin to forge a more positive view of the *city* of Jerusalem, but their attitude towards the *Temple* remained remarkably constant. This distinction between the city and the Temple would become quite important. Eusebius had argued that Jesus' prophetic words in Luke 19:41–46 indicated his judgement upon both the Temple and city. Cyril now saw them focused exclusively on the Temple.[7] This would pave the way for the rebuilding of the city and the rehabilitation of Jerusalem within the Christian consciousness. Yet it made it even more necessary that the Temple site should then be left deserted, as the one remaining focal point which visibly endorsed Jesus' words of judgement. So the Byzantines never built on the site.

There were others in Palestine, however, who had their own alternative plans for the site. During the brief reign of Julian the 'Apostate' (361–363) some of the Jewish population in Palestine seized the opportunity of a non-Christian emperor to attempt a rebuilding of the Temple. In the end the project was aborted, but it caused quite a sensation in Jerusalem for a while.[8] Some Christians began speculating whether this was a sign of the coming of the Antichrist – evidently apocalyptic notions relating to the Temple are nothing new.

But it was a 'false dawn' and the Temple platform area would remain deserted until the seventh century, with the arrival of Islam. For the Muslims this large area of prime land, conveniently left undeveloped, was too good an opportunity to be missed. Without needing to damage the rest of the city, they could construct two impressive buildings on this commanding site, which would both emblazon the news of Mohammed's victory and also give to his followers a lasting holy site.

In this way the religious tensions, felt so keenly today, were embedded in Jerusalem's stones. Judaism (symbolized by the Temple as it existed in the days of Jesus) gave way to Christianity (the Temple

---

[7] On this vital distinction, see my *Holy City, Holy Places?*, pp. 376–401, and now 'Pilgrimage in the Early Church' in C. Bartholomew (ed.), *Explorations in a Christian Theology of Pilgrimage* (Aldershot: Ashgate, 2004).
[8] On this fascinating episode, see Wilken, *The Land Called Holy*, pp. 139–40 and a recently discovered letter attributed to Cyril of Jerusalem: see S. P. Brock, 'The Rebuilding of the Temple under Julian: A New Source', *Palestine Exploration Quarterly* 108 (1976), pp. 103–7. The Hebrew graffito carved in the Western Wall of the Temple platform, with words from Isaiah 66, may well date to the time of this incident.

area being left deserted), which in turn gave way to Islam (the Temple area being redeveloped for the El-Aksa Mosque and the Dome of the Rock). Would history have taken a very different course if, for some reason, the Byzantine Christians had instead built over the site, rather than leaving it vacant? We can never know. Yet the result was that something which was intended as a sign vindicating Jesus' prophetic power became instead an opportunity for others to promote the claims of their own, quite different, prophet.

7. AN IMPORTANT CONTRAST

This brief summary of early Christian approaches to the Temple is instructive. For it brings to the fore what may justly be called the 'classical' Christian interpretation of this theme: the Temple is valued as a central part of Old Testament revelation but is now seen as fulfilled and rendered redundant by the coming of Christ.

The biblical theology of the Temple that you will find in these pages instinctively follows this line of reasoning, highlighting what is technically referred to as either the 'Christological' or 'covenantal' approach to the Old Testament. It insists that the Old Testament must be read in the light of the New Covenant and that the Temple finds its true fulfilment in Christ.

This stands in marked contrast to the approach of dispensationalism, which appears as a relatively modern idea and is founded on what many sense is an unhelpful division between Israel and the church. If space had allowed, it would have been good to have an extended examination of dispensationalism. It is one thing to describe the end result of this way of thinking (as Sizer's essay does so well), another to lay bare the fallacies at its root. Such work needs urgently to be done.[9] But will anyone hear? Academic discussions seldom become best sellers in the same way as do books such as the current *Left Behind* series. Sensationalism in a time of anxiety is popular, but it is not always safe. It is also important that Christian academics speak to these situations and don't bury their heads in history, without seeing the relevance of their work for the present.

So, although this volume is not the last word on the subject, it is a very good place to start some serious biblical study investigating this key theme. Read this book to be moved more deeply into an understanding of the Bible, to be made aware of some key issues and to become better informed on a vital debate. For, as should now be abun-

---

[9] Some useful treatments which touch on this issue include D. E. Holwerda, *Jesus and Israel: One Covenant or Two?* (Grand Rapids/Leicester: Eerdmans/Apollos, 1995) and O. P. Robertson, *The Israel of God: Yesterday, Today and Tomorrow* (Phillipsburg: Prebyterian & Reformed, 2000).

dantly clear, this is not a merely 'academic' issue! How we interpret the Bible inevitably affects how we relate to the modern land of Israel / Palestine. And at the heart of the land lies the site of the Temple. Quite apart from this, however, we discover that the Temple is a central theme within the pages of Scripture, a right understanding of which can flood lots of light on other themes within its pages.

8. THE TEMPLE AND GOD'S PRESENCE TODAY

But, finally, a word on a brighter note. One of the most important themes associated with the Temple is that of God's presence. What we learn in these pages is that, through the mystery of the gospel, this divine presence is something which has been spread abroad from the Temple. Even now those who are in Christ are indwelt by God's presence and so can rightly be called 'living stones' within God's Temple (1 Pet. 2:5). May the reading of these pages not just inform our minds but renew our hearts with a sense of God's gracious and empowering presence with us as we face an uncertain future in this troubled world. As Jesus said, 'I am with you always even to the end of the age' (Matt. 28:20); 'My peace I give you … In this world you will have trouble, but take heart! I have overcome the world' (John 14:27; 16:33). In this lies the only true hope not just for Jerusalem, but also for New York and the 'ends of the earth'.

1
EXODUS AND THE BIBLICAL THEOLOGY
OF THE TABERNACLE

JAMES PALMER

The account of the Tabernacle in Exodus 25–40 gives the instructions that Moses received from God when he was on Mount Sinai. Chapters 25–31 describe the design of the Tabernacle, the ark, the altar and the lampstand, the making of anointing oil, incense, the priests' robes and ordination. This material is substantially repeated in chapters 35–40, showing that the Israelites were careful to obey all the commands that the LORD had given them through Moses.[1] The story of Moses at the Mountain of God (Exod. 32–34) breaks this account in two. This apparent 'interruption' in the canonical form of the book invites the reader to reflect on the relationship between the cultic life of Israel and the story of Israel. As Brevard Childs puts it: 'the canonical function of Exodus 32–34 is to place the institutions of Israel's worship within the theological framework of sin and forgiveness'.[2]

We will start by looking at the Tabernacle account, considering how it serves to provide a context for Exodus 32–34 (part 1), then turn to look at Exodus 32–34 considering how it, in turn, provides a theological framework for the cultic material (part 2). Finally, we will turn to examine briefly how the concerns of this Old Testament passage are reconfigured in John's Gospel in the light of Christ, using John 1:14 as a starting point (part 3). My thesis, put bluntly, is that the theological concerns raised by the story of Moses on Sinai are continued in Israel by means of the Tabernacle and fulfilled in and transformed by Christ.

---

[1] The text of 35–40 is not identical to 25–31, and the LXX of Exodus 35–40 is significantly shorter than the equivalent in the MT. For an outline of positions and bibliography, see E. Tov, *The Text-Critical Use of the Septuagint in Biblical Research* (Jerusalem: Simor, 1997²), pp. 256ff.

[2] B. S. Childs, *Introduction to the Old Testament as Scripture* (London: SCM Press, 1979).

1. THE ACCOUNT OF THE TABERNACLE AS CONTEXT FOR EXODUS 32–34[3]

In his study of *The Dwelling of God* Craig Koester suggests three main functions of the Tabernacle. He sees the Tabernacle as being a place of revelation, the place where sacrifices would be offered and atonement made and the place where God's presence would remain as a sign of his covenant faithfulness.[4] Koester suggests, first, that the Tabernacle was a place of revelation. This is primarily because of Exodus 25:22: 'There, above the cover between the two cherubim that are over the ark of the testimony, I will meet with you and give you all my commands for the Israelites.' The ark of the testimony is not only the focus of the Tabernacle and God's presence with Israel; it is also the focus of revelation. This function of the Tabernacle is reflected in the rest of the Pentateuch: it was the place where God made known the instructions about the different sacrifices (Lev. 1:1–17), confirmed Moses' status as a prophet (Num. 12:1–9) and foretold the future apostasy of Israel (Deut. 31:14–21; cf. 2 Chr. 1:6–13). Childs notes the continuity of the Sinai tradition and the Tabernacle on this issue, pointing out that the tablets of the Decalogue were kept in the ark, which 'testifies to the continuity between God's past revelation of his will and his ongoing, continual revelation to Israel in the Tabernacle'.[5] If, with Calvin, we see the Law as revealing the character of God,[6] then we can see the holiness of God from the fact that there needs to be sacrifice and atonement, we can see the justice of God from the fact that sin must be dealt with, not ignored, and we can see the grace and compassion of God from the fact that he provides a means of accepting his people. This category is, perhaps, the least significant of the three for our understanding of the Tabernacle. In any case, it overlaps quite substantially with the others.

The second function of the Tabernacle suggested by Koester is that it was a place where sacrifices would be offered and atonement made. He sees this as being most clearly presented in Exodus 29:38–43 and 30:7–10. The first of these two texts gives the regulations for the daily sacrifice of lambs in the Tabernacle (the *Tamid*). One lamb was to be

---

[3] For a verse-by-verse approach to the Tabernacle chapters, see N. M. Sarna, *Exodus* (JPS Torah Commentary; Philadelphia: Jewish Publication Society, 1991). See also T. D. Alexander, *From Paradise to the Promised Land: An Introduction to the Pentateuch* (Carlisle/Grand Rapids: Paternoster Press/Baker Book House, 2002²), ch. 15 and B. S. Childs, *The Book of Exodus* (OTL; Louisville: Westminster Press, 1974), pp. 512–52, 625–38.

[4] C. R. Koester, *The Dwelling of God: The Tabernacle in the Old Testament, Intertestamental Jewish Literature, and the New Testament* (CBQMS 22; Washington: Catholic Biblical Association of America, 1989), p. 7.

[5] Childs, *The Book of Exodus*, p. 541.

[6] J. Calvin, *Institutes of the Christian Religion* (tr. Henry Beveridge; London: SCM Press, 1940), especially book II, chapters 7 and 8.

sacrificed in the morning, the other at twilight (according to Josephus, between 3 p.m. and 5 p.m.).[7] The second text starts with regulations on the daily burning of incense and concludes with Exodus 30:10: 'once a year Aaron shall make atonement on [the altar's] horns. This annual atonement must be made with the blood of the atoning sin offering for the generations to come.' This last verse refers to the yearly rituals of the Day of Atonement where the incense altar is purified.[8] As with revelation, the sacrificial importance of the Tabernacle is mentioned elsewhere in the Pentateuch (e.g. Lev. 1:5; 4:7; 15:29–31; 16:1–34) and in the rest of the Old Testament (Josh. 22:19–29; 1 Chr. 16:1).[9] The Exodus Tabernacle account mentions most of the types of sacrifice,[10] which are more fully explained in Leviticus 1–7.[11] Sacrifice was central to the cultic life of Israel, expressing the Israelites' need to be clean in the sight of the holy God. Closely linked to this point is the role of the Aaronic priesthood. Exodus 28 and 29 emphasize the importance of the priesthood to the relationship of the people with the LORD. The complex rituals of the priests underlie the need for holiness before the LORD and the importance of mediation.

The third function of the Tabernacle suggested by Koester is that it was a place where God's presence would remain. This is seen explicitly in Exodus 25:8 and 29:44–46, where God says that he will dwell with his people in the Tabernacle. Exodus 25:8ff. reflects an understanding of the Tabernacle as the house of God: 'then have [the Israelites] make a sanctuary for me and I will dwell in the midst of them. Make this Tabernacle and all its furnishings exactly like the pattern I will show you.' The Tabernacle is to be made exactly according to the pattern given to Moses, highlighting the fact that it is an earthly reflection of God's heavenly dwelling (as was the common understanding in the ancient Near East, cf. Heb. 8:5). Exodus 29:44–46 goes a little further in claiming that the purpose of the exodus was that God might dwell with Israel:

> so I [the LORD] will consecrate the Tent of Meeting and the altar and will consecrate Aaron and his sons to serve me as priests. And I will dwell in the midst of the Israelites and be their God. Then they will know that I am the LORD their God, who brought them out of Egypt so that I might dwell in the midst of them. I am the LORD their God.[12]

---

[7] Josephus, *War* VI:9:3.
[8] Sarna, *Exodus*, p. 195, cf. Leviticus 16. See Alexander, *From Paradise to the Promised Land*, ch. 17, especially pp. 223ff.
[9] Koester, *The Dwelling of God*, pp. 8, 20.
[10] ḥaṭṭā't, 29:14, 36; 'ôlâ, 29:18, 42; šᵉlāmîm, 29:28; minḥâ, 29:41.
[11] See G. J. Wenham, *The Book of Leviticus* (Grand Rapids: Eerdmans, 1979), pp. 47–129, and especially 'The Theology of Leviticus', pp. 15–32.
[12] This seems to underwrite the argument used by Moses in his intercession with God (Exod. 32:11; 33:16).

This understanding of the Tabernacle as the dwelling of God has been challenged by Nahum Sarna in his commentary on Exodus. Sarna notes that the phrases *wešākantî bětôkām* ('and I will dwell in the midst of them', Exod. 25:8) and *wešākantî bětôk běnê yiśrāy'ēl* ('and I will dwell in the midst of the Israelites', Exod. 29:45) do not explicitly specify the *Tabernacle* as the place where God would dwell. He suggests that:

> the sanctuary is not meant to be understood literally as God's abode, as are other such institutions in the pagan world. Rather, it functions to make perceptible and tangible the conception of God's immanence, that is, the indwelling of the Divine Presence in the camp of Israel, to which the people may orient their hearts and minds.[13]

There are two difficulties with this way of putting things, one conceptual, the other exegetical. First, unless we wish to attribute to the text the belief that God had a material body, it is difficult to see what the implied opposition of 'literal' and 'non-literal' presence is meant to mean. Asking whether the Tabernacle is the 'literal abode of God' or not is probably incoherent. It is perhaps better to ask in what way a non-material being can dwell in a material, spatial-temporal world. Secondly, though it is true that God was present generally in the camp (e.g. Num. 5:3), the language used of the Tabernacle implies that it is rather more than the material focus of 'the conception of God's immanence'. Exodus 25–31 imply or state explicitly four times that careless behaviour related to the Tabernacle will cause death (Exod. 28:35, 43; 30:20, 21). This is not death inflicted by the community (cf. the death penalty for Sabbath breaking, Exod. 31:14ff.; 35:2), but is tied to the particular presence of God in the Tabernacle (cf. Lev. 16:2). It therefore seems acceptable to speak of God 'living' in the Tabernacle as long as it is understood that this is metaphorical and does not imply a simplistic understanding of what it might mean to say that God is present.[14] Exodus 40:34 is another significant text regarding the presence of God in the Tabernacle. There is a close parallel between this verse, where the cloud that often represents the presence of God in the Exodus (Exod. 13:21; 14:19, 24; cf. 33: 9ff.) descends on the Tent of Meeting and the glory of God fills the Tabernacle, and Exodus 24:17ff. implying that 'the presence of God which once abode on Mount Sinai, now dwells in the sanctuary and accompanies Israel on her way'.[15]

One aspect of the Tabernacle that is not brought out by Koester's categories is the link between creation and the Tabernacle. This connection is very clearly seen in the literature of the Second Temple

---

[13] Sarna, *Exodus*, p. 158.
[14] I suspect that this may be the point that concerned Sarna.
[15] Childs, *The Book of Exodus*, p. 638.

period, though is less explicit in the Old Testament itself.[16] There are two related points: the Tabernacle as 'heaven on earth' and the connections between the Tabernacle and creation and the Garden of Eden. First, there is the idea of the Tabernacle as a microcosm of creation, or 'heaven on earth'. This was the view held by, for example, Philo and Josephus, and in modern scholarship has been argued for by Jon Levenson, among others.[17] Secondly, the Tabernacle has points of comparison with creation. This can be seen, for example, in the way that Leviticus 26:11ff. uses the language of the LORD walking amongst his people in connection with the Tabernacle. This strongly recalls the Genesis account of Adam and Eve (cf. Gen. 2:15; 3:8).[18]

The general contention that the Tabernacle/Temple can be seen as strongly linked with creation is plausible on the grounds of ancient Near Eastern parallels and from the muted, though still present, witness of the Old Testament, especially when read in the light of early Jewish interpretation. However, this symbolism is not explicitly picked up and developed in Exodus and we should note Childs' opinion that there is a danger of 'failing to distinguish sharply enough between material simply found in the Old Testament and the explicit use which Israel made of this material'.[19] To put it differently, it is not clear that this reading takes the *canonical* context of the Tabernacle account of Exodus seriously enough.

2. EXODUS 32–34 AS THEOLOGICAL FRAMEWORK FOR THE TABERNACLE ACCOUNT

As it stands, the Pentateuch contains its cultic and legal material in the context of the story of creation, the Patriarchs and the early history of Israel. For this reason we have little hope of grasping the canonical significance of the Tabernacle unless we read it in its canonical context in the book of Exodus. We will focus on chapters 32–34, for though the context of the Tabernacle account is all of Exodus, these chapters break the Tabernacle account in two and may, therefore, be seen as especially important in its interpretation. In Childs' words, cited above, Exodus 32–34 provides a 'theological framework' for the interpretation of the Tabernacle account. The second chapter of Walter Moberly's *At the Mountain of God*[20] offers a 'close reading' of the story of Moses and the

---

[16] See C. T. R. Hayward, *The Jewish Temple: A Non-biblical Sourcebook* (London: Routledge, 1996), and the essay by G. K. Beale in this volume which deals with this in more depth.

[17] E.g., J. D. Levenson, *Creation and the Persistence of Evil: The Jewish Drama of Divine Omnipotence* (Princeton: Princeton University Press, 1988), especially ch. 7.

[18] See the detailed discussion of these points in Beale's essay.

[19] Childs, *The Book of Exodus*, p. 539.

[20] R. W. L. Moberly, *At the Mountain of God: Story and Theology in Exodus* (Sheffield: JSOT, 1983), pp. 32–4, 44–113.

golden calf that is to be found in Exodus 32–34. Building on Moberly's account, I intend to draw out three of the issues raised by the Moses narrative that are also dealt with by the Tabernacle material: how a holy God can live with a sinful people, the revelation and knowledge of God, and the presence of God.

One of the main concerns that Moberly raises in his reading of Exodus 32–34 is the question of how the LORD can continue to live with his people after they break the covenant, made only shortly before, by their idolatrous behaviour. Exodus 32–34 suggests three ways in which this is possible: the mediation of Moses, the nature of God and the provision of the cult. In a series of intercessions Moses persuades the LORD not to destroy his people Israel. He does this on the basis of God's reputation before the nations (Exod. 32:12; cf. Num. 14:13ff.), his promise to Abraham (Exod. 32:13; cf. Gen. 12:7; 15:5; 22:16) and his character as revealed in the Exodus (Exod. 32:11ff.). God finally relents and does not destroy the people (Exod. 32:14) because he is 'pleased with Moses and knows him by name' (Exod. 33:17). The acceptance of the people is dependant on the relationship of God with his chosen mediator.[21] This is especially the case after Israel's idolatry. The second way that the text answers the question of how God can continue to live with his people is suggested by Moses' first intercession in chapter 32. It is possible because of the character of God revealed by the exodus and the promise that was made to Abraham. The LORD can continue to live with Israel because he is a God who is:

> compassionate and gracious, slow to anger, abounding in love and faith-fulness, maintaining love to thousands and forgiving wickedness, rebellion and sin. Yet [a God] who does not leave the guilty unpunished. He punishes the children and their children for the sin of the fathers to the third and fourth generation (Exod. 34:6ff.).

God will show mercy because he is a merciful God. Thirdly, God will live with the Israelites if they keep the covenant made at Sinai by living and worshipping in conformity with the Law (Exod. 34:10–28).[22] They are not to marry or make treaties with the inhabitants of the land (Exod. 34:12, 15ff.) and they are not to be influenced by pagan worship (Exod. 34:13ff.), especially in the matter of idols (Exod. 34:17). There are also instructions about annual feasts (vv. 18, 22ff.), correct sacrifice (v. 25,

---

[21] Ibid., p. 75.
[22] See the comments on the importance of worship in these chapters in G. I. Davies, 'The Theology of Exodus' in E. Ball (ed.), *In Search of True Wisdom* (Sheffield: Sheffield Academic Press, 1999), especially pp. 143ff. More generally, see D. Peterson, *Engaging with God: A Biblical Theology of Worship* (Leicester: Apollos, 1992), ch. 1 and Y. Hattori, 'Theology of Worship in the Old Testament' in D. A. Carson (ed.), *Worship: Adoration and Action* (Grand Rapids/Carlisle: Baker Book House/Paternoster Press, 1993), pp. 21–50.
[23] Exodus 34:25 pointing to the whole cultic procedure, see Leviticus 1–7 for fuller details. Cf. n. 10 above.

possibly 19ff.)[23] and the Sabbath (v. 21).[24] Israel is to be holy as the LORD her God is holy (cf. Lev. 11:44ff.; 19:2; 20:26). Exodus 32–34 presents two pictures of worship, one idolatrous, the other true.[25] The making of the golden calf and the worship offered to it form a paradigm of false worship. However, the theophany of Exodus 34:6–7 leads to Moses worshipping the LORD in a way that may also be paradigmatic. Moses' worship is in response to the LORD's self-revelation (Exod. 34:8) and it is worship of the LORD alone. The commandments which follow are primarily focused on correct worship: Israel is not to worship other gods, as the LORD is a jealous God (Exod. 34:14). There is a pointed reminder a few verses later that the people should not make any idols.[26]

A second area of concern in these chapters is the question of the revelation of God. This is most apparent in Exodus 33. In verse 18 Moses asks if he can see God's glory. God responds: 'I will cause my goodness to pass in front of [Moses] and I will proclaim my name the LORD in [Moses'] presence. I will have mercy on whom I will have mercy and I will have compassion on whom I will have compassion' (Exod. 33:19). God's promise to do this is kept in Exodus 34:6ff., where he passes in front of Moses. The covenant name 'the LORD' is tied to the special relationship of God with Israel, so it is appropriate that it is used after God has accepted Israel back after her unfaithfulness. The glory of God is revealed in moral terms, that is, in the goodness, mercy, compassion, grace, faithfulness, patience, love and justice of God. Moses is told that he can only see God's back and not his face (Exod. 33:20, 23). This apparently contradicts Exodus 33:11, where we are told that 'the LORD would speak to Moses face to face, as a man speaks with his friend'.

The 'contradiction' of Exodus 33:11 and 33:20, 23 is initially problematic. It could be that the two texts come from sources that disagreed over whether God's face could be seen ('E' and 'J'?). If this were true, it would only be another way of putting the problem: what, then, did the final redactor of the text mean by putting two apparently contradictory texts in the same chapter? Perhaps one statement is 'literal' and the other 'non-literal', though it must be admitted that there is no clear way of deciding which is 'literal' and which is not, or indeed what 'literal' might mean in this context. Both statements are supported elsewhere in the canon: Numbers 12:8 and Deuteronomy 5:4, 34:10 say that Moses spoke with God face to face, Genesis 32:30 [Heb. 32:31], Judges 6: 22ff. and 13:22 all assume that seeing God leads to death. Privileging

---

[24] The Sabbath was a sign of covenant (Exod. 31:13) and witnessed to the holiness of Israel. It was closely tied to the Tabernacle, as shown by the bracketing of the Sinai narrative with Sabbath commands (Exod. 31:12–18; 35:1–3): Childs, *The Book of Exodus*, pp. 541ff.

[25] Peterson, *Engaging with God*, pp. 30–42.

[26] *Massēkâ*, as in Exodus 32:4.

one claim over the other (especially if we feel this to be 'obvious') is arbitrary. More significant, perhaps, is the fact that *both* statements are metaphors that speak of God on the basis of a human model,[27] though we still need to account for the 'contradictory' nature of the metaphors. In the light of the subject matter, it seems probable that the intention was to point to the reality and intimacy of Moses' knowledge of God whilst at the same time stressing its limits and the fact that knowledge of God is not straightforward. The dynamic of affirmation and denial has similarities with a later stream of Christian theology ('negative theology').[28]

This 'contradiction' may be read as a good illustration of the nature of the 'reality depicting' capability of metaphor and the limits of human knowledge of God. In her *Metaphor and Religious Language* Janet Soskice points out that 'The great divine and the great poet have this in common: both use metaphor to say that which can be said in no other way but which, once said, can be recognised by many.'[29] The bold 'contradictory' metaphors used in this narrative do just this. Moses is able to see God's face yet is shielded from the glory of God so that he does not see God's face, for this would kill him. This language of 'facing' God suggests powerfully to the imagination that Moses could know God truly and intimately, yet not exhaustively. Exodus 34:6–7 is the fullest expression of the character of God in the Old Testament and it is remarkable that this revelation of his character is marked so strongly by the emphasis on the limitation of this revelation.[30]

The final area that I wish to emphasize from these chapters is the presence of God. This may be seen most clearly in the crucial revelation of Exodus 34:6–7, which is articulated primarily in terms of God proclaiming his name to Moses (Exod. 33:19; cf. 34:5). The two ideas of revelation and presence are very closely related: for God to reveal himself is for him to be present in some way.[31] The presence of God in these chapters is tied to a specific place. This is either the tent of meeting, which Moses would pitch outside the camp (Exod. 33:7–11; possibly 34:34), or, as in the case of the theophany of Exodus 34:6–7, at Sinai. In chapter 32 Moses ascends the mountain and the people make an idol (Exod. 32:1ff.). Judging from Aaron's words 'these are

---

[27] J. M. Soskice, *Metaphor and Religious Language* (Oxford: Clarendon Press, 1985), p. 55.

[28] See the exposition of the Latin *'via negativa'*, which suggests that Exodus may have been one of its sources, in D. Turner, *The Darkness of God* (Cambridge: Cambridge University Press, 1995). Cf. the reference in n. 38.

[29] Soskice, *Metaphor and Religious Language*, p. 153.

[30] I owe this last point to R. W. L. Moberly's biblical theology lectures in Durham, 1999–2000. See also R. W. L. Moberly, 'How May we Speak of God? A Reconsideration of the Nature of Biblical Theology', *Tyndale Bulletin* 53.2 (2002), pp. 198–9.

[31] This may be seen in the way that the Lord speaks with Moses, Exodus 32:7, 9, 33; 33:1, 9, 11, 14, 17, 19, 21; 34:1, 6, 10, 27, 34; cf. Deuteronomy 4:12. See the comments of Strange in this volume.

your gods O Israel who brought you up out of Egypt' (Exod. 32:4), the Israelites seem to understand the calf's role as representing the LORD, or as mediating his presence. Aaron then announces a festival to the LORD in the presence of the calf idol; it is seen as the way in which God is present with his people. Moberly suggests that the golden calf also serves as a replacement for Moses, since 'it arises out of the prolonged absence of Moses on the mountain', and like Moses it is said to have brought the people out of Egypt (Exod. 32:1, 4).[32] In Exodus 34:29–35 Moses returns the second time from Sinai and his face is shining from his exposure to the LORD. He reflects and mediates to the people the glory of the LORD: 'the implication is that the Israelites see the glory of Yahweh in the face of Moses. As Moses was not able to see the face of Yahweh, so the Israelites can hardly endure to look on the face of Moses (v. 30) ...'[33]

The positioning of this narrative, which is concerned with questions of how God can be present with and reveal himself to a rebellious people, in the middle of the Tabernacle account serves to ground our understanding of the cultic life of Israel in the story of Israel: 'the function of the Tabernacle was to create a portable Sinai, a means by which a continual avenue of communication with God could be maintained'.[34] Just as the cloud of God's glory covered mount Sinai (Exod. 24:15), so the cloud covered and filled the Tabernacle (Exod. 40:34ff.), indicating God's presence with Israel. In Childs' words, 'what happened at Sinai is continued in the Tabernacle'.[35]

3. CHRIST AS TABERNACLE IN THE GOSPEL OF JOHN

John's Gospel makes it very clear that it considers the Old Testament to be a book about Jesus. This is seen explicitly in John 5, which reports the encounter between Jesus and the Jews. Jesus attacks what was, in effect, a non-Christological reading of the Old Testament, saying that the Scriptures testified about him and that if the Jews believed Moses, as they claimed to, they would believe Jesus, for Moses wrote about him (John 5:39, 46). It is also implicit in the fact that John draws so deeply on the Old Testament institutions and events to articulate the significance of the life and death of Jesus. The prologue to John also contains one of the relatively rare allusions to the Tabernacle in the New Testament.[36] We are told that: 'The Word became flesh and

---

[32] Moberly, *At the Mountain of God*, p. 46.
[33] Ibid., p. 106.
[34] Sarna, *Exodus*, p. 237.
[35] Childs, *The Book of Exodus*, p. 540.
[36] The others are found in Acts, Hebrews and Revelation. See the relevant chapters of this volume.

tabernacled[37] among us. We have seen his glory, the glory of the One and Only, who came from the Father, full of grace and truth' (John 1:14). We now turn to look at how the theological significance of the Tabernacle is reworked around the person of Christ by John. To put the point somewhat differently: what does John mean when he says that Jesus 'tabernacled' amongst us? We will look at this question using the three categories suggested by Koester: revelation, sacrifice and atonement, and divine presence. It is quite impossible in this context fully to examine these three concepts in John's theology, yet it seems inappropriate to offer a biblical-theological reading of the Tabernacle account without some hints as to how it fits with the New Testament and broader theological questions.

John's Gospel is, on any account, concerned with the concept of revelation. This is apparent in many different ways, though summarized in the idea that the glory of the Father is exclusively revealed through the Son (John 1:14, 18; 12:45; 14:6, 9 etc.). The revelation is made most fully in the incarnation and passion. However, the Father is not revealed to all, for even though many look, few actually see (John 1:5). Jesus' death and resurrection are tied together as his 'glorification' (John 7:39; 12:16, 23; 13:31ff.): in the cross we see in the most profound way how the grace, compassion, mercy and love of God are a revelation of the glory of God. John's theology of glory is a theology of the cross; the glory of God is seen in the shame of the cross. This is a denial of the world's understanding of what 'glory' looks like.[38]

The second area for consideration is sacrifice. John twice calls Jesus the Lamb of God (John 1:29, 36),[39] picking up the sacrificial ideas of the cult and much early Christianity.[40] However, he does not have a developed articulation of this in the same way as, for example, Paul. As

---

[37] This is a deliberately tendentious translation of the Greek *skenoo* (to dwell). See the essay by Bill Salier in this volume for arguments for the link between this part of the prologue and Exodus 25–40.

[38] 'The man who perceives the visible rearward parts of God as they are seen in suffering and the cross does, however, deserve to be called a theologian.' Luther, Thesis 20 of the Heidelberg Disputation. (Note the clear allusion to Exod. 33ff.) See the exposition of Luther's theology of the cross in A. E. McGrath, *Luther's Theology of the Cross* (Oxford: Blackwell, 1985), chs 5 and 6, especially pp. 149ff. It is especially interesting that Rowan Williams (in the section on Luther in *The Wound of Knowledge* [London: Darton, Longman & Todd, 1990²], pp. 140–61, esp. p. 149) refers to Luther's *theologia crucis* as 'an experiential and historically orientated restatement of the tradition of negative theology'.

[39] See the discussion in C. K. Barrett, *The Gospel According to St John: An Introduction with Commentary and Notes on the Greek Text* (London: SPCK, 1978²), pp. 176ff.

[40] See M. Turner, 'Atonement and the Death of Jesus in John – Some Questions to Bultmann and Forestall', *EQ* 62.2 (1990), pp. 99–122, p. 121. Note that Richard Bauckham's thesis that the gospels were not 'community dependant' in the way envisaged by much New Testament scholarship would serve to strengthen the point that John was alluding to the wider understanding of the death of Christ. Cf. R. Bauckham (ed.), *The Gospels for all Christians* (Edinburgh: T&T Clark, 1998), especially ch. 5.

is well known, Bultmann thought that John had subsumed the death of Jesus under the general category of revelation.[41] In one place he goes as far as to say that the idea of Jesus' death as an offering for sin 'plays no part' in John's understanding.[42] Though it is quite true that John does primarily think of salvation and eternal life in terms of revelation, Bultmann's statements are too sweeping and one sided.[43] For, as Caiaphas misunderstood so well,[44] it is better for one man to die than for the whole nation to perish (John 11:50; 18:14; cf. also John 6:51; 10:15). The related cultic aspect of worship is now refocused as worship of Jesus in response to this fuller revelation of God in Christ (John 20:28; cf. 9:38), just as Moses worshipped the LORD in response to the revelation he had received (Exod. 34:6–8). Worship is not to be tied to the Temple on the mountain (John 4:21), but is to take place in Spirit and truth (John 4:23). Nor is it tied to festivals, since Jesus 'fulfils' the Sabbath (John 5), the Passover (John 6), the Feast of Tabernacles (John 7–9) and the Dedication of the Temple (John 10; cf. 1 Macc. 4:41–61).[45]

The last of the three functions of the Tabernacle in Koester's scheme is that of God's presence. For John this is seen most obviously in the incarnation, which he describes as the 'tabernacling' of God with his people (John 1:14): the presence of God is no longer tied to places or buildings, but to a person. Jesus is the new Tabernacle, the new Temple and the new Bethel (John 1:14; 1:51; 2:22; cf. Gen. 28:16). After the glorification of Jesus the presence of God is primarily mediated through the Spirit of Jesus (John 14:16–18; 15:26). In fact, the Spirit cannot come until Jesus has returned to the Father (John 7:39; 16:7). Thus God in Christ lives in his church by means of his Spirit. As in the Exodus material, there is an awareness of the difficulty of divine presence language, especially the tension between presence and absence: Jesus' ongoing presence in the church is dependent on his 'literal' absence.

These outlines of a biblical-theological reading of the Tabernacle raise important theological and philosophical questions. The main issue at stake seems to be that of the presence of God and the related questions of under what conditions God can be present and in what way he is present. The answer to these questions would need to consider many interrelated areas: how God relates to creation (matter, time and

---

[41] R. Bultmann, *Theologie des Neuen Testaments* (Tübingen: J. C. B. Mohr UTB [Paul Siebeck], 1984), p. 406: '*der Tod Jesu ist unter den Offenbarungsgedanken gestellt; in ihm handelt Jesus selbst als der Offenbarer und ist nicht das leidende Objekt einer göttlichen heilsverantstaltung*'.

[42] Ibid., p. 407. '*Jedenfalls spielt der Gedanke vom Tode Jesu als dem Sühnopfer bei Johannes keine Rolle; und sollte er ihn aus der Gemeindetradition übernommen haben, so wäre er bei ihm ein Fremdkörper.*'

[43] See Turner, 'Atonement and the Death of Jesus in John' and J. Ashton, *Understanding the Fourth Gospel* (Oxford: Clarendon Press, 1991), ch. 13, especially pp. 485–501.

[44] D. A. Carson, 'Understanding Misunderstandings in the Fourth Gospel', *Tyndale Bulletin* 33 (1982), pp. 59–89.

[45] Peterson, *Engaging with God*, p. 100.

space); what difference the doctrines of incarnation and Trinity might make to our articulation of the problem; and how discussions of the Eucharist and the church might effect and be effected by our answers to these questions. All this would serve as an exposition of the statement that, as God dwelt with his people in the Tabernacle, he dwelt – and dwells – with his people in Christ.

2

FROM TENT OF MEETING TO TEMPLE

Presence, Rejection and Renewal of Divine Favour[1]

PEKKA PITKÄNEN

1. DIVINE PRESENCE AND THE ROLE OF THE TENT OF MEETING AND THE TEMPLE

1.1 Ancient Near Eastern background

In order to understand the meaning and role of the tent of meeting and the Temple in Israel, we shall examine how the Israelites understood divine presence in relation to them. As the Israelites shared a common cultural background with their surrounding nations, we shall first make an overview of ancient Near Eastern concepts of divine presence in order to see how these can help us understand Israelite concepts better.

In the ancient Near East gods were thought to be present both in heaven and on earth. The Mesopotamian sun god Shamash was present in heaven in the sun,[2] Ishtar was seen as the goddess of the morning and evening stars,[3] and ancient Near Eastern mythologies clearly speak of various actions of gods in the heavenly realm. On the other hand, the most important and conspicuous place where a god could be present on the earth was a temple, and a temple was considered an earthly house of a god. The presence of a god in a temple occurred through a cult object, which could either be an anthropomorphic[4] or a theriomorphic[5] statue representing the

---

[1] Adapted from P. M. A. Pitkänen, *Central Sanctuary and the Centralization of Worship in Ancient Israel from the Settlement to the Building of Solomon's Temple* (Piscataway, NJ: Gorgias Press, 2003), pp. 25–67, 127–58.
[2] See, e.g., T. Jacobsen, 'The Graven Image' in P. D. Miller, Jr and S. D. Hanson (eds), *Ancient Israelite Religion: Essays in Honor of Frank Moore Cross* (Philadelphia: Fortress Press, 1987), pp. 15–32 (p. 17).
[3] Ibid., pp. 17–18.
[4] So especially in Mesopotamia.
[5] So often in Egypt, see e.g. E. Hornung, 'Ancient Egyptian Religious Iconography' in J. M. Sasson (ed. in chief), *Civilizations of the Ancient Near East III* (New York: Scribners, 1995), pp. 1711–30.

god, a divine symbol[6] or a cult stela.[7] The cult object was made and dedicated to provide a locus for the god's presence.[8] The presence of the god in the cult object was usually seen as continuous.[9]

A god's presence in heaven and earth could be simultaneous. This is demonstrated by the fact that, for instance, the sun god Shamash still remained in the sky even if he was present in his sanctuary.[10] Also, a god could be simultaneously present in more than one locality on earth.[11]

The favour of the gods was important for the prosperity of the people concerned, and the favourable disposition of a god was connected with its presence. The worst that could happen to a city or land was that its god or gods would become angry. Such an anger would in general be a portent of a catastrophe, such as an enemy invasion and the destruction of the city or land. A number of Sumerian laments and other texts describe gods abandoning their temples and the troubles that ensue.[12] A violation of a god's sanctuary or the sin of a ruler or people could be the cause of divine abandonment, even though there are also examples where no clear reason for divine temple abandonment is given.[13]

Mesopotamian divine temple abandonment often involved the departure of the image from the temple in question.[14] As Block des-

---

[6] For Egypt, see Hornung, 'Ancient Egyptian Religious Iconography'; for Mesopotamia, see A. Green, 'Ancient Mesopotamian Religious Iconography' in Sasson (ed.), *Civilizations of the Ancient Near East III*, pp. 1837–55.

[7] See T. N. D. Mettinger, *No Graven Image?: Israelite Aniconism in its Ancient Near Eastern Context* (CBOTS 42; Stockholm: Almqvist & Wiksell, 1995); see also M. Hutter, 'Kultstelen und Baityloi: Die Ausstrahlung eines syrischen religiösen Phänomens nach Kleinasien und Israel' in B. Janowski, K. Koch and G. Wilhelm (eds), *Religionsgeschichtliche Beziehungen zwischen Kleinasien, Nordsyrien und dem Alten Testament* (OBO 129; Freiburg/Göttingen: Universitätsverlag/Vandenhoeck & Ruprecht, 1993), pp. 87–108.

[8] See e.g. Jacobsen, 'The Graven Image'; D. Lorton, 'The Theology of Cult Statues in Ancient Egypt' in M. B. Dick (ed.), *Born in Heaven, Made on Earth: The Making of the Cult Image in the Ancient Near East* (Winona Lake: Eisenbrauns, 1999), pp. 123–210.

[9] For exceptions, see Lorton, 'The Theology of Cult Statues in Ancient Egypt', pp. 179–201; cf. Hornung, 'Ancient Egyptian Religious Iconography', pp. 72–3, 95–6.

[10] See Jacobsen, 'The Graven Image', pp. 17–18; Lorton, 'The Theology of Cult Statues in Ancient Egypt'.

[11] Jacobsen, 'The Graven Image', p. 17; Lorton, 'The Theology of Cult Statues in Ancient Egypt', p. 134, n. 14.

[12] For an overview of these, see D. Block, *The Gods of the Nations: Studies in Ancient Near Eastern National Theology* (ETS Monograph Series 2; Jackson, Mississippi: Evangelical Theological Society, 1988).

[13] See ibid.

[14] See ibid., pp. 134–5; J. J. Niehaus, *God at Sinai: Covenant and Theophany in the Bible and Ancient Near East* (Carlisle: Paternoster Press, 1995), pp. 139–40. On the other hand, the entrance of the god into the temple (*tērubat bītim*) forms the high point of temple dedication ceremonies (see e.g. V.[A.] Hurowitz, *I Have Built You an Exalted House: Temple Building in the Bible in Light of Mesopotamian and Northwest Semitic Writings* [JSOTSS 115; Sheffield: Sheffield Academic Press, 1992]).

cribes it, even if the event was on the human level to be seen simply as a spoliation of the image, on the cosmic level the party which had lost the image interpreted the event as the god himself having arranged it.[15] If the image was received back, it was interpreted as a sign that the god returned of its own volition.[16]

Thus it is clear that it was important for the ancient Near Eastern people to secure divine favour and presence. In this, the cult of the god was instrumental.[17] The principal locality where the cult took place especially in Egypt and Mesopotamia was the temple where, as discussed above, the god was considered to be present.[18]

Divine presence was also important for war and for oaths and treaties. Statues or divine emblems were carried by the king to the battle.[19] Oaths were taken in a temple or at the vicinity of a divine emblem in Old Babylonian times.[20] Treaties were typically deposited in the presence of gods, and this often naturally implies a sanctuary or sanctuaries of these gods as a place of deposit.[21]

We may summarize that in the ancient Near East divine presence was an important aspect of religious life. It guaranteed safety and prosperity, including in times of war, and was important regarding the making of oaths and treaties. A god could be present on earth above all through its image (or symbol), and a temple was an earthly house of a god where the god resided through its image (or symbol).

1.2 *The role of the ark, the Tent of Meeting and the Temple*

Having clarified general ancient Near Eastern conceptions of divine presence, we may state that the ark of the covenant was the Israelite functional equivalent of an ancient Near Eastern god image,[22] and that

---

[15] Block, *The Gods of the Nations*, pp. 134–5.

[16] Ibid., p. 135.

[17] See F. A. M. Wiggermann, 'Theologies, Priests, and Worship in Ancient Mesopotamia' in Sasson (ed.), *Civilizations of the Ancient Near East III*, pp. 1857–70; H. te Velde, 'Theology, Priests, and Worship in Ancient Egypt' in ibid., pp. 1731–49 (p. 1731); G. McMahon, 'Theology, Priests, and Worship in Hittite Anatolia' in ibid., pp. 1981–95 (p. 1993).

[18] See Wiggermann, 'Theologies, Priests, and Worship in Ancient Mesopotamia', p. 1859; McMahon, 'Theology, Priests, and Worship in Hittite Anatolia', p. 1981.

[19] See especially B. Pongratz-Leisten, K. Deller and E. Bleibtreu, 'Götterstreitwagen und Götterstandarten: Götter auf dem Feldzug und ihr Kult im Feldlager', *Baghdader Mitteilungen* 23 (1992), pp. 291–356.

[20] See, e.g., Codex Hammurabi, §§ 9, 23; J. N. Postgate, *Early Mesopotamia: Society and Economy at the Dawn of History* (London and New York: Routledge, 1992), pp. 280–1.

[21] See, e.g., G. Beckman, *Hittite Diplomatic Texts* (SBL Writings from the Ancient World 7; Atlanta: Scholars Press, 1996), p. 125 (§ 6–7) regarding a treaty between Ramses II and Kupanta-Kurunta.

[22] Cf. P. D. Miller, Jr and J. J. M. Roberts, *The Hand of the Lord: A Reassessment of the 'Ark Narrative' of 1 Samuel* (Baltimore and London: Johns Hopkins University Press, 1977), p. 9 and *passim* on this role of the ark.

the Tent of Meeting and the Temple of Solomon were the equivalent of an ancient Near Eastern temple as a house of god.[23] This can be seen in a number of ways. First, if we think of the biblical accounts of the building of the Tabernacle and the building of the Temple in the Old Testament, in both cases Yahweh's *kābôd* takes residence in the new building after the ark has been brought into the Tabernacle or the Temple (see Exod. 40:21, 34–35 for the Tabernacle; 1 Kgs. 8:6–10 [cf. 2 Chr. 5] for the Temple).[24] Thus, the bringing in of the ark to the Tent of Meeting/Temple corresponds to an Assyrian *tērubat bītim*, the entry of the god to the house.[25] On the other hand, when the ark is captured from the Israelites at the battle of Aphek (1 Sam. 4), Phinehas's wife, at her last, utters *gālâ ḵāḇôḏ miyyiśrāʾēl* (1 Sam. 4:21, 22), signalling that Yahweh has left the land.[26] Similarly, there is a description of the departure of God's *kābôd* in Ezekiel 8–11 from the Temple before its destruction by the Babylonians.[27]

Furthermore, the role of the ark in battle is similar to that of ancient Near Eastern divine symbols. According to Numbers 10:33–36 Yahweh's actions are connected with the movements of the ark. In Numbers 14:41–45 the ark, and thus the presence of Yahweh, does not move with the people, resulting in defeat (cf. Deut. 1:42). In Joshua 1–8 the ark is carried in front of the people (e.g. Josh. 3:6; 6:8–9) and in 1 Samuel 4:7, when the ark comes to the Israelite camp, the Philistines are described as being afraid because God has come to the camp.[28]

Yet differences between the ark and ancient Near Eastern god images make the ark a unique cult object. Whereas most of the ancient Near Eastern god images were anthropomorphic (or perhaps theriomorphic) representations of the corresponding deity, the ark is not a representation of Yahweh or what he might look like, in line with the aniconic character of Israel's religion (Exod. 20:4–5; Deut. 5:8–9; cf. Deut. 4:12–19).[29] Also, whereas in the ancient Near East gods take their

---

[23] Cf. M. Haran, *Temples and Temple-Service in Ancient Israel: An Inquiry into the Character of Cult Phenomena and the Historical Setting of the Priestly School* (Oxford: Clarendon Press, 1978), according to whom the tent of meeting was a 'portable temple'.

[24] So expressly Hurowitz, *I Have Built You an Exalted House*, pp. 267–8.

[25] See ibid., pp. 260–77. See also Miller and Roberts, *The Hand of the Lord*, pp. 79–81 for a text describing the entrance of Marduk to Babylon.

[26] Cf. T. N. D. Mettinger, *The Dethronement of Sabaoth: Studies in the Shem and Kabod Theologies* (CBOTS 18; Lund: CWK Gleerup, 1982), p. 121; Miller and Roberts, *The Hand of the Lord*, pp. 64, 66.

[27] See Block, *The Gods of the Nations*, pp. 150–9; see also Mettinger, *The Dethronement of Sabaoth*, pp. 97–103. One should also note that even though the ark is not mentioned in the passage, it was lost at the time of the destruction of the First Temple.

[28] Cf. Miller and Roberts, *The Hand of the Lord*, pp. 32–36 for 1 Samuel 4:1–12. Note also that in 2 Samuel 11:11 the ark accompanies the Israelites on their campaign to Rabbah.

[29] One should also note that there is no record of a ritual for the initiation of the ark such as the 'opening of mouth' rituals of the ancient Near East (for these, see e.g. Jacobsen, 'The Graven Image'; Lorton, 'The Theology of Cult Statues in Ancient Egypt').

residence *in* the god image, Yahweh is not present *in* the ark but *at* the ark. Yet it is not clear how Yahweh is present at the ark. The expression *yōšēb hakkerūbîm* (1 Sam. 4:4) does not indicate any specific location as the preposition is missing.[30] One should also note that there existed only one ark of the covenant, the symbol of Yahweh's presence. This strongly implies that there could at one time be only one 'house of Yahweh' where the ark and thus Yahweh himself would be present. This of course does not take away the possibility that Yahweh could manifest himself in a theophany, as he did to Elijah at Horeb (1 Kgs. 19) and at other places and occasions during the history of Israel. Nevertheless, the Tent of Meeting containing the ark as the *locus specificus* is *the* place where Yahweh dwells among his people Israel (Exod. 25:8),[31] and the same applies to the Temple of Solomon (1 Kgs. 8:10–13).

We should also note here that ancient Near Eastern parallels suggest rather that Deuteronomy does not deny the presence of Yahweh in the Temple or the Tent of Meeting, given that there is no explicit denial of Yahweh's presence in a sanctuary in Deuteronomy.[32] The picture of the ark in Deuteronomy is compatible with Yahweh's divine presence at the ark, especially as the Law tablets are deposited in the ark (Deut. 10:1–5; 31:26; cf. Exod. 25:21) in line with the ancient Near Eastern custom of depositing treaty tablets in the divine presence.[33] Furthermore, we have to remember that heaven, especially in Egypt, was the primary dwelling place of gods,[34] and consequently it would not be odd if Deuteronomy emphasized this aspect of divine presence.

---

[30] Cf. M. H. Woudstra, *The Ark of the Covenant from Conquest to Kingship* (PhD Thesis, Philadelphia, Westminster Theological Seminary, 1961), pp. 85–7. Note, however, Exodus 25:22.

[31] Cf. also J. Joosten, *People and Land in the Holiness Code: An Exegetical Study of the Ideational Framework of the Law in Leviticus 17–26* (Leiden: E. J. Brill, 1996), pp. 125–7, referring especially to Leviticus 26:11.

[32] For a review of the problem of divine presence in Deuteronomy, including history of scholarship, see J. G. McConville and J. G. Millar, *Time and Place in Deuteronomy* (JSOTSS 179; Sheffield: Sheffield Academic Press, 1994), pp. 110–16. See also G. von Rad, *Studies in Deuteronomy* (Studies in Biblical Theology 9; Chicago: Henry Regnery Company, 1953), pp. 37–44 (English translation of *Deuteronomium-Studien* [Göttingen: Vandenhoeck & Ruprecht, 1948]); M. Weinfeld, *Deuteronomy and the Deuteronomic School* (Winona Lake: Eisenbrauns, 1972), pp. 191–209; I. Wilson, *Out of the Midst of the Fire: Divine Presence in Deuteronomy* (SBL Dissertation Series; Atlanta: Scholars Press, 1995).

[33] Also, for instance, if the Deuteronomic editor of 2 Samuel 7 or 1 Kings 8 wanted to polemicize against Yahweh's dwelling on earth, one has to consider his polemics as very clumsy, since he left intact 2 Samuel 7:5–7 and 1 Kings 8:10–13, which affirm Yahweh's presence on earth.

[34] According to Lorton, 'The Theology of Cult Statues in Ancient Egypt', p. 134, n. 14, 'considering only the example of the sun-god, it should be obvious that the essence of the deity was first and foremost in the sun itself, while only part of it could be in his cult statue'.

In summary, the ark and the Tent of Meeting/Temple are analogous to ancient Near Eastern god images and temples. Yahweh is
continually present on earth at the ark, which is normally kept in the
Tent of Meeting or Temple, the house of Yahweh.

1.3 Local altars

In order to understand further the role of the Tent of Meeting and
Temple, let us consider the function of local altars. The main passage
dealing with local altars is the altar law of Exodus 20:22–26. If we look at
Exodus 20:22–26 from the standpoint of divine presence, first of all, we
should note that an altar is generally associated with offerings and thus
cult, whether private or public. Also, the cultic activities of an ancient
Near Eastern temple and of the Israelite Tent of Meeting/Temple were
intended to occur in the divine presence. Throughout the ancient Near
East and in Israel divine presence was associated with blessing (cf. Lev.
26:11) and they are clearly linked in the context of Exodus 20:22–26.
Exodus 20:24 indicates that Yahweh will 'come' to the worshipper and
bless the worshipper in every place where he 'causes his name to be
remembered'.

In the context of the altar law of Exodus 20:22–26, this means that
Yahweh will be present at an altar described in the passage, if the
altar is erected at a suitable place and offerings offered on it. In other
words, an altar, as described in Exodus 20:22–26, acts as a *locus* at which
Yahweh's presence is manifested.[35]

Also, when we recall that in the ancient Near East gods were usually
perceived as dwelling in heaven, Yahweh's 'coming' suggests that he
'comes' to the local altar from heaven and not from another earthly
locality.[36] The earthen altar serves as a meeting place between heaven
and earth.

---

[35] Cf. B. A. Levine, '*Lpny YHWH* – Phenomenology of the Open-Air-Altar in Biblical
Israel' in *Biblical Archaeology Today, 1990: Proceedings of the Second International Congress
on Biblical Archaeology* (Jerusalem: IES/Keterpress, 1993), pp. 196–205 (p. 199), who
states, 'In the earliest performances of cultic rites associated with outdoor altars, it
was assumed that the deity was not automatically to be found at the site of worship.'
Moreover, according to Levine (ibid., p. 204), in a relevant place, the 'dramatic appearance of the deity in response to sacrificial worship' is 'a phenomenon which occurs
anew each time the deity is ritually invoked, or attracted', and, 'This is what it meant
to say that a worshipper stood *lpny YHWH* "in the presence of YHWH"' (cf. ibid., pp.
199–203).
[36] Cf. Levine (ibid., p. 199), who suggests that the deity which normally resides in
the heavens descends to earth and arrives at the site in response to his worshippers.
Levine also points out Genesis 18:21–22 (Yahweh's descent to Sodom and Gomorrah);
Micah 1:3 (Yahweh's descent to tread the high places of the earth); Judges 13:20
(Manoah and the angel's ascent heavenward in the sacrificial flame of fire); 1 Kings
18:24, 38 (the fire from heaven at Carmel) and Genesis 28 (the ascension and descen-
sion of angels between heaven and earth and the descent and presence of Yahweh with

Moreover, it is by no means clear how Yahweh 'comes' to be present in the place where the altar is. Whereas Yahweh is somehow localized above the ark, there is no indication of Yahweh's exact location or mode of presence when he 'comes' to the worshipper. This suggests that Yahweh is rather present freely at the location, and this is compatible with the accounts of Yahweh's theophanies outside the context of local altars, the ark, the Temple and the Tent of Meeting.[37] This freedom of Yahweh gives further ground for the prohibition of images, as an image is a cult object inside which a deity takes its dwelling. Images are not necessary as *loci* of Yahweh's presence, but the offering of sacrifices at an earthen altar is sufficient to secure Yahweh's presence and blessing. For this same reason, a *massebah*, as a seat of Yahweh's presence, would not be compatible with orthodox / canonical Israelite worship,[38] even if one might say that a *massebah* is strictly speaking not an image.[39]

Thus, the ark, the Tent of Meeting and the Temple differ from local altars as described in Exodus 20:22–26. Whereas Yahweh is present in the Tent of Meeting or Temple at the ark, local altars are merely places where Yahweh 'comes' to meet the worshipper. Whereas the Tent of Meeting and the Temple with the ark are elaborate constructions with an elaborate priestly cultus, local altars are of simple nature, and no priestly injunctions or prerogatives exist for them in the biblical texts. Thus, the ark, the Tent of Meeting and Temple far outshine the external form and purpose of local altars, and the 'system' of the ark together with the Tent of Meeting or the Temple is worthy of a designation *central sanctuary*, a place where Yahweh dwells among his people Israel.

2. FROM TENT OF MEETING TO TEMPLE

2.1 Rejection

Having examined Israelite concepts of divine presence in their ancient Near Eastern context and having noted the special importance of the

---

Jacob) as expressing the 'vertical dimension' of divine presence (ibid., pp. 199–203), and Numbers 23 as an example where the deity arrives to Balaam in response to offerings (B. A. Levine, *In the Presence of the Lord: A Study of Cult and Some Cultic Terms in Ancient Israel* [Leiden: E. J. Brill, 1974], p. 23).

[37] E.g. Genesis 18; 1 Kings 19:9–18; Exodus 33:9; Numbers 12:5; Deuteronomy 31:15.

[38] That *masseboth* were used in Palestine as a seat of divine presence and / or as a representation of a god is suggested by a number of factors: see e.g. the finds at Arad from Iron Age II (see e.g. Mettinger, *No Graven Image?*, pp. 143–9) and Hazor from Late Bronze Age (see e.g. ibid., pp. 178–81), where *masseboth* were found at the 'holy of holies' of the cultic site. Cf. also G. J. Wenham, *Genesis 16–50* (WBC; Dallas: Word, 1994), p. 224; Hutter, 'Kultstelen und Baityloi', pp. 91–9.

[39] However, a standing stone could be erected as a sign or witness, or could even mark a sacred area as long as it was not seen as a seat of Yahweh (see esp. Josh. 4:6–8, 21–24; Deut. 27:1–8).

ark, the Tent of Meeting and the Temple, let us examine how these concepts help us understand the mutual relationship of the Tent of Meeting and the Temple as revealed by the events which start with the capture of the ark by the Philistines at the battle of Aphek and end with the building of Solomon's Temple. While these events are described in most detail in 1 Samuel 2–1, Kings 6, Psalm 78:55–72 reveals most about their theological meaning.

Psalm 78:55 notes how God gave the land to the Israelites, in addition to his other past good deeds towards them. Yet the Israelites continue to act faithlessly. They behave just as their fathers did in the wilderness (v. 57). They test God, rebel against him and do not keep his commandments (v. 56). Moreover, once they have settled in the land, they build illegitimate places of worship (*bāmôt*, v. 58) and worship idols.[40]

In verses 58–60 the psalm expresses that God utterly rejected the Israelites because of their idols and high places. An important part of this is God's rejection of Shiloh as his dwelling place (v. 60). 1 Samuel starts with Shiloh being presented as an important sanctuary, with the ark located there (1 Sam. 3:3; 4:4). Moreover, according to the Masoretic text of 1 Samuel 2:22, the tent of meeting was in Shiloh during the time of Eli and Samuel.[41] Also, Joshua 18:1 and 19:51 state that the tent of meeting was set up at Shiloh during the time of Joshua, and according to 1 Kings 8:4 the tent of meeting was later taken into the Jerusalem Temple.[42]

Next, according to verse 61, Yahweh 'gave his strength to captivity, his splendour to the hand of the enemy'. The reference to the strength (`oz) of Yahweh naturally refers to the ark, as the Philistines captured the ark in 1 Samuel 4–6, and as Psalm 132:8 speaks of the ark as the strength (`oz) of Yahweh.[43] From an ancient Near Eastern perspective, as described above, the loss of a god image was a sign that the god had abandoned his sanctuary and city, perhaps even

---

[40] Cf. Judges 2; 1 Samuel 8:8.

[41] See D. G. Schley, *Shiloh: A Biblical City in Tradition and History* (JSOTSS 63; Sheffield: Sheffield Academic Press, 1989), p. 232, n. 10 for a full discussion of 1 Samuel 2:22, including the similarity of the verse to Exodus 38:8; Numbers 25:6–10.

[42] The historical reality of the tent of meeting has been denied by many (see e.g. ibid. *passim* for a survey of opinions and scholars, including J. Wellhausen, *Prolegomena zur Geschichte Israel* [Berlin: Georg Reimer, 1905⁶ (1878¹)]). However, there are also extra-biblical reasons to think that the concept of the tent of meeting may be based on historical reality. For instance, in Ugarit, El evidently has a tent shrine (see R. J. Clifford, 'The Tent of El and The Israelite Tent of Meeting', *CBQ* 33 [1971], pp. 221–7), and the Late Bronze–Early Iron Age finds at Timna have suggested that there was a tent shrine at the location of the temple of Hathor (see B. Rothenberg, *Timna: Valley of the Biblical Copper Mines* [London: Thames & Hudson, 1972]).

[43] So most commentators.

the whole land. Thus, the capturing of the ark, the Israelite seat of Yahweh's presence, was a sign that Yahweh had abandoned Israel and his sanctuary in Shiloh (vv. 59–61).[44] This abandonment is also expressed in 1 Samuel 4:21–22 by the exclamation of Phinehas's wife: 'Glory has departed from Israel … because the ark of God had been taken' (vv. 21–22).

According to verses 56–58, the reason why Yahweh abandoned Shiloh was the sins of the people. 1 Samuel 2–3 reveals that the sons of Eli neglected the proper procedures of the offerings (1 Sam. 2:12–17) and conducted themselves improperly with the women who were part of the service of the tent of meeting (1 Sam. 2:22). Then, according to 1 Samuel 2:27–36 and 3:10–14, the disaster at Aphek was part of Yahweh's judgement against the house of Eli. This judgement started with the death of Hophni and Phinehas, which also served as a sign of it (1 Sam. 2:34; 4:11). The judgement was continued by the slaughter of the priests at Nob (1 Sam. 22; cf. 1 Sam. 2:30–33) and completed by the expulsion of Ebiathar by Solomon (1 Kgs. 2:26–27; cf. 1 Sam. 2:36).[45] Verses 62–64 refer to the start of this demise, the defeat at Aphek and the resulting casualties (vv. 62–63), and the death of Hophni and Phinehas (v. 64), with the latter part of verse 64 according well with the plight of Phinehas's widow (1 Sam. 4:19–22).[46]

Even though in Psalm 78 it is the sins of the people and their high places and idolatry, whereas in 1 Samuel 2–3 it is the sin of the priesthood, which causes Yahweh's anger and rejection, the viewpoints of Psalm 78 and 1 Samuel 2–3 are mutually compatible. Moreover, when one considers that both Psalm 78:56–58 and 1 Samuel 2–3 indicate that the sins of the people and of Hophni and Phinehas were of cultic nature and that in general a violation against cult was one of the worst things that the leaders or people could do against gods in the ancient Near East, it is not surprising that Yahweh is portrayed as greatly angered (Ps. 78:59; 1 Sam. 3:11–14) and as rejecting the tent of meeting, Shiloh and Israel.

2.2 Renewal of divine favour

According to Psalm 78:65, Yahweh next awakes as from sleep and restores Israel's fortunes (v. 66). The return of the ark from the land of the Philistines (1 Sam. 6) is part of this process.

---

[44] See also A. F. Campbell, *The Ark Narrative (1 Sam 4–6; 2 Sam 6): A Form-Critical and Traditio-Historical Study* (Dissertation Series 16; Missoula: SBL and Scholars Press, 1975), p. 185; Miller and Roberts, *The Hand of the Lord*, pp. 60–75.

[45] So also R. W. Klein, *1 Samuel* (WBC; Waco: Word, 1983), p. 27.

[46] Cf. M. E. Tate, *Psalms 51–100* (WBC; Dallas: Word, 1990), p. 294; and see also R. P. Carroll, 'Psalm LXXVIII: Vestiges of a Tribal Polemic', *VT* 21.2 (1971), pp. 133–50 (p. 145).

The ultimate part of the restoration of the fortunes of Israel is the election of David and of Judah and Jerusalem (vv. 68–72). Verse 67 provides a contrasting background for this election: the tribe of Ephraim, which had been the leader during the pre-monarchical period, has been rejected together with Shiloh and is not chosen again.[47]

The prominence of Joseph and Ephraim in the pre-monarchical period and the change of focus from Ephraim to Judah is confirmed by the Old Testament record outside Psalm 78 and 1–2 Samuel, and is also suggested by the archaeological record. In Genesis 48 Jacob sets Ephraim before Manasseh, and according to Deuteronomy 33:16 Joseph is a 'prince of his brothers', which accords with Genesis 37–50 (see especially Joseph's dreams in Gen. 37:5–11). Moreover, judging from the tribal origin of the individual judges and from other internal considerations of the book of Judges, Ephraim and the northern and Transjordanian tribes seem to be strong for most of the Judges period.[48] On the other hand, except for the initial period of the judges, as Miller and Hayes point out, the southern tribes are less prominent.[49] Also, as Carroll notes, Joshua and Samuel were Ephraimites.[50] Finally, one should not lose sight of the fact that Shiloh was in the territory of Ephraim, and it is worth noting that Bethel, where at least the ark was for a time according to Judges 20, was not in the territory of Judah.

Moreover, according to Finkelstein, surveys and excavations have shown that during Iron Age I the number of settlements found in the northern hill country was reasonably large, whereas not many settlements were found in the southern hill country.[51] On the other hand, there was a considerable increase of settlements in Judah in the beginning of Iron Age II.[52] Thus the archaeological record speaks for the prominence of the north in the pre-monarchical period, and for a shift of prominence from north to south at the threshold of the monarchy.

In verses 70–72, God's choice of David is affirmed. Overall, according to Psalm 78, the fall of the old tribal order including the abandonment of the leadership of Ephraim and the sanctuary at Shiloh in Ephraim's territory was God's judgement on Israel (Ps. 78:56–64). Then, God in his grace set up a new order in Judah and Jerusalem, with the establishment of kingship and the Temple in Jerusalem (Ps. 78:67–72).

This view of the events fits very well with the contents of the books of Samuel. Above all, the main focus of the books of Samuel is on

---

[47] Cf. Tate, *Psalms 51–100*, pp. 294–5.
[48] See J. M. Miller and J. H. Hayes, *A History of Ancient Israel and Judah* (London: SCM Press, 1986), pp. 94–8.
[49] Ibid., p. 103.
[50] Carroll, 'Psalm LXXVIII', p. 140.
[51] I. Finkelstein, *The Archaeology of the Israelite Settlement* (Jerusalem: IES, 1988), especially pp. 47–55, 121–204.
[52] Ibid., pp. 326–7.

describing how the old system, where judges ruled Israel, ended and changed to a new system of kingship under David, Yahweh's chosen king.[53] However, it should not come as a surprise that the change of the cultic order constitutes a vital part of the portrayal of the events which result in the emergence of the Davidic monarchy, fully in line with the general ancient Near Eastern emphasis on cultic matters. First, the place of worship changes. Whereas at the beginning of 1 Samuel the central place of worship is Shiloh, with David's capture of Jerusalem the scene is set for the ark to be transported there. Eventually, the ark is brought to Jerusalem in a joyous procession (2 Sam. 6). Moreover, David wishes to build a Temple for the ark (2 Sam. 7), and the matter is fulfilled by his son Solomon, as the books of Kings describe (2 Sam. 7:12–13; 1 Kgs. 5–8).[54] Secondly, the priesthood changes. Whereas at the beginning of 1 Samuel the Elide priesthood officiates, at the end of 2 Samuel only Abiathar is left of the Elide line (1 Sam. 22:20),[55] and he too is banished in the beginning of the reign of Solomon in favour of Zadok (1 Kgs. 2:26–27).[56] Both Abiathar and Zadok officiate during the time of David (2 Sam. 8:17; 20:25), a transitional time between the fall of Shiloh and the building of the Temple in Jerusalem.

Thus Psalm 78 speaks about the rejection of Ephraim and Shiloh in the light of God's choice of Judah and Jerusalem. This implies that Shiloh and Jerusalem were successive sanctuaries in Israel. The rejection of Shiloh and the tent of meeting started a chain of events where the old pre-monarchical system of worship was replaced in the early monarchic period with the Jerusalem Temple becoming the centre of Israel's worship. Instead of dwelling in the tent of meeting, Yahweh would henceforth dwell among his people Israel in the Temple in Jerusalem.

3. CONCLUSION

We have seen that an examination of Israelite concepts of divine presence in their ancient Near Eastern context provides a framework

---

[53] Overall, the books of Samuel in general have been seen as a legitimation of the Davidic monarchy; see especially L. Rost, *The Succession to the Throne of David* (Historic Texts and Interpreters in Biblical Scholarship I; Sheffield: Almond Press, 1982). English translation of *Die Überlieferung von der Thronnachfolge Davids* (Stuttgart: Kohlhammer, 1926).

[54] Note that, as the status of the central sanctuary is ambiguous, this naturally implies that worship at local altars is legitimate during this transitional time (cf. 1 Sam. 7:3–4, 9:11–14).

[55] Cf. A. Cody, *A History of the Old Testament Priesthood* (AnBib 35; Rome: Pontifical Biblical Institute, 1969), p. 89; Schley, *Shiloh*, pp. 142–3 and *passim* for issues involved in scholarly discussion regarding the connection of Abiathar to Eli.

[56] It seems reasonable to think that Abiathar has been added to the list of 1 Kings 4:4 since he officiated during the time of Solomon before his banishment; cf. R. D. Patterson, and H. J. Austel, *1, 2 Kings* (EBC 4; Grand Rapids: Zondervan, 1988), pp. 1–300 (p. 50).

for understanding the Old Testament texts that describe the historical events where the focus of Israel's religious and political life changes from Shiloh and Ephraim to Jerusalem and Judah. An understanding of the importance of the favour and presence of gods in the ancient Near East linked to an understanding that the central sanctuary was the sole place where Yahweh dwelt among his people in Israel helps us appreciate the tremendous importance of the central sanctuary in Israel. Since religion was closely tied with all aspects of life in ancient Israel, the location of the central sanctuary could not but be of tremendous importance as well. As Psalm 78 and other Old Testament texts describe, the central sanctuary was set in Shiloh after the settlement, and Ephraim, in whose territory Shiloh lay, had the overall leadership within the twelve-tribe confederation that composed Israel. However, the loss of the ark to the Philistines in the battle of Aphek was seen as a sign that Yahweh had rejected Israel and Shiloh due to their faithlessness. The ark never returned to Shiloh, but, as described in 1–2 Samuel, was taken to Jerusalem by David after a transitional period during which Israel's political system changed. The enthronement of David, the taking of the ark to Jerusalem and the building of the Temple were seen as demonstrations of the grace of Yahweh, who once again favoured Israel. While these events marked an important stage in the process by which the divine redemption of creation would be fulfilled, future developments would include the destruction of the Temple and the punishment of the house of David in the sixth century BC.

Nevertheless, the legacy of the tent of meeting, the First Temple and the Davidic monarchy lived on, finding its fulfilment in the person of Jesus Christ. After Christ the king from the line of David tabernacled in the flesh (John 1:14) and established a New Covenant, the New Covenant people became the Temple of God where God's spirit dwells (1 Cor. 3:16; 6:19; 2 Cor. 6:16; cf. Eph. 2:20–22).

3

'DID I EVER ASK FOR A HOUSE OF CEDAR?'

The Contribution of 2 Samuel and 1 Chronicles 17
to the Theology of the Temple

CARL E. ARMERDING

1. INTRODUCTION

The 'Temple', as we know it, appears to have burst upon the biblical story with the shift from decentralized judgeship to established monarchy. On the surface, it sprang, full-grown, from a desire of king David, when he 'was settled in his palace [house] and Yahweh had given him rest from his enemies' (2 Sam. 7:1), to address the contrast between Yahweh's tent and his own new palace. When David shared the idea with Nathan, the prophet's initial response was positive, but after a night of revelation David's seer returned with a sharply modified word.

The ensuing divine speech, though building on David's desire for a 'house' for his God, takes the conversation in a sharply different direction, and only toward the end (v. 13) is the Temple concept approved. In the following Samuel narrative (the so-called Succession Narrative), the idea of a Temple is only reintroduced after Solomon's accession (1 Kgs. 5; cf., however, 1 Chr. 22ff.). The point remains that, in contrast to the Tabernacle, which is presented in Exodus 25ff. as a divinely inspired public works project, the Temple idea is humanly conceived, and in the text receives at best luke-warm support. This is all the more intriguing in light of the fact that the Temple assumed such a central place in later Jewish history and thought.

It must not be thought, however, that the idea of Yahweh, or Elohim, having a dwelling place is a new one. From the beginning the God of the Bible is seen as a being who, though infinite, can inhabit some kind of space. Nor have other metaphors of a divine dwelling generated the same polemical discussion as have the ideas connected with what became Solomon's Temple. What was it about the Temple itself, in contrast to other figures of divine presence, which initially provoked Yahweh's disinterest, if not displeasure? In this paper we shall attempt to set Temple questions in the context of the longer history of the biblical idea of divine dwelling, and thus provide a context for the Davidic Covenant, both in its 2 Samuel 7 setting (the Deuteronomic History)[1] and in its parallel, 1 Chronicles 17.

In pursuing this line of questioning, it must be acknowledged that the Temple did become a central focus of Israel's life, both before and after the exile, and that Yahweh repeatedly extended promises to Israel connected with his name in that place. Nevertheless, the question must be asked, 'Was what David proposed and Solomon built a necessary development in Yahwistic faith or a distraction from Yahweh's ideal programme?' The question posed to David by Yahweh, through Nathan (2 Sam. 7:7), remains: 'Wherever I have moved with all the Israelites, did I ever say to any of their rulers whom I commanded to shepherd my people Israel, "Why have you not built me a house of cedar?"' Does Yahweh dwell in 'temples made with hands' (Acts 7:48–49; cf. Isa. 66:1–2; 1 Kgs. 8:27), or is there something inimical about the whole idea, as recognized by Solomon in his dedicatory prayer, and picked up by Isaiah, Stephen and then the Apostle Paul (Acts 17:24). Why had Yahweh never asked for a house of cedar?

The broader issues are those of divine dwelling in general. How does Yahweh normally 'appear among' or 'dwell within' his people? Where is he to be found? And worshipped? Although, at the beginning, the heavens and the earth are Yahweh's true habitation, he appears to his creatures in a variety of forms (e.g. Gen. 18), culminating within Israel's history prior to the Temple in the focus given to the ark and its tent (Tabernacle).[2] In contrast to the typical random theophany, the ark becomes the normal locus for divine–human encounter amongst the Israelites (Exod. 25:22), and the central feature of the Tabernacle shrine. Various other 'tent' shrines are mentioned, the most prominent of which is the 'tent of meeting'.[3] What is important is that none of these institutions are comparable to either the biblical or ancient Near Eastern temples, which were fixed, generally national, shrines, typically housing the image of a deity. Although various temples

---

[1] This widely accepted term (hereinafter abbreviated DH) incorporates the historical books from Joshua to 2 Kings, and in the hands of various scholars can signify anything from theories of a unified historical corpus, largely the work of exilic or post-exilic writers, with its own theological stance (so Martin Noth), to a convenient way to describe what appears to be a series of sequential historical books.

[2] Called in Exodus 25:8 a 'sanctuary' (*miqdāš*) and in verse 9 a 'dwelling place / tabernacle' (*miškān*). The instructions (Exod. 25–30) given for the Tabernacle, including the ark, were provided by Yahweh to Moses on Mount Sinai, according to a 'pattern' provided (Exod. 25:9). Cf. the 'tent of meeting' below.

[3] The 'tent of meeting' (*'ōhel mô'ēd*) appears first in Exodus 27:21, and is the place where Yahweh regularly meets Moses, who becomes Yahweh's channel for communication between the people and himself. Its relationship to the tabernacle, and indeed the whereabouts of the ark and the various tents of Scripture, is complicated, especially since all were movable shrines for a nomadic people. For our purposes, the symbolism of the ark, the tabernacle and various tents, including their portability, is more important than their specific histories, for which consult Bible dictionaries.

are known to the biblical record (e.g. Judg. 9), never to this point has Yahweh required a Temple for himself.

But when a Temple does come, Yahweh promises to fill it with his glory (1 Kgs. 8:10ff.), establishing a signal presence (or absence) that will become a litmus test for Israel's covenant life. Throughout the monarchy, the state of Jerusalem's Temple and its worship often reflects the spiritual health, or sickness, of the nation.[4] The prophetic critique (cf. Isa. 1; Jer. 7) of Israel's covenant unfaithfulness at times appears close to a complete rejection of the Temple and its worship (Jer. 7:12–15), though such passages are interspersed with promises of a bright future in which a restored Temple takes centre stage in the eschatological Jerusalem (Isa. 2:1–5). With these promises in mind, for the exiles looking back on the ruined Temple (Lam.), its restoration will literally be 'life from the dead', though even the hopes attached to the Second Temple (e.g. Hag. 2:6–9) would themselves eventually be dashed, and dispersed Judaism would develop other institutions, for example, synagogue and Torah, that would effectively take the place of the Jerusalem Temple in the cult, if not in the longings of its adherents.

With the Qumran sectarians and into the New Testament era, the situation is further complicated. Spiritualizing tendencies regarding the Temple dominate both, and in the New Testament the literal Temple gives way to other metaphors of the presence of God among his people, re-enforced by the desolation of the physical shrine in Jerusalem. Finally, at the very end of the New Testament we are introduced to a different kind of city, in which there is no need of a Temple, given that the Lord Almighty and the Lamb are resident there (Rev. 21:22).

So, we must ask, was a Temple ever really a biblical idea? Does God need a 'house of cedar' that we can build for him? In the remainder of this essay, I propose to look at the narrative context of the Davidic Covenant, in both 2 Samuel 7 and 1 Chronicles 17, to attempt some evaluation of the theological basis for the Temple in each account. Although the two texts vary little (see below), the context surrounding each provides a key to how the covenant, and the Temple, functions within the narrative.

2. THE TEMPLE QUESTION IN LIGHT OF THE DAVIDIC COVENANT IN 2 SAMUEL 7 AND 1 CHRONICLES 17

2.1 *The texts themselves*

The Samuel and Chronicles accounts of the discourse between David and Yahweh, through the prophet Nathan, are clearly recensions of

---

[4] Though in the prophets (e.g. Jer. 7) a situation is envisaged where the outward health of the Temple stands in stark contrast to the inner spiritual health of the nation and its covenant.

a single original, though they contain numerous minor rhetorical differences, most of which little affect the subject of this study. In light of what will be developed below, however, four verses invite comment, as reflecting something of a *Tendenz* within the documents where they are found.[5]

2.1(i) 2 Samuel 7:1 (cf. 1 Chr. 17:1)

Following the common phrase 'After the king [Chronicles: 'David'] was settled in his palace', 2 Samuel 7:1 adds 'and Yahweh had given him rest from all his enemies round about'. As we will observe, the concern of the DH is the establishment of a covenant king ruling in peace and justice over the people of Israel; thus the notice of 'rest' in Samuel is consistent with phraseology which has marked the DH from the conquests of Joshua onward. Rest from their enemies is the goal of Yahweh's raising up kingship, and thus part of the context leading into the Davidic Covenant dialogue. By contrast, the concern of the Chronicler is to present an ideal worshipping community, focused on the Jerusalem Temple, and presided over by a Davidic monarch and Levitical priesthood, in which 'rest from enemies' under a covenant king can be assumed.

This is quite consistent with the rest of the Deuteronomist's account, as we have already seen. Immediately following the Davidic Covenant, David's string of victories (2 Sam. 8) confirm that he has been given rest, at least in the sense of victory, and '*pax Davidica*' is established, with just rule (2 Sam. 8:15–18) as the fruit of these conditions.[6] The Temple itself will not again be introduced until 1 Kings 5, when Solomon contracts with Hiram in Tyre for building materials, and gives as reason for David's failure to build the constant warfare that surrounded him. Solomon's greater 'state of rest' (1 Kgs. 5:4) is seen as a natural progression from Davidic times, rather than a deficiency in David himself, in possible contrast to the Chronicler's account (2 Chr. 2:3–5; cf. 1 Chr. 22:6–10), as noted below. Futher to the point, when the threshing floor of Araunah is purchased and dedicated (2 Sam.

---

[5] Bibliography on these two chapters, as might be expected, is extensive, with summaries available in the respective volumes of the Word Biblical Commentary series. A. A. Anderson, *2 Samuel* (WBC 11; Waco: Word, 1989) and R. Braun, *1 Chronicles* (WBC 14; Waco: Word, 1986). References quoted here are from the CD-ROM edition (Dallas: Word, 1998).

[6] Many scholars suggest literary and theological rather than chronological reasons for chapter 7's appearance here, and especially the note of completed victory for David's kingdom. Extensive discussion of the literary pre-history is to be found in the 'Form/ Structure/Setting' section of Anderson, *2 Samuel*. That 2 Samuel 7 represents both the literary and theological apex of the David narrative, and probably the entire DH, is obvious, so its placement in the DH prior to the succession conflicts that follow is most appropriate.

24:24–25), there is still no mention of the Temple, and less yet of any reasons why David might not be the builder.[7]

By contrast, the Chronicler, with a different interest, and writing long after David's wars have ceased and Solomon has already built the Temple, has less immediate reason to concentrate on the historical situation facing David. It is not, however, that the wars of David have been forgotten: quite the opposite, according to at least one commentator. H. G. M. Williamson[8] and others have pointed out that the Chronicler's failure to mention the 'rest' provided by Yahweh through David's conquests may be a deliberate omission, inasmuch as his subsequent chapters (18–20) contrast the 'man of war'[9] with his idealized son, the peaceable Solomon, who will, finally, build the Temple and establish the dynasty. One might say, then, that it is not through David's wars that 'rest' is to be found, but through Solomon's construction of the Temple for the worshipping community.

2.1(ii) 2 Samuel 7:5/1 Chronicles 17:4

The same point may be re-enforced in 2 Samuel 7:5 (contra 1 Chr. 17:4). In the former Nathan has Yahweh enquiring about David's intention to build a house ('Are you going to build me a house to dwell in?'), in contrast to Chronicles, where David is emphatically told he will *not* build a house for Yahweh. Instead, it will be 'one of his sons' (v. 12), making clear that the restriction on Temple building is not absolute but temporary, and tied to who will be the actual builder. Yahweh's objection, in that case, is not to a Temple, in preference for a movable tent-shrine,[10] but to David as builder. A careful reading of the Samuel text may demonstrate a significant difference in emphasis between the Deuteronomists and the Chronicler, with the crux turning on whether the opening phrase of Yahweh's word in 2 Samuel 7:5 is to be taken in essential agreement with the Chronicler (emphatic *you*, indicating that the negation concerns, primarily, the person ... rather than the action),[11]

---

[7] Also completely missing in the DH, at the conclusion of 2 Samuel 24, is any charge to Solomon concerning the Temple, an event writ large in the parallel account in 1 Chronicles 22.

[8] H. G. M. Williamson, 'Eschatology in Chronicles', *Tyndale Bulletin* 28 (1979), pp. 115–54.

[9] On the surface, 1 Chronicles 18–20 parallels 2 Samuel 8–11, but the wider context develops the accounts in different directions. The precise reference to David's warlike career comes not in the Chronicler's account of the dialogue with Hiram (2 Chr. 2), which is quite silent on the reasons for the Temple not being built earlier, but at the start (1 Chr. 22:6–13) of the long addition (1 Chr. 22 – 29:20), following from the threshing floor incident, in which David charges his officials and Solomon to build the Temple.

[10] So von Rad, *The Problem of the Hexateuch and Other Essays* (Edinburgh: Oliver & Boyd, 1966), p. 119, quoted in Anderson, *2 Samuel*.

[11] Anderson, *2 Samuel*, 'Comment' on v. 5.

or whether, as the immediate context (*vis-à-vis* the later verses) implies, a complete rejection of the idea. As with so much of this discussion, the tension remains, and it seems facile simply to wipe out the strong objection to a Temple in verses 5–7 by harmonizing Nathan's somewhat ambiguous question in 2 Samuel 7:5 with the clear negative found in 1 Chronicles 17:4.

2.1(iii) 2 Samuel 7:14/1 Chronicles 17:13

A third significant difference is found in 2 Samuel 7:14's balancing of the promise to David's offspring with a specific threat of chastening for disobedience. Although in the full light of verse 15, with its parallels in Chronicles, the 'covenant'[12] with David is clearly unconditional,[13] the tension that exists in 2 Samuel 7 is noticeably absent in 1 Chronicles 17. Consistent with the Chronicler's rosier picture of the Davidic royal house, the phrase may appear out of place, and in any event its resolution has more to do with the Deuteronomist's concern for a righteous king in perpetuity than the Chronicler's focus on a worshipping community in the Temple. The vicissitudes of human frailty will affect both the royal line and the Temple, and are not absent from either source's larger history, but it seems quite consistent with the Chronicler's *Tendenz* to omit it here. He has little theological need to concentrate on the potential failures of a son of David; his more immediate concern will be the preservation of the Temple and its worship.

2.1(iv) 2 Samuel 7:19/1 Chronicles 17:17

The fourth, and final, significant difference presents a clear textual contrast, but is notoriously difficult to interpret. At the end of a common word of thanksgiving to Yahweh because 'you have spoken about the future of the house of your servant', the Samuel text adds the enigmatic *weʾzōʾṯ tôraṯ hāʾāḏām*, translated by the NIV as 'Is this your usual way of dealing with man?' The NRSV renders it 'May this be instruction for the people', while the RSV appears to omit it completely. The Chronicler's parallel line reads *ûreʾîṯanî keṯôr hāʾāḏām hammaʿălâ*, and is translated by the NIV as 'you have looked on me as though I were the most exalted of men', by the NRSV as 'you regard me as someone

---

[12] Though the word 'covenant' (*berîṯ*) is not used in the chapters, scholars have consistently viewed this as one of the great covenants of Scripture (see extensive bibliography in the notes on 2 Samuel 7:1 in Expositors' Bible Commentary (EBC) [Grand Rapids: Zondervan, various dates], here cited from CD-ROM edition, Zondervan Reference Software). Significantly, the passage is frequently referred to in other Scriptures (2 Sam. 23:5; 1 Kgs. 8:23; 2 Chr. 13:5; Ps. 89:3, 28, 34, 39; 132:12; Isa. 55:3; Jer. 33:21) as a covenant, a conclusion with which few would argue.

[13] Even a partial listing of the discussion would be inadequate (see EBC, introductory comment on 2 Sam. 7), and is, in any case, irrelevant to this article.

of high rank' and is again ignored completely by the RSV.[14] Regarding the Samuel passage, one commentator[15] agrees with S. R. Driver[16] that 'all proposed emendations of the MT here, whether or not based on the parallel in 1 Chronicles 17:17 ("You have looked on me as though I were the most exalted of men"), are unsatisfactory', while going on to suggest that the best proposal to date is that of W. C. Kaiser,[17] who paraphrases verse 19b 'This is the charter by which humanity will be directed.' Taking Kaiser's point, the Samuel passage highlights the Davidic Covenant, with its messianic implications, as the foundation for all subsequent working of God in history. 2 Samuel 7 becomes, with the Abrahamic Covenant (Gen. 12, 15 and 17), the universal 'charter' by which Yahweh will confirm the universal promise of blessing ('to all nations') already articulated through Abraham.

If this interpretation of 1 Samuel 7:19 is accepted, the expression in 1 Chronicles 17:17 makes a bit more sense. Though Chronicles gives pride of place to Solomon when it comes to Temple building, David's exaltation is an important part of the theological development in the story. In the DH, the focus of blessing will be on the king, and thus eventually on the Messiah. By contrast, in Chronicles, the focus is on Yahweh's presence in the worshipping community, gathered in the Jerusalem Temple. In either case, an idealized David, and David's son(s), are fundamental to the process.

2.2 The narrative context in Samuel and Chronicles

Having looked at significant differences in the texts themselves, we return to the wider context, with the goal of discovering whether either setting provides an answer to the basic question, 'Did Yahweh ever ask for a house of cedar?' Each collection, that of the DH[18] and the Chronicler,[19] is written with a specific set of theological concerns, and our study needs to be informed by them. Before considering what may divide the two corpuses, it may be helpful to remind ourselves

---

[14] R. Braun, ad loc. in *1 Chronicles*, follows RSV, and labels all proposed emendations unconvincing, both of the Chronicles and the Samuel passages.

[15] Footnotes to EBC, ad loc. (CD-ROM edition).

[16] S. R. Driver, *Notes on the Books of Samuel*, p. 277, as cited in EBC.

[17] W. C. Kaiser, 'The Blessing of David, The Charter for Humanity' in J. H. Skilton (ed.), *The Law and the Prophets* (Nutley: Presbyterian & Reformed, 1974), p. 311. EBC (ad loc.) examines the language of the passage in light of proposed Assyrian and Hebrew vocabulary, and concludes that Kaiser's contention is not without merit.

[18] I assume some form of unified final DH editing, while retaining the integrity of individual books (e.g. B. Webb, *The Book of Judges: An Integrated Reading* [Sheffield: JSOT, 1987], ch. 1).

[19] Again, despite considerable debate, for present purposes we take the Chronicler's work to include only the books called by that name. Ezra and Nehemiah, while reflecting many common concerns, do not contain the chapter in question, and will be left to another study.

that both share the common biblical concern of redemptive history: that is, that God is at work in the people of Israel to create from the seed of Abraham a unified nation, living in unbroken relationship with its God, ruled over in righteousness by a divinely appointed leader, and able to fulfil the divine purpose of witness to the world of God's original creation mandate. Within this rubric the DH has a primary concern for kingship and righteous government, while the Chronicler's vision is for a worshipping community, with the role of the righteous king assumed. Let's take each in turn.

2.2(i) The Deuteronomic history

As we have seen, the DH is dominated by the search for a righteous king, specifically what can be called 'charismatic, covenant kingship'. This designation combines, in my view, the two streams of concern for kingship from Joshua onwards and indeed backward to Deuteronomy itself. The charismatic element, that is, that the leader must be raised up and gifted by Yahweh, requires the support of an active covenant relationship, in which the leader and people live under Yahweh's rule in obedience to righteous laws and statutes. The search for a leader, which actively begins during the period of the judges, continues through Samuel, Saul and David, until in the latter's reign the ideal is, at least for a time, reached. This typology ensures, for the DH at least, that 2 Samuel 7 will function as the apex of the entire history.[20] The ideal for this righteous covenant-keeping king is found in Deuteronomy 17:14–20, in which the king reads and obeys the Law, lives among rather than above his brethren and accumulates neither horses nor wives nor gold.

Israel as a worshipping community and the places where worship is conducted are secondary concerns of the DH. Specifically, nothing in this picture prepares us for the idea of building a Temple. The focus in this part of Samuel is on David's rise to power as the true covenant, charismatic king. After the relative failure of the old system of judges, whose charismatic calling and gifts were not supported by covenant keeping, whether in the ruler or the tribes behind him/her, the narrative moves swiftly through Samuel, his sons, the popular call for kingship, Saul, and finally David. Along the way, together with the failures of the covenant people and their leaders, we encounter several signal failures of the cult system,[21] but none point to a Temple as the answer. As early

---

[20] It probably also provides the reason why the more tawdry side of David's career (e.g. the Nathan and Bathsheba account) is introduced in 2 Samuel only after the Davidic Covenant.

[21] Notorious are the more tawdry 'cult' events of Judges, like Micah's shrine and the Danite/Levite participation, but we could add the Elide priesthood of 1 Samuel 1–3, the captivity of the ark (1 Sam. 4) and Saul's lapse (1 Sam. 13).

in the narrative as the end of Judges, we find references to a 'house of God' (Judg. 18:31), while references to the ark are common throughout the conquest narratives in Joshua; both come together in 1 Samuel 3:3 at Shiloh. Although we must await references in the latter prophets for an explicit answer to what happened to Shiloh,[22] it is clear that sometime near the beginning of the monarchy the shrine is destroyed. Nothing in the narratives indicates a particular nostalgia for Shiloh, although the plight of the ark (1 Sam. 4:18) as well as the failure of kingship (2 Sam. 1:19–27) are both lamented. At most, David, whose rise brings hope for the true king, indicates a desire to incorporate the ark, theretofore completely transportable, into his new capital city of Jerusalem (2 Sam. 6), and has pitched some form of tent in which the ark will be housed (2 Sam. 6:17). This scene, of course, provides the immediate context for the Davidic Covenant in the DH, but until this time we have had no indication, either from Yahweh or from one of his charismatic leaders, that the ark needed any house beyond what was available. Indeed, just as Abimelech (Judg. 9) and Micah (Judg. 17–18) function as the antithesis of judgeship and kingship, one might argue that the presence of temples in both episodes function as the antithesis of true worship in Israel. The focus of the DH is on the king and covenant, not a Temple, and not even the ark or the Tabernacle, which are merely the means of grace through which God's covenant presence is manifested. And so it will continue in the Davidic Covenant, despite the concern of David in 2 Samuel 7:1 that initiates the discussion.

To sum up the context for David's request that he build a Temple for Yahweh, and focus attention again on the role of 2 Samuel 7 in the DH narrative, we recall that little or nothing in the narrative demands a central sanctuary. Neither Shiloh nor any other cult centre is clearly identified with Yahweh's choice of a 'place for my Name', an idea powerfully expressed in Deuteronomy.[23] In any case, Deuteronomy's central covenant teaching does not fall on the place, but on the presence of the Name among God's people as an impetus to faithful living (Deut. 28:58) and a witness to the world (Deut. 28:10). All of this is consistent with Israel's missionary purpose as the seed of Abraham (Gen. 18:18–19) and the emphasis of the David Covenant as expounded above. Although in the later prophets Israel's worldwide mission will be

---

[22] Jeremiah 7:12–14; 26:6–9.
[23] Deuteronomy 12:5–21; 14:23–24; 16:2–11; 26:2. Questions of the dating of Deuteronomy and its relation to the centralization of worship under Josiah cannot be discussed here, though for purposes of this paper we assume that Deuteronomy reflects a centralizing tradition with its roots much earlier in Israel's history as a people. It is important to recall other strands in the DH, such as the Gibeon sanctuary, which balance any exclusive or absolute claims for Jerusalem. Again, the point is that it is Yahweh and his covenant, not the sanctuary, that claim ultimate loyalty, a theme which dominated prophets like Jeremiah.

served by people coming up to the Jerusalem Temple, another consistent prophetic strain envisages the Law going out from Jerusalem (Isa. 2:3/ Mic. 2:4), and Yahweh's name/glory being praised throughout the earth (Isa. 24:14–16; 42:1–7; Mal. 1:11, 14). The former locates Yahweh's worship and presence in a single place, the Jerusalem Temple,[24] while the latter preserves and expands the concept of Yahweh's universal presence, and indeed the whole earth as his dwelling.

It is not surprising, therefore, that Nathan's prophecy (2 Sam. 7:5–16) has its focus on the 'house' Yahweh is building for David (and Israel) rather than on the 'house' David (or Solomon) will build for Yahweh. Up to the time of David, Yahweh has indeed dwelt in a tent, whether in Shiloh or Gibeon, and his ark has moved with the people of God through deserts and mountains, through war and peace, always with its message of relationship and grace. The rationale for a Temple in this section of the DH, it seems, is not that Yahweh needs a 'house of cedar', but that David is concentrating his power in Jerusalem. Whether the concentration of royal power in a royal citadel and sanctuary is a step forward or backward in achieving charismatic, covenant kingship might be argued either way, but that it is happening in the narrative is unambiguous. David has now established a fortress city as his capital, built himself a palace of cedar (2 Sam. 5:11), taken wives and concubines (2 Sam. 5:13), and, we might add, begun to look a bit more like the 'kings of the nations' whose lifestyle and habits came under the light of Samuel's earlier criticism (1 Sam. 8:10–18). In such circumstances, adding a royal sanctuary is just one more accoutrement of power. Little wonder that the prophetic oracle gives its short shrift in the text! The idea will, of course, surface much later in 1 Kings 5,[25] but only when, under Solomon, the process of developing monarchy has moved far beyond the simple formulae of covenant kingship outlined in Deuteronomy 17 and expressed in the transition passages of 1 Samuel. That God will adapt the idea and use the Jerusalem Temple, and indeed fill it with his presence and glory, is consistent with his gracious attitude toward the earlier request for a king. But whether a 'house of cedar' was ever a requirement for Yahweh's purposes in Israel any more than was a royal palace needs still to be asked, especially in light of the struggle Israel had, later, to detach itself from the wrong-headed ideas of divine dwelling that grew up around the Jerusalem Temple. Just as Israel itself needed to return to the wilderness (Hos. 2) to learn again its love relationship with Yahweh, so its institutions, like the Temple, needed to be seen in their original context. For the Temple, this was the truth that

---

[24] Whether the Temple of Solomon (1 Kgs. 8:41–43; 2 Chr. 6:32–33), the post-exilic Temple (Zech. 8:20–23) or the eschatological Temple of Ezekiel, with it river flowing out of Jerusalem.

[25] In sharp contrast to 1 Chronicles, where after a few chapters (18–20) the Temple narrative is taken up.

Yahweh indeed 'tabernacles', or 'dwells', amongst his people, a feature of his life with them in the desert that was given new meaning in the exile. For all of this, a tent serves as well as a house of cedar.

2.2(ii) The Chronicler

In contrast to the DH, the central focus of Chronicles is on Israel as a worshipping community, with developed institutions of priesthood, Temple and cult. Everything else, including the Davidic Covenant, is brought under these rubrics, and it can be argued that even the prominence given to the Davidic line serves the Temple more than the reverse. Throughout the account, even before the actual building of the Temple begins, language of the 'house of God' or 'house of Yahweh' is predominant,[26] though often in the early chapters such vocabulary is combined with language of Tabernacle or tent. In 1 Chronicles 9:23, even the 'house of Yahweh', presumably in the context the one rebuilt in Jerusalem, is called 'the house of the tent' (*bêt-hā'ōhel*).

A secondary focus in 1 Chronicles is, of course, the Davidic line, but David himself appears as the heroic warrior-king who will bring up the ark and set the stage for Solomon's construction of the Temple. The book jumps quickly from the heroes of antiquity, at the beginning of world history, to some spotty genealogies of parts of Israel, with the story coming into a clearer focus in chapter 6 with the sons of Levi. Again, partial genealogies follow, until chapter 9 introduces those who resettled Jerusalem after the exile, again moving quickly to priests, Levites and Temple servants. Chapters 10–16 move through Saul's reign to David and his retinue, culminating in the extensive coverage of the ark's restoration to Jerusalem (chs 15–16), all of which set the scene for the Davidic Covenant passage in chapter 17.

Following the covenant with David (ch. 17), as we have noted, there is a relatively brief record of David's victories (chs 18–20), omitting completely the succession struggles that dominate the long interlude in Samuel between Nathan's oracle and the eventual building of the Temple under Solomon. Along the way, David and his mighty men acquire large quantities of bronze, silver and gold (18:7–11), which are in turn dedicated to Yahweh (18:8) and will eventually be used in the construction of the Temple.[27] This all culminates in 1 Chronicles 21, in which the incident of numbering the fighting men turns quickly to a focus on the Jerusalem Temple site and its divine authorization. The angel of Yahweh, whose function in 2 Samuel 24 is to carry out the punishment, assumes a much more prominent role here, directing the action which leads to David's taking the threshing floor for the forth-

---

[26] A third to a fourth of all Old Testament references occur in the books of Chronicles.
[27] 1 Chronicles 22:2–4 adds David's preparation for workmen, cut stone, cedar logs, nails, etc.

coming 'house of Yahweh'. The angel directs Gad to instruct David
to build an altar on the threshing floor (1 Chr. 21:18), after which he
appears to Ornan (Araunah) and his sons (v. 20), preparing them for
the eventual disposition of their property. The immediate account
comes to an end in verse 26, with God answering David's prayer by fire
on the altar, in contrast to 1 Samuel 24:25's simply staying the plague.
The Chronicler then adds a postscript (1 Chr. 21:28 – 2:1), not found
in the DH account, providing a rationale for putting the 'house of
Yahweh' (clearly, in prospect, the Temple) at the place of the threshing
floor, though as the text points out both the Tabernacle and the altar of
burnt offering were still at the high place in Gibeon.

As the story has unfolded, Israel now has two cult centres: the
High Place at Gibeon and the ark in its tent in Jerusalem. Already in
1 Chronicles 16:39–42 we have been reminded that, despite the ark's
removal to Jerusalem and the subsequent liturgical requirements it
generated (1 Chr. 16:37–38), there was also a functioning shrine at
Gibeon, replete with a Zadokite priesthood, an altar and Levitical
singers. But with 1 Chronicles 22:1, the tension between the various
'tent' sanctuaries had been resolved, and the remainder of 1 Chronicles
recounts David's further preparations for what Yahweh had commissioned.

An important point is to be noted in 1 Chronicles 22:6–10, where
the Chronicler makes explicit the reason why Solomon, not David, will
build the Temple: that is, that David was a man of war; while Solomon
will be a man of peace. It is Solomon, not David, who is given 'rest from
his enemies on every side' (22:9), and even his name means peace.[28]
Here, then, is the explanation for two of the differences in the text of
the Davidic Covenant noted above. The explicit prohibition to David
in 1 Chronicles 17:4 shifts the focus from whether a Temple should be
built at all, as in 2 Samuel 7, to who is qualified to build it. Secondly, the
Chronicler's omission of the rest formula attached to David in 2 Samuel
7:1 appears deliberate, and is quite consistent with the context.

3. CONCLUSION

What, then, can we conclude from these studies? First, it seems quite
evident that the question of the Temple idea's legitimacy is much closer
to the surface in the Samuel account. Like kingship, which in the DH
is accepted only with considerable reservations and qualifications, the
Temple is not a natural development. That is not to say that some of
the ideas behind the Temple, like those that led to kingship, are foreign
to the DH and its theological thrust. If we recall that 'charismatic,
covenant leadership' is the goal of the DH's history, we can see that the

---

[28] See the probable sound association in the text (*kî šelōmô yihyê šemô wešālôm* ...).

tension between institutions like the judges and the developed idea of a king like David is inevitable. The Davidic Covenant, for the deuteronomic historians, resolves some of that tension, even while creating further anomalies.

Equally, in the DH's treatment of the Temple there is a commitment to the concept of Yahweh dwelling among his people in a relationship of unbroken faithfulness and pure worship. The institutions of the developing cult are presented as the means of grace, through which this relationship functions, and in which Yahweh actively comes down to his people. As the story has progressed, there are some obvious anomalies, specifically related to the possibility that the One God might be worshipped in a variety of shrines. At one level, this is no problem, for Yahweh is everywhere present, and in the language of the poets of the Old Testament, his dwelling is all heaven and earth. But he has also chosen to dwell between the cherubim above the ark of the covenant/testimony, and he meets his representative Moses at the door of a particular Tent of Meeting.

It is the genius of the Temple to bring all of these functions together. Furthermore, to express them through a unified cult, under the patronage of a divinely ordained king, gives shape to the city-state that the people of Israel had become in the land. This is the picture the Chronicler also celebrates, and provides the context for Nathan's oracle in chapter 21.

But other questions need also to be asked, and these come to the surface in the DH, with its sober examination of the failures of kingship and covenant. When these institutions have broken down, but Yahweh's love continues, what are the elements that cannot be shaken? In such a time as the exile, with no Temple and no king, the old idea of Yahweh as a dynamic deity who goes with his people in all their ups and downs, living with them in tents or in prison, needs to be recalled. It is Yahweh himself, and his covenant promises, that remain when all else fails, and the houses of cedar have turned to dust. This is the message of 1 Samuel and the context for the Davidic Covenant in chapter 7.

At the close of the DH (2 Kgs. 25:27–30) there is no mention of the Temple, but hope is raised that there will again in Israel be a manifestation of the promise for a king.[29] By contrast, 2 Chronicles 36:23 ends with the promise of a renewed Temple. It should not be surprising, then, that the same themes dominate each narrator's telling of the Nathan oracle and David's response to it.

---

[29] We recognize that the question of hope in the Jehoiachin notice has brought a variety of answers, summarized recently in D. F. Murray, 'Of All the Years the Hopes – or Fears?: Jehoiachin in Babylon (2 Kings 25:27–30)', *JBL* 120.2 (Summer 2001), pp. 245–65). My own view is that the reason for the notice must have to do with hope kept alive.

4

A CURIOUS SILENCE

The Temple in 1 and 2 Kings

ROBERT FYALL

Like the dog that failed to bark, the relative neglect of the Temple in 1 and 2 Kings after the Solomon narrative is one of those thundering silences which calls for exploration. This paper sets out to examine the role of the Temple in the overall pattern of Kings and seeks to draw some conclusions about the writer's overall purpose.[1] In the introductory part we shall look at the author's overriding concerns and comment on the striking contrast with the Chronicler. Then four major areas of the writer's theology of Temple will be addressed and some conclusions drawn.

Nearly one-fifth of the book is devoted to Solomon, and of that three long chapters (1 Kgs. 6–8) are devoted to the Temple. Thereafter it is scarcely mentioned, apart from in 2 Kings 12 and 18ff. Plainly the author's concern lies somewhere else. We would expect him to show his hand fairly early in the narrative and, indeed, given the significance of David, before the king's death at the end of 1 Kings 2. The opening chapters of 1 Kings 1–2 deal with the palace intrigues and counter-intrigues, as a result of which Solomon ascends the throne. Much of this material is vivid and circumstantial narrative, but it is difficult to find a controlling thread or to discern what the writer wants to say. However, in 2:2–4 there occurs a little passage which gives us our bearings not only for this chapter but for the rest of the book.

David emphasizes that the story of his dynasty will flourish in direct proportion to its faithfulness to the Torah of Moses – the Temple is not mentioned. By contrast, the Chronicler omits these words, although in 1 Chronicles 29:19 he does pray that Solomon will have 'wholehearted devotion to keep you commands, requirements and decrees'. Yet, significantly, to that is added 'and to do everything to build the palatial structure for which I have provided'. Moreover, chapters 22–28 have

---

[1] Throughout this paper I shall use the term 'writer'; 1–2 Kings plainly has many sources, but in my view the canonical text bears the mark of one controlling mind. Similarly, the term 'book' will refer to both parts of Kings, unless otherwise stated.

outlined the huge involvement of David in the preparations for the Temple. We shall return to this contrast between Kings and Chronicles, but suffice it to say for the moment that Kings emphasizes Torah more than it does Temple.

1. WHAT IS THE SIGNIFICANCE OF TEMPLE IN THE FLOW OF 1 AND 2 KINGS?

After an introduction in 1 Kings 5 outlining Solomon's preparations for his building project, chapters 6–7 deal with Temple and palace and chapter 8 with the prayer of dedication. The details of building probably come from Temple archives now lost beyond trace and the account is marked by great clarity as the writer moves from structural design to interior furnishings. In chapters 6–7 four matters call for attention.

The first is that the project begins well: the Temple is 'for the LORD' (6:2) and the detail in verse 7 about dressed stone shows scrupulous obedience to the Torah (see Exod. 20:25 and Deut. 27:5–6). This is re-inforced by 6:11–13, where Yahweh himself underlines the words spoken by David in 2:2–4. Thus obedience, humility and gratitude rather than bricks and gold are to be the true fabric of the Temple.

Secondly, the lovingly executed work is reflected in the way our author lingers over the details of the building. Many of the technical terms of construction and architecture are imperfectly understood, yet this does not diminish the impression of care and devotion. Further, the details suggest a sense of authenticity, reading rather like the leaflets available to visitors to cathedrals and other large churches.

Thirdly, a warning bell rings loudly as chapter 7 opens: 'It took Solomon thirteen years, however, to complete the construction of his palace.' The significant *vav* in 7:1 is usefully rendered in the NIV as 'however', to emphasize the implied contrast between seven years of Temple building and the thirteen years of palace building.[2] It seems that the Temple was only a fairly modest part of the whole scene; it would hardly dominate the city like Durham Cathedral or York Minster. It is hard to avoid the impression that the Temple was in many ways a kind of royal chapel, an adjunct to Solomon's power and prestige (see also 11:7–8).

Fourthly, in 7:15–22, prominence is given to the gigantic pillars which towered almost as high as the Temple. *Yakin* (the Hiphil Imperfect of *kwn* – 'to be firm, established') possibly alludes to such phrases as 'I will establish the throne of his kingdom forever' (2 Sam. 7:13) and 'I have sworn to David my servant: I will establish your line

---

[2] See also Provan's useful note on the use of the phrase 'two houses'. I. W. Provan, *1 and 2 Kings* (NIBC Old Testament series; Peabody/Carlisle: Hendrickson/Paternoster Press, 1995), pp. 69–70.

forever' (Ps. 89:3–4). Boaz may be *be'oz* – 'with strength' – and allude to the opening and closing lines of Psalm 21. Thus the pillars would symbolize true wisdom and stability.

Chapter 8 represents the high-water mark of Solomon's story with the dedication of the Temple and the accompanying prayer. We shall return to this chapter in the final section of this essay, but two matters call for comment here.

The first is that the ark finds a home (8:1–9). Without it, the Temple was a shell. Up to now the ark had been in the tent sanctuary in the city of David. We last heard of it in 3:15 when Solomon sacrificed before it after the LORD's appearance to him in Gibeon. Verse 9 is a crucial one for our author's theology. The ark is empty except for the stone tablets, the heart of Torah, which are a tangible reminder of David's words to Solomon to walk in the ways of the LORD.

The second is 8:27–30, especially verse 27: 'But will God really dwell on earth? The heaven, even the highest heaven, cannot contain you. How much less this temple I have built!' Here is a true and profound grasp of the transcendence of God (a point to be referred to later).

We could wish that Solomon's story had ended there, but we cannot ignore chapter 11 and its relevance to the Temple theme. The relevant verses are 7–8, where Solomon now builds multiple shrines for foreign deities. This was doubtless made easier by the disturbing relegation of the Temple to the status of a royal chapel in chapters 6–7. The verbs in verse 8 suggest repeated actions. This was no temporary lapse: full-blown syncretism, where Yahweh simply becomes another godlet, is now the order of the day.

After Solomon, for many chapters the Temple is virtually ignored, and when it does occur the references are brief and rather cryptic. In 1 Kings 14:25–28 we read of Shishak of Egypt's invasion and plundering of the Temple. Rehoboam then replaces the gold shields of Solomon with bronze shields. This is an actual incident, but surely also an eloquent commentary on the shabby and downbeat nature of the regime. The shields may have looked the same from a distance, but the reality was far different. But what is striking is that apparently Temple liturgy was maintained (v. 28). In the midst of idolatry and apostasy (vv. 22–24), the king was still going through the motions of orthodoxy with a supporting cast.

We next hear of the Temple in 1 Kings 15:15, where Asa refurbishes it. However, almost immediately the refurbished items are removed again as part of a bribe to the king of Aram (vv. 18ff.). The Temple, it appears, is at the centre of no one's agenda.

But more significant still is the dramatic turn of events in 1 Kings 17. The focus switches to the great prophetic ministries of Elijah and Elisha, which run until Elisha's death in 2 Kings 13. These chapters are overwhelmingly concentrated on the northern kingdom, and especially on the way that Torah is to the fore, as in the preaching of Elijah we have Moses *redivivus*. Thus the great central section of the book ignores the Temple.

2. WHAT ABOUT 2 KINGS 12?

Just at the end of Elisha's story we have, unexpectedly, the Temple thrust centre stage. Jehu, an army commander, has bloodily extirpated both the dynasty of Ahab and Baal worship in the north, which included the destruction of the temple of Baal built by Ahab (1 Kgs. 16:32). Athaliah, daughter of Ahab, who had married Jehoram of Judah (2 Kgs. 8:18), attempted to destroy the Judahite royal line. She was herself overthrown by a conspiracy headed by Jehoiada the high priest, and Joash or Jehoash was placed on the throne. 2 Kings 12 tells of this ultimately unsuccessful attempt to restore the Temple, and it is to this we now turn.

This story is fascinating more for what it does not say than for what appears on the surface. It looks, Janus-like, to both Solomon and Josiah. In some ways the forty-year reign of this king mirrors on a small scale that of Solomon in his concentration of the Temple and his eventual backsliding. Likewise it points forward to Josiah in his standing by a pillar and being presented with a covenant scroll when he comes to the throne as a child. Yet, as we shall see, the contrasts are more striking and fundamental, and indeed are probably the key to this story. Why does this king go so badly wrong?

We are not given a clear idea of Joash's motivation; indeed, he is a very shadowy figure. A clue comes in 2 Kings 12:2: 'Joash did what was right in the eyes of the LORD all the years Jehoiada the priest instructed him.' This is a very qualified approbation: he is not compared to David and his faith is second-hand and temporary. This is to be reflected in his attitude to the repair of the Temple. Three considerations mark this narrative. The first is an overemphasis on money and fabric. There is no sense of vision or excitement (contrast 1 Kgs. 8). Here is only a job to be done and money raised and fabric repaired. Joash is the patron saint of those who imagine that the way to do God's work is to have a fabric committee and a fund-raising programme.

Secondly, there is a total silence about prayer and Torah. Nowhere is there a call for renewed faithfulness, nowhere is there a mention of returning to the LORD. Indeed, they waited twenty-three years to do anything about the project he had initiated. Admittedly, Joash was only seven when crowned, but it is hard to believe that this project was at the heart of his agenda.

Thirdly, there is no mention of personal faith, nothing said about Joash's heart. Solomon's heart was often fickle and unstable and led him badly astray. However, at the high-water mark in 1 Kings 8 he shows a genuine and warm spirituality. Joash appears to have had no heart for God at all.

In any case, it is not long before Joash has to surrender many of the Temple artefacts to buy off the king of Aram. The Chronicler speaks of Joash's later apostasy, and his reign ends in shame and failure (2 Chr. 24:17ff.).

Here we have Temple without Torah. When we remember that for Solomon in 1 Kings 8 the Temple was significant only because it contained the ark of the covenant, which in turn contained the tablets of the Law, we realize the deficiencies here. Later in the Josiah story we are to see how the heart of the reform is to be the Book of the Law. Here with Joash we have merely the repair of a building. This is reflected in the very matter-of-fact style and the absence of any colour or emotion in the portrayal of the characters – 'the professional language of the accountant'.[3] This kind of 'interest' in the Temple will lead down a cul-de-sac.

3. WHAT WAS ITS IMPORTANCE TO THE GREAT REFORMING KINGS?

The closing action of the Kings narrative is dominated by the two great reforming kings, Hezekiah and Josiah. Our purpose now is to examine what part the Temple played in their activities. We begin in 2 Kings 16, in the reign of Hezekiah's father, Ahaz. Verses 10–20 of that chapter describe Ahaz's ill-judged meeting with Tiglath Pileser of Assyria at Damascus. There he sees an altar which takes his fancy, and he has a replica made for the Temple. On his return to Jerusalem, he assumes a Solomon-like role (1 Kgs. 8:62–64), and offers the full range of sacrifices upon the new altar. These are followed by other innovations such as removing the bronze bulls supporting the Sea. The reason given is 'deference to the King of Assyria'. Ahaz fears Assyria more than Yahweh; this is to be strikingly reversed by his son. We seem further away than ever from a true understanding of Temple theology.

Hezekiah's story is told in 2 Kings 18–20 and the focus is clearly on how this new Davidic king stood up to the Assyrian Goliath. However, for our purposes, there are two short passages which are relevant. First, 18:4 briefly mentions the cultic reforms, with an emphasis on the removal of the high places.[4] The Chronicler, by contrast, devotes three long chapters (2 Chr. 29–31) to Hezekiah's cultic reforms. Of these, chapter 29 specifically deals with the Temple and with the opening of its doors, which Ahaz had closed. Here, our author focuses on one issue relating to the Temple – the removing and destruction of the bronze snake. This fits in with the overall thrust of the Kings narrative, which accepts the Temple and its furniture, but is always conscious of the

---

[3] T. R. Hobbs, *1, 2 Kings* (Word Biblical themes; Dallas: Word, 1989), p. 149.
[4] The text is emphatic: 'It was he ...', 'He was the one ...' who removed the high places.

danger of faith being placed in material objects. This will be developed in the final section.

The other relevant passage (2 Kgs. 19:14–19) is one which has no parallel in Chronicles. Here Hezekiah receives Sennacherib's insulting letter. He took this to the Temple 'and spread it out before the Lord'. Here, like Solomon in 1 Kings 8, Hezekiah recognizes both the unique relationship of Yahweh with the Temple and his independence of it. 'Enthroned between the cherubim' he is especially encountered in the ark of the covenant. Yet he is the creator and the Lord of history and not simply the God in Jerusalem. Significantly, Hezekiah's words echo those of David to Goliath, 'the whole world will know that there is a God in Israel' (1 Sam. 17:46), and Elijah to the prophets of Baal, 'so that these people will know that you, O Lord, are God' (1 Kgs. 18:37). It is the word of Yahweh, Lord of all, who will deal with this threat.

Before looking at Josiah, a word is necessary on Manasseh, Hezekiah's son and 'Judah's Ahab' (2 Kgs. 21:3). In 2 Kings 21 our author shows how Manasseh systematically dismantles all his father's reforms and directly challenged the faith and loyalty to Yahweh, which had been at the heart of his father's reign. The Temple is filled with all the appurtenances of paganism: Asherah pole(s), altars to other deities and occult practices. The net effect of all this is to reduce Yahweh to a local godlet. The wholesale abandonment of Torah is seen as deliberate and calculated (vv. 7–10). Ominous prophetic warnings of the fall of Jerusalem now appear, and the example of the destruction of Ahab's dynasty recalled. The Temple has become an idolatrous shrine. This activity continues in the insignificant and dismal two-year reign of his son Amon.

In spite of this apostasy, the light shines again as the crown is placed on the head of an eight-year-old boy, Josiah, worthiest of David's sons to sit on his throne. Much could be said, but three matters relate particularly to our subject. The first is the commendation of a David-like figure. There is, however, a significant phrase in 2 Kings 22:2, used of none of the other kings: 'not turning aside to the right or to the left'. This is an allusion to Deuteronomy 17:20, where the ideal king is one who does not deviate either left or right of Torah. Here we have not only the new David, but the new Moses. Torah is to govern and be the standard for everything, including the Temple.

Secondly, we have the notice of Temple repairs, which echo those of Joash (2 Kgs. 12:4–16). At this stage it seems little more than that. However, unlike Joash, our author's comment on this king leads us to expect something better, and we are not to be disappointed.

This third element comes in 2 Kings 22:8: 'Hilkiah the high priest said to Shaphan the secretary: "I have found the Book of the Law in the temple of the Lord."' This provides the impetus for the further far-reaching reforms. This is not the place to discuss in detail the controversy surrounding the precise nature and dating of the Book of the Law. If this were indeed not a rediscovery but a new product of a reforming group it is difficult to explain why earlier kings were condemned (e.g. Jehu in 2 Kgs. 10:31) or commended (e.g. Hezekiah in 2 Kgs. 18:6) for their attitude towards it. A strong probability must be that it was suppressed during the long and apostate reign of Manasseh. Further, it seems likely that it was at least part of Deuteronomy, as the reforms which follow, especially the covenant renewal ceremony (2 Kgs. 23:1–3), return to that book and the reforms are driven by it.

Ultimately, because of Manasseh's apostasy, exile is inevitable (2 Kgs. 23:26–27). The Temple will not be saved, nor will the city. The curtain is about to fall.

2 Kings 25 tells the story of the sack of Jerusalem and the destruction of the Temple in a very matter-of-fact way, which adds to the sense of bleakness. Two matters call for comment. The first is the description of the removal of the Temple artefacts in verses 13–17. We have not heard of some of these since the days of Solomon in 1 Kings 6–8, and we sense here the fulfilment of judgement. The Temple has gone and its most glorious days will not return.

The other noteworthy point is the last few verses of the book (25:27–30). A ray of hope shines as the Babylonian king releases Jehoiachin and invites him to the royal table. The reader will remember the promises to the house of David and the prayer in 1 Kings 8:22–53 looking beyond the exile. The story is not over. Interestingly, the Chronicler ends by looking to the rebuilding of the Temple (2 Chr. 36:23); here in Kings it is the words of promise to the dynasty.

4. WHERE DOES THE KINGS EMPHASIS FIT CANONICALLY?

We have outlined the author's theology of Temple and one important area remains: where does this fit canonically? The following comments are not exhaustive – other papers in this volume should be consulted – but there are three issues which can be explored a little.

The first is how Temple expresses the nature of God originally adumbrated in Genesis 1 and 2. Genesis 1 shows the transcendence of God, who speaks and a universe springs into being, and who is outside and greater than the universe he has created. This is further reflected in some of the Psalms: for example, 29:9, 'in his temple all cry, "Glory!"', and 93:5, 'holiness adorns your house for endless days, O LORD'. Both these psalms speak of God's unapproachable sovereignty over creation and 'Temple' or 'house' is primarily creation itself. However, in Genesis 2, God comes down into his creation, he walks and talks with his people. He creates in the universe one particular planet, in that planet places a garden, and there he comes. So in the fallen world there is a country, in that country a mountain citadel, in that citadel a building, in that building a room, and in that room a box with the tablets of Torah. This blend of transcendence and immanence is what lies at the heart of a true theology of Temple. Solomon, in his greatest moment in 1 Kings 8, grasped this: 'the heaven, even the highest heaven, cannot contain you. How much less this temple I have built' (1 Kgs. 8:27). Yet God has placed his name there and Solomon is able to speak of 'praying towards this place'. Hezekiah, faced with crisis, also recognizes this in 2 Kings 19:14–19, where he goes to the Temple and prays to the God who is met there, yet who reigns over heaven and earth. This perception avoids two errors. The first is collapsing the transcendence of God into vagueness and using the belief that he is everywhere as an excuse to avoid him anywhere. The second is to try to confine him locally to a shrine, which is idolatry.

The second area requires more reflection on the differences of Kings and Chronicles. Probably the Chronicler's basic theology of Temple is embodied in Abijah's address in 2 Chronicles 13:4–12, where its fundamental connection with the Davidic dynasty is underlined. The Kings author makes no mention of this speech. Similarly, the great emphasis on the Passovers of Hezekiah and Josiah (2 Chr. 30:1–13; 35:17–18) shows the Chronicler's concern for united Temple worship as the means to restore the sense of post-exilic Israel's identity as the people of God. His strong emphasis on David's extensive preparations for the Temple (1 Chr. 22–29) shows that it was virtually a joint project with Solomon. The connection of king and Temple is powerful and unmistakable.

The Kings author, however, insists on Torah. This is an emphasis which began as far back as 1 Samuel 3 where the word of the LORD is 'rare' and then firmly established by the call and ministry of Samuel. This is reiterated in 2 Samuel 7 where two meanings of 'house' are played on. God will build a 'house', that is, a dynasty for David, rather than David building a house, that is, a Temple for the LORD. It is difficult to avoid the impression that in Samuel/Kings the Temple, like kingship, is something that God is prepared to accept, rather than being seen as the best. The emphasis in 2 Samuel 7:5–7 is on the best, and that is to become the emphasis of the New Testament when Christ himself embodies the glory of God.

This is linked to the strong emphasis on the prophetic word most fully expressed in the ministries of Elijah and Elisha and underpinned by the discovery of the Book of the Law in 2 Kings 22. Yet although this Book has been for some time hidden, this does not mean that it only emerged during Josiah's reign. As we noted above, Hezekiah is commended for keeping the Law (2 Kgs. 18:6), and the crucial words of David in 2 Kings 2:2–4 make better sense if we understand that the book had been available for kings to consult and had been suppressed during Manasseh's long reign. Indeed, the Kings account of Josiah's reformation makes the discovery of the Book and the events flowing from it central to the narrative. Here is the missing element which makes the reformation so utterly different from Joash's mere repair of fabric.

Moreover, the Chronicler ends his account with the decree of Cyrus, which focuses on building a 'temple for him at Jerusalem in Judah' (2 Chr. 36:23). In Kings, as the tragic events of the exile unfold, our author sees these as 'in accordance with the word of the LORD proclaimed by his servants the prophets' (2 Kgs. 24:3).

A third issue is the way the Temple recedes in importance thereafter. The post-exilic prophets Haggai and Zechariah both speak of it. Haggai shows the danger of not rebuilding the Temple, reflecting as it does a general spiritual apathy, but soon strikes an eschatological note (2:9), and the book ends with the emphasis again on the word of the LORD. Zechariah underlines the danger of mere physical rebuilding without change in inward attitude. The author of Hebrews draws from Tabernacle, rather than Temple, and the theme culminates, as we shall see in Beale's chapter, in Revelation 21:22: 'I saw no temple in the city …' Canonically, there the particular emphases of Kings find their fulfilment.

5. SOME OBSERVATIONS

The author of Kings has not identified Temple as of major significance in his unfolding story of the life of the covenant community. He has certainly not ignored it, but nor has it been the centre of gravity. Three observations can usefully be made.

The first is that ultimately Temple, unlike Torah, is not absolutely essential for the life of faith. This is perhaps most readily seen in a book like Esther, where the life of faith is seen at its most minimalist. There is no cultic framework, no Temple or liturgy to sustain the life of the faith community. Yet underneath the surface there are canonical links with earlier Scriptures and the whole flow of narrative echoes, among other things, the Joseph story.[5] Faithfulness to Yahweh is possible without Temple but not without Torah.

A second observation flowing from this is a word on the attitude to 'institutions' which emerges in 1 Samuel – 2 Kings. The author of Kings regards the Temple in a similar way to that of the author of Samuel to kingship. Both these institutions are not part of God's primary purpose, but both can be manifestations of his rule and his presence. Both have the inherent danger of focusing on the wrong object, but both, at their best, can point to ultimate reality. We have

---

[5] Another such echo can be found in Esther 3:12. There the royal secretaries write out the decree aimed at the destruction of the Jews 'on the thirteenth day of the first month' (cf. Ex. 12:6). This immediately raises the question as to whether the God of the Exodus could save them now.

noted how Solomon, in 1 Kings 8, grasps that reality, but subsequently this was often obscured.

The third observation is a development of the above. The theology of the Temple with which the author of Kings operates is adumbrated most clearly in 2 Samuel 7, where God's word to David through Nathan plays on the two meanings of 'house': the Temple and the Davidic dynasty. The key is in verse 11b: 'the LORD himself will establish a house for you'. Ultimately the initiative is from God and the Temple can only be a temporary manifestation of his own glory and presence.

Our author recognizes the place of the Temple, but it is not the centre of his agenda. At its best it is a visible and tangible reminder of the presence of Yahweh and his choice of Zion. As long as that presence is not identified with the bricks and mortar and the institution, all is well. It was to take the bitter experience of exile to show that Yahweh could not be confined to any building, nor his presence trapped in any locality.

5

THE TEMPLE IN EZEKIEL

JOHN B. TAYLOR

It comes as a surprise to many readers of the book of the prophet Ezekiel that a man who professed to have spent half of his life and the whole of his prophetic ministry as an exile from Jerusalem in the deserts of Babylonia should have been so preoccupied with the welfare of his home city and its Temple. Jerusalem is mentioned no less than twenty-six times in the course of his forty-eight chapters and there are endless references to the Temple and the mountains of Israel. The holy city with its guilty past and its restored future are made the main theme of twenty-two of the chapters. Why this should have so dominated his writing is a well-known problem that has been met with a variety of possible solutions.

Several earlier commentators questioned whether the book of Ezekiel was a literary unity at all,[1] or had been reworked by a later hand in the light of the experiences of the exile.[2] Others believed that the prophet exercised a double ministry, first in Jerusalem from the date of his call to the fall of Jerusalem, and then in captivity in Babylonia.[3] A modification of this view was that while in exile Ezekiel received his call to go to the house of Israel and made the journey to Jerusalem described in 8:3 as having taken place in a kind of trance state while he was surrounded by the elders of the exiles.[4] This of course begs the practical question of how permission for such a return might have been granted and obtained from the Babylonian authorities.

Those who have argued for the integrity of the evidence provided in the book[5] point to Ezekiel's having been a priest or the son of a

---

[1] So R. Kraetzschmar, *Das Buch Ezechiel* (Gottingen: Vandenhoeck & Ruprecht, 1900).

[2] V. Herntrich, *Ezechielprobleme* (BZAW Beihefte 61; Giessen: Töpelmann, 1932).

[3] A. Bertholet, *Hesekiel* (Handbuch zum Alten Testament; Tübingen: J. C. B. Mohr, 1936).

[4] O. R. Fischer, *The Unity of the Book of Ezekiel* (unpublished dissertation, Boston University, 1939); followed by R. H. Pfeiffer, *Introduction to the Old Testament* (New York: Harper, 1941); P. Auvray, *Ezechiel* (Paris: les Editions du Cerf: La Sainte Bible de Jerusalem, 1949); and H. G. May in *Interpreters Bible* (vol. 6; New York: Abingdon, 1956).

[5] Among those commentaries in this category are: G. A. Cooke, *A Critical and Exegetical Commentary on the Book of Ezekiel* (ICC; Edinburgh: T&T Clark, 1936); C. G. Howie, *The Date and Composition of Ezekiel* (JBL Monograph Series IV; Society of Biblical Literature:

priest (1:3), and that he would therefore have been brought up in the apprenticeship of the Temple and its priestly lore before being exiled to Babylon. They also evidence the strong emotional attachment felt by the exiles for their native city, witnessed both by their concern for news of Jerusalem's welfare and the conviction of some that they would speedily return there after the briefest of exiles. And they rightly point out that Ezekiel was far from being the only member of a priestly family in exile and that hundreds of his fellow exiles were of priestly descent. It would therefore have been totally understandable that they were preoccupied with thoughts of Jerusalem, the Temple and a return to the worship of God in his sanctuary.

A key factor in the interpretation of Ezekiel is the significance of his opening words, 'In the thirtieth year', which as the text stands is identified with the fifth year of the exile of king Jehoiachin. Although this is a notorious *crux interpretum*, the best solution seems to be to regard it as the thirtieth year of Ezekiel's life, a proposal dating back to Origen.[6] This would make his age at the start of his captivity as twenty-five; he would have been thirty-four when his wife suddenly died (24:18); and fifty when he had his closing vision of the restored land and Temple (40:1). The thirtieth year would have suggested the age of his adulthood when he might otherwise have been expected to begin the full exercise of his priesthood, of which he had been deprived by the exile, and gives a new significance to God's call to him to be a prophet of the word of God instead of being a priest entrusted with Temple liturgy and Temple Torah.

If this is indeed so, Ezekiel's interaction with the theme of the Temple was no mere theological nicety. It was deeply personal to him, and would have been the prime focus of his early apprenticeship right up to the time when he was so unceremoniously taken away from it and deposited in a prison camp in far-off Babylonia, wondering if he would ever return to fulfil his life's vocation.

Philadelphia, 1950); G. Fohrer, *Ezechiel* (Handbuch zum Alten Testament; Tübingen: J. C. B. Mohr, 1955); W. Zimmerli, *Ezechiel* (Biblischer Kommentar; Neukirchener Verlag des Erziehungsvereins: Neukirchen-Vluyn, 1969); W. Eichrodt, *Ezekiel: A Commentary* (tr. C. Quin; London: SCM Press, 1970); J. W. Wevers (ed.), *Ezekiel* (Century Bible; London: Nelson, 1969); K. W. Carley, *The Book of the Prophet Ezekiel* (Cambridge Bible Commentary; London: Cambridge University Press, 1974); R. H. Alexander, 'Ezekiel' in F. Gaberlein (ed.), *Expositors Bible Commentary* (Grand Rapids: Zondervan, 1976); M. Greenberg, *Ezekiel 1–20* (Anchor Bible; New York: Doubleday, 1983); L. Allen, *Ezekiel 20–48* (WBC; Dallas: Word, 1990); B. Vawter and L. J. Hoppe, *A New Heart: A Commentary on the Book of Ezekiel* (International Theological Commentaries; Grand Rapids: Eerdmans, 1993); D. I. Block, *The Book of Ezekiel: Chapters 1–24* (NICOT; Grand Rapids: Eerdmans, 1997); also T. Renz, *The Rhetoric Function of the Book of Ezekiel* (supplement to VT vol. LXXVI; Leiden: Brill, 1999).
[6] Supported among others by Eichrodt, Carley, Allen, Vawter and Hoppe, and Block. Most commentators discuss the various possibilities without coming down on one particular solution.

Within that context of dashed hopes and frustrated expectations, we now turn to consider his vision of the glory of God with which he begins his prophecy. Quite apart from the puzzling nature of the description of the vision, which has sorely tried the ingenuity of artists illustrating our children's bibles, the key considerations are its timing, its location and its significance in retrospect. We have already remarked on its timing: it came to Ezekiel five years into his and his people's captivity, and it happened in his thirtieth year. If the latter figure does indeed indicate his priestly coming of age, the former points to those five years of sheer perplexity as Ezekiel and his fellow exiles reflected on the question of the divine presence in Jerusalem which had for so long been axiomatic in their beliefs. Yahweh's apparent defeat by the forces of Babylon must have shattered the exiles, as year on year they contemplated both their past and their likely future.

We have already noted that, according to Jeremiah 29, a prevailing view among the exiles was that the captivity was to be of brief duration because Yahweh would not allow it to be long and would certainly restore them to Jerusalem so that city and Temple could continue to be the centre of their world. The fact that this view may have had Isaianic authorization did not impress Jeremiah, and he stated explicitly that the exile was to be viewed as a long-term punishment to be thought of in terms of seventy years rather than a year or two. The exiles were instructed by letter to reconcile themselves to settling into life in Babylon, cultivating their crops, bringing up their families and developing a civic sense of belonging to their host community.[7]

Assuming that there was some limited degree of interchange of information, if not of personnel, between Jerusalem and the exiles, as his prophecy certainly implies, Jeremiah's words could well have reached Ezekiel's ears. He would have agreed with Jeremiah's assessment of the situation, not so much in terms of the length of time they would have to endure being in exile, but in the heinousness of Israel's behaviour that justified so exemplary a punishment. The Babylonian captivity was to Ezekiel more than just another blip on the screen of Israel's history, which would speedily be righted by the mercy of God, but a serious malfunction of the covenant which could not be allowed to be glossed over. It is noteworthy that Ezekiel makes several references to current attitudes both among the exiles and among those left behind in Jerusalem, all of which indicate that the true seriousness of the situation had completely passed the people by. For example, there are the two 'proverbs' widely quoted (and responded to in 12:21–28), which state 'the days grow long and every vision comes to nought' (i.e. nothing disastrous is going to happen) and 'the vision that he sees is for many days hence, and he prophesies of times far off' (i.e. the doom

---

[7] See Jeremiah 29:4–9.

is all eschatological, but we are living in the present). There is also the oracle about the meat in the cauldron (11:2–12), attributed to those still living in Jerusalem, which implies that they consider themselves to be the choice of God's people and that they are now the rightful inheritors of Yahweh's good promises, over against the supposedly disinherited citizens in exile.

In all these respects Ezekiel was swimming against the tide of public opinion and there is no suggestion in his writing that he had any sympathy with the prevailing optimism about the outcome of the exile. In this he was following – or independently agreeing with – his contemporary Jeremiah in expressing the belief that the inviolability of Jerusalem was not sacrosanct. The divine presence was a matter of covenant grace, not of covenant obligation, and thus the possibility of the divine absence was never far away.

John E. Kutsko has written impressively on this subject in his monograph *Between Heaven and Earth: Divine Presence and Divine Absence in the Book of Ezekiel*,[8] which is probably the study most germane to the theme of this chapter. He summarizes the whole of the first eleven chapters of Ezekiel under the subtitle 'From Divine Presence to Divine Absence'. The so-called *kābôd* theology of chapters 1 and 10 is the way 'Ezekiel enlists various means to describe the presence of God in order to make God mobile and to reassure his audience that Yahweh is present despite his seeming absence.'[9] While one would question his use of the word 'enlist', with its implication that Ezekiel's vision was a device rather than a real and dramatic theophany, it is undeniable that the vision as the prophet described it expresses a number of features about Yahweh, of which mobility is one. Here was an experience of God, not just appearing in a burning bush (as with Moses) or in the Temple (as with Isaiah), but moving as if on a mission, coming out of the north, conveyed by winged creatures and supported on wheels that turned as they went. Other memorable features of the vision are Yahweh's indescribability (the language is consciously imprecise, as if words are inadequate to express what the prophet saw); his dazzling wonder, with references to flashing fire, gleaming bronze, shimmering wings and the gleam of chrysolite; and his capacity for moving in every direction at will (or as the Spirit directed).

The striking fact of the vision is of course that it occurred in Babylonia, and far away from Jerusalem, where it might more under-standably have been encountered. What then was the vision and what was its significance? A number of features identified it with the God of the Temple, despite the deep underlying suspicion that Yahweh was

---

[8] John E. Kutsko, *Between Heaven and Earth: Divine Presence and Divine Absence in the Book of Ezekiel* (Biblical and Judaic Studies UCSD 7; Winona Lake: Eisenbrauns, 2000).
[9] Ibid., p. 2.

invisible as well as indescribable and unencounterable in the normal run of things. The first was that it appeared 'out of the north', the direction to which one looked if expecting a visitor from the land of Judah (the direct route from west to east being impossible and the so-called Fertile Crescent route being the only viable option). The second feature, and probably the most telling, is the description of the strange living creatures that attended the deity and supported the chariot-throne. These, with their part-human, part-animal appearance, were reminiscent not only of the seraphim of Isaiah's Temple vision (with wings featuring prominently) but were known to have resonances with the rarely seen, but doubtless often spoken about, cherub-figures bowing over the lid of the ark of the covenant, and also with the interior decoration of the Temple itself, with which any priestly entrant would have been familiar.

To this may be added the swift, darting mobility of the wheels turning in any and every direction, which must have suggested to Ezekiel and to those to whom he communicated his vision that Yahweh was not confined to the Temple, though located there, and that he was in visionary form visiting his displaced people in exile. The impact of this and its theological significance would not have taken long to dawn on the prophet and his fellow exiles. If their God could appear to them in the place that spoke to them of defeat, humiliation and the power-lessness of Yahweh before the all-conquering might of the Babylonian armies and their gods, there was hope.

At this stage there is no indication in Ezekiel that the appearance of Yahweh's *merkābâ* or chariot-throne implied that he had abandoned Jerusalem in favour of some other location. This was more a statement that the divine presence could be encountered in the land of exile than that he had taken leave of the Temple. As such it constituted a heartening reassurance to the prophet that he and his fellow exiles were nevertheless within the reach of the mercy and care of God, even though this was soon to be tempered by the commission that was given him of being sent 'to the people of Israel, to a nation of rebels, who have rebelled against me ... and you shall speak my words to them, whether they hear or refuse to hear; for they are a rebellious house' (Ezek. 2:3–5). Such a mission anticipated hostility, rejection and stub-bornness from his hearers and necessitated a forehead 'like adamant harder than flint' (Ezek. 3:9) on the part of Ezekiel. The content of the message, symbolized by the scroll that he was given to eat, consisting of words of lamentation and mourning and woe, all written unusually on both sides of the parchment, implied that his future ministry was to be full to overflowing with doom and condemnation.

This was the experience, both uplifting and depressing, heartening and daunting, reviving and perplexing, that left Ezekiel 'in bitterness in the heat of my spirit' (Ezek. 3:14) to sit with the exiles by the river Chebar 'overwhelmed among them for seven days' (Ezek. 3:15).

The full significance of the vision would have taken all of that time to dawn upon the prophet's mind. It was startling, innovative, contradictory, baffling. It had no precedents in Israelite prophetic experience, except perhaps for Moses at the burning bush. Since the days of the Tabernacle and the consecration of the Temple, there was only one place where visions of God might reasonably be expected. But now Yahweh appeared to have crossed his traditional boundaries. Why was this and what did it signify?

We are all familiar with Ezekiel's conclusion. The punishment of Israel's disobedience, of which the deportation of 597 BC was but a foretaste, had a long way yet to go before it was exhausted. The sins, both of his fellow exiles and of those left behind in Jerusalem, merited much more by way of retribution, and God's wrath would not be satisfied until the city and its Temple and its walls were totally destroyed. Inconceivable as it may sound to devotees of Yahweh and the Temple, this to Ezekiel was the inevitable outworking of God's justice. Jerusalem was doomed.

He then sees himself as not merely a prophet to Israel but as the watchman for the house of Israel, under obligation to warn both righteous and unrighteous in the community to repent and to refrain from sin so that they may save their lives. Only by fulfilling his role as watchman will Ezekiel himself escape the blood-guiltiness that might otherwise fall on him.

Then the prophet, recommissioned and reinvigorated by the Spirit of God (3:22), and in spite of the bonds that restrict his movements and the ritual dumbness that prevents him from uttering anything but the words God is to give him, begins his play-acting ministry of signs and dramatic symbolism. The theme is now unquestionably the prospect of siege for Jerusalem, starvation diet during famine, prolonged captivity and near-total devastation and destruction of the city's population. It develops in chapters 4–7 and reaches its climax in the second of Ezekiel's visions where he is transported to Jerusalem (in imagination as we must suppose, despite the well-known views to the contrary) to view the forms of idolatry being committed in the Temple.

It is not impossible that the four examples of idolatry described in Ezekiel 8 (the image of jealousy alongside the altar; the portrayal of unclean creatures in the darkened recesses of the Temple; the women weeping for Tammuz; and the twenty-five sun worshippers) were purely imaginary or at best typical of the Temple's wrongdoings. Much depends on the degree of communication that was thought to exist between Ezekiel and the exiles and the people left behind in Jerusalem. On the evidence of Jeremiah 29 and the exchange of letters that may have accompanied it, and the message of the fugitive of Ezekiel 33:21, it seems not unlikely that a certain amount of news did pass between Jerusalem and Tel Abib, whether by individuals or in letters conveyed by such imperial Babylonian postal service as may have existed. If there was nothing but the rarest communication, it would make Ezekiel's credibility the more difficult to establish. The fact that he could be so precise in some of his details, and naming of names, including especially the death of Pelatiah (11:13), and not apparently be greeted with a torrent of scepticism, leads one to suppose that his network of information, available both to him and the elders of the exiles, was better than we might otherwise suppose. So one is inclined to think that what he describes in chapter 8 had substance in reality, or at least was sufficient to strike chords, if not of memory, then of likelihood, in the minds of his hearers.

At the same time, the evidence of these four acts of idolatry has a typical side to it, condemning the priests, the elders, the women and lay worshippers in turn. The idolatry of Jerusalem has become so multifaceted and embraces so many sections of the population that the conclusion can only be drawn that the holy place had become totally corrupted and both the city and the building must go. How Ezekiel came to this despairing conclusion is a subject that justifies further study, though it must remain in the realm of speculation. It clearly stemmed from a sense of horror at the way in which Yahweh worship had degenerated over recent years. It also grew out of a heightened sense of the holiness of God, which was appreciated by prophets like Jeremiah and Ezekiel in a way that neither priests nor laity ever felt it. The exempting mark on the foreheads of those who were to be saved from the destruction of the executioners in chapter 9 was for those few who 'sigh and groan over all the abominations that are committed in it' (Ezek. 9:4). The generality were unsurprised by what went on and were condemned for their complacency at this affront to God's purity and holiness.

Yet to come to the conclusion that this sorry state of affairs justified not only Nebuchadnezzar's wholesale deportation of a large section of the population but went beyond that to the prospect of the city's utter devastation was to appear to run counter to the very covenant of God with Israel. This had been the mainstay of Israel's faith and confidence all through the hazards of Hezekiah's reign, with the armies of Sennacherib at the very gates of the city. The record of Isaiah 36–37 (2 Kgs. 18:13–20:11) gives a graphic account of the threats uttered by the invading army at the very gates of Jerusalem. The Assyrian army commander's words, spoken 'in the language of Judah', and the fear they inspired in Hezekiah and the people of Jerusalem are only just countered by a robust response from Isaiah, as he assures both king and people that Yahweh would not abandon his holy city. 'Like birds hovering, so the LORD of hosts will protect Jerusalem; he will protect and deliver it, he will spare and rescue it' (Isa. 31:5). The fact that the threat evaporated, as by a miracle, became for later generations a precedent which left them with an almost doctrinaire conviction that Jerusalem was forever safe. The covenant had held, and the city had been delivered, because Yahweh was its guarantor and the Temple was his dwelling place.

In the light of this, I am inclined to the view that it was only the vision of Yahweh's appearing in Babylonia that enabled Ezekiel to entertain the unbelievable belief that the God who was present in Jerusalem could be the God who would also take his leave. He was no longer apparently bound to the Temple there. He could move. So the vision in the plain freed the prophet to deliver the message that worse was yet to come and provided him with the justification that the people's idolatry constituted virtually an annulment of the age-old covenant of God with Israel. Hence his two allegories of the foundling child[10] and of Oholah and Oholibah[11] do not tell of the nation's transition from a state of relative innocence to one of disobedience and corruption, but present a picture of Israel as having been decadent and unclean from the very beginning, and the covenant of grace as a potential disaster from the outset on account of the nature of the people to whom it was so graciously and generously given.

A further witness to Ezekiel's theology of divine judgement and the justification of God in abandoning Jerusalem is the language he uses of idols and idolatry, supremely in his use of *gillûlîm*. Kutsko makes particular play on this, describing the word as 'a highly pejorative expression connoting a quite literal grossness; that is, these objects lack any associative value or merit, and they convey uncleanness'. He goes on to argue that Ezekiel's frequent references to idols offered the exiles a theological proposition: 'the physical presence of idols indicates their powerlessness, and the absence of Yahweh's presence indicates God's power'.[12]

Despite this, the text of Ezekiel's vision betrays an element of reluctance about the departure of Yahweh from his Temple. At the end of chapter 10 the *kābôd* vision, which though described in somewhat greater detail is said to be identical with what was seen by the river Chebar, 'went forth from the threshold of the house and stood over the cherubim. And the cherubim lifted up their wings and mounted up from the earth in my sight as they went forth, with the wheels beside them; and they stood at the door of the east gate of the house of the LORD; and the glory of the God of Israel was over them.' Three points are worth noting: (i) the laconic expression *wayyēṣēʾ kᵉbôd yhwh*, the glory of Yahweh went forth, with its Ichabod[13] echoes of finality; (ii) 'the glory over the cherubim' contrasted with the Temple pattern of the cherubim revering the glory over the mercy seat (the *hilasterion*);

---

[10] Ezekiel 16:1–63.
[11] Ezekiel 23:1–49.
[12] Kutsko, *Between Heaven and Earth*, p. 75.
[13] The story of Ichabod, literally 'no glory', 'or the glory has departed', is found in 1 Samuel 4:21.

(iii) Ezekiel's unusual use of the phrase *bêt-yhwh*, house of the LORD, instead of just *bāyit*, the house, as if to draw attention to the movement of the LORD's glory from the LORD's house. Yet it was only a partial departure: from inner sanctum to threshold, as if the LORD is reluctant to leave and is almost pressurized into moving further away from the idolatrous epicentre that was once his dwelling place.

The next stage is reached at the end of chapter 12 after the further denunciation of the twenty-five and the death of Pelatiah. This time it is expressed as 'the glory of the LORD went up from the midst of the city' (it is not just the Temple that is being abandoned) 'and stood upon the mountain which is on the east side of the city' (as if to reflect some continuing concern, a watching brief over the city that for all its idolatry has not yet been completely cut off from Yahweh's covenant care). The suggestion is not that Yahweh has decamped to dwell permanently where he appeared to Ezekiel in Babylon, but that he has released himself from the Jerusalem Temple and has, as it were, gone walkabout. His absence from the Temple means his presence here, there and everywhere, in Babylon or anywhere, yes, or even in Jerusalem and Judah.

We now turn to the vision of the restored land and the new Temple of chapters 40–48,[14] regretfully glossing over the intervening chapters. Because of its futuristic tone and combination of architectural detail and practical unfeasibility, this has proved a problem for exegetes and expositors. There is no doubt that in terms of space and descriptive style Ezekiel set great store by these chapters. They provide him with the grand finale to his book, with the great culminating name change from *Yerushalayim*, Jerusalem, to *Yahweh-Shammah*, the LORD is there. He incorporates both a design for an idealized replacement Temple and a set of pseudo-Mosaic regulations about the ways in which worship shall be conducted there. He reallocates the land among the tribes as if he is rewriting the book of Joshua. He reverses the Mosaic division by ensuring that the Levites do have an inheritance of land near to the city. He pictures the outflow of divine grace and blessing from the heart of the new Temple as the trickle of water from beneath the altar, the place of sacrifice, flows eastwards gaining depth and momentum as it does

---

[14] Among recent monographs dealing with this part of Ezekiel are those of J. D. Levenson, *Theology of the Program of Restoration of Ezekiel 40–48* (Harvard Semitic Monograph Series 10; Missoula: Scholars Press, 1976); M. Haran, 'The Law Code of Ezekiel XL–XLVIII and its Relation to the Priestly School', *Hebrew Union College Annual* 50 (1979), pp. 45–71; S. Niditch, 'Ezekiel 40–48 in a Visionary Context', *CBQ* 48 (1986), pp. 208–24; S. S. Tuell, 'The Temple Vision of Ezekiel 40–48: A Programme for Restoration?', *Proceedings, Eastern Great Lakes and Midwest Biblical Society* 2 (1982), pp. 96–103 and *The Law of the Temple in Ezekiel 40–48* (Harvard Semitic Monograph Series 49; Atlanta: Scholars Press, 1992); D. Stevenson, *Vision of Transformation: The Territorial Rhetoric of Ezekiel 40–48* (printed dissertation; Ann Arbor: Scholars Press, 1995).

and bringing healing and fructifying grace to the barren badlands of the Dead Sea valley.

The question inevitably arises as to whether or not this was meant to be an architect's or a town-planner's design for an actual new city and Temple. Both Judaism and Christianity have strands of opinion (not to say dogma) that expect or intend that one day this will be their aim. It is easy to dismiss such claims as being hopelessly unrealistic, but they persist and it is right for us to spend a few pages in rebuttal.

The first thing to note is that there is no indication in Ezekiel that the construction of such a city and such a Temple was authorized by God. As Allen observes, 'Significantly there is no call to rebuild the temple, only to observe the regulations for rites and offerings ... The new Temple was to be Yahweh's creation built for rather than by his people, as a model of his own being and of his relationship with them.'[15] Instead, Ezekiel is presented with a scenario prepared by God, which he is shown around by his interpreting angel-guide. The new Temple is God's doing. The prophet's only task is to describe it in as full detail as he can.

Secondly, the sheer impracticability of much of the vision leads one to the view that its message is in the symbolism, not in its architecture or in the literal partitioning of the land. One commentator summed it up as Ezekiel's concern being 'not for a new geography of real estate but for a new human geography – of the LORD's rule and the governance of Israel within the land'. Among those impractical features may be listed the 'very high mountain' of 40:2, 'on which was a structure like a city opposite me' (so LXX), which most commentators are inclined to see as poetic licence for Mount Zion or as a symbolical parallel to Moses on the high mountain of Sinai (so Vawter, Levenson and others). Moshe Greenberg, who also compares Ezekiel in relation to the exiles with Moses in relation to those rescued from Egypt, notes that in terms of a Temple blueprint Ezekiel's Temple provides only a ground plan and no other dimensions, omits reference to Temple furniture and equipment (no bronze Sea or lavers and no internal furnishing except the altar of wood), and finds only gatehouses (of 'ridiculous' disproportion) and no partition wall around the inner court.[16] Vawter notes the uneasy marriage of vision and legislation and concludes: 'These visions had no

---

[15] Allen, *Ezekiel 20–48*, p. 214. He also refers to W. Zimmerli, '*I am Yahweh*' (tr. D. W. Stott; ed. W. Brueggemann; Atlanta: John Knox, 1982), pp. 115–16, and quotes approvingly John Skinner, *The Book of Ezekiel* (Expositors Bible; London: Hodder & Stoughton, 1909), who wrote: 'The temple that Ezekiel saw ... is a house not made with hands; it is as much a part of the supernatural preparation for the future theocracy as the "very high mountain" on which it stands, or the river that flows from it to sweeten the waters of the Dead Sea' (p. 392).

[16] See M. Greenberg, 'The Design and Themes of Ezekiel's Program of Restoration', *Interpretation* 38 (1984), pp. 181–208.

effect on the actual rebuilding of the temple and the reordering of the liturgical life of Judah after the exile.'[17] Lind even more categorically writes: 'Though some interpreters think that Ezekiel intended that the temple be built according to these specifications, there is no hint in the vision that this is so.'[18] He also underlines the symbolism both of the measurements employed in the layout and of the restructuring of the land's geography.

More positively, let it be noted that Ezekiel's chief concern, as befits his priestly upbringing, appears to be that in Israel's restored future, worship is to be the prime concern of the covenant community led by its prince, and Yahweh is to be central both to the city and to the land. This is brought out supremely in the description of the river of life flowing from beneath the threshold of the Temple. The thought of a spring of water emerging from a mountaintop is far-fetched enough, but a stream that deepens as it goes, without the aid of tributaries (which in any case would contradict the intended symbolism), is beyond belief. So all this is of a piece with the interpretation of these nine chapters as idealized and essentially symbolic in character and intention. Those literalists who cherish the hope that they will one day be able to turn them into some kind of fulfilment in a Third Temple are doing a disservice both to the text and to the intention of the prophet.

An episode that has not often been noticed is the brief paragraph in which the glory of the LORD takes up his residence in the future Temple. With repeated assurances that this vision is the same as the one he saw in chapters 1 and 10 (so 43:3), Ezekiel tells how from his privileged place in the inner court he saw the glory of the LORD entering the Temple by the gate facing east and filling the Temple. A literary artist might well have deferred this statement to the very end of his book, matching it with the vision of chapter 1, but instead of placing it at chapter 48, we find the story appearing in chapter 43, with more yet to come. Clearly the return of the LORD to the very heart of his people was important to Ezekiel (or his editor), but equally clearly it was not the final message. That was left to the miraculous effect that the renewed Temple and the deity who presided there would have on the people and the land and in particular on the archetypal barren wilderness of the Arabah and the Dead Sea, transformed into a place of never-ending fruitfulness and healing properties.

Ultimately it is the people who matter. As each tribe has its own gate for entry into the presence of the LORD, the message is that everyone will be there who should be there, each with freedom of access, each a stakeholder in the city of tomorrow. And at the heart of it all, Yahweh Shammah.

---

[17] Vawter and Hoppe, *A New Heart*, p. 187.
[18] M. C. Lind, *Ezekiel* (Believers Church Bible Commentary; Scottdale: Herald Press, 1996).

I would not want to end this brief survey of the Temple in the book of Ezekiel without touching on a few of the many echoes, parallels and developments of Ezekiel's teaching which are found elsewhere in Scripture. Parallels with Moses and Sinai have already been mentioned and more could be adduced, for example, like Moses, Ezekiel views the promised future from a Pisgah of his own, seeing it from afar but not, so far as we know, seeing the return from exile and the way the Temple was rebuilt. (Would he, I wonder, have approved?) There are also strong links with the Eden story, as Levenson has made clear and as is witnessed by the streaming waters of chapter 47, the mineral resources of the land and its trees, as well as in the specific references of 31:9–18 (the parable of the cedar in Lebanon) and the language of the lament over the king of Tyre in 28:13ff.

But it is to the many influences on the New Testament that we shall feel bound to look most closely, of which our Lord's memorable words on the great day of the feast in John 7 are perhaps the most significant. Jesus, like Ezekiel, predicted the destruction of the Temple of his day, but unlike Ezekiel he never projected an architectural vision of its replacement. Instead he took the fulfilment upon himself. As the glory of the Lord was present in his body, so the divine presence would live on in the body of the church, and then ultimately in heaven. So the way is prepared for the rich development of Ezekiel's symbolism in the book of Revelation. This is for another to expound, but we have begun to see in Ezekiel some of the theological markers that will be developed by later writers in formulating a fully Christian theology of the presence of God.

Ezekiel's great legacy was that he freed Israel from the last vestige of a belief in the localized presence of God in a building in Jerusalem, however this may have been understood, to the possibility that Yahweh was a God of movement (as he had always been in the days of the Tabernacle and the wilderness wanderings) and that he was forever moving on with his people. He would remain with his people in exile, in resettlement and in dispersion, and one day he would appear supremely in the body of his Son, Jesus Christ, in whom deity, the divine presence and the long-awaited Davidic king would be incarnate.

6

THE TEMPLE RESTORED

R. T. BECKWITH

1. THE RESTORED TEMPLE IN PROPHECY

The looting and burning of the Temple at Jerusalem in 587 BC had been a culminating horror in the Babylonian conquest and captivity of Judah. The prophet who had most insistently predicted the exile, Jeremiah, had also, remarkably enough, set a definite term to it; but for explicit predictions of the restoration of the Temple we must look to two other prophets, Isaiah and Ezekiel. Jeremiah has only an implicit prediction, in Jeremiah 33:11.

In Isaiah 44:24–28 the LORD, the creator of the world, foretells by his servant and his messengers apparently impossible things, thus confounding human wisdom and false prophecy: Cyrus will be the LORD's shepherd, to perform all his pleasure; Jerusalem and the cities of Judah will be built and inhabited, all obstacles being removed; and the foundation of the Temple will be laid. The prophet foretells the situation at and immediately following the decree of Cyrus and the initial return of the exiles, as recorded in Ezra 1–3.

A much more visionary and elaborate prediction of the restored Temple is made by one of the prophets in exile, Ezekiel, in Ezekiel 40–48. Here the Temple is already built and ready for use, and the prophet is conducted round it by an angel. The glory of the LORD enters the house, and the prophet is bidden to set the vision before the people as a pattern of holiness for them to follow. The Temple, if taken with its enclosure, is very much larger than the Temple of Solomon, and though on a similar plan (with the building divided into holy of holies and holy place, with the altar of burnt offering facing its entrance in the surrounding court), it differs in various other respects; and its visionary character is emphasized by the water springing out of its threshold, which becomes a river flowing down into the Arabah and making the waters of the Dead Sea fresh.

Ezekiel's vision is taken up again by Zechariah, after the building of the Second Temple, and is seen by Zechariah as still belonging to the future. In Zechariah 14 a time is foreseen when living waters will go out from Jerusalem, not only towards the eastern sea but also towards the western, and when every pot in the Lord's house, and in Jerusalem and Judah also, will be as holy as the bowls before the altar.[1]

2. THE RESTORED TEMPLE IN FACT

The decree of Cyrus the Great, founder of the Persian Empire, in 538 BC, following his capture of Babylon the previous year, was part of a general edict of toleration towards local religions. It had the wonderful result of enabling Sheshbazzar, the 'prince of Judah', Zerubbabel (also of the royal house) and Jeshua the high priest to return, with other companions, to their own land, taking with them the plundered vessels of the Lord's house and gifts which they had been given, and to reinstitute, on the site of the Temple, the sacrificial worship laid down in the Law of Moses. They began by rebuilding the altar of burnt offering and restoring the daily sacrifices, after which they restored the festal offerings. The next step was to lay the foundation of the Temple itself. The work on the Temple was interrupted by the officious interference and then opposition of the syncretistic occupants of the Samaritan territories, but after some years Zerubbabel and Jeshua resumed it at the urging of the prophets Haggai and Zechariah, and it was completed in 516 BC in the reign of Darius I. All this is recounted in Ezra 1–6, and there is a parallel but by no means identical account in 1 Esdras 2–7.

3. COMPARISONS AND CONTRASTS

The information which we are given about the Second Temple is not sufficient to enable us to compare it in detail with Solomon's Temple, though a comparison of Ezra 6:3 with 1 Kings 6:2 indicates that it was twice as high, and other differences will appear later. At the same time, it did not have the idealistic dimensions of Ezekiel's Temple, nor did it have the magnificence of Solomon's Temple, to judge from the reactions it inspired (Ezra 3:12–13; Hag. 2:3; Zech. 4:10; cf. Tobit 14:5). The apparent inferiority was not simply one of adornment, for, as the rabbis were afterwards to point out: 'The Second Temple lacked five things which the First Temple possessed, namely, the fire, the ark, the Urim and Thummim, the oil of anointing and the Holy Spirit [of prophecy].'[2]

The 'fire' is the supernatural altar-fire, which fell from heaven (2 Chr. 7:1–3). In the version of the saying given by the Babylonian Talmud, the 'oil of anointing' is replaced by the 'Shekinah' (literally 'dwelling'),

---

[1] Compare also Joel 3:17–18.
[2] These items are listed in the Jerusalem Talmud (Taanith 2:1; Makkoth 2:4–8) and the Babylonian Talmud (Yoma 21b).

which means the visible manifestation of God's presence in Solomon's Temple by way of the glorious cloud (1 Kgs. 8:10–11; 2 Chr. 5:13–14; 7:1–3). The loss of the ark at the Babylonian exile was a calamity which the people naturally felt with especial acuteness, and many legends gathered round its fate (2 Macc. 2:4–8; 2 Baruch 6:3–9). Josephus states in so many words that the holy of holies was now empty (*War* V:219). So the Second Temple contained none of the visible tokens of God's presence that there were in Solomon's Temple: his presence was now purely a matter of faith.

Compared with Ezekiel's Temple, the Second Temple differed not just in size but in sanctity. The priests who followed Jeshua – though with exceptions like Ezra – were not outstanding for piety. Both Ezra and Nehemiah had serious problems with the priests (Ezra 9:1; 10:18–22; Neh. 13:4–9, 28–31) and the prophet Malachi found them violating the law of sacrifice and neglecting their task of teaching (Mal. 1:6 – 2:9).

4. PRIESTHOOD AND RITUAL IN THE RESTORED TEMPLE

But for the strong reaction of Ezra and Nehemiah, it is possible that the priesthood would have brought back the syncretism which had been the besetting sin of Israel and Judah before the exile. In the event, this did not happen – not, at least, until the Hellenizing crisis of the second century BC, when the opponents of syncretism had priests for their leaders, no less than the promoters of it. Instead, a serious effort was made by the returned exiles, priests and people alike, to live by the written Law of Moses. As regards the priesthood and the ritual, the evidence of this determination begins with the earliest return of the exiles,[3] though the work of Ezra and Nehemiah consolidated what had already been begun.

The neglect of their teaching role by the priesthood, criticized by Malachi, must have been one of the causes of the rise to prominence of lay scribes in the intertestamental period. Pharisaism, which was always a predominantly lay movement, and which gloried in being traditional, was probably the most direct descendant of the early lay scribes, whereas Sadduceeism and Essenism, which were led by priests, seem likely to have been reform movements within the priesthood, possibly provoked to jealousy by Pharisaic activity. All three movements of piety, of which Pharisaism was much the largest, probably had a prehistory, before their definite emergence in the mid-second century BC, and they may all be embraced in the Hasidim or 'pious' who had a little earlier supported Judas Maccabaeus in resisting Greek persecution (1 Macc. 2:42; 2 Macc. 14:6). The three movements, though they

---

[3] See Ezra 3:1–5, 8–11; 6:15–22; 1 Esdras 5:44–62; 7:6–15.

had other differences, were basically three schools of thought about the interpretation of the Pentateuchal Law, including, of course, the law of priesthood and ritual. Here the Essenes and Sadducees had a great deal in common, since they agreed in contradicting Pharisaic interpretations which were or seemed perverse, and often (though not always) agreed in what they substituted. The Sadducees, however, largely agreed with the Pharisees and disagreed with the Essenes on the liturgical calendar and on the cycle of priestly courses which the calendar controlled.[4]

5. THE DESTINY OF THE RESTORED TEMPLE

The prophet Haggai, when responding to those who remembered the Temple of Solomon and regarded the Second Temple as nothing, declares: 'The latter glory of this house shall be greater than the former, saith the LORD of hosts; and in this place will I give peace, saith the LORD of hosts.' The way this will come about is:

> Yet once, it is a little while, and I will shake the heavens, and the earth, and the sea, and the dry land; and I will shake all nations, and the desirable things of all nations shall come, and I will fill this house with glory, saith the LORD of hosts. The silver is mine, and the gold is mine, saith the LORD of hosts (Hag. 2:6–9).

This is a new form of the old prophetic promise that in the latter days all nations shall flow to the mountain of the LORD's house, to be taught his ways, and to cease from warfare against one another (Isa. 2:1–4; Mic. 4:1–5), and that his house will become a house of prayer for all peoples (Isa. 56:7); but the promise is now applied specifically to the Second Temple.

How it will come about is further explained by Malachi:

> Behold, I send my messenger, and he shall prepare the way before me: and the Lord, whom ye seek, shall suddenly come to his temple; and the messenger of the covenant, whom ye delight in, behold, he cometh, saith the LORD of hosts (Mal. 3:1).

The Lord, preceded by his forerunner, whom we now know to be John the Baptist, will personally appear in the Second Temple. It is doubtless when that happens that the Gentiles will be won to the true faith. But when that happens, his own people will not be unaffected either. As the next five verses go on to say, it will be a time of just but merciful

---

[4] This interpretation of intertestamental religious history is set out at length in chapter 7 of my book *Calendar and Chronology, Jewish and Christian* (Leiden: Brill, 1996). Chapters 4 and 5 expound the differences between the Jewish schools of thought on the calendar and on the cycle of priestly courses.

judgement upon the priests and Levites, and also upon sinners in the nation at large.[5]

One more thing is foretold with regard to the Second Temple: it is to be destroyed. At the end of the seventy weeks from the rebuilding of Jerusalem to the great act which brings sin to an end, as foretold by Gabriel to Daniel, we learn that 'the people of the prince that shall come shall destroy the city and the sanctuary' (Dan. 9:26).

6. DESECRATION, REDEDICATION AND ELABORATION

After the conquest of Palestine by Alexander the Great in the late fourth century BC, Greek influence became strong in the region, and this led to a revival of the old policy of religious syncretism by the high priests Jason and Menelaus. Their persuasion of the people proving inadequate, it was succeeded by violent persecution. The desecration of the Second Temple by Antiochus Epiphanes, the Hellenistic king of Syria, in 167 BC was the climax of his campaign to destroy the Jewish faith. The desecration is several times referred to in prophecy (Dan. 8:11–14; 11:31; 12:11) and is narrated in the books of Maccabees (1 Macc. 1:20–64; 2 Macc. 5:11 – 6:11). The king had previously removed from the Temple the lampstand, the shewbread-table, the veil and other sacred objects.[6]

The story of the successful resistance to Antiochus' campaign, against enormous odds, by the priestly Maccabee family and their companions is told with simple grandeur in 1 Maccabees: it is a narrative of dedication and faith which has few equals. They were able to cleanse the Temple and replace its defiled or stolen furnishings and to recommence its services after an interval of three years. They put it in the hands of faithful priests and fortified it against further profanation (1 Macc. 4: 36–61; 2 Macc. 10:1–8).

It was restored as it had been before, with its single lampstand and shewbread-table, and its curtains, and with an altar of uncut stones, of the kind authorized in Exodus 20:24–26, as well as the brasen altar, and probably serving as its base (1 Macc. 4:45–51). Several of the same features are described from an earlier period in one of the probably

---

[5] The Messianic understanding of Old Testament prophecy which prevailed in inter-testamental times was the basis on which the claims of John the Baptist and Jesus (new though those claims were) rested. It is assumed here that such an understanding was sound, and that the determination of some modern exegetes to give short-term inter-pretations to all Old Testament predictions is misguided.

[6] The Second Temple evidently had a single great lampstand and table, and curtains, like the Tabernacle, and not ten smaller lampstands and tables, and wooden doors, like Solomon's Temple. See Exodus 25:23–40; 26:31–37; 36:35–38; 37:10–24; 1 Kings 6:31–35; 7:49; 2 Chronicles 4:7–8, 19–20; though according to 2 Chronicles 3:14 Solomon gave the Holy of Holies a veil as well as doors.

genuine fragments of the historian Hecataeus of Abdera, quoted by Josephus (*Ag. Ap.* I:198).[7]

The final major restoration of the Second Temple was that undertaken by Herod the Great and commenced in 19 BC. Though Herod's work was as much a work of rebuilding as of repair, and took a very long time (the forty-six years mentioned in John 2:20 were not the end of it), it seems from the accounts given by Josephus and in the Mishnah (Tractate Middoth) to have adhered closely to the pattern of the Second Temple except in two main particulars, and in these to have been influenced by Scripture.

Josephus says that one of Herod's main aims was to double the height of the porch, so that it equalled the height of that in Solomon's Temple (*Ant.* XV:385; cf. 2 Chr. 3:4). Josephus also says that Herod, 'by erecting new foundation walls, enlarged the surrounding area to double its former extent' (*War* I:401), which, though inaccurate, may tie in with the Mishnah's figures, also inaccurate, of 500 cubits by 500, presumably based on Ezekiel's vision (*m. Midd.* 2:1; cf. Ezek. 45:2).[8]

The Mishnah again follows Ezekiel's vision in saying that the holy place had doors (Middoth 4:1, quoting Ezek. 41:23, 24), and Josephus says that it had doors behind its curtain (*War* V:211–212), thus giving to the holy place the same sort of double protection as Solomon's Temple gave to the holy of holies. The Second Temple seems already to have had this arrangement before Herod, judging from the Letter of Aristeas 85–86. The holy of holies, however, appears only to have had its curtain or veil, which would be torn in two when Jesus died (Mk. 15:38).

The enormous stones, still surviving, from which Herod constructed the platform for his Temple, and the white marble and gold from which he constructed the Temple itself, easily explain the admiration of the apostles: 'Master, behold, what manner of stones and what manner of buildings!' But the Lord's reply is, 'Seest thou these great buildings? There shall not be left here one stone upon another, which shall not be thrown down' (Mk. 13:1–2). There had been a sad decline since the days of the early Maccabees, and beauty is no compensation if God's house has been made a den of robbers. During his ministry Jesus had acknowledged the Temple as his 'Father's house' and as 'a house of

---

[7] Hecataeus of Abdera was a Greek historian contemporary with Alexander the Great. His book 'On the Jews', of which only fragments remain, is not indisputably genuine, but it is certainly old. This is the source of Josephus' quotation.

[8] The units are not stated in Ezekiel 45:2. The immediate context suggests cubits, though a comparison with Ezekiel 42:15–20 seems to make reeds more probable. For other possible links between Herod's Temple and the Old Testament, especially Ezekiel's vision, see F. J. Hollis, *The Archaeology of Herod's Temple* (London: J. M. Dent & Sons, 1934), appendix 2.

prayer for all the nations' (Mk. 11:17; Lk. 2:49). He had attended the festivals and taught there, but he had not been recognized as its Lord, and even when he had cleansed it the fact had only been resented. So now it was doomed.

7. THE SUPERSEDING OF THE RESTORED TEMPLE

Jesus' cleansings of the Temple at the beginning and end of his ministry, and his warning of its coming destruction, in accordance with Daniel's prophecy, were only the culmination of a dissatisfaction with the Second Temple which had extended over a long period. Tobit, which, with its Persian background, is probably the oldest book of the Apocrypha, makes its hero on his deathbed foretell the exile and the return:

> And they shall again build the house, but not like the first house, until the time that the time of the seasons is fulfilled. And after these things they shall all return from their captivity and shall build Jerusalem with honour, and the house of God shall be built in her, as the prophets of Israel spoke concerning her (Tobit 14:5, Codex Sinaiticus).

The book foresees a new Jerusalem and a new Temple, more glorious than the returned exiles had achieved, understanding the 'prophets of Israel' (Ezekiel and Zechariah in particular, probably) as having foretold this.

The same hope is expressed in the third book of 1 Enoch, the Book of Dreams, where Jerusalem is pictured as a house and the Temple as a tower: it tells of the burning of the tower and the destruction of the house at the exile, of how the sheep did not enter the house any more, and of how at the rebuilding of the tower all the bread placed on the table before it was polluted and not pure (1 Enoch 89:66–67, 73). This seems to speak of the sacrifices being offered in the Second Temple according to an interpretation of the Law incompatible with Essene ideas. Then the writer looks to the future and says:

> And I stood up to see till they folded up that old house, and carried off all the pillars, and all the beams and ornaments of the house were at the same time folded up with it, and they carried it off and laid it in a place in the south of the land. And I saw till the Lord of the sheep brought a new house greater and loftier than the first, and set it up in the place of the first which had been folded up: all its pillars were new, and its ornaments were new and larger than those of the first, the old one which he had taken away, and all the sheep were within it (1 Enoch 90:28–29, Charles' translation).

The Qumran Temple Scroll indicates that the dissatisfaction of the Essene school with the Second Temple extended well beyond the way the ritual was conducted there. The Scroll is written in the person of Moses, and provides as detailed a pattern for the Temple as the Pentateuch had provided for the Tabernacle. Much of it consists of a harmonized conflation of the Law of Moses, according to the Essene interpretation, but much else of it inevitably consists of inference, providing explicit instructions about how the Temple and its services ought to be, although there are no explicit instructions on the subject in Scripture, only certain recorded examples. Such instructions would apply equally to the Temple of Solomon and to the Second Temple, though the contemporary application would of course be to the latter. We have seen how the builders and restorers of the Second Temple sometimes turned to the account of the Tabernacle or to Ezekiel's vision, probably for lack of explicit instruction: the Temple Scroll meets the same problem by providing explicit instruction; but only if the Essene school had become the most influential could any practical use have been made of it.

How literal the hopes of Tobit and 1 Enoch for a future new city and Temple were, we cannot be quite sure, but the prophecies of Ezekiel and Zechariah on which they depended (especially the latter) have much about them which is symbolic or visionary, and the same is true of the Revelation of John, in which those prophecies are taken up and endorsed. John says of the New Jerusalem, come down from heaven to earth, 'I saw no temple therein, for the Lord God the Almighty, and the Lamb, are the temple thereof' (Rev. 21:22). Just as the LORD was a sanctuary for a little while to his people in exile (Ezek. 11:16), so will he be for evermore. A Temple is where God is, and if God is to be in the New Jerusalem, we need search no further for its Temple. Since God dwells especially in heaven, his presence makes heaven also a Temple. John refers several times to the Temple in heaven and to various features of the Temple there, including the ark of the covenant and the incense altar.[9] The writer to the Hebrews has the same conception and develops it fully. Jesus is the holy high priest, who has entered the presence of his Father in the heavenly Temple with the blood of the once for all sacrifice for sin which he offered on earth, and there he ever lives to make intercession for his people (Heb. 7–10). And it is there that his people also must now draw near with their prayers, rather than to the Temple at Jerusalem.[10]

The earthly Temple, like the Tabernacle, was a 'Tent of Meeting' where the LORD met with his people. But symbolically it was also God's house or dwelling place. At the incarnation, the body of Jesus became indeed God's dwelling place, and is therefore called a Temple (John 2:18–22). And at Pentecost, this miracle was extended also to his people, when the Holy Spirit came to dwell within them.[11] There had

---

[9] Revelation 8:3–5; 9:13; 11:19; 14:17; 15:5.
[10] Hebrews 4:14–16; 10:19–22; 13:12–14; cf. John 4:21–24.
[11] 1 Corinthians 3:16–17; 6:19; 2 Corinthians 6:16; Ephesians 2:20–22.

been hints of this wonder in the Old Testament, as in Psalm 114, hints which had been taken up by the men of Qumran (1QS 8:5–9; 9:5–6), but the church of Jesus Christ was its ultimate fulfilment.

7

GOD'S IMAGE, HIS COSMIC TEMPLE AND THE HIGH PRIEST

Towards an Historical and Theological Account
of the Incarnation

CRISPIN H. T. FLETCHER-LOUIS

A central problem which has driven biblical studies in the modern period has been the perceived incompatibility between the Christ of faith and the Jesus of history. That incompatibility is nowhere more sharply focused than on the central Christian belief that Jesus of Nazareth was God incarnate. How could a first-century Jewish joiner be both a good monotheistic Jew and the Chalcedonian Son of God? How could Jesus' earliest Jewish disciples, for whom the prohibition against idolatry was axiomatic, have believed Jesus was Israel's God and as such the worthy recipient of their devotion? How could the fully human Jesus, raised amidst the thoroughly *this*-wordly social, political and economic struggles of his people, have had the audacity to have thought himself the *other*-worldly divine being of later Christian piety? Since the scholarly consensus has long been that the historical Jesus lived, moved and had his being in a theological world far from removed from later Christological orthodoxy, there follow interminable theological and historical difficulties in making sense of the transition to the kind of incarnational theology that is clearly assumed in the writings of the New Testament. Behind these difficulties there stands the larger question for biblical theology: how can we explain and justify the movement from Israel's monotheism to the New Testament's incarnational vision of God? Is not the notion of God incarnate fundamentally a category mistake given that the Old Testament reveals the one God to be a creator absolutely and qualitatively distinct from his creation?

Throughout the modern period when conservative and orthodox scholarship has been vexed by these questions the role of the Temple in Israel's life and its significance for New Testament theology has been ignored if not actively denigrated. The reasons for this modern marginalization of Temple are not hard to see. Among others, the Jewish Old Testament scholar Jon Levenson has clearly seen the problem, and his essays *Sinai and Zion* and *Creation and the Persistence of Evil* are classic and seminal attempts to rehabilitate the relevance of the Temple for biblical theology.[1] He, and a growing number across the Old Testament, post-biblical and New Testament disciplines are now recognizing both the centrality of the Temple for Israel's life and practice and that the Temple cult stands at the centre of a complex cosmological mythology. To my knowledge, however, no one has yet attempted a thoroughgoing examination of the relevance of this Temple mythology for the early Christian belief in the incarnation.[2]

Here I offer a series of theses which draw, in very broad brush-strokes, the larger conceptual picture of the role of the Temple in a history of the incarnation which begins in Genesis and has a high point in the Pentateuchal vision of the Tabernacle long before it reaches (for Christians) its apogee in the life and death of Jesus. Each of these theses would need a much fuller discussion for their demonstration, but I have tried where necessary to offer exegesis which explains and supports the case.

1. THESIS 1: THE ISRAELITE CULT (TABERNACLE AND TEMPLE) IS A MIRROR IMAGE OF CREATION

This, I hope, is the least controversial and most widely – if not univers-ally – accepted of my theses. Both accounts of creation in Genesis 1–3 describe the contents and order of creation in terms of ancient temple building in general and Israel's peculiar vision of sacred space in particular. 'The whole universe must be regarded as the highest and, in truth, the holy temple of God' (Philo, *De spec. leg.* I:66) just as the cult (the Tabernacle and Solomon's Temple) is a microcosm of the whole of creation. Tabernacle and Temple are organized to reflect Israel's understanding of the structure of the cosmos, and the worship and rituals of the cult actualize and guarantee the God-intended order and stability of creation.[3]

---

[1] Jon D. Levenson, *Sinai and Zion* (Minneapolis: Winston, 1985) and *Creation and the Persistence of Evil: The Jewish Drama of Divine Omnipotence* (San Francisco: Harper & Row, 1988).

[2] Margaret Barker is, in this respect, a lone and too-often ignored exception and what follows owes a great deal to her insights into the relationship between cult and incarna-tion. See especially *The Gate of Heaven: The History and Symbolism of the Temple in Jerusalem* (London: SPCK, 1991); 'Temple Imagery in Philo: An Indication of the Origin of the Logos?' in William Horbury (ed.), *Templum Amicitiae: Essays on the Second Temple Presented to Ernst Bammel* (JSNTS 48; Sheffield: Sheffield Academic Press, 1991), pp. 70–102; *The Great Angel: A Study of Israel's Second God* (London: SPCK, 1992); 'The High Priest and the Worship of Jesus' in Carey C. Newman, James R. Davila and Gladys S. Lewis (eds), *The Jewish Roots of Christological Monotheism: Papers from the St. Andrews Conference on the Historical Origins of the Worship of Jesus* (JSJSup 63; Leiden: Brill, 1999), pp. 93–111; *The Revelation of Jesus Christ* (Edinburgh: T&T Clark, 2000).

[3] See Crispin H. T. Fletcher-Louis, 'The Destruction of the Temple and the Relativization of the Old Covenant: Mark 13:31 and Matthew 5:18' in K. E. Brower and M. W. Elliott (eds), *'The Reader must Understand': Eschatology in Bible and Theology* (Leicester: Apollos,

2. THESIS 2: HUMANITY IS CREATED TO FUNCTION AS GOD'S IDOL IN THE COSMOS AS MACRO-TEMPLE

My second thesis is based on the first and the work of several recent treatments of the 'image of God' language in Genesis 1:26.[4] What does it mean that God creates humanity in his image and likeness? This is an old *crux interpretum*. With a number of recent commentators we must now take seriously the fact that 'image' language is cult statue or idol language. This is how the word *ṣelem* is normally used in the Old Testament (e.g. Num. 33:52; 1 Sam. 6:5; 6:11; 2 Kgs. 11:18) and in the cognate Akkadian phrase *ṣalam ili/ilani*. Given that (i) other parts of Genesis 1 are a polemic against the polytheism of pagan cosmogonies and (ii) the Genesis 1 account of creation has its *Sitz im Leben* in the priestly view of the cult and its liturgy,[5] to use language otherwise reserved for idols for the creation of humanity is either dangerously obtuse or deliberately subversive.

Deliberate subversion must then be the intention: the Israelite view of the cosmos has at its apex the human being – not the sun, moon, stars, animals or other created realities – as the concrete physical form and manifestation of the one creator God. Over against zoomorphic paganism Genesis 1 sets up anthropomorphic monotheism with a vision of creation as a temple in which all the antechambers for lesser gods and their statues have been emptied less the sight of the creator God in his human 'statue' in the central and highest holy of holies be obscured. As J. Kutzko and others have recently seen, the point here is to give the biblical prohibition of idolatry its strongest possible rationale: *for us to make an idol is foolish because it fails to appreciate that, according to the original and intended order of creation, it is humanity which is to function in relation to the one and only creator god as do pagan statues and idols in relation to their gods.*[6]

To appreciate the full force of this *image-of-God-in-humanity* theology we must have in mind the role of idols in ancient Near Eastern religion.

1997), pp. 145–69 and *All the Glory of Adam: Liturgical Anthropology in the Dead Sea Scrolls* (STDJ; Leiden: Brill, 2001), ch. 3 for a fuller discussion and bibliography.

[4] I have discussed this more fully elsewhere: 'The Worship of Divine Humanity and the Worship of Jesus' in Newman, Davila and Lewis (eds), *The Jewish Roots of Christological Monotheism*, pp. 112–28. Besides the literature cited there, see Iain Provan, 'To Highlight all our Idols: Worshipping God in Neitzsche's World', *Ex Auditu* 15 (1999), pp. 19–38 (esp. pp. 25–6) and Ulrich Mauser, 'God in Human Form', *Ex Auditu* 16 (2000), pp. 81–100 (esp. pp. 90–2).

[5] See especially Moshe Weinfeld, 'Sabbath, Temple and the Enthronement of the Lord: The Problem of the Sitz im Leben of Genesis 1:1–2:3' in A. Caquot and M. Delcor (eds), *Mélanges bibliques et orientaux en l'honneur de M. Henri Cazelles* (AOAT 212; Kevelaer/Neukirchen-Vluyn: Butzon & Bercker/Neukirchener Verlag, 1981), pp. 501–11.

[6] See John Kutsko, *Between Heaven and Earth: Divine Presence and Absence in Ezekiel* (Biblical and Judaic Studies UCSD 7; Winona Lake: Eisenbrauns, 2000).

In the contemporary religious practice of Israel's neighbours (and, in all probability, her own pre-exilic, 'heterodox', cultic life) an idol is set up in a sacred place or building to be the real presence and visible form of the god. Because the god really does inhabit the image its proper care (clothing, washing, feeding) and veneration guarantees the god's benefits and protection for the worshipping community. The divinized statue has both rights and responsibilities in relation to its community. Without the right worship of the image by the community their social, economic and military welfare is jeopardized. If the statue of a patron deity is captured by an enemy then the god abandons the community as he is defeated by a superior god.[7] The role of the god and its statue in the socio-political sphere is then mirrored in the cosmological sphere. If the pagan statue of the supreme creator god is not properly attended then creation itself is liable to return to chaos. With this understanding of divine images assumed the so-called priestly account of creation has a remarkably high theological anthropology: it is humanity who is to be the eyes, ears, mouth, being and action of the creator God within his creation. Humanity is given both the freedom of the cosmos, is entitled to be fed from its produce, is to fill it with God's presence and is to exercise the creator's own divine rule over his creation (Gen. 1:28–29).

Loosely speaking, then, Genesis 1 is an 'incarnational' cosmology. Although the precise role of 'flesh' in the picture is not clear, it is humanity which has the peculiar responsibility for bearing divine presence and carrying out the divine will. This might offend Christian (and Jewish) theological orthodoxies. It might be objected, for example, that to claim that humanity in general has an incarnational role within creation undermines the peculiarity and uniqueness of *the* incarnation in Jesus of Nazareth. There is in conservative theological circles a piety which guards against humanity making too grandiose a claim for itself. If this exegesis of Genesis 1 amounts to the claim that humanity is created divine, is that not an abrogation of the absolute qualitative distinction between God and humankind, between creator and creature? Does this kind of a theological anthropology not lead to an overbearing and self-satisfied ecclesiology and a Pelagian soteriology? Is it no different an anthropology from that of the promethean pretensions of nineteenth- and twentieth-century modernity?

---

[7] This understanding of idols and divine presence is humorously illustrated by the behaviour of the Phoenician citizens of Tyre during Alexander's siege of the city in 332 BC. According to Plutarch: 'And many of the Tyrians dreamed that Apollo was going away to Alexander, since he was displeased at what was going on in the city. Whereupon, as if the god had been a common deserter caught in the act of going over to the enemy, they encircled his colossal figure with cords and nailed it down to its pedestal, calling him an Alexandrist' (*Alex.* 34:3–4). Although relatively late, this story accurately reflects the logic of age-old Levantine idol worship.

There is not space here adequately to answer these questions. But a genuinely submissive respect for the biblical text is bound to consider the *critique* of some would-be pious objections which this reading of the text itself presents: the priestly *image-of-God-in-humanity* theology says that idolatry is ruled out of court because *to locate divine presence and action in another part of creation or in that which we create is to absolve ourselves of our own responsibility to bear divine presence and action.* The idolatrous humanity, like Narcissus, clings to those objects made in its own image which it believes will affirm its being and guarantee its security and prosperity. The true humanity in the biblical vision is one which affirms, gives security to and makes multiply the life of creation. The mark of the former is passivity and that of the latter activity. Any pious restriction of divine (privilege and) *responsibility* for the one human Jesus Christ must therefore be mindful of the besetting danger at the root of idolatry; a self-absolution from the responsibility given to us at creation of bearing divine presence. It is, of course, possible to make an idol of Jesus.

3. THESIS 3: GOD'S TRUE HUMANITY IS RESTORED IN ISRAEL, HIS IDOL

There is another obvious question which this reading of Genesis 1 poses: if this is how humanity was created, what relationship does the post-lapsarian humanity have with the pre-lapsarian one? Where in the later biblical account of human history is there to be found the humanity which God intended? Before the Christian version of the story presents Jesus as the answer to that question the Old Testament already replies that it is in Israel that the true humanity is restored.[8]

In at least one passage this means that Israel, like the original humanity, is to be God's idol. Ezekiel is a representative of the priestly tradition who, as Kutzko has shown, shares P's *image-of-God-in-humanity* theology.[9] In one passage its *Israel-as-true-Adam* rhetoric reaches a high point of exquisite literary power.[10] Near the beginning of the long allegory of Israel's relationship with Yahweh in Ezekiel 16 there is a dyptich in which the nation's idolatrous treatment of her idols is contrasted with the way she has been treated by Yahweh:

---

[8] See N. T. Wright, *The New Testament and the People of God* (London: SPCK, 1992), pp. 262–8.

[9] Kutsko, *Between Heaven and Earth*.

[10] Here I develop Kutsko's wider discussion of the way in which Ezekiel places Israel, as the true humanity, in the position of God's true image and idol.

3.1 Ezekiel 16 and the Travesty of Idolatry

[4]As for your birth, on the day you were born your navel cord was not cut, nor were you washed with water to cleanse you, nor rubbed with salt, nor wrapped in cloths. [5]No eye pitied you, to do any of these things for you out of compassion for you; but you were thrown out in the open field, for you were abhorred on the day you were born. [6]*I passed by wā'e 'ĕbōr you*, and saw you *flailing about in your blood*. As you lay in your blood, I said to you, 'Live! [7]and grow up like a plant of the field.' You grew up and became tall and arrived at full womanhood; your breasts were formed, and your hair had grown; *yet you were naked and bare.*

[8]I passed by you again and looked on you; you were at the age for love. *I spread the edge of my cloak over you, and covered your nakedness: I pledged myself to you and entered into a covenant with you, says the* LORD *God, and you became mine.*	[15]But you trusted *in your beauty bᵉyopyēk and played the whore* because of *your fame šᵉmēk, and* lavished *your whorings on any passer-by 'ōbēr.*
[9]Then I bathed you with water and *washed off the blood from you*, and anointed you with oil.	
[10]I clothed you with embroidered cloth *riqmâ* and with sandals of fine leather *tāḥaš*; I bound you in fine linen *šeš* and covered you with rich fabric. [11]I adorned you with ornaments: I put bracelets on your arms, a chain on your neck, [12]a ring on your nose, earrings in your ears, and a beautiful crown upon your head.	[16]You took some of your garments, and made for yourself colourful shrines, and on them played the whore; nothing like this has ever been or ever shall be.
[13]You were adorned *with gold and silver*, while *your clothing was of fine linen šeš, rich fabric, and embroidered cloth riqmâ.* You had *choice flour sōlet and honey and oil for food.* You grew exceedingly beautiful, fit to be a queen.	[17]You also took your beautiful jewels of *my gold and my silver* that I had given you, and made for yourself male images *ṣalmê*, and with them played the whore; [18]and you took your embroidered garments *riqmātēk* to cover them, and set *my oil* and my incense before them. [19]Also *my bread that I gave you – I fed you with choice flour sōlet and oil and honey – you set it before them as a pleasing odour*; and so it was, says the LORD God.
[14]*Your fame šem* spread among the nations *on account of your beauty bᵉyopyēk*, for it was perfect because of my splendour that I had bestowed on you *bahādārî 'ăšer śamtî 'ālayik*, says the LORD God.	[20]You took your sons and your daughters, whom you had borne to me, and *these you* sacrificed to them to be devoured. As if your whorings were not enough! [21]*You slaughtered my children* and delivered them up as an offering to them.

[22]And in all your abominations and your whorings you did not remember the days of your youth, when *you were naked and bare, flailing about in your blood.* [23]After all your wickedness (woe, woe to you! says the LORD God), [24]you built yourself a platform and made yourself a lofty place in every square; [25]at the head of every street you built your lofty place and prostituted your beauty, offering yourself to every passer-by, and multiplying your whoring.

Some of the parallels between the account of what God does to Israel and what she does to her images *ṣalmê* are obvious; others need a little explanation.[11] In the same way and with the same materials that God clothes and feeds Israel she clothes and feeds her male images. With these she initiates sexual promiscuity, like a prostitute selling her wares to every passer by, whereas God had initiated his betrothal to her when he passed by and found her in her vulnerability. God had washed off from Israel the blood in which she was born. For this altruistic care for an abandoned child, Israel's sacrificial murder of its own children stands in antithetical parallelism. The effect of Israel's idolatry is to undo the redemptive work of God. Where the naked Israel had been clothed by God, she has now taken off her clothes for her lovers and is once more naked. By the end of the tale the nation finds itself back in a worse place than the one from which it started; not just abandoned by her parents, but now also murdered.

As a critique of the tragedy and folly of idolatry this passage only works because in doing what she does to her idols Israel does what God has already done to her. As the queen of the divine king she has everything, as an idolater she gives away everything to her idols. The description of idolatry in verses 15–19 is a neat cameo of the way in which statues and idols were worshipped in the ancient Near East; clothing, feeding and burning of incense being the essential features of the daily care of the gods in Mesopotamia and Egypt. There is nothing extraordinary in these verses: they are entirely true to the realities of ancient religious life.[12] What is a little more extraordinary, however, is that all the features of this picture of pagan idolatry are already present in verses 8–14. Much of the imagery in the first half of the dyptich fits the allegorical account of Yahweh's relationship with his people in terms of a marriage. But the washing and anointing of the woman does not.[13] And, although Yahweh's spreading his garment over Israel might be well-known betrothal imagery (Ruth 3:9), his clothing his queen and adorning her with ornaments is less obviously a constituent element in the marriage allegory. Both of these are best explained as a deliberate

---

[11] For the parallels and their chiastic structure, see Julie Galambush, *Jerusalem in the Book of Ezekiel: The City as Yahweh's Wife* (SBLDS 130; Atlanta: Scholars Press, 1992), pp. 96–101; Daniel I. Block, *The Book of Ezekiel: Chapters 1–24* (NICOT; Grand Rapids: Eerdmans, 1997), p. 472.

[12] See, e.g., A. Leo Oppenheim, *Ancient Mesopotamia* (Chicago: University of Chicago Press, 1977²), pp. 183–98; J. Cerny, *Ancient Egyptian Religion* (New York: Hutchinson's University Library, 1952), pp. 101–4.

[13] Ruth 3:3 and Susanna 17 do not help here (S. Greengus, 'Old Babylonian Marriage Ceremonies and Rites', *JCS* 20 [1966], p. 484). Whilst the exchange of goods and various rites of washing and anointing play an important part in the Mesopotamian service, there is no evidence that the groom would wash, anoint and clothe the bride. In Middle Assyrian Laws §§42–43 (*ANET* 61–62) only the *father* of the groom anoints his son's bride.

anticipation of the language of idolatry in verses 15–19, such that *God's treatment of Israel is regarded as a kind of cultic veneration.*
At the very least, the fact that the care of the gods stereotype is already used of God's treatment of his people means that Ezekiel adopts the same profound critique of idolatry to that of the priestly tradition: idolatry is a folly and a tragedy because it means giving up to another what is already one's (Israel's, Adam's) own. But, more than that, Ezekiel also wants to say that Israel *really* is the genuine bearer of divine presence and, as queen to her king, the rightful wearer of God's glory. This is why the first half of the piece climaxes with the statement that Israel's beauty was perfect because God bestowed his own splendour on her. And this is why the food which God gives to his queen is not simply the food of royalty. The choice flour *sōlet* and oil which she receives are normally constituent parts of cultic offerings (e.g. Lev. 2:7; Num. 6:15; 7:13, 19; 8:8).[14] And in antiquity honey is normally the food of the gods. So the passage claims that, in an analogical manner of speaking, *God worships Israel.*[15]

Contrary to the then generally accepted rationale of the ritual for the consecration of a man-made idol (the Washing or Opening of the Mouth), the passage as a whole says that pagan idols possess nothing more than the borrowed garments of their own worshippers. For a genuine impartation of divine being – which all idols were believed to possess – only Israel qualifies since the true creator God has graciously bestowed upon her his own character, power, privilege and life.

If, in a prophetic allegory, Israel can be depicted as the idol of her god, was that anything more than a flight of poetic fantasy? Did the theology of Ezekiel 16 have anything to do with the everyday life of Israel's cult in which Israel was treated as her god's idol? To answer these questions we turn to our fourth thesis.

4. THESIS 4: ISRAEL'S ROLE AS GOD'S IDOL IS WORKED OUT BY HER HIGH PRIEST IN THE TEMPLE-AS-MICROCOSM

Since Ezekiel is taken by some scholars to be closely related in time and theology to the priestly material in the Pentateuch, we should not be surprised to find his theology of God's image worked out in the cultic material in Exodus 25 – 40, where detailed instructions for the building of the Tabernacle and ordination of its priesthood are given.

---

[14] Galambush, *Jerusalem in the Book of Ezekiel*, p. 95; Block, *The Book of Ezekiel*, p. 486.
[15] This rather than the notion that 'Jerusalem's use of her food (Temple offerings) and clothing (Temple furnishings) in encounters with 'other gods' specifically violates her function as Yahweh's cult center' (Galambush, *Jerusalem in the Book of Ezekiel*, p. 96) is the point of the dyptich. It is not so much that Israel plays the role of cultic *place* in vv. 8–14 as that she plays the role of cultic *object*.

In the temples of ancient Near Eastern antiquity the idols play a role without which a temple cannot properly function. They are the object of devotion in their respective shrines and they are carried around and outside the sanctuaries when a ritual enactment of their roles in creation and history are required. The symbolism of their place, attire and activities is inseparable from the belief that their temples are maps of the cosmos. If, as is usually thought, Israelite religion is utterly aniconic then its cult is, in terms of the history-of-religions, an oddity.[16] Oddities are the stuff of history and should not be dismissed out of hand by the historiographer. However, I suggest that P's challenge to contemporary patterns of religious behaviour is more radical than odd because *in Israel's Temple (and Tabernacle) the role of the cult statute is played by the high priest who is the visible and concrete image of the creator within the Temple-as-microcosm.* To explain and justify this thesis I offer the following ten interpretative observations.[17]

4.1 The creation of light and Aaron's tending of the Menorah

The Exodus account of the instructions given to Moses for the building of the Tabernacle is widely recognized to mirror the order and details of the account of creation in Genesis 1:1–2:4. To the seven days of creation there correspond in Exodus 25–31 (the first of the two blocks of Tabernacle material in Exod. 25 – 40) seven speeches to Moses (Exod. 25:1–30:10; 30:11–16; 30:17–21; 30:22–33; 30:34–38; 31:1–11; 31:12–17). In a seminal, but yet to be fully appreciated, article P. J. Kearney high-lighted the redactional significance of this heptadic structure for P and argued that each of these seven speeches contains the cultic equivalent of the seven days of creation.[18] The third and seventh speeches obviously fit such a creation–Sinai intratextuality, since the former describes the making of the bronze laver, otherwise known as 'the Sea' (1 Kgs. 7:39), as a parallel to the creation of land and sea on the third day of creation (Gen. 1:10–11), and in the latter God tells Moses to tell the Israelites that they must keep the Sabbath, just as God himself had rested on the seventh day of his creation (Gen. 2:2–3).

For the first speech to Moses (Exod. 25:1–30:10) Kearney argued that P makes a connection between Aaron's tending the Temple lampstand

---

[16] The attempt by T. N. D. Mettinger (*No Graven Image?: Israelite Aniconism in its Ancient Near Eastern Context* [CBOTS 42; Stockholm: Almqvist & Wiksell, 1995]) to find a wider pattern of Levantine aniconism is unconvincing.

[17] Theological anthropology has been a blind spot of those Old Testament commentators who have discussed the relationship between Exodus 25–40 and Genesis 1. Since the image-of-God-in-humanity stands at the heart of the theological vision of P this has meant that much of the intratextuality between these two parts of P has been missed and the literary case has been weakened.

[18] 'Creation and Liturgy: The P Redaction of Exodus 25–40', *ZAW* 89 (1977), pp. 375–87.

and God's creation of light on the first day of creation (Gen. 1:3–5). There are two references to Aaron's responsibilities for the menorah (27:20–21 and 30:7–8). These make an inclusio around the account of Aaron's garments (ch. 28) and his ordination (ch. 29). Kearney suggested that by this inclusio P wants to say that just as 'God brought forth light into darkness (Gen 1:2–3) so Aaron causes light to shine throughout the night'.[19] In both these instances the menorah is to be tended in the 'evening' and the 'morning' and so this cultic action marks the primal boundary which results from the creation of light on the first day of creation. God's creation of light in Genesis 1:3–5 is recapitulated by the priest in the cult-as-microcosm: the high priest plays the role of the creator on the cultic stage.[20]

4.2 The ephod

Exodus chapter 28 provides a detailed account of Aaron's garments. Prominent among these is the *ephod*. There is general agreement that in older biblical material, outside of P, the ephod is a garment or solid covering for a statue of a god (Judg. 17:5; 18:14–20; Hos. 3:4; cf. 2 Kgs. 23:7).[21] Commentators who reckon with this older use of the word assume that with the purging of Israelite idolatry the ephod's associations with an idol are simply lost or ignored when the word describes a priestly garment. However, I suggest that P's use of the term for Aaron's attire is deliberately subversive: Aaron is truly God's idol, his image, and thus deserves to be dressed as such.

4.3 Aaron's garments are the Israelite version of the golden garments of the gods

This leads us to a consideration of Aaron's clothing as a whole. The idols of the Levant, Mesopotamia and Egypt are typically dressed in glorious, multicoloured, gold and silver jewel-studded garments. The dressing of the garments at the statutes' consecration and regularly thereafter is an essential feature of the care and veneration of the gods.[22] I suggest that this is what Aaron's garments are, generically speaking.

---

[19] Ibid., 375.

[20] The later rabbinic tradition according to which the Temple is the place where the first light was created no doubt relies on this older biblical material. See Peter Schäfer, 'Tempel und Schöpfung: Zur Interpretation einiger Heiligtumstraditionen in der rabbinischen Literatur' in Peter Schäfer (ed.), *Studien zur Geschichte und Theologie des rabbinischen Judentums* (AGJU 15; Leiden: Brill, 1978), pp. 122–33.

[21] See D. N. Freedman (ed.), *Anchor Bible Dictionary* (vol. 2; New York: Doubleday, 1992), p. 550; *HALAT* and the survey of modern commentators in C. Houtman, *Exodus* (vol. 3; Kampen: Kok, 2000), pp. 479–82.

[22] On the golden garments of the gods tradition, see A. Leo Oppenheim, 'The Golden Garments of the Gods', *ANES* 8 (1949), pp. 172–93.

Although the twelve stones of the breastpiece and the two onyx stones of the shoulders have their own specific symbolic significance they are a component part, along with the fabrics in gold, blue, purple and crimson, of Israel's version of the golden garments of the gods convention.

This not only accords with P's pre-history, it is also consistent with post-biblical interpretation. As late as the *Midrash Rabbah* the rabbis remembered that Aaron's garments were God's garments (*Gen. Rab.* 38:8). And, time and again, in earlier post-biblical literature where the high priest's garments appear this assumption seems to be present.[23]

4.4 *The Urim and Thummim and God's supernal, light-filled clothing*

One specific detail of the priestly attire which identifies Aaron's garments as those belonging to God himself is the mysterious Urim and Thummim. What this (or these) is (or are) we are not sure. But some connection between the Urim *ûrîm* and light *'ôr* is usually assumed in later translations and interpretation.[24] We also regularly find the view that the high priest's garments, particularly the stones, are iridescent, light-giving garments, which means that, at least in the text's *Receptionsgeschichte*, the Urim (and Thummim) are identified with the garments and that an association with God's own glorious light-filled garments is implied. The gods of Israel's neighbours are clothed in light or luminescent garments. And, so, also Yahweh is 'clothed with honour and majesty, wrapped in light as with a garment' (Ps. 104:1–2).[25]

An intriguing aspect of the instructions for the Urim and Thummim is the fact that, unlike all the other sartorial details of Exodus 28, Moses is not told to *make* them.[26] Is this a deliberate omission? There is solid evidence that early readers of the texts thought so. In one Qumran text the Urim and Thummim is somehow identified with the primal light, the perfect light (*'ortm*) which God himself creates for his dwelling on the first day of creation (4Q392 frag. 1 lines 4–5).[27] Perhaps related is

---

[23] See, e.g., Sirach 50:1–21; *Aristeas* 99; 1QSb 4:24–28 and the discussions in Fletcher-Louis, *All the Glory of Adam*; 'The Worship of the Jewish High Priest by Alexander the Great' in L. T. Stuckenbruck and W. Sproston North (eds), *Exploring Early Christianity and Jewish Monotheism* (Edinburgh: T&T Clark, 2004); and 'The Temple Cosmology of P and Theological Anthropology in the Wisdom of Jesus ben Sira' in C. A. Evans (eds), (SSEJC 8; Sheffield: Sheffield Academic Press, forthcoming).

[24] See the survey in Cornelis van Dam, *The Urim and Thummim: An Old Testament Means of Revelation* (Winona Lake: Eisenbrauns, 1993) and the discussion of Qumran material in Fletcher-Louis, *All the Glory of Adam*, chs 7 and 11.

[25] This verse has probably influenced the description the high priest's garment and appearance in Sirach 50:11 (see Fletcher-Louis, 'The Temple Cosmology of P', ad loc.).

[26] Though see the Samaritan text of Exodus 28:30 for Moses told to make the Urim and Thummim.

[27] On this text see Fletcher-Louis, *All the Glory of Adam*, pp. 232–7.

the tradition, which C. T. R. Hayward has shown is already present in Sirach 45:11,[28] that the stones of the breastpiece are of divine origin.[29]

4.5 The irony of Exodus 32 and Ezekiel 16

If the garments Aaron wears are those appropriate for God's image then there emerges a clear literary and conceptual relationship between, on the one hand, the P material in Exodus 25–31 and 35–40 and the older account of the worship of the golden calf in Exodus 32 and, on the other, the theology we have teased out of Ezekiel 16.

If our reading of Exodus 25–31 is right, then the making of the golden calf in Exodus 32 is a highly ironic and tragic portrayal of Israel's idolatry: Aaron leads the people in *making* a lifeless divine image of wood and gold which is to be the god to lead Israel into the promised land, whilst atop Sinai God gives to Moses a vision for the true cult in which Aaron himself, the representative of his people, is to *be* the image – idol – of God. Furthermore, the way in which the people divest themselves of their *own* garments and jewellery for the making of the calf parallels precisely the inversion of divine clothing in Ezekiel 16. In Exodus 32:2–4 Aaron makes a calf from the gold earrings of Israel's wives, sons and daughters. It is of the same jewellery that, presumably, the nation is to make an offering for the materials of the Tabernacle and for Aaron's garments according to Exodus 25:1–7. In God's sanctuary (above) the people (represented by their priesthood) are bedecked with golden garments; in the idolatrous cult (below) the idol is made from the same materials which previously adorned the people.

The narrative and conceptual structure is equivalent to that in Ezekiel 16. And, indeed, it is well known that the language which Ezekiel 16 uses to describe Israel's garments is that which is otherwise peculiar to P's account of the Tabernacle and Aaron's garments.[30] The words *šēš* ('fine linen') and *riqmaî/ma'ăśê rōqēm* (embroidery / work of an embroiderer) only appear together outside Ezekiel 16 in the description of the Tabernacle, its furnishings and Aaron's garments (Exod. 28:39; 39:29).[31] The relatively infrequent word *nezem* for the earrings which

---

[28] C. T. R. Hayward, *The Jewish Temple: A Non-Biblical Sourcebook* (London: Routledge, 1996), p. 69.

[29] Cf. Philo, *Quis Heres* 176; *b. Git.* 68a; *b. Pesah.* 54b; *Sifre Deut.* 355; *Mek. R. Ishmael Vayassa'* 6:43–60.

[30] See Galambush, *Jerusalem in the Book of Ezekiel*, p. 95 and already the Targum of Ezekiel, ad loc. (S. H. Levey, *The Targum of Ezekiel* [ArBib 13; Edinburgh: T&T Clark, 1987], p. 63).

[31] The commentators, e.g. Galambush, *Jerusalem in the book of Ezekiel*, pp. 95–6, wrongly focus on the similarity between the garments and the materials of the tabernacle structure where the use of the materials of Ezekiel 16 for the high priest are of more immediate interpretative significance.

the people provide for the molten calf (Exod. 32:2–3) is also used both for the materials which the Israelite's offer for the building of the sanctuary (Exod. 35:22) and for the noserings God gives Israel in Ezekiel 16:12.[32] These shared linguistic peculiarities and the fact that the word *tāḥaš*, 'fine leather', for the sandals Israel wears in Ezekiel 16:10, appears elsewhere only for the materials of the Tabernacle must mean that, together with the theological overlap, Ezekiel 16 and Exodus 25–40 have a common literary tradition.

Excursus: The first day of creation and the Chaoskampf

In addition to these five interpretative observations there are others which support the view that in the first speech to Moses Aaron's priestly office gives him the position as God's idol in the Temple-as-microcosm. These all depend on us recognizing that in Genesis 1, especially verses 2–5, creation takes place as an act of ordering out of primaeval chaos. The relevance of the ancient Near East's *Chaoskampf* tradition for the priestly account of creation is, of course, much disputed, and whilst space prevents a detailed engagement with the discussion of Genesis 1 here, sensitivity to the importance of the divine warrior's victory in P's vision of creation opens up several important interpretative insights for Exodus 25–31.[33]

There is widespread evidence that in the royal and cultic institutions of Near Eastern antiquity the sacral king acted out the role of the divine warrior – Baal, Marduk, Asshur, Ningirsu et al – in state rituals.[34] For P this royal rite is taken over by the priest who in other respects adopts in the exilic period the role played by the king in the pre-exilic period. We have already seen how God's creation of light is mirrored in Aaron's tending of the lampstand. The dividing of time between day and night, and the setting up of the boundaries evening and morning as the first act of creation, should be seen in their wider

---

[32] The use of this word in the account of the making of the idol in Judges 8 (vv. 24–26) suggests a wider (and older) literary topos is being employed in Ezekiel and Exodus.

[33] For the *Chaoskampf* behind Genesis 1, see John Day, *God's Conflict with the Dragon and the Sea: Echoes of a Canaanite Myth in the Old Testament* (Cambridge: Cambridge University Press, 1985); Bernard F. Batto, *Slaying the Dragon: Mythmaking in the Biblical Tradition* (Louisville: Westminster John Knox, 1992), ch. 3.

[34] For Mesopotamia, see R. J. Tournay and S. Saouaf, 'Stèle de Tukulti-Ninurta II' *Annales archélogiques de Syrie* 2 (1952), pp. 169–90 and H. Frankfort, *Kingship and the Gods: A Study of Ancient Near Eastern Religion as the Integration of Society and Nature* (Chicago: University of Chicago Press, 1948), p. 327. For the Hittites, see, e.g., Robert L. Alexander, *The Sculpture and Sculptors of Yazilikaya* (Newark: University of Delaware Press, 1986), p. 97. For Ugarit, see Mark S. Smith, *The Ugaritic Baal Cycle: Volume I. Introduction with Text, Translation and Commentary of KTU 1.1–1.2* (Supplements to VT; Leiden: Brill, 1994), pp. 102–8, and see now generally N. Wyatt, *Myths of Power: A Study of Royal Myth and Ideology in Ugaritic and Biblical Tradition* (UBL 13; Ugarit-Verlag: Münster, 1996), pp. 127–94, 301–2.

history-of-religions context where light plays a prominent role in the creator god's victory over chaos.[35]

4.6 The ephod: the divine warrior's garment?

We have seen how Aaron's garments, particularly the stones of the breastpiece, also adopt the symbolism of God's primal light. These stones, perhaps themselves the Urim and Thummim, are a part of the ephod. Besides being a covering for a cult statue in biblical tradition there is some evidence that in cognate Canaanite religious mythology an ephod is a garment worn by the divine warrior Baal when he slays the chaos monster. In a well-know passage of the Ugaritic Baal Epic we read how:

> Although you [Baal] defeated Lotanu [= Leviathan], the fleeing serpent, destroyed the coiling serpent,
> the Tyrant with the seven heads [cf. Isa. 27:1],
> you were uncovered, the heaven came loose like the girdle of your cloak [*ĕipdk*]! ...
> (CTA 5:I:1–5; cf. CTA 5:V:2–4, 24)

The translation of the crucial line is uncertain. But if this text assumes that an *'ipd* is a garment worn, in a cosmogonic context, by the divine warrior as he defeats the forces of chaos then it is all the more appropriate for Aaron to be given this garment in the first speech to Moses in Exodus 25–31: Aaron is dressed as the divine warrior who stands behind Genesis 1:1–5.

4.7 Josephus' view of the sash, pomegranates and golden bells

Later post-biblical interpretation of Aaron's garments recorded by the aristocratic priest Josephus further supports the notion that Aaron is dressed as the divine warrior. His description of the sash worn by the high priest (*Ant.* III:154–6) appears to have in mind an image of a conquered Leviathan draped around its victor's torso.[36] Josephus tells us that the pomegranates around the hem of the high priest's garments recalled the lightnings and the bells that accompanied them evoked the sound of thunder (*War* V:231; *Ant.* III:184). Although a connection between pomegranates and lightning is hardly self-evident, the image of the high priest moving around a cosmic stage accompanied by thunder and lightning immediately evokes the stereotypical portrayal of the divine warrior in Israelite and wider ancient Near Eastern texts (cf. e.g. Ps. 29:3, 7; 77:18; Job 37:4).

---

[35] See, e.g., Day, *God's Conflict with the Dragon and the Sea*, pp. 101–3, 121–2.
[36] See the discussion of this text in Crispin H. T. Fletcher-Louis, 'The High Priest as Divine Mediator in the Hebrew Bible: Dan 7:13 as a Test Case', *SBLSP* (1997), pp. 161–93, 190–1.

4.8 Blood splattering

In Exodus 29 the ordination of Aaron and the other priests includes their garments being sprinkled with the blood of a ram (vv. 19–21; cf. Lev. 8:30). The ceremony is unique and otherwise the priests' garments are to be kept scrupulously clean from blood (Lev. 6:26, cf. *Jub.* 22:17). So why be splattered with blood during ordination to the priesthood? I suggest that at his ordination Aaron becomes the divine warrior whose garments are splattered with the blood of his enemies. The besplattered blood of the warrior was no doubt a familiar sight in antiquity and it is no less a well-established theme in the *Chaoskampf*. For example, in the Mesopotamian myth of Anzu when the storm god Adad defeats the chaos bird Anzu:

> Adad roared like a lion, his din joined that of Anzu. A clash between battle arrays was imminent, the flood-weapon massed. *The armour-plated breast was bathed in blood.* Clouds of death rained down, an arrow flashed lightning (Anzu II).[37]

Aaron is ordained at Mount Sinai and thenceforth he officiates in the Tabernacle as the people journey through the wilderness and enter the promised land. The nation is arranged in a military formation and we are reminded of those biblical texts where the LORD comes up from Sinai and the region of Edom as a divine warrior surrounded by 'myriads of holy ones' (Deut. 33:2–3; cf. Judg. 5:4–5; Ps. 68:8–9, 18). In particular, the ordination of Aaron in this narrative setting evokes the scene in Isaiah 63:1–6 where the divine warrior marches in great might from Edom stained with the blood of his enemies which has 'spattered' (*yēz*) his crimson garments. The same relatively infrequent verb (*nzh*) is used for the ordination of Aaron (Exod. 29:21).

The sight of Aaron ordained as the visible image of the divine warrior who leads the people into the promised land then provides sacramental assurance for the promise at the end of the chapter:

> I will dwell among the Israelites and I will be their God. And they shall know that I am the LORD their god, who brought them out of the land of Egypt that I might dwell among them; I am the LORD their God (Exod. 29:45–46).

4.9 Post-biblical interpretation

Confirmation that this is the right reading of Exodus comes from post-biblical interpretation where in many and diverse sources the (true) high priest is portrayed as the divine warrior. The high priest's exit

---

[37] Stephanie Dalley, *Myths from Mesopotamia* (Oxford: Oxford University Press, 1989), p. 213.

from the inner sanctuary to the gathered community seems to have been understood as a dramatization of the LORD's powerful setting forth from his holy habitation (cf. Isa. 26:21; Mic. 1:3). In Sirach 45:6–8 (Hebrew text) the high priest is described in terms of the divine warrior of Numbers 23:22 and 24:5–8 leading his people out of Egypt back to the promised land.[38]

4.10 High Priest as Adam and image of God

Finally, we should note that a correlation between Adam's role as God's idol in creation (Gen. 1) and the high priest's part as God's idol in the drama of the cult-as-microcosm is natural given that the high priest was also believed to be the true or second Adam. This idea is probably present already in Ezekiel 28:12–16 and is otherwise clearly attested in Sirach 49:16 – 50:1 (Hebrew text).[39]

5. THESIS 5: THE GOD'S IDOL THEOLOGICAL ANTHROPOLOGY WAS WELL KNOWN AND AXIOMATIC FOR THE THEOLOGY OF THE EARLY CHURCH

Was this theology of the divine image in humanity well known in the first century and did it play a significant role in early Christology? There is plenty of evidence that in the post-biblical period the theology of the divine image and the role of the high priest in the Temple-as-microcosm I have sketched was well known.[40] Its potential significance for an understanding of the theological shape and historical origins of the New Testament belief in the incarnation should be obvious and Acts 17 suggests that this theology was axiomatic for the early church.

In Acts 17 Luke records the contents of the speech Paul preached on the Areopagus in Athens. The speech is generally reckoned to be a fine piece of missionary apologetic in which Paul raids the philosophical language of his learned audience in order to accommodate the Christian gospel as far as possible to those not initiated into the basics of a Jewish theological framework. But, in using the language of the Stoic poets to claim that all human beings 'live and move and have their being' in the one true God, whose offspring we all are (v. 28), the Lukan Paul has also been accused of a natural theology utterly at odds with both a genuine Jewish way of thinking and the thought of the historical Paul.

---

[38] See generally Barker, 'The High Priest and the Worship of Jesus' and Fletcher-Louis, *All the Glory of Adam*, chs 3, 7 and 11.

[39] See Hayward, *The Jewish Temple*, pp. 45–6 for later texts.

[40] See Fletcher-Louis, *All the Glory of Adam* and 'The Worship of the Jewish High Priest by Alexander the Great' for some of the material from the intertestamental period.

For all the detailed investigations of its conceptual background the flow of Paul's argument in this chapter has not been properly appreciated. The occasion for the speech is important. Paul is exasperated at the sight of all the idols in Athens (v. 16). As he mingles (in good Socratic fashion) and converses with Epicurean and Stoic philosophers they think that his message about Jesus and the resurrection means he is proclaiming 'foreign gods' (v. 18). So, when Paul is invited to address the Areopagus *he* is concerned about idolatry and his audience, on the other hand, have the impression that Paul also wishes to introduce the veneration of Jesus as a, to them, foreign deity. Clearly, in what follows Paul preaches a thoroughly Jewish attack on the worship of any image of gold, silver or stone 'formed by the art and imagination of mortals' (v. 29). This might lead to the conclusion that he is also concerned to negate the impression that he believes Jesus is divine; a god who demands cultic veneration.[41] However, were that the case, it would conflict with the rest of Luke's account of early Christianity since everywhere else Luke is quite clear that Jesus is divine and worthy of human devotion.[42] In fact, I suggest, Paul adopts precisely the argument against idolatry we have investigated thus far *so that*, implicitly, his own worship of Jesus can be theologically justified.

In verses 27–28 Paul says that the one true God is not far from each and every one of us because, in fact it is 'in him' that 'we live and move and have our being', 'because we are also his kind'. Either Paul is a sloppy apologist who is unaware of the meaning such language has in its original Stoic context or he deliberately claims a theological anthropology according to which humanity is fundamentally a partaker in the divine nature. The latter is clearly the case since Paul then proceeds – 'being *therefore* of God's kind we ought not to think that the deity is like gold, or silver, or stone, an image formed by ...' The logic assumes the biblical image-of-God-in-humanity theology: it is we ourselves who are the locus of divine presence in creation; not things of stone, silver and gold or things which we create mentally or by hand.[43] And so, when in verses 24 and 26 Paul had spoken of God as creator of heaven and earth, the creation of humanity 'from

---

[41] So, e.g., J. D. G. Dunn, *The Acts of the Apostles* (Epworth Commentaries; Peterborough: Epworth Press, 1996), p. 231.

[42] See Crispin H. T. Fletcher-Louis, *Luke–Acts: Angels, Christology and Soteriology* (WUNT 2:94; Tübingen: Mohr Siebeck, 1997).

[43] It also, probably deliberately, evokes the famous justification for Ruler Cult given by the Anthenians in 290 BC when they hymn their saviour Demetrius Poliocrates as follows: 'For the other gods are either far away (*makran*, cf. Acts 17:27) or do not have ears, or do not exist or do not pay attention at all to us, but you we see present, not of wood or stone but real. And so we pray to you' (Athenaeus, *Deip.* VI:253e).

one' and the setting up of temporal and demographic boundaries, he probably has in mind the very specific theology of creation laid out in Genesis 1.[44]

This *preparatio evangelica* is, then, thoroughly Jewish.[45] It receives two notable Christian modifications. First, and most obviously, it leads to a warning of coming judgement by a man, Jesus, whom he has already raised from the dead (v. 30). Since in classical antiquity the defining feature of divinity is immortality the idea seems to be that by his resurrection Jesus is shown to be the one genuine instance of an anthropology which we would all live by if we did not worship silly idols. Here, in Jesus, is the true instance of the genus god-man; a genus according to which we all (Jew and Gentile) were originally created (vv. 26–28). The thought sequence is tightly packed, but a concern to relativize the universal in the light of the particular is patent; indeed, that is probably what it means that the world is to be *judged by* one appointed man. Jesus uniquely embodies the anthropological standard by which we are all to be judged. Only of this human can the words of the Stoic poets be truly said.[46]

Secondly, the Jewish theological structure is modified by a critique of the ancient understanding of temples which has profound implications for the whole narrative sweep of the biblical theology of the incarnation. In verse 24 the Jewish critique of idolatry entails not just a rejection of the idea that gods dwell in statues but also that they dwell in any peculiar way in a temple shrine. In both Jewish and classical antiquity it was axiomatic that gods – or God – dwelt in a peculiar way in a temple, its shrine(s) and their cultic objects. The Christian rejection of (literal) temple space as sacred space is a feature of Luke's account of early Christianity (cf. Acts 7:47–50) and, of course, is ultimately a defining feature of New Testament theology: sacred *space* is overtaken by sacred *person(s)*.

On the one hand, this peculiarly Christian theological position is Christological in origin. The *person* Jesus of Nazareth and his community, his body (cf. Acts 9:4), is now the locus of divine presence, not the Jerusalem (or some other rival) Temple. On the other hand,

---

[44] For the Pauline knowledge of the Priestly cosmology and theological anthropology, see Crispin H. T. Fletcher-Louis, 'Wisdom Christology and the Partings of the Ways Between Judaism and Christianity' in Stanley E. Porter and Brook W. R. Pearson (eds), *Jewish-Christian Relations through the Centuries* (Sheffield: Sheffield Academic Press, 2000), pp. 52–68.

[45] Hans-Josef Klauck, *Magic and Paganism in Early Christianity* (Edinburgh: T&T Clark, 2000), p. 90 comes closest to grasping the logic of Paul's argument and he rightly compares Wisdom 15:16–17.

[46] In the rest of Acts (and Luke) it is clear that those who follow him, who live in his Spirit (Acts 18:9) and who are conformed according to his character (esp. Acts 7), can then also rightly claim that they live and move and have their being in the One God whose name they now carry (e.g. Acts 9:15–16).

the relativization of the Temple can be understood as a legitimate (re-) reading of the biblical narrative. According to the Pentateuch it is pre-eminently *humanity* – the true humanity – which uniquely embodies divine presence in creation (Gen. 1). The Christological fulfilment of this *ab creatio* vision is anticipated by a biblical Israelology according to which God's chosen people are his visible, concrete presence in history and creation (Ezek. 16). At Sinai the vision is refracted through a still narrower lens in the singular embodiment of divine presence in Aaron and his successors. There, according to the conventions of antiquity, the divine image – Israel's high priest – is set up in the god's shrine (the Tabernacle). But according to the logic of the biblical narrative this is only a prophetic dispensation. Whilst the theological *anthropology* of Exodus 25–40 is both an anticipation of the Christological climax to the biblical story and a *fulfilment* of its cosmological opening (Gen. 1), the *Temple* cosmology of the Tabernacle is not strictly required by the narrative, even in its own narrower Old Testament terms. That is to say, Genesis 1 leads, through Exodus 25–40, to an incarnational theology of the kind adopted by the New Testament, but it does *not* demand that God and his image be located in a temple. In Pauline terms the *promise* (Gen. 1:26 in context) came before the *command* (the Tabernacle-Temple of Exod. 25–40) and when the time of the promise is fulfilled the *command* (temple sacred space) is obsolete. This narrative substructure is probably implicit in Acts 17: the God who creates and is Lord of heaven and earth (Acts 17:24a–b) did not *then* and does not *now* (17:24c) dwell in shrines made with human hands.[47] Rather he is present in the one person Jesus of Nazareth.

Because of the limitations of space Acts 17 will have to suffice as a case study which demonstrates the importance for early Christian beliefs about Jesus of the older biblical view that humanity as a whole was created to function, incarnationally, as God's image or idol. Much more will have to be done to establish whether and in what ways this thinking was pivotal throughout early Christianity. But it should at least now be clear that a proper understanding of the Temple and its understanding of divine presence in biblical religion is likely to have had considerable significance for the early Christian doctrine of the incarnation.

---

[47] The Lukan Paul omits the biblical, Israel given, time in-between *then* and *now*, since for his Gentile audience it is an unnecessary chapter in the story.

8

THE TEMPLE IN LUKE'S GOSPEL

PETER HEAD

1. INTRODUCTION: LUKE, THE TEMPLE, THE SETTING AND THE SCHOLARS

Luke's interest in the Temple is sufficiently clear and widely acknowledged as to need no more than a few general comments by way of introduction. The Gospel opens in the Temple with Gabriel's dramatic appearance to Zechariah during his priestly service (1:5ff.); it takes its tone and theme from Simeon's outbursts of praise and warning at the sight of the infant Jesus in the Temple (2:25–35); and it closes after Jesus' resurrection with his joyful disciples praising God in the Temple (24:62ff.). The Temple thus provides an important narrative focus for the whole Gospel, a focus that is maintained at the outset of the second volume, but which is qualified in various ways as the story moves on through Acts. We shall have more to say about vocabulary in a moment; for now we simply note that Luke uses the general term for temple (*to hieron*) more than the other three Gospels combined, and that he uses a greater variety of terms for the Jerusalem Temple than any of the other Gospels.

Luke's apparent interest in the Temple is matched by a corresponding interest in the city of Jerusalem in which the Temple resides. This is clear not only in terms of vocabulary statistics,[1] but also in the attention given to Jerusalem as the goal of Jesus' fate from the point at which Jesus 'set his face to travel to Jerusalem' in 9:51 (also v. 53), through the prolonged travel narrative of the central chapters of the Gospel, up to his approach (19:11) and lament over the city (19:41–44) immediately prior to his entry into the Temple (19:45ff.). This interest is also carried through into the Acts of the Apostles, as the progress of the Gospel is traced in its movement 'beginning from Jerusalem' (Luke 24:47–49; Acts 1:8) to the ends of the earth.

---

[1] Luke refers to Jerusalem thirty times in the Gospel and fifty-seven times in Acts, while Matthew refers to Jerusalem ten times, Mark fourteen times and John thirteen times.

While we would therefore be on safe ground in asserting that Luke is interested in the Temple (indeed, that he is sufficiently interested to justify two chapters here on his treatment of the Temple and no separate treatment of Matthew or Mark), it is nevertheless the case that this 'interest' does not translate immediately into clarity about the place of the Temple in Luke's theology. Nevertheless, 'interest' in the Temple was also characteristic of Judaism at the time, even when 'attitudes' to the Temple differed markedly, and as an aid to setting Luke into his context a brief survey of attitudes to the Temple will follow.

Within the Old Testament, as previous chapters have shown, Solomon's Temple in Jerusalem served as the cultic centre of Israel's faith and life; as the place of sacrifice, atonement and pilgrimage; where the covenant obligations of Israel might be joyfully rendered to the LORD (e.g. Deut. 12, 16, 26). It also served as the centre for the administration of law and justice (Deut. 17; cf. Hag. 2:11–13), even as an archive and a treasury. The Temple was the locus of God's divine presence with Israel (1 Kgs. 8), the place where God chose for his name to dwell (Deut. 12:21; 1 Kgs. 8:29; Ps. 132), and thus a place for prayer and divine revelation.[2] Herod's rebuilding of the Second Temple, reconstructed at vast expense and over many years, aimed to recapture the glory of the Solomonic Temple (Josephus, *Ant.* XV:385).[3] In this, at least, Herod's vision seems to have been realized: the stones were imposing (Mk. 13:1ff.), the decorations beautiful (Luke 21:5), the gold-work magnificent enough to justify oaths (Matt. 23:16), and the magnificence of the edifice of polished white marble was widely acknowledged by visitors and pilgrims alike.[4] Josephus wrote, 'the exterior of the building wanted nothing that could astound either mind or eye' (*War* V:222). The rabbis said 'he who has not seen the temple of Herod has never in his life seen a beautiful building' (*b.B.B.* 4a; *b. Sukk.* 41b).

Most Jews accepted the legitimacy of the Second Temple and continued to order their faith and life around its cultic activity. The Temple came to be regarded as the symbolic centre of the entire cosmos

---

[2] Note the prophetic description of the Temple as God's house (Isa. 2:2ff.; Jer. 23:11; Ezek. 8:14, 16; Joel 1:13–16; Mic. 4:1ff.; Hag. 1:14) and his dwelling place (Joel 4:17, 21; Hab. 2:20; cf. Ezek. 9:3; 43:5–9). For prayer in (or to) the Temple, see 1 Kings 8, especially vv. 44–49; Daniel 6:10; Jonah 2:5, 8 (cf. earlier Josh. 7:6–9; 1 Sam. 1:10–16; 2 Sam. 7:18–29); and, eschatologically, Isaiah 27:13; Jeremiah 31:6; 33:10ff., and with a view to the nations, Isaiah 2:2ff.; 56:6ff.; 55:20, 23. For revelation in the Temple, see Isaiah 6:1ff. (and cf. 1 Sam. 3:4ff.; Josephus, *Ant.* XIII:282).

[3] Begun in the eighteenth year of Herod's reign, 20–19 BC (Josephus, *Ant.* XV:380 [cf. *War* I:401, which refers to the fifteenth year]). The basic structure was completed in eight years (Josephus, *Ant.* XV:20), although some work was still proceeding forty-six years later (John 2:20, probably AD 27), and the whole was not completed until even later.

[4] Note the emphases in Josephus, *Ant.* XV:391–402 (visible for a great distance, splendidly adorned with gold, the greatest wall ever heard of) and *War* V:184–226 (esp. 222ff., part of which is cited above); and see also *m. Midd.* Tacitus described it as a Temple of immense wealth (*Histories* V:8).

(Ezek. 38:12; 1 Enoch 26ff.; *Jub.* 8:12).[5] For Jews in the Mediterranean diaspora, the Temple, although physically distant, remained symbolically prominent, as can be seen in the respect for the Temple in the literature of the diaspora, the continued enthusiasm for the pilgrimage feasts (especially Tabernacles and the Day of Atonement) and the apparently scrupulous observance of the annual collection of the half-shekel tax for the Jerusalem Temple (Exod. 30:11–16; Neh. 10:32ff.; 2 Chr. 24:6).[6] As Barclay notes, 'the uniqueness for Jews of the Jerusalem temple ("one temple for the one God", Philo, *Spec Leg* 1.67; Josephus, *C Ap* 2.193) suggests that its symbolic value was powerful even when its impact on daily life was weak'.[7] The special reputation of the Jerusalem Temple also made an impact on some Gentiles, whose admiration for the Temple went beyond any general enthusiasm for oriental cults, and is noted several times by Josephus.[8]

We should also note that dissatisfaction with the Temple in Jerusalem, with the legitimacy of the priests, with the problems posed by Roman occupation and Pompey's defilement of the Temple, and/ or with the purity of the cultic practice itself, is also attested within Judaism. Quarrels about legitimacy could give rise to an alternative cult centre, such as that established by Onias IV in Leontopolis in reaction to perceived inadequacies in the Maccabean restoration of the

---

[5] This idea is found in a variety of rabbinic traditions, e.g. the saying attributed to R. Shemuel, 'This world is like unto the human eye, for the white is the ocean which girds the earth; the iris is the earth upon which we dwell; the pupil is Jerusalem; and the image therein is the Temple of the Lord' (*Bereshith Rabbah* 63.14, as cited in Z. Vinay, *Legends of Jerusalem* [vol. 1; Philadelphia: Jewish Publication Society, 1973], p. 6); cf. more fully L. Ginsberg, *The Legends of the Jews* (vol. 5; Philadelphia: Jewish Publication Society, 1925), pp. 14–16 (note 39 to vol. 1, p. 12). The cosmic significance of the Temple is demonstrated in a range of Second Temple literature discussed by C. T. R. Hayward, *The Jewish Temple: A Non-biblical Sourcebook* (London: Routledge, 1996), especially pp. 6–13 for a summary (note also Philo, *Moses* II:84–88); also M. Barker, *The Gate of Heaven: The History and Symbolism of the Temple in Jerusalem* (London: SPCK, 1991).

[6] For the literature, see e.g. *Ep. Ar.* 83–120; 3 Maccabees; Sibylline Oracles; Philo, *Legatio ad Gaium*; cf. J.M.G. Barclay, *Jews in the Mediterranean Diaspora: From Alexander to Trajan (323BCE–117CE)* (Edinburgh: T&T Clark, 1996), p. 420; Hayward, *The Jewish Temple*; for the pilgrimage feasts see J. Jeremias, *Jerusalem in the Time of Jesus: An Investigation into Economic and Social Conditions during the New Testament Period* (London: SCM Press, 1969), pp. 62–71; Barclay, *Jews in the Mediterranean Diaspora*, pp. 415ff.; for the Temple tax, see Josephus, *Ant.* XIV:110; *War* VII:281; cf. *m. Shek.* 1:4 and note Tacitus' comment (*Histories* V.5.1); evidence from Cyrenaica, Asia, Egypt, Rome, and the Eastern diaspora is collected by Barclay, *Jews in the Mediterranean Diaspora*, p. 417 (cf. also S. Mandell, 'Who Paid the Temple Tax when the Jews were under Roman Rule?', *HTR* 77 [1984], pp. 223–32).

[7] Barclay, *Jews in the Mediterranean Diaspora*, p. 419.

[8] Josephus, *War* V:17 and IV:262; *Ag. Ap.* I.198f; II:138; cf. Suetonius, *Augustus* 93; see more generally S. J. D. Cohen, 'Respect for Judaism by Gentiles in the Writings of Josephus', *HTR* 80 (1987), pp. 409–30; E. Schürer, *The History of the Jewish People in the Age of Jesus Christ*, Geza Vermes, Fergus Millar and Matthew Black (eds) (vol. 2; Edinburgh: T&T Clark, 1973), pp. 309–14. The Torah itself presumes that Gentiles will make sacrifices (Lev. 22:25; cf. 1 Kgs. 8:41–43; *m. Shek.* 1:5; 7:6).

Temple (1 Macc. 4:36ff.; 2 Macc. 10) and with a view to fulfilling Isaiah 19:18–22. This temple, modelled on that in Jerusalem, and set within a small town built on the model of Jerusalem, functioned as a cult centre from 170 BC to AD 71.[9] Perceived problems relating to purity might give rise to an emphasis on eschatological hopes for a renewed Temple.[10] Qumran texts attest an emphasis on the impurity of the Jerusalem Temple (CD 4:18; 5:6; 20:23; 1QpHab. 12:7–9), an eschatological hope in a new or restored Temple (CD 4:1–12; War Scroll 2:1–6; 12:12–18; 19: 5–8; Temple Scroll), with a belief that the community itself could be likened to the Temple (1QS 5:4–7; 8:4–7, 8–10; 9:3–6; 4QFlor.).[11]

From this necessarily brief survey of attitudes to the Temple in Jerusalem we turn to an equally brief survey of some recent work on the subject of Luke's attitude to the Temple, which should make this clear and highlight some of the issues to be tackled in what follows.[12]

On the one hand, some scholars have argued that Luke sees a fundamental incompatibility between the Temple and its cult and the Christian faith. As might be expected, this has taken somewhat different forms in recent years. Conzelmann argued that the Lukan Jesus, having cleansed the Temple, could then occupy it as its rightful owner; while following Jesus' rejection and death the Jews occupy it unlawfully, it is a profane building, destined for destruction, a destruction which 'is the clear refutation of Judaism'.[13] Baltzer argued that the Temple is displaced in Luke's thought by the presentation of Jesus as

---

[9] Josephus, *War* I:31–3; VII:420–36; *Ant.* XII:387ff.; XIII:62–73, 285; XIV:131ff.; XX:235–7. See G. Bohak, *Joseph and Asenath and the Jewish Temple in Heliopolis* (EJL 10; Atlanta: Scholars Press, 1996). Ancient alternatives had also existed on Mount Gerizim (Samaritan, from *c.*330 BC) and at Elephantine (for fifth century BC), but were no longer in use in the first century.

[10] As for example in the Psalms of Solomon: 1:8; 2:3; 8:12; cf. the messianic renewal in 17:28–33; cf. also Ecclesiasticus 36:13ff.; 2 Maccabees 2:4–8; Tobit 13:10; 14:5; *T. Levi* 17:10; Jubilees 23:21.

[11] Cf. B. Gärtner, *The Temple and the Community in Qumran and the New Testament: A Comparative Study in the Temple Symbolism of the Qumran Texts and the New Testament* (SNTSMS 1; Cambridge: Cambridge University Press, 1965); P. N. W. Swarup, *An Eternal Planting, a House of Holiness: The Self-Understanding of the Dead Sea Scrolls Community* (PhD thesis, Cambridge University, 2002).

[12] There does not seem to be a really adequate treatment of the history of research in this area. Useful introductions to key scholars and their treatment of Judaism in Luke–Acts can be found in J. B. Tyson, *Luke, Judaism, and the Scholars: Critical Approaches to Luke–Acts* (Columbia: University of South Carolina Press, 1999); but he makes no attempt to highlight treatments of the Temple. F. D. Weinert, who lists a few relevant books and articles, nevertheless complains that although 'the role of the Temple in Luke–Acts is widely recognized by commentators as a prominent motif in Luke's work ... few have pursued this topic with any rigor'. 'Luke, the Temple, and Jesus' Saying about Jerusalem's Abandoned House (Luke 13:34–35)', *CBQ* 44 (1982), pp. 68–76 (here from p. 68)

[13] H. Conzelmann, *The Theology of St. Luke* (ET; Philadelphia: Fortress Press, 1982), p. 78. It is clearly significant that Conzelmann did not regard either Luke 1–2 (pp. 118, 172; cf. 16, n. 3) or 24:50–53 (p. 94) as original parts of the Gospel.

endowed with glory.[14] Esler argued that Luke's attitude to the Temple was ambivalent, his positive treatments sprang from a desire to connect Christianity to Israel's antiquity, but the story he tells of the Gentile mission ultimately reveals a fundamental incompatibility between the Temple cult and the messianic faith.[15] Walker argued that, while Luke affirms the Temple's past, he denies the Temple a future. In particular he takes Jesus' comment 'your house shall be left you' (Luke 13:35) as introducing, at a pivotal point in Luke's travel narrative, the notion of divine abandonment of the Temple. This note is then further developed in Stephen's speech (Acts 7) and the comment, taken as climactically important by Walker, that the Temple doors were closed behind the arrested apostle (Acts 21:30).[16]

On the other hand, a number of writers have argued (against Conzelmann in particular) that Luke's perspective is quite different. Weinert argued that Luke did not hold a negative view of the Temple, but regarded it as an appropriate place for Israel to pray; that the Temple, while not indispensable, may nevertheless serve God's purposes if the worshippers have the right attitude.[17] Bachmann held that the Temple maintained a key role for Luke as the sacred place for Jewish Christians (central for prayer, teaching, pilgrimage, Torah observance,

---

[14] K. Baltzer, 'The Meaning of the Temple in the Lukan Writings', HTR 58 (1965), pp. 263–77. This article, which pays special attention to the Old Testament background to Luke's thought, was important in showing that important issues relating to Luke's view of the Temple might be raised in passages where the Temple itself is not mentioned, i.e. that the question needs to be answered on the level of Luke as a whole, but the argument is not sufficiently developed to be persuasive.

[15] P. F. Esler, Community and Gospel in Luke–Acts: The Social and Political Motivations of Lucan Theology (SNTSMS 57; Cambridge: Cambridge University Press, 1987), pp. 131–63. Esler deals almost entirely with Acts, especially Acts 7.

[16] P. W. L. Walker, Jesus and the Holy City: New Testament Perspectives on Jerusalem (Cambridge/Grand Rapids: Eerdmans, 1996), pp. 57–68. Walker follows F. F. Bruce's treatment of Acts 21:30 (see p. 68); he also nods in the Baltzer's direction when he suggests that the cloud of the divine presence around Jesus (Luke 9:35; Acts 1:9) might indicate that Luke saw Jesus as the 'new Temple' (p. 68, n. 47); cf. also mutatis mutandis E. Franklin, Christ the Lord: A Study in the Purpose and Theology of Luke–Acts (London: SPCK, 1975), pp. 90ff. (although Franklin does not regard Luke as hostile or negative towards the Temple); N. Taylor, 'Luke–Acts and the Temple' in J. Verheyden (ed.), The Unity of Luke–Acts (BETL 142; Leuven: Leuven University Press and Peeters, 1999), pp. 709–21 ('Rather than affirming hopes for the restoration of Temple and cult, Luke expounds a view of the Temple that has been superseded by other manifestations of the divine presence, in the person of Jesus and in the life and expansion of the Church in the power of the Holy Spirit', p. 712).

[17] F. D. Weinert, 'The Meaning of the Temple in Luke–Acts', BTB 11 (1981), pp. 85–9; 'Luke, the Temple, and Jesus' Saying about Jerusalem's Abandoned House (Luke 13:34–35)', pp. 68–76; 'Luke, Stephen, and the Temple in Luke–Acts', BTB 17 (1987), pp. 88–90 (articles based on his 1979 dissertation). In general most of his arguments are negative in this context: passages which have been appealed to as evidence on Lukan negativity are not rightly interpreted.

etc.), but not for Gentile Christians.[18] More recently, Chase has argued that Luke's positive appreciation of the Temple is based on its historic role in the advent of God's eschatological salvation and its anticipated future eschatological restoration.[19]

It is fairly obvious, even from such a brief survey, that Luke–Acts contains material that can be understood to be favourable to the Temple, as well as material that seems more negative. Whether Luke provides sufficient signals to determine his general theological attitude is obviously a question we want to pose as we proceed through the text. Although it would be an oversimplification to say that the positive material appears in the Gospel and the negative material in the Acts, it is nevertheless clear that no general conclusions about the place of the Temple in Luke's theology can be reached from the Gospel alone. This essay thus needs to be read in conjunction with Steve Walton's essay that follows. We shall take the evidence in the order in which the Gospel presents it to us, with half an eye on comparative material in Matthew and Mark, and see what hints are given as to the status and significance of the Temple. One other preliminary issue must be tackled before we launch into the investigation proper.

2. THE TEMPLE: LUKE'S VOCABULARY

We have already noted the prominence of Temple vocabulary in Luke (when compared with the other Gospels), and it is time to present the basic evidence and discuss Luke's vocabulary choices. Luke uses four different terms to refer to the Temple:[20]

2.1 *To hieron (11–9–14+25–10 [and 1 in Paul] = 70)*

This is Luke's generally favoured term, used rather broadly to describe the whole Temple precinct, including the various courts and ancillary buildings.[21] Indeed, Luke never uses this term in contexts which require that the inner sanctuary is specifically included (Luke 2:27, 37, 46; 4:9; 18:10; 19:45, 47; 20:1; 21:5, 37, 38; 22:52, 53; 24:53). Only five of the

---

[18] M. Bachmann, *Jerusalem und der Tempel: Die geographisch-theologischen Elemente in der lukanischen Sicht des jüdischen Kultzentrums* (Stuttgart: Kohlhammer, 1980). Bachmann also argued (against Conzelmann) that Luke depicts Jerusalem's identity not independently of but as defined by the Temple.

[19] J. B. Chance, *Jerusalem, the Temple, and the New Age in Luke–Acts* (Macon: Mercer University Press, 1988).

[20] In the following lists I use a standard format to indicate the number of times each word appears in each of the Gospels, with a New Testament total and an occasional note of other New Testament writers. Thus: Matthew–Mark–Luke+Acts–John … = New Testament total.

[21] BAGD, 372; *TDNT*, III:235–7.

fourteen occurrences could plausibly be attributed to the influence of written sources (Mark and 'Q'); the other nine occur either in uniquely Lukan material, or only in Luke's form of the triple tradition.[22] In the bulk of the Greek Old Testament this term is mostly used for pagan shrines and practically never for the Jerusalem Temple (for which *oikos* or *naos* are used). This observation led Schrenk to suggest that the general preference of New Testament writers for such a term shows that the Temple is regarded as 'the outdated shrine, with no attempt to mark it off from the religious world around'.[23] This view, however, appears to share in the markedly negative attitude to Judaism shared by many contributors to the pre-war volumes of the *TDNT*; it takes no account of the evidence of the contemporary usage in the Maccabean literature, Philo and Josephus, where such a pejorative connotation cannot at all be detected; and it certainly fails as an explanation of Luke's usage, especially considering the basically positive way the term is introduced in 2:27 and 37 (as we shall argue below).[24]

2.2 Ho naos (9–3–4+2–3 [8 in Paul; 16 in Apoc.] = 45)

In Luke–Acts this term always refers to the sanctuary proper (Luke 1:9, 21, 22; 23:45 [= Mk. 15:38]; Acts 17:24; 19:24) as distinct from the Temple precincts (for which *to hieron* is used).[25] This distinction, which is not observed by other New Testament writers, is also sometimes questioned in relation to Luke. BAGD cite Luke 1:21ff. in favour of a broader meaning for *naos* ('of the temple at Jerusalem' ... 'of Herod's temple' ... 'also of the whole temple precinct'),[26] but

---

[22] 2:27 (Luke), 37 (Luke), 46 (Luke); 4:9 (=Matt. 4.5); 18:10 (Luke); 19:45 (Mark 11:15), 47 (Luke); 20:1 (=Mark 11:27); 21:5 (=Mark 13:1); 21:37 (Luke), 38 (Luke); 22:52 (Luke); 22:53 (=Mark 14:49); 24:53 (Luke).

[23] *TDNT*, III:235.

[24] The material from Maccabees, Philo and Josephus is noted by Schrenk (pp. 233ff.), but its significance is not credited. On the broader issue, see P. M. Casey, 'Some Anti-Semitic Assumptions in the Theological Dictionary of the New Testament', *NovT* 41 (1999), pp. 280–91.

[25] R. C. Trench argued that the distinction between *naos* (= sanctuary, Holy of Holies) and *hieron* (= Temple precincts) was 'always assumed in all passages relating to the temple at Jerusalem, alike by Josephus, by Philo, by the Septuagint translators, and in the N.T.' *Synonyms of the New Testament* (London: Kegan Paul, Trench, 1886[10]), p. 11. Support for this was drawn by Trench both from references to pagan temples (e.g. Herodotus, *Histories* I:181,183; Thucydides, *History of the Peloponnesian War* IV:90; V:18; Acts 19:24, 27); and the explicit testimony of Josephus (*Ant.* VIII:95–97). This distinction is then 'brought to bear with advantage on several passages in the N.T.' (p. 11, includes e.g. Matt. 27:5, p. 12). The general attempt must be pronounced a failure (cf. esp. Matt. 27:5 [NB v. l.], 27:40 // Mark 15.29; John 2.20).

[26] For *naos* referring to the whole Temple precinct BAGD cite 'Bell. 6, 293, C. Ap. 2, 119; Mt 23: 17, 35; 27: 5, 40; Mk 14: 58 (...); 15: 29; Lk 1: 21f; J 2: 20; Ac 7: 48 t.r.; Rv 11: 2; 1 Cl 41: 2; B 16: 1ff; GP 7: 26'.

this is not the most obvious interpretation for this passage where the more restrictive sense surely still applies (note 1:10: the people were praying 'outside' – *exō*; while Zechariah was delayed *en tō naō*).[27] The distinction also functions in relation to the temple of Artemis in Ephesus, hence the silver shrines are *naoi* (Acts 19:24), while the whole temple is *to hieron* (v. 27). Luke uses this term twice in Acts of pagan shrines, but this should hardly control our interpretation of its use in the Gospel.[28]

2.3 Ho oikos (10–13–32 + 24–4)

It is generally fairly clear that this term, 'house', is used in a wide variety of Hellenistic sources to refer to a temple generally, and parallels exist in Hellenistic Jewish literature for its use for the Jerusalem Temple.[29] While when used generally, for someone's house, this is clearly favoured vocabulary for Luke, the small subset of these references which involve reference to the Temple are more evenly distributed (4–3–5+2–3). Whether all five Lukan passages are actually referring to the Temple is uncertain and will be discussed more fully later. For the moment we note that all five appear to have been found in Luke's sources,[30] and that all five occur 'in contexts where there is conflict with the Jewish establishment', although this conflict is not always directly related to the status of the 'house'.[31]

2.4 Ho topos (ho hagios) (only in Acts 6:13ff.; 7:7, 49; 21:28 [bis])

Only the first and the last of these use the adjective.

---

[27] This view of Luke's usage is widely held among commentators, e.g. I. H. Marshall, *Commentary on Luke* (NIGTC; Exeter/Grand Rapids: Paternoster Press/Eerdmans, 1978), p. 54; J. B. Green, *The Gospel of Luke* (NICNT; Grand Rapids/Cambridge: Eerdmans, 1997), p. 70, n. 30; L. T. Johnson, *The Gospel of Luke* (SP; Collegeville: Liturgical Press, 1991), p. 55; also O. Michel, *TDNT*, IV:885.

[28] N. H. Taylor argues that *naos* 'occurs after the appearance of Gabriel to Zechariah only in contexts where divine residency is denied and the notion thereof derided'; this suggests (at least to Taylor) that 'with the events of the Gospel inaugurated in the appearance of Gabriel to Zechariah, Luke understands the special significance of the Temple under the old covenant as having come to an end' ('Luke–Acts and the Temple', p. 713). It is difficult to be convinced that one other usage of the term in the Gospel (when the curtain of the Temple is torn in two, 23:45) is a sufficient basis for these claims.

[29] Josephus, *War* IV:28; 3 Km 7:31; Justin, *Dial.* 86:6; LXX (acc. BAGD). More broadly BAGD refers to Euripides, Herodotus, Plato and inscriptions, etc. as attesting the meaning 'temple'.

[30] Luke 6:4 (David entered 'the house of God' [= Mark 2:26] [not specified in 1 Sam. 21]); 19:46 (*bis*) ('my house shall be a house of prayer' [= Mark 11:17]); 11:51 (*re* Zech. [= Matt. 23:35 has *naos*; Q: *oikos*]); 13:35 ('your house shall be left [desolate]' [= Matt. 23:38, Q] [if refers to Temple, see below]); Acts 7:47,49 [here quoting Isa. 66:1ff.]. Luke 2:49 might be taken as implying *oikos*, but this would not seem to explain the plural article (see below).

[31] Taylor, 'Luke–Acts and the Temple', p. 713.

Some preliminary observations may be drawn from this survey of the Lukan vocabulary. First, it is important simply to note the diversity of vocabulary and the probability that this reflects, at least partly, the diverse vocabulary of the Lukan sources. While this may reflect Luke's relatively conservative treatment of his source materials, it also represents something of a challenge to a full-blooded redaction-critical approach. If Luke was not concerned to make his vocabulary uniform, he may equally not have been concerned with imposing a clear and transparent theological perspective on his Temple materials.

Secondly, although our concentration will be on passages where the Temple is specifically referred to in one way or another, we should not think that this covers everything important about Luke's view of the Temple. There are a number of other important terms and concepts, such as 'priest', 'glory', 'rock', 'mountain', which could evoke Temple traditions in certain contexts. Even silences can be significant: for example, Jesus' offer of forgiveness, expressed independently of the Temple and the priestly cult, suggests some ambivalence to the Temple and its cult, as currently practised.

Thirdly, given Luke's ability to distinguish between the sanctuary itself and the whole Temple precincts (using *naos* and *hieron* respectively), it seems likely that he would equally be able to distinguish the Temple and the city in which it was located, Jerusalem. Of course, the destiny of the two are intertwined, and Conzelmann's radical separation of the two was ill-conceived, but it does not follow that the two should be regarded as substantially merged in Luke's thought. The standard Jewish view, expressed in Josephus and the Mishnah, could speak in graded terms of the relative holiness of the sanctuary, the Temple courts, the city and the land, all conceived of as a series of concentric circles, and it is not impossible that Luke's conception was somewhat analogous.[32]

3. THE TEMPLE IN THE BIRTH NARRATIVES

Luke's birth narrative opens and closes with scenes set in the Temple: Zechariah's encounter with the angel Gabriel (1:5–25) and Jesus' encounter with the teachers (2:40–52). The important further scene of Jesus' presentation in the Temple introduces the reader to groups of expectant Jews in and around the Temple associated with Anna and Simeon (2:22–29).

---

[32] *m.Kelim* 1:6–9 speaks of ten degrees of holiness while Josephus speaks of seven zones (*War* I:26; V:227; *Ag. Ap.* II:102ff.); cf. Green's comment in *The Gospel of Luke* on Luke 1:21–23: 'Luke has focused our attention narrowly on the events inside the temple sanctuary, but now provides a transition back into the outside world – the temple area (vv. 10, 21) and, indeed, Judea (vv. 5, 23; cf. v39)'.

Zechariah is a priest of the order of Abijah (cf. 1 Chr. 24:7–19). Elizabeth, his wife, is also of priestly lineage and together they live in a righteous, explicitly Law-observant relationship with the LORD (like figures such as Noah, Gen. 6:9; Abraham, Gen. 17:1; David, 1 Kgs. 9:4; or Job, Job 1:1). Zechariah's priestly service is described positively as a service 'before God' (*enanti tou theou*, 1:8; the same preposition is used in the description of priestly duties in relation to the altar of incense in Exod. 30:8, LXX). At the time of the incense offering the people are in prayer (outside the *naos*, v. 9, but within the Temple precincts), and the angel of the Lord refers as well to Zechariah's prayer for a child (v. 13). The sanctuary is the place of revelation, as Gabriel, who later claims to stand in the presence of God (v. 19 [note the perfect participle]) appears in the sanctuary and stands at the right side of the altar of incense before his announcement of the good news to Zechariah. The whole account has the flavour of, and contains numerous parallels to, the story of Hannah and Elkanah in 1 Samuel 1–2, an account with a strong and positive Temple setting.

This description suggests not a neutral portrayal of the Temple, but a positive one, as the place of prayer, of the revelation, even of the presence of the Lord.[33] It would certainly suggest that Luke would have to give his presumably predominantly Gentile readers quite explicit signals about a change in the role and status of the Temple. Nevertheless, it is worth noting that Gabriel's message of good news about John presumes that the people of Israel are in some manner alienated from the Lord and need to be turned to the Lord (1:16) and prepared for him (1:17). John will accomplish this in the Spirit and power of Elijah, a figure distinctly unconnected with the Temple, as John himself will turn out to be.

The presentation of Jesus in the Temple provides another example of Torah observance on the part of Jesus' parents (2:22–24 could hardly be more emphatic on this point except that the point is further reinforced in v. 27 and v. 39; cf. Exod. 13:2, 12, 15; Lev. 12:8).[34] Here Luke notes only Jerusalem as the location, suggesting that the Lord is present in some manner in Jerusalem (v. 22: 'they brought him up to Jerusalem to present him to the Lord'). The context strongly suggests that the Temple is in view; although the consecration of the firstborn may not presume a Temple location (cf. Exod. 13:11–16; cf. Num. 18:15ff.), the offering for purification after childbirth clearly does (i.e. in Lev. 12:6–8), and the subsequent account makes this quite explicit as Simeon comes into the Temple in order to encounter Jesus (2:27). Something

---

[33] The general point is widely acknowledged; cf. similarly Green, *The Gospel of Luke*, pp. 61ff.
[34] Note ibid., pp. 140ff.

of the same conflation of Jerusalem and Temple is present throughout this account. Simeon is a man of Jerusalem who comes to the Temple; Anna never departs from the Temple and speaks to those looking for the redemption of Jerusalem.

In this account too the Temple is the location of God's presence (2:22), the place of praise in the face of divine revelation (2:28–32), of worship with fasting and prayer (2:37) and of proclamation (2:38). But it is also the location for eschatological hopes of renewal and restoration: not admittedly hopes involving any explicit mention of the Temple, but hopes in Simeon's case for the consolation of Israel (v. 25), which means the fulfilment of Isaiah's time of salvation (cf. Isa. 40:1; 61:2; cf. Isa. 49:13; 51:3; 52:9; 66:13; 57:18: 'I have seen their ways, but I will heal them; I will lead them and repay them with comfort'; esp. LXX); and in the case of Anna's audience, hopes for the redemption of Jerusalem (2:38). The revelation of the Lord's Messiah brings forth both Simeon's song of praise celebrating the arrival and universal scope of God's salvation (cf. Isa. 11:11; 40:5; 42:6; 46:13; 49:6; 52:9ff.; cf. Ps. 98) and his solemn word to Mary (2:34ff.): Israel's consolation, her salvation and her glory will be met with a divided response among those in Israel: 'this child is destined for the falling and rising of many in Israel'.[35] The Temple is the setting, but the message is that God's Messiah and God's time of salvation have arrived.

The account of Jesus in the Temple at age twelve also begins with an account of the regular pilgrimage observance of his parents (2:41ff.). Here they come to Jerusalem for the Passover (cf. Deut. 16:16), and Jesus stayed behind in Jerusalem: he was eventually found in the Temple (presumably here understood by Luke to be a subset of Jerusalem), amazing the teachers with his understanding (NB the emphasis on Jesus' wisdom in 2:40, 52 and cf. expectation of the Messiah endowed with wisdom in Isa. 11:2; 1 Enoch 49:3; Pss. Sol. 17: 37, etc.). Is this the first sign of Luke's positive view of the Temple as a place of teaching and learning (cf. later in the Gospel, and also Acts 5:25)? We should note that Jesus' saying often translated 'Did you not know that I must be in my Father's house?' (2:49) does not actually include such a clear (and approving) reference to the Temple: 'do you not know that I must be among the things of my father' (*en tois tou patros mou*).[36]

---

[35] Green suggests irony, 'this location helps to legitimate the universal reach of the Gospel: precisely in the center of the world of Israel, the Jerusalem temple, God discloses that salvation for Israel includes salvation for the Gentiles' (*The Gospel of Luke*, p. 146). Whether it is irony, or rather the first indication that the divine salvation begins in Jerusalem (cf. Luke 24:47–49; Acts 1:8), is a difficult question.

[36] D. D. Sylva, 'The Cryptic Clause, *en tois tou patros mou dei einai me* in Luke 2:49b', *ZNW* 78 (1987), pp. 132–40.

4. THE TEMPLE IN THE CENTRAL SECTIONS OF LUKE

Luke's version of the temptation of Jesus in the wilderness has a notable order for the three temptations (especially compared with the apparently more logical order in Matthew), which places the temptation in the Temple at the climactic final point: 'then the devil took him to Jerusalem and placed him on the pinnacle of the temple (*to hieron*) …' (4:9). Doubtless this anticipates the way in which Jerusalem is the climactic destination of Jesus' travel narrative, where Jesus' final temptation will take place, since Luke will utilize the terminology of temptation repeatedly in chapter 22 (e.g. vv. 3, 28, 31, 39–46, 53).

Just as the devil departs (both from Jesus and the narrative) until an opportune time (4:13), so does the Temple with only one important but disputed reference before the narrative of entry and the passion. Nevertheless, just as the absence of the devil has been overrated in some circles, the absence of explicit textual references to the Temple should not be taken as an indication that the symbolic system associated with the Temple is not actually in view more or less throughout the story. For example, when Jesus tells the cleansed leper to go and show himself to the priest, and, as Moses commanded, make an offering for his cleansing (5:14), I presume this would require, according to Leviticus 14:10–32, attendance at the Tent of Meeting, that is, the Temple; and further that Jesus obviously supports, to some extent, the system that is already in place. Notably the following passage (the healing of the paralytic, 5:17–26) has Jesus claiming (implicitly over against the Temple cult system) the authority to forgive sins. Some of the passages which deal with the radical table fellowship adopted by Jesus and the parables relating to it (i.e. chapters 14–15) could also profitably be related to some implicit Temple themes. We should also note Luke 6:4, where Jesus appeals to the example of David who 'entered the house of God and took and ate the bread of the presence, which it is not lawful for any but the priests to eat, and gave some to his companions'. It is interesting that the account in 1 Samuel 21:1–6 does not specify that David entered the Tabernacle. Where Matthew makes a comparison with the Temple explicit (albeit with a neuter form: 'something greater than the temple is here'); Luke perhaps takes the view that the incident in 1 Samuel took place on the Sabbath, the day when the bread was changed over (cf. 1 Sam. 21:6, which refers to changing the bread in general).

Throughout Luke's central travel narrative the goal (for Jesus and the narrator) is the departure (exodus) which he was going to accomplish at Jerusalem (9:31). Indeed, the section is defined at the outset by the repeated comment that 'he set his face to go to Jerusalem' (9:51; cf. v. 53), and is followed up with references to Jerusalem throughout the travel section (13:22, 33ff.; 17:11; 18:31; 19:11). Jerusalem is the city which kills the prophets and is to be for Jesus the place of rejection and death. In this the Temple also has its place. In the Lukan woe against the lawyers (11:51) 'this generation' is charged with the blood of all the prophets from Abel to Zechariah who perished between the altar and the house (Luke: *oikos*; Matthew: *naos*; NRSV: sanctuary).[37] This suggests that the Temple takes its share in the rejection and in the subsequent rejection. We might note the comment of Jesus about the eighteen people killed in Jerusalem when the tower of Siloam collapsed: 'do you think that they were worse offenders than all the others living in Jerusalem? No, I tell you; but unless you repent, you will all perish just as they did' (13:4ff.).

A particularly crucial text occurs in Jesus' lament over Jerusalem in 13:31–35. After twice affirming that his ministry will have a climactic finish in Jerusalem (13:32ff.) he says:

> Jerusalem, Jerusalem, the city that kills the prophets and stones those who are sent to it! How often have I desired to gather your children together as a hen gathers her brood under her wings, and you were not willing. See, your house is left to you. And I tell you, you will not see me until the time comes when you say, 'Blessed is the one who comes in the name of the Lord' (13:34ff.).

A number of scholars have taken the reference to the 'house' here (*oikos*, in 13:35) as a reference to the Temple and its destruction.[38] For Walker this also is of pivotal importance as the first statement of Jesus on the subject of the Temple and one of huge structural importance in Luke's travel narrative.[39] In view of our previous comments on 11:51 and the close connections between the two passages (both of which speak of the killing of the prophets and apostles/sent ones, 11:49 // 13:34) and the connection between Temple and Jerusalem exhibited in Luke's usage, it would seem likely that the *oikos* here does refer to the Temple (as in 6:4 and 19:46). Some objections to this reading might be discussed briefly.

First, it does seem clear that the Lukan text should be read as here, without *erēmos* (which has a stronger claim to be read in Matt. 23:38). Without *erēmos* there is no strong allusion to Jeremiah 22:5 (LXX), where *oikos* or 'house' refers primarily to 'the house of the king of Judah' (as in Jer. 22:1, 6), and secondarily to the royal palace and the whole city (as in Jer. 22:4, 6b–8).

Secondly, the possessive pronoun 'your' house is sometimes taken to exclude direct identification with the Temple, which Luke else-

---

[37] Cf. 2 Chronicles 24:20–22 (presumably); although Zechariah 1:1 may be another candidate (cf. Matt. 23:25).
[38] E. E. Ellis, *The Gospel of Luke* (NCB; London/Grand Rapids: Marshall, Morgan & Scott/ Eerdmans, 1981), p. 191 (note others listed in Marshall, *Commentary on Luke*, p. 576).
[39] Walker, *Jesus and the Holy City*, pp. 57–68.

where identifies as belonging directly to God.[40] This approach may be a little overoptimistic regarding Luke's freedom with his sources and is in any case not true of 11:51. Nevertheless, we might ask about the implications of the pronoun. There is no completely obvious natural antecedent. The plural subject of the previous verb is presumably in view ('you were not willing'); this in turn looks like a plural reference to Jerusalem (rather than Jerusalem's children). The question then is what is referred to by 'Jerusalem's house'? A reference to the Jewish leadership is not completely excluded, but nor can an association with the Temple. Perhaps as also seems to be the case in the Matthean parallel, a play precisely like that in Jeremiah 22 is in operation.

It is perhaps worth pointing out that the meaning of the phrase itself has not yet been determined! Luke's placing of the material is important (to credit Weinert), and the tone is more of prophetic lament rather than inevitable judgement. If this is along the right lines then we might compare the material in 13:6–9 and in 13:32ff.: the current establishment is under threat for its rejection of the prophets, but has some more time: note the reprise of verse 35 later in Luke's narrative of the entry in 19:38, and the second lament over Jerusalem in 19: 41–44. Matthew's placement (immediately before the Olivet discourse in ch. 24) enhances the immediacy of the crisis whereas Luke's placement seems to allow for more time. Some sort of interplay between the Temple and the city is presupposed here.[41] The ambiguity of this passage suggests that we allow the three later passages which treat the subject of Jerusalem's rejection to clarify the Lukan intention (19:41–44; 21:20–24; 23:27–31).

5. THE ENTRY AND 'CLEANSING' OF THE TEMPLE

The long narrative journey to Jerusalem moves forward from Jesus' third passion prediction in 18:31–33 with numerous indications of actual progress towards the city (Jericho, 18:35; 19:1; near Jerusalem, 19:11; going up to Jerusalem, 19:28; Bethphage and Bethany, Mount of Olives, 19:29; within sight of the city, 19:41) and climaxes in Jesus' royal entry into the Temple (19:45).[42] Immediately prior to the entry of Jesus

---

[40] Marshall, *Commentary on Luke*, p. 576 (referring to SB 1:943ff.); Weinert, 'Luke, the Temple, and Jesus' Saying about Jerusalem's Abandoned House (Luke 13:34–35)', pp. 68–76.

[41] Cf. BAGD: *oikos* here used in a wider sense meaning 'city' (cf. the note on POxy 126:4; Jer. 22:5; 12:7; *T. Levi* 10:5).

[42] The kingship of Jesus, although hinted at earlier in various ways (e.g. 1:32ff.), comes into prominence in this entry movement (cf. 19:27 and v. 35ff. – where the spreading of the garments echoes the anointing/coronation of Jehu as king over Israel [2 Kgs. 9:13]; and the straightforward royal acclamation of v. 38 – only partly dependent on Ps. 118:26), and plays an important role in the passion narrative (22:16, 18, 29ff.; 23:2, 3, 37ff., 42); cf. Acts 13:22; 17:7.

into the Temple comes the second lament passage (19:41–44) in which devastation of the city is predicated on the lack of recognition of the divine visitation in Jesus.[43] It is notable that one aspect of the promised threat against the city, 'they will not leave within you one stone upon another' (19:44), seems to be picked up from the traditions concerning the destruction of the Temple (cf. e.g. Luke 21:6).

Jesus' entry into the Temple answers to Malachi 3:1: 'the Lord whom you seek will suddenly come to his temple'. He takes possession of the Temple as 'my house' (19:46; cf. Isa. 56:7), first to effect a brief demonstration, but more emphatically to teach there.[44] The so-called 'cleansing of the Temple' is given a very abbreviated treatment by Luke, which minimizes the elements of hostility and rejection present in Mark's account,[45] and focuses positively on the role of the Temple as a house of prayer (Isa. 56:7), a role which the Temple has already played (cf. 1:10, 13; 2:29–32, 37; 18:9–14) and which it will shortly have again (24:53; Acts 3:1; 22.17). Luke's account of Jesus' teaching in the Temple is marked off by an *inclusio* between 19:47: 'every day he was teaching in the temple', which opens the two-chapter section of teaching set in the Temple precincts; and 21:37: 'every day he was teaching in the temple', which draws the section to a close (cf. 20:1; 21:1, 5; cf. 22:53).[46]

The conflict material included here by Luke does not at first sight connect directly to the Temple itself. Nevertheless, the material has Christological significance as Luke claims for Jesus divine authority to teach (20:1–8), a climactic role as the rejected beloved Son (20:13), and the status of Lordly Messiah (20:41–44).[47]

Luke's placement of the parable of the wicked tenants, and its connections with preceding and following stone sayings, connects

---

[43] The background to much of the terminology is, as Dodd demonstrated, several passages of the Old Testament concerning divine judgement against the city (e.g. Isa. 29:3; Ezek. 4:1–3), see C. H. Dodd, 'The Fall of Jerusalem and the "Abomination of Desolation"', reprinted (from *JRS* [1947]) in *More New Testament Studies* (Manchester: Manchester University Press, 1968), pp. 69–83.

[44] Cf. Conzelmann, *The Theology of St. Luke*, p. 76.

[45] Mark carefully interleaves (or 'sandwiches') the Temple viewing (11:11), the barren fig tree (11:12–14), the Temple 'cleansing' (11:15–18) and the withered fig tree (11:20ff.), suggesting an interpretation of the Temple as barren and facing judgement (cf. W. R. Telford, *The Barren Temple and the Withered Tree: A Redaction-Critical Analysis of the Cursing of the Fig-Tree Pericope in Mark's Gospel and its Relation to the Cleansing of the Temple Tradition* (JSNTSS1; Sheffield: JSOT, 1980), widely followed in the commentaries.

[46] Mark describes Jesus as residing outside of Jerusalem and entering the Temple on particular occasions, for demonstration and teaching (e.g. 11:11, 12, 15ff., 19, 27), with the eschatological discourse set on the Mount of Olives 'over against the temple' (*katenanti tou hierou*, 13:3). Luke acknowledges the fact that Jesus was accommodated outside of Jerusalem (Luke 21:37), only after a narrative that has been set, from the point of view of the reader, completely within the Temple (Luke 19:47; 20:1, 9, 45; 21:1, 5).

[47] Conzelmann: 'It is in the Temple that the final manifestation of who Jesus is now given in view of his imminent Passion' (*The Theology of St. Luke*, p. 78).

the quotation of Psalms 118:22 in 20:17 – 'The stone that the builders rejected has become the cornerstone' – very closely to the Temple (as of course does the Psalm itself, see Ps. 118:19ff., 26ff.; cf. also *T. Sol.* 22:7 – 23:4).[48] The rejection of the stone by the Temple builders, in view of the two other occurrences of this verb in Luke (see 9:22; 17:25), must mean the rejection of Jesus, the beloved Son of the parable (20:13; cf. 3:22). The transformation of the rejected stone into the cornerstone corresponds to Jesus' vindication after his rejection (i.e. his resurrection). This vindication–resurrection of Jesus will thus establish him as the centre-piece of a restored 'temple'. Precisely how Luke conceives of this 'temple' is not yet clear; we should probably take this as a hint and anticipation of a theme to be developed more fully in Acts, both explicitly in Acts 4:10–12 (where the text is cited again) and implicitly elsewhere.[49]

Also located within the Temple (in a broad sense) is the Lukan version of the discourse concerning the destruction of the Temple and Jerusalem (21:5–36). At the outset the focus is on the Temple and its beautiful stones (v. 5), in the statement 'the days will come when not one stone will be left upon another; all will be thrown down' (21:6). This comment rehearses an element of the earlier threat against the city (19:44), and suggests that the Temple participates in the judge-ment consequent on failure to recognize and heed the divine visitation in Jesus (as perhaps also suggested in relation to the Temple builders by 20:17ff.). But the focus does not remain on the Temple but quickly broadens out to include discipleship and mission before the eschato-logical crisis (vv. 9–19), the destruction of Jerusalem (vv. 20–24), and thence to the whole world (vv. 25–33). The crisis faced by Jerusalem is paralleled to universal cosmic crisis (21:35).

The crucifixion narrative contains the next reference to the Temple, in the tearing of the Temple veil (23:45). Clearly the crucifixion scene is of pivotal importance for Luke and a number of crucial themes are focused here. The 'crowds' or 'people', hitherto distinguished by

---

[48] The vineyard parable of Isaiah 5:1–7, on which the parable of the tenants is clearly based, was already understood as referring to the Temple in *Targ. Is.* 5:2; *t. Suk.* 3:15 and (probably) 4Q500; J. M. Baumgarten, '4Q500 and the Ancient Conception of the Lord's Vineyard', *JJS* 40 (1989) pp. 1–6; cf. Swarup, *An Eternal Planting, a House of Holiness.*

[49] At Qumran the new temple/stone is the elect community (see 1QS 8.7; cf. also 1QH 6/XIV.25–29; 7/XV.8f; cf. also Eph. 2:20–22; 1 Pet. 2:4–7); Gärtner, *The Temple and the Community in Qumran and the New Testament,* pp. 133–6. For this general perspective applied to Mark's account, see Joel Marcus, *The Way of the Lord: Christological Exegesis of the Old Testament in the Gospel of Mark* (Edinburgh: T&T Clark, 1993), pp. 114–27 (cf. also J. Jeremias, *TDNT,* IV:276 on Luke). Marcus argues that the eschatological community of Jesus' followers is in view in the immediate context in the 'others' to whom the vineyard is given (Mark 12:9 // Luke 20:16). He writes: 'Mark ... views Christ's resurrection, the exaltation of the rejected stone to the head of the corner, as the creation of a new Temple composed of the resurrected Lord in union with his eschatological community of "others"' (p. 123).

a positive or at least enquiring attitude to Jesus, which limited the options for the authorities (cf. 19:47ff.; 20:6, 19, 26, 45; 21:38; 22:2), now form a temporary alliance which leads directly to the crucifixion (22:4ff., 13–25; cf. vv. 27, 35, 48, 51).[50] Jesus, the innocent one (22:4, 14ff., 22, 41, 47), remains firm in his resolve and final confidence (23: 28, 34, 43, 46).[51] In Luke the tearing of the Temple curtain is reported straight after the mention of darkness over the whole land and before Jesus' final statement and last breath.[52] The Temple had two curtains, but it seems most likely, given the use of *naos* and *katapetasma*, that Luke means to refer to the veil before the holy of holies.[53] What significance should be attached to the tearing of the Temple curtain remains disputed, however, and three main lines of interpretation have emerged: (i) that it was a portent of the destruction of the Temple;[54] (ii) that it was a sign of the end of the Temple cultus 'as a sacred symbol of socio-religious power' (in view of the death of Christ);[55] and (iii) that it was a sign of open access to God through Jesus' death.[56] Sylva argued, primarily on the basis of the parallels between Jesus' passion and the

---

[50] Cf. also Acts 2:22ff., 36; 3:12ff.; 4:10; 5:30; 10:39; 13:27ff. J. T. Carroll, 'Luke's Crucifixion Scene' in D. Sylva (ed.), *Reimaging the Death of the Lukan Jesus* (BBB73; Frankfurt-am-Main: Anton Hain, 1990), pp. 108–24.

[51] B. E. Beck, 'Imitatio Christi and the Lucan Passion Narrative' in W. Horbury and B. McNeil (eds), *Suffering and Martyrdom in the New Testament: Studies Presented to G. M. Styler by the Cambridge New Testament Seminar* (Cambridge: Cambridge University Press, 1981), pp. 28–47. D. Schmidt relates the innocence of Jesus to the righteous one of Isaiah 53:11: see 'Luke's "Innocent" Jesus: A Scriptural Apologetic' in R. J. Cassidy and P. J. Schasper (eds), *Political Issues in Luke–Acts* (Maryknoll: Orbis, 1983), pp. 111–21.

[52] Mark has darkness (15:33), the cry of desolation (v. 34), the bystanders thinking he calls Elijah (v. 35), the sponge on a stick (v. 36) then the loud final cry (v. 37) followed by the Temple curtain torn in two, from top to bottom (v. 38), before the final declaration of the centurion (v. 39). Matthew has an identical order, with additional material relating to the earthquake and the resurrection of the saints between the tearing of the Temple curtain (27:51) and the statement of the centurion (27:54). Many of the unique features of the Lukan account may, like much else in the passion narrative, suggest dependence on (an) additional source(s). For a thorough (!) survey, see J. M. Harrington, *The Lukan Passion Narrative: The Markan Material in Luke 22,54 – 23,25. A Historical Survey: 1891–1997* (NTTS XXX; Leiden: Brill, 2000). Codex Bezae (D 05) restores Luke's tearing of the Temple curtain to the customary place after Jesus' death.

[53] Although *katapetasma* is used of the curtain between the forecourt and the sanctuary (Exod. 26:37; 38:18; Num. 3:26), the initial and predominant use is of the curtain between the sanctuary and the holy of holies (Exod. 26:31–35; Lev. 21:23; 2:3; Sir. 50:5; also Philo, *Moses* II:86; Josephus, *Ant.* VIII:75), this is also meant in the only place where the two terms both occur (1 Macc. 1:22).

[54] So Marshall, *Commentary on Luke*, p. 875; M. D. Goulder, *Luke: A New Paradigm* (JSNTSS 20; Sheffield: Sheffield Academic Press, 1989, 1994), p. 769; J. B. Tyson, *The Death of Jesus in Luke–Acts* (Columbia: University of South Carolina, 1986), p. 108.

[55] J. B. Green, 'The Demise of the Temple as "Culture Center" in Luke–Acts: An Exploration of the Rending of the Temple Veil', *RB* 101 (1994), pp. 495–515.

[56] D. Sylva, 'The Temple Curtain and Jesus' Death in the Gospel of Luke', *JBL* 105 (1986), pp. 239–50: p. 241, n. 7 has a list of scholars holding various views.

death of Stephen in Acts 7, especially the way that the heavens opened so that Stephen could commit his spirit to the Lord revealed in the open heaven (Acts 7:55ff.), that the tearing of the Temple curtain enables Jesus access to and communion with the God who reveals himself in and from the Temple at the moment of his committal (Luke 23:45b–46 belong together on this view).[57] The evidence in support of this view, despite the positive verdict of Nolland, remains weak, and it does not seem possible to give a definitive verdict on Luke's intention here.[58]

6. THE TEMPLE AND THE TRANSITION INTO THE ACTS

After the resurrection appearance and the Lukan form of the commissioning of the disciples, the Gospel closes with a short passage in which Jesus leads the disciples to Bethany, blesses them and then ascends into heaven (24:50ff.; cf. Acts 1:6–11);[59] Luke then has the disciples worshipping Jesus (a Christological highpoint of the Gospel) before they return to Jerusalem with great joy and the Gospel closes with the disciples in the Temple.[60] They were there constantly (*dia pantos*), within the Temple precincts (*hieron*), praising God (24:52ff.).[61] The notes of joy and

---

[57] Sylva also appeals to Acts 3:1; 10:30, which suggest that Luke regarded the ninth hour (the time of Jesus' death) as the hour of Temple prayer (ibid., p. 245). Sylva is followed by J. Nolland, *Luke* (WBC, 3 vols; Dallas: Word, 1989, 1993, 1993), pp. 1157ff.

[58] It is worth noting Josephus' discussion of various events in and around the Temple, including the spontaneous opening of the eastern gate of the inner court, which produced a range of different contemporary interpretations which are reported by Josephus (see *War* VI:286–315; referred to by Sylva, 'The Temple Curtain and Jesus' Death in the Gospel of Luke', p. 239, n. 2).

[59] The language of 24:50 echoes a number of passages in which priestly blessings are bestowed (e.g. Lev. 9:22: *exaras ... tas cheiras ... eulogēsen autous*; Sir. 50:20–22: *Epēren cheiras autou ... dounai eulogian*), which has led some scholars to suggest that Luke may be presenting Jesus as a priest: see most recently and fully A. G. Mekkattukunnel, *The Priestly Blessing of the Risen Christ: An Exegetico-Theological Analysis of Luke 24, 50–53* (EUS XXIII.714; Bern: Peter Lang, 2001). Again, however, the evidence is not really sufficient to secure such a wide-ranging conclusion, especially when there are not hints of Jesus as priest elsewhere in Luke (notwithstanding the attempted demonstration of the contrary by Mekkattukunnel, pp. 176–81), and as the language of blessing (if not the posture) is also appropriate in a range of other contexts, including farewell discourses (e.g. Gen. 49:28; Deut. 33:1, etc.), see especially Nolland, *Luke*, pp. 1227ff.

[60] Among the large number of textual variants in these two verses (possibly due to dislocation of Luke from Acts) the original text of Alexandrinus (A 02) lacks *en tō hierō*. M. C. Parsons argued that the Western non-interpolations, the shorter readings in 24:3, 6, 12, 36, 40, 51 and 52 are all original: *The Departure of Jesus in Luke–Acts: The Ascension Narratives in Context* (JSNTSS 21; Sheffield: JSOT, 1987), pp. 29–52. For a recent treatment, see A.W. Zwiep, 'The Text of the Ascension Narratives (Luke 24.50–3; Acts 1.1–2, 9–11', *NTS* 42 (1996), pp. 219–44.

[61] *Dia pantos* always has the sense of 'constantly' in the New Testament (cf. Matt. 18:10; Mark 5:5; Acts 2:25; 10:2; 24:16; Rom. 11:10; 2 Thess. 3:16; Heb. 2:15; 9:6; 13:15).

praise in the Temple serve to link the conclusion of the Gospel with its introduction, as well as anticipating the early chapters of the Acts.[62]

7. CONCLUDING REFLECTIONS

It is hardly appropriate to offer any definitive conclusions at this point. Luke affirms the role of the Temple in many ways, as a place of prayer and revelation, as in some respects central to God's dealings with the cosmos. At the same time the Temple, like the city in which it resides, stands under the threat of judgement inasmuch as it partakes in the rejection of God's beloved Son. His vindication beyond rejection elevates him to a key position as cornerstone of a renewed Temple, but the story still has some distance to run before the relationship between the two Temples becomes clearer. For that we need to turn to Luke's second volume.

---

[62] For *eulogeo*, see 1:42, 64; 2:28, 34 (the last three set in the Temple); for *chara*, see 1:14; 2:10 (*chara megalē* as in 24:53). For continual presence in the Temple see 2:37 (Anna in the Temple day and night). For early references in Acts see 2:46; 3:1–10; 5:20, 25, 42.

9

THE TEMPLE IN THE GOSPEL ACCORDING TO JOHN

BILL SALIER

1. INTRODUCTION

Everything in the Fourth Gospel is recorded for the purpose that Jesus will be recognized as Israel's divine Messiah who brings life (20:30–31). This recognition is essential for any who would attain to this life and the status of being a child of God (1:12–13) that it entails. The very essence of life as stated in the Gospel is the knowledge of God and the one he has sent, Jesus Christ (17:3). John presents Jesus as the embodiment of the presence of God and the means by which God is revealed and therefore known. He does this in a variety of ways through the course of his narrative presentation of the historical events of the life of Jesus, aware that through a combination of prophetic insight and Spirit-led understanding these events are pregnant with spiritual meaning. Not only the events of Jesus' life are pressed into service. As John presents Jesus in his historical context, he presents him in the context of the Jewish faith with all of its practices and institutions. Through these practices and institutions he presents the same essential truth that Jesus is the divine Messiah, the revealer of the Father and therefore the lifegiver. The Temple is one of these institutions.

In this brief examination of the Temple in the Fourth Gospel its place will first be considered with respect to the narrative programme of the Gospel. It is a significant setting for much of the action in the first twelve chapters of the Gospel. It is the place where the divine Messiah reveals his identity and his relationship with the Father who sent him. It is also the place where this revelation is questioned and eventually rejected by his interlocutors and opponents, 'the Jews'.[1] It is the place

---

[1] This is a controversial term in the interpretation of the Fourth Gospel and the literature is voluminous. See, e.g., U. Wahlde, 'The Johannine Jews: A Critical Survey', *NTS* 28 (1982), pp. 33–60. The view taken here is that the expression refers to a 'composite character' in the narrative that epitomizes the *kosmos* (world) in its opposition to Jesus. It has its roots in the historical opposition to the mission and person of Jesus. Cf. A. T. Lincoln, *Truth on Trial: The Lawsuit Motif in John's Gospel* (Peabody: Hendrickson, 2000), p. 19 and J. W. Pryor, *John: Evangelist of the Covenant People – The Narrative & Themes of the Fourth Gospel* (Downers Grove: IVP, 1992), p. 184.

where the narrative programme foreshadowed by 1:9–11 is played out.

Following this, the part that the Temple has to play within the Christological programme of the Gospel will be examined. The Temple is a highly significant structure within the Jewish religious framework and John explores Jesus' relationship to it, using its significance within this religious framework to help shed light on the portrait of Christ that he is painting. There are also implications suggested for the Temple itself that form a part of the Gospel's teaching as well. The Temple imagery of the Gospel helps to elucidate the mission of the Son and is one, amongst many, of the institutions of 'the Jews' that Jesus is portrayed as fulfilling and replacing as he goes about this mission.

Finally, two observations will be made concerning the use of Temple imagery in the programme of the Gospel. The first will point to an area where the potential for reflection has been underexploited while the second will point to reflection that ought to be more cautiously conducted.

An examination of the place of the Temple in the Fourth Gospel demonstrates one of the ways in which a New Testament writer can creatively use an Old Testament motif in the service of his own Christological presentation. This is more than simply a literary technique. An understanding of fulfilment and replacement is also employed. The implications for understanding both Jesus and the Temple are explored within the sweep of God's purposes.

2. GOING TO THE TEMPLE

The Temple provides the physical setting for several passages of the narrative of the Fourth Gospel. These passages will be briefly examined in order to discern features of John's presentation of the Temple.

2.1 John 2

The Temple first appears as a narrative setting in the Gospel in the account of the Temple cleansing (2:12–22). Jesus travels to Jerusalem and is immediately situated in the Temple (2:14). The move between Jerusalem and Temple in 2:13–14 is so casually phrased that it almost appears that for Jesus to go to Jerusalem means that he will go to the Temple.

Upon finding those selling sacrifices and changing money for the Temple tax in the Temple environs, Jesus promptly clears them out (2:15). This action is explained for the reader by the narrator, via the disciples' reminiscence, in terms of zeal 'for his father's house' (2:17). When challenged as to the provision of a sign to justify his actions Jesus refers, in an enigmatic statement, to the destruction of the Temple and its reconstitution in three days (2:19). Once again the narrator supplies an interpretative comment in order to help the reader understand that what was being referred to in this comment was the body of Jesus (2:22).

For the reader familiar with the Temple and its symbolism there might be a surprise in terms of the comparison with the previous incident at Cana (2:1–11). There Jesus is spoken of as manifesting his glory (2:11), an activity that one might expect to be more naturally associated with the Temple, based on Old Testament expectations of manifestations of the glory of God in the Temple and Tabernacle (Exod. 40:34 ff.; 1 Kgs. 8:10–11). There is no statement of any such manifestation connected with the Temple. The question/demand of the Jews (2:18) seems to distance the cleansing incident itself from the category of sign narrative. The possibility that the cleansing itself is the sign offered does not seem to be suggested within the narrative itself.[2] The sign offered, while having reference to the Temple, will be 'performed' outside the Temple environs.

The initial impression of the Temple in the narrative is as the setting for a demonstration of the zeal of Jesus for his Father's honour. It is thus the setting for an intimation, at least, of his relationship with the Father, whatever other significance might be drawn. As a physical setting it moves from being full to being empty as Jesus clears the paraphernalia of sacrifice and money changing away. It is then metaphorically 'replaced' in his enigmatic utterance.

2.2 *John 5*

In John 5 Jesus is once again depicted as going up to Jerusalem in words reminiscent of 2:13. The familiarity of the phrase might lead the reader to expect another visit to the Temple, so it comes as somewhat of a surprise to see that Jesus instead goes to the pool by the sheep gate (5:2). Jerusalem and the Temple are not thereby entirely synonymous in the thinking of the evangelist. However, it is not long before the action moves to the Temple. Jesus meets the man whom he has just healed in the Temple (5:14) and there is no indication that the ensuing discourse moves from this location. In the controversy that follows (5:16ff.) Jesus replies to his accusers with an extended exposition of the nature of his relationship to the Father. This is an intensely 'revelatory' discourse where the equality and subordination of the Son to the Father are outlined in comprehensive fashion. In the sequence of this chapter the sign occurs outside the Temple while Jesus' revelatory word is spoken within the Temple environs before the Jews (5:18; cf. 2:18).[3] The Temple is the place of revelation, but this is revelation in word and not sign.

---

[2] See A. Köstenberger, 'The Seventh Johannine Sign: A Study in John's Christology', *BBR* 5 (1995), pp. 87–103, for a vigorous defence of the sign nature of the incident.
[3] Although the healing is not labelled a sign in 5:18, the later references in 7:21, 31 seem to refer back to this incident in those terms.

2.3 John 7–8

After an interlude teaching at the synagogue at Capernaum in chapter 6, the action again finds its setting in the Temple in the extended controversy with the Jews that continues through chapters 7 and 8.

After a delayed start Jesus goes up to the Temple (7:1–10). A sense of anticipation for his arrival is promoted through the dispute with his brothers over his attendance at the festival (7:2–8) and then speculation amongst the Jews and the crowds concerning his identity (7:10–13). In the middle of the Festival of Booths, Jesus is at the Temple and he begins to teach (7:14). There is no monologue this time but a freewheeling and open debate where Jesus makes claims concerning both himself and his audience, and these are alternately discussed, questioned, refuted and accepted by different portions of the audience (7:10–12, 26–27, 31, 40–44). It is no longer Jesus and 'the Jews' who are present in the Temple as has been the case in the first two incidents. There are references to the people (7:25), the crowds (7:12), the Pharisees (7:32) and the Temple police (7:45). In two bold statements Jesus claims to embody two of the significant symbolic aspects of the feast that he is attending (7:37–39, 8:12). The heat of the debate rises as Jesus accuses his opponents of being children of the devil (8:44) and he finally departs the Temple following the attempt to stone him (8:58–59).

This is a dynamic and contentious account as the varying reactions to the proclamations of Jesus are presented. Jesus is engaged with in both dialogue and accusation, and he responds in vigorous fashion as the heat in the debate rises through the two chapters. The issue remains the identity of Jesus and his relationship to the Father but the debate is broadened to encompass the issue of relationship with the Father with respect to his audience. The Temple has become the place of assessment and rejection as well as proclamation.

2.4 John 10 and beyond

The Temple is once again the setting for an appearance by Jesus in chapter 10. At yet another feast, the Feast of Dedication, Jesus appears. The transition from Jerusalem to Temple is effected in a manner similar to 2:13 (cf. 10:22). Jesus is questioned once again as to his identity (10:22–24). He speaks once more and the response from his opponents is purely negative. His departure from their hands marks his last appearance, in the narrative, at the Temple (10:39).

The Temple is only specifically mentioned once more in the narrative. It is alluded to in the phrase 'this place' (11:48) as Caiaphas speaks better than he knows in the context of the events happening around him, but the final mention occurs during the brief account of the interrogation of Jesus by the high priest (18:19–24). Jesus states that he has spoken openly and always taught in the synagogues and at the Temple 'where all the Jews come together' (18:20).

This statement prompts the realization that the public teaching ministry of Jesus has been largely conducted in the Gospel in either the synagogue or the Temple.[4] This is especially emphasized by the narrative of chapters 5 to 8, where virtually every occurrence of the verb 'teach' and the noun 'teaching' appear.[5] In each of these public settings, in the Temple and the synagogue, Jesus has spoken of his identity and his mission. He has revealed himself by word in the Temple and the synagogue. According to his testimony to the high priest, the Temple and synagogue were the places of openness and revelation, they are the places where the Jews 'come together' (18:20).[6] Of the two, the Temple appears to be far more significant for the narrator, with the main teaching action centred there.[7]

Jesus has been assessed and rejected in both Temple and synagogue. The Temple supremely, and synagogue to a certain extent, are the setting where the narrative programme anticipated in the prologue at 1:11 is fulfilled. Jesus has come to his own and been rejected.[8]

3. REPLACING THE TEMPLE

While the Temple figures prominently in the narrative programme it also serves to advance the Christological/theological programme of the Gospel as well.

At the very least the Temple is portrayed as the place where the revealer reveals himself in word. This much is clear from the remark made in 18:20, as well as the content of the sequence from chapter 5 through to chapter 8. The theological programme of the prologue is thus fulfilled in the Temple environs as God makes himself known, through his Son, in the Temple. This is to be expected with the Temple representing the locus of divine presence.[9]

However, John portrays Jesus as not only revealing the divine presence in the midst of the Temple, but also replacing the Temple as the locus of divine presence. This replacement joins with a number of other

---

[4] The only exception to this occurs in John 12 where Jesus speaks in front of the assembled crowd (12:23–36). Perhaps the reader is meant to assume that this occurs in the Temple, but this is not specified.

[5] The exceptions are 9:34 and 14:26 for the verb 'teach'; 'teach' in 18:20 and 'teaching' in 18:19 are obviously related to the point being made in context.

[6] Cf. 5:16, 18; 6:41, 52; 7:11, 15, 35; 8:22, 48; 10:24.

[7] J. Lieu, 'Temple and Synagogue in John', *NTS* 45 (1999), pp. 51–69. See especially p. 67, 'Thus the synagogue serves only to reinforce the Temple themes, almost as a pale shadow thereof.'

[8] Ibid., p. 69 tentatively suggests that the Temple might even be considered Jesus' own *patris* (homeland). However, this downplays even further the mention of the synagogue. The more general reference back to 1:11, his own place and his own people, would seem to be in mind in this expression.

[9] Ibid., p. 68.

implied replacements to form part of a conceptual web that portrays, through the narrative, the point that Jesus has come as the fulfilment of the plans and purposes of God in the Old Testament revelation.[10] The various strands of this web include replacements of holy space (e.g. 1:51; 2:22; 4:23)[11] and holy times (e.g. 5:1; 6:4; 7:2) as well as allusions to other motifs from the Old Testament Scriptures (e.g. 10:11; 15:1). The basis of this web is established in the important words of the prologue, 1:14–17, a passage that is also significant for thinking about the replacement of the Temple.

3.1 John 1:14–17

The importance of the prologue to the rest of the Gospel is universally acknowledged, even if details of its structure and the precise relationship to the rest of the Gospel continue to be debated.[12] The prologue is best viewed as an overture to the Gospel, providing an overview of its general shape, as well as introducing snatches of tunes to be heard throughout the rest.[13] Jesus is clearly portrayed as the divine and pre-existent *logos* (word) who reveals the Father (1:1, 18). The first major section of the prologue (1:1–13) records in universal (1:1–5) and then historical terms (1:6–11) the coming of the divine word to, respectively, the *kosmos* (world) and his own people and meeting ignorance and rejection. This rejection is counterbalanced by the mention of those who believe and are given the right to become children of God, born of the will of God (1:12–13).

This manner of this coming is described and its significance reflected upon in the second major section (1:14–18). The key verse is 1:14. The reintroduction of the term *logos* and the change in person to plurals signal a new section.[14] This reflection extends through to verse 18 and it is clear that the thought of Exodus 32–34 is present throughout. The use of the verb *skenoō* (to dwell) recalls the substantive *skēnē* (tent, dwelling), used to denote the Tabernacle throughout the Exodus account. While not decisive by itself,[15] the combination with *doxa* (glory) in the same verse, the connection with the name, previously mentioned in verse 12, and the following references to Moses (1:17) all

---

[10] For the notion of a conceptual web, see the work of J. G. van der Watt, *Family of the King: Dynamics of Metaphor in the Gospel According to John* (BIS 47; Leiden: E. J. Brill, 2000).

[11] An extended discussion can be found in W. D. Davies, *The Gospel and the Land: Early Christianity and Jewish Territorial Doctrine* (Berkeley and Los Angeles: University of California Press, 1974), pp. 288–335.

[12] For an overview, see E. Harris, *Prologue and Gospel: The Theology of the Fourth Evangelist* (JSNTSupp 107; Sheffield: Sheffield Academic Press, 1994), pp. 9–25.

[13] G. R. Beasley-Murray, *John* (WBC 36; Waco: Word, 1987), p. 5.

[14] W. J. Dumbrell, *The Search for Order: Biblical Eschatology in Focus* (Grand Rapids: Baker Book House, 1994), p. 237.

[15] *Skēnē* is used in a variety of Old Testament contexts.

point to Exodus 32–34, where these elements are present. In Exodus 32–34, between the giving of the plans for the Tabernacle and its construction, occurs the incident with the golden calf. This incident poses a number of problems for the ongoing relationship between Yahweh and his people, which are resolved in the ensuing discussion between Moses and Yahweh.[16] Following his successful intercession on behalf of the people of Israel, Moses asks for a vision of God's glory. This is denied him in full (Exod. 33:18–23) but Moses is instead promised the divine name (Exod. 33:19), which appears to be less than a full theophany.[17] Glory seems to connote the divine majesty of God that is somehow dangerous and therefore unapproachable, while the name connotes 'accessibility, availability, and approachability in worship'.[18] While the mention of the name of Jesus (1:12), essential for belief, picks up on these latter concerns, the glory of God is also present in the flesh of the Word/Jesus. In him, what was not possible in the time of Moses has become possible.

The Tabernacle was a significant symbol of the rule of God amongst his people, the focal point for their worship and a potent symbol of his presence.[19] From this point on the reader is aware that Jesus embodies all that the Tabernacle stood for: the rule of God, the focus of the knowledge of God and the locus of the true worship of God. In him are made manifest the name and glory of God. A new Tabernacle is present.

As the reflection in the prologue moves on there is a further dimension added as John draws a contrast between the revelation that was given Moses and that which came about through Jesus Christ (1:17). This is summarized as *charis anti charitos* (grace upon grace) (1:17). The force of the preposition *anti* most likely suggests a notion of replacement, as the contrast stated in 1:17 also suggests.[20] The statement preserves the gracious nature of the Law but at the same time points to its replacement by that to which it pointed in any case (5:45–47).[21] The idea of gracious replacement is played out through the narrative with respect to the various institutions of Israel. Amongst these will be the Temple. In a sense the Temple is already in view with the mention of the Tabernacle. While distinct entities, it is also clear that the two are conceptually similar in their function and symbolism. This is apparent at the account of the dedication of the Temple in 1 Kings 8. The ark is

---

[16] See the discussion by James Palmer in this volume.
[17] G. McConville, 'God's "Name" and God's "Glory"', *Tyndale Bulletin* 30 (1979), pp. 149–68.
[18] Dumbrell, *The Search for Order*, p. 239.
[19] Ibid., p. 238.
[20] See R. E. Brown, *The Gospel According to John* (AB 29; Garden City: Doubleday, 1966), vol. 1, p. 16 and D. A. Carson, *The Gospel According to John* (Leicester: IVP, 1991), pp. 131–2 for the major interpretative options and their relative merits.
[21] Carson, *The Gospel According to John*, p. 133.

transferred to the inner sanctuary of the Temple, the glory of the LORD fills the house (1 Kgs. 8:11) and the name of the LORD is said to dwell there (1 Kgs. 8:17, 18, 19, 20, 29). The function and symbolism of the Tabernacle has passed to the Temple.

Jesus is depicted in the prologue as the 'embodiment of the rule of God, as the replacement for the Tabernacle of the exodus, as the true Temple, that is the focus of true worship'.[22] He is the locus of divine presence and therefore the revelation of God as he reveals himself as the unique Son (1:18).[23]

3.2 *John 2*

The theme of replacement is then played out through the rest of the narrative. The most explicit reference to the Temple in this respect occurs in chapter 2. When challenged to produce a sign justifying his action in cleansing the Temple, Jesus refers to the Temple of his body, using the term *naos* (temple, sanctuary). This could imply a more specific reference to the sanctuary of the Temple as opposed to more general environs, but the presence of a distinction is disputed.[24] What does appear to be significant is Jesus' use of the term not so much for what it connotes as for providing the change in terminology that provide the basis that enables the narrator to help the reader to perceive the layers of meaning that will soon develop.[25]

An explicit identification is made between Jesus' body and the Temple. An exchange takes place conceptually between the two such that the reader is invited to think of Jesus' body in Temple terms from this point forward in the narrative. There is a tension here to be explored in that Jesus performs the action of cleansing as an expression of his zeal for the Temple and what it represents. There appears to be no criticism implied of the Temple as an institution: rather, the opposite is the case. At the same time, however, the import of his reply to his interlocutors is that the Temple will become obsolete and replaced by his own body. Is this in fact an oblique prophecy of the destruction of the Temple?[26]

---

[22] Dumbrell, *The Search for Order*, p. 239. Lieu, 'Temple and Synagogue in John', pp. 66ff. rejects any idea of judgement or the establishment of a new Temple.

[23] Dumbrell, *The Search for Order*, p. 239.

[24] Carson concedes a possible difference but is generally reticent, *The Gospel According to John*, p. 181. Lieu, 'Temple and Synagogue in John', is emphatic: 'the switch from ἱερόν ... to ναός is surely deliberate: the shrine is the locus of divine presence', p. 66.

[25] F. J. Moloney, *The Gospel of John* (Sacra Pagina 4; Collegeville: Liturgical Press, 1998), p. 78. M. G. W. Stibbe, *John* (Readings; Sheffield: JSOT Press, 1993), pp. 51–2 emphasizes the movement from *hieron* (temple) to *oikos* (house) to *naos* (temple, sanctuary) to *sōma* (body) that leads the reader into the explicit identification being made.

[26] As suggested for example by P. W. L. Walker, *Jesus and the Holy City: New Testament Perspectives on Jerusalem* (Cambridge/Grand Rapids: Eerdmans, 1996), p. 165. Cf. also C. K. Barrett, *The Gospel According to St John: An Introduction with Commentary and Notes on the Greek Text* (London: SPCK, 1978²).

Probably not in the sense of a judgement. Jesus does not say that he will destroy the Temple; rather his challenge is voiced in response to the demand for a sign. Plainly his accusers read it as a reference to the physical Temple,[27] but the overall context and then the interpretative comment from the narrator distance Jesus from any threat or prophecy of destruction. The connection is rather with his death. The paradigm established by 1:17 leads to the view the statement here is one of replacement in the sense implied by '*charis anti charitos*'. Jesus can therefore be presented as positive about the Temple as his Father's house and, at the same time, point towards its replacement in his own body.

There may be a further implication to be drawn from the idea of the replacement of the Temple by Jesus. The Temple was also the place where the relationship between a holy God and a sinful people was maintained through the sacrificial system. In John 2 we see the Temple cleared of the animals necessary for this to take place, and in their place standing the one who has just been announced as the lamb of God, who takes away the sin of the world (1:29). The theme of replacement of the Temple may be read in even more comprehensive terms in view of the potential connections to be made with the sacrifices offered there. Not only does Jesus replace the Temple as the locus of divine presence, but he will also fulfil its function as the place where reconciliation with a holy God can be achieved through sacrifice.[28]

3.3 Other connections

The theme of the replacement of the Temple is alluded to briefly in the midst of the conversation with the Samaritan woman in John 4. The topic of conversation has switched to worship of God and the issue of place has arisen. The background is the dispute between the Samaritans and the Jews concerning the proper place for worship – Jerusalem or Mount Gerizim. Jesus' adjudication on this particular matter is unequivocal as he points forward to a new form of worship

---

[27] Perhaps what is being suggested is along the lines of the interpretation offered by Ridderbos. He interprets the imperative as a challenge to the Jews along prophetic lines to complete the 'destruction' they are already engaged in and Jesus will raise the Temple but in a more profound sense than they can begin to imagine. H. N. Ridderbos, *The Gospel According to John: A Theological Commentary* (Grand Rapids: Eerdmans, 1997), p. 119.

[28] So Carson: '(Jesus is) ... the focal point of the manifestation of God to man, the living abode of God on earth, the fulfilment of all the Temple meant and the centre of all true worship. In this 'Temple' the ultimate sacrifice would take place', *The Gospel According to John*, p. 182. Cf. also J. Neusner, 'Money Changers in the Temple: The Mishnah Explanation', *NTS* 35 (1989), pp. 287–90. He suggests that Jesus' action 'represents an act of the rejection of the most important rite of the Israelite cult, the daily whole offering, and therefore, a statement that there is a means of atonement other than the daily whole-offering, which is now null', p. 290. Cf. also C. Koester, *Symbolism in the Fourth Gospel: Meaning, Mystery, Community* (Minneapolis: Fortress Press, 1995), pp. 83–4.

in the coming time that will occur at neither place (4:21). Rather, true worship will be conducted in spirit and truth. While the topic of conversation is Jerusalem, Jesus' statement has clear implications for the Temple which is the focal point of worship in the city of Jerusalem.[29] It has already been flagged in chapter 2 that Jesus' body is the Temple of God. The time is now indicated when worship of God will be conducted without ties to places. The two mountains and the two temples are to be superseded because Jesus is the source of the Spirit and the truth that make possible the worship the Father desires.[30]

The claims made by Jesus during the Feast of Tabernacles in John 7–8 suggest implications for the theme of Temple replacement.[31] Tabernacles was an important feast where thanks was given for the time in the blessing in the wilderness under Moses. It was also an anticipation of the time when God would again bless his people in a similar way. At the heart of the festival was a water-pouring ceremony reminding Israel of the past provision of water in the wilderness and the future time when water would flow from Jerusalem and the Temple.

In 7:37–39 Jesus stands on the great day of the feast and declares himself to be the place from which living waters will flow. The so-called 'Christological reading' is adopted here in view of the overall focus of the Gospel on the person of Christ, the observation that never in the Fourth Gospel are believers said to be the source of the Spirit (except perhaps in an attenuated sense, 15:26–27) and the context in which the statement is proclaimed.[32]

Standing as he does in the midst of the Temple, with the water pouring ceremony in the temporal vicinity,[33] the reference to the Scripture (7:38) is best taken as reflecting not a single Scripture but a variety of scriptural witnesses.[34] These include the reference to the water flowing

---

[29] Contra Lieu, 'Temple and Synagogue in John', p. 59 who suggests that Jerusalem only is in view.

[30] D. Peterson, *Engaging with God: A Biblical Theology of Worship* (Leicester: Apollos, 1992), pp. 98ff.

[31] Contra Lieu, 'Temple and Synagogue in John', p. 67 who denies any significance for the Temple and claims that the festivals are simply occasions for the gathering together of the Jews.

[32] Following Pryor, *John*, pp. 39–40. For a lengthy discussion of the options and an exposition of the alternate reading that sees the believer as the source of the flow of living water, see Carson, *The Gospel According to John*, pp. 321–8. Despite the differences in the two readings, Carson helpfully points to the common ground the two positions share, not the least being the point that whichever way the verse is punctuated Jesus remains the source of living waters.

[33] See the background in Brown, *The Gospel According to John*, vol. 1, p. 326 and the more extended treatment in G. MacRae, 'The Meaning and Evolution of the Feast of Tabernacles', *CBQ* 22.3 (1960), pp. 251–76.

[34] For the singular 'Scripture' not necessarily referring to a particular Scripture, see John 20:9. Carson also points out the tremendous variety with which John introduces his various citations of Scripture in his 'John and the Johannine Epistles', in D. A. Carson

from the rock during the Exodus (Exod. 17) and the water flowing from the Temple in Zechariah 14 and Ezekiel 47.

With this statement, and its interpretation by John in terms of the eschatological gift of the Spirit (7:39), Jesus is again presented as the new Temple. From him will flow the rivers of water promised to flow from that future Temple, bringing life to all they touch.

In John 10 Jesus is described as the one whom the Father has sanctified. At a festival celebrating the rededication of the Temple following defilement[35] again a note of replacement is struck in terms of Jesus being the truly 'dedicated one'.

The theme of replacement is important in the narrative framework and touches the Temple at the points examined. Not only does John use the Temple and its associated imagery to help illuminate his portrait of Jesus, but he also allows the consequences to be traced for the Temple itself. By the end of chapter 10 the Temple has been set aside within John's narrative.[36]

4. TWO THOUGHTS

Having seen these two broad areas it remains to trace out two other possible implications connected with our theme.

4.1 The Temple for the nations

The theme of the Temple is also connected to the wider perspective evinced by the Gospel. As Jesus replaces the Temple for Israel there are also hints that he will fulfil the role of the Temple with respect to the nations. The expansive view of the Gospel is signalled from the opening verses as the opening presentation of the mission of Jesus is cast into the widest possible context of creation (1:1–5). At many points the language of *kosmos* injects a universal note into the narrative (e.g. 3:16; 4:42) and while there is plainly a relationship between 'the Jews' and the *kosmos* in the Gospel,[37] the term does also point to the wider concerns of the mission of Jesus. The universal scope of Jesus' mission is referred to when he states that his mission as the messianic shepherd will be to gather sheep who 'do not belong to this fold' (10:16).

---

and H. G. Williamson (eds), *Scripture Citing Scripture: Essays in Honour of Barnabas Lindars* (Cambridge: Cambridge University Press, 1988), pp. 245–64. Cf. also Beasley-Murray, *John*, p. 116.

[35] See Brown, *The Gospel According to John*, vol. 1, p. 402 for details.

[36] Walker, *Jesus and the Holy City*, p. 169.

[37] Cf. Lieu, 'Temple and Synagogue in John', p. 55: 'the relationship between the "world" and "the Jews" for John is never entirely clear – which determines the boundaries of the other?'

This same sentiment is expressed in the editorial comment concerning Caiaphas' unintended prophecy at 11:52.

In terms of connection with passages associated with the Temple, the more general theme of replacement makes its contribution to this universal aspect. The statement in John 4:21–23 before the Samaritan woman indicates the possibility of the worship of God beyond the borders of Israel. This possibility is facilitated by the lack of ties to a physical location and is immediately reinforced by the ensuing mission amongst the Samaritan villagers.

Even more explicit is the statement of Jesus in John 7 that points to his position as the one from whom rivers of living water will flow. In both Zechariah 14 and Ezekiel 37 this image of water flowing from the Temple extends beyond the borders of Israel for the benefit of the nations. This picks up some of the thought of the Old Testament prophets who depicted the eschatological hope of the restored Temple as the centre of the nations (Isa. 2:2–4; Mic. 4:1–3; Jer. 3:17).[38]

It is the presence of Greeks at the feast that precipitates Jesus' knowledge that the fateful hour has arrived. It is interesting to note that the Greeks, who have come to Jerusalem in order to worship at the festival, are presented as seeking Jesus, while the Temple is not mentioned in the text. Doubtless they would have gone to the Temple eventually but the narrative suggests an implied replacement for the location where God may be found and worshipped. Following this request Jesus speaks of his own death as being the seed that dies in order to bear much fruit and that in his lifting up all men will be drawn to him (12:32). The destruction and raising of the Temple, foreshadowed in 2:22 and fulfilled in the events of the death and resurrection of Jesus, will be the means by which the nations are eschatologically gathered.

While it is clearly the Jerusalem Temple that is in view, the significance of the theme of temple replacement would not be lost on non-Jewish readers of the Gospel, who would be well aware of the function of a temple.[39] In this respect the choice of temple replacement as one of the many images bearing the truth about Jesus is a logical choice in a Gospel that evidences concern that as wide a range of readers as possible might have access to the truths it contains.

4.2 The Temple presence of Jesus beyond the cross?

It has been suggested that the Temple theme is extended in the farewell discourse to include the disciples and eventually the Christian church

---

[38] Cf. also the discussion in McKelvey concerning Jewish understandings of the Temple as a world centre. R. J. McKelvey, *The New Temple: The Church in the New Testament* (Oxford Theological Monographs; Oxford: Oxford University Press, 1969), Appendix A, pp. 188–92.

[39] See the discussion in L. Hartman, '"He Spoke of the Temple of His Body" (John 2.13–22)', *Svensk Exegetisk Årsbok* 54 (1989), pp. 70–9.

when Jesus mentions the fact that his Father's house has many rooms and he goes there to provide a place for them. While the resonance of the phrase 'my father's house' with the statement in the Temple at 2:14 is evocative and perhaps suggests some notion of heaven as the Father's heavenly Temple,[40] one wonders if this is not overreading the motif in a Gospel that remains very much Christologically centred. Certainly the language of intimacy and relationship abounds throughout the farewell discourse, but it does not appear to draw in the imagery of the Temple such that the disciples replace the Temple in any sense through their association with Jesus.[41] This is language for other voices in the New Testament.[42]

Jesus remains very much the locus of the revelation of God. He is the replacement Temple and all that that means. If we are to speak of the ongoing Temple presence of Jesus beyond the resurrection and connect it with the disciples, then perhaps the better connection will be via the Spirit promised to the disciples as the replacement presence of Jesus with them. This presence will enable knowledge of the Father and the disciples will be drawn further into the life of the Father and Son. How will this presence be experienced?

At least one of the functions of John 14–16 is an extended apology for the veracity of the contents of the Gospel. It performs this function as it demonstrates the commissioned and Spirit-inspired nature of the recollections and interpretation of the disciples. This will apply specifically to the disciple whom Jesus loved and who is responsible for the contents of the Gospel. At the same time the ongoing mission of the disciples is outlined in both continuity and discontinuity with the mission of Jesus.[43] Their chief aid for mission will be the word concerning Christ, brought to their remembrance and comprehension by the Spirit (15:27; 16:8; 16:20).

How will the 'Temple presence' of Jesus continue amongst the Christian community and the nations? It will be through the ministry of the Spirit and the word. The Spirit and the word will maintain the Temple presence of Jesus in the midst of the community that bears his name and through them to the nations beyond. It will be by receiving this word and believing its message concerning Jesus that the revelatory programme of the prologue with its life-giving benefits will continue (John 20:29–31).

---

[40] See J. McCaffrey, *The House with Many Rooms: The Temple Theme of Jn. 14,2–3* (AnBib 114; Roma: Editrice Pontificio Istituto Biblico, 1988). The referent of 14:2–3 as being heaven is contentious. See the discussion in Carson, *The Gospel According to John*, pp. 488ff.

[41] Contra, e.g., M. Coloe, 'Raising the Johannine Temple (John 19.19–37)', *AusBR* 28 (2000), pp. 47–58, and Walker, *Jesus and the Holy City*, pp. 170ff.

[42] E.g. 1 Corinthians 7; 1 Peter 2.

[43] A. J. Köstenberger, *The Missions of Jesus and the Disciples according to the Fourth Gospel: With Implications for the Fourth Gospel's Purpose and the Mission of the Contemporary Church* (Grand Rapids: Eerdmans, 1998).

5. CONCLUSIONS

The Temple is integral to both the narrative and theological interests of the Fourth Gospel. The focus throughout the Gospel is clearly upon Jesus as the one who will bring about the gracious replacement and fulfilment of the hopes of Israel and therefore the world. One of the ways in which this theme is expressed is through an extended reflection on the relationship of Jesus to the Temple. The Temple forms the physical setting for the revelation of the Son of God in his teaching ministry and is the place where he is also rejected. It is clear that Jesus comes to represent all that the Temple meant for the people of Israel. He is the locus of divine revelation, worship and presence. And he will be that for the world. While there is criticism of practices associated with the Temple, it is not subject to criticism as an institution. Rather it will be graciously replaced; the grace of God expressed through it for the Old Covenant people of God gives way to the grace of God expressed through the mission of the Son. A person has replaced a place and all that it meant.

The presentation of the Gospel looks in two directions. It looks backwards to the Old Testament and the Tabernacle and Temple of Israel and shows how these two institutions foreshadow Christ and are fulfilled by him. The Gospel also anticipates the final and surprising conclusion to the development of the Temple theme throughout the canon of the Christian Scriptures in Revelation 21:22 and as such makes a significant contribution to this biblical theological theme.[44]

---

[44] Perhaps a comment on John's approach to the Old Testament is in order at this point. John testifies that the Scriptures bear witness to Jesus and he demonstrates this with a variety of approaches. A brief examination of the Temple in the Gospel shows that at least one arrow in his biblical theological quiver is typological. Not only are individual Scriptures fulfilled, but a whole range of institutions and events are also capable of being seen as illuminating the life and significance of Jesus, as well as apparently finding their goal in him. Cf. Carson, 'John and the Johannine Epistles', p. 254.

10

A TALE OF TWO PERSPECTIVES?

The Place of the Temple in Acts

STEVE WALTON

'Things take time.' This slogan of those who have studied the management of change aptly summarizes the development of early Christian
thought and praxis in relation to the Jerusalem Temple in Acts. Luke
portrays the earliest Christians as going to the Temple to pray (Acts
2:46),[1] but also presents Paul as stating that God 'does not live in
shrines made by human hands' (17:24). Is Luke consistent in Acts? Can
these strands be held together within a wider view?

The aim of this paper is to examine these questions by, first, carefully
examining Luke's usage of Temple language in its various contexts,
highlighting both positive and negative views, and then by attempting
to place these texts within a wider Lukan framework in order to see
how they might hold together. The first of these tasks will necessitate
a sustained engagement with Stephen's speech, which has been a
storm centre in scholarship on this question. Finally, we shall reflect
very briefly on the place of Acts' view of the Temple in wider biblical
theology.

1. NAMING THE TEMPLE

In Acts there are four main terms used for the Jerusalem Temple and
other temples: 'temple' (*hieron*), 'shrine' (*naos*), 'house (*oikos*) and 'this
[holy] place'.[2]

While Luke uses 'shrine' (*naos*) in his Gospel for the central shrine or
sanctuary of the Jerusalem Temple (Luke 1:9, 21ff.), he never uses this
word in relation to the Jerusalem Temple in Acts – presumably partly,
at least, because he has no occasion to describe events taking place
in the shrine. Rather, 'shrine' is a generic term used in Paul's Athens
speech of places where God does not live (17:24), and in describing the
silversmiths' models of the temple of Artemis (19:24, 27). Thus this term

---

[1] References henceforward in this paper are to Acts unless stated otherwise.
[2] Cf. discussion (of these names and other issues concerning the Temple) in Peter Head's
paper on Luke in this volume, coming to (unsurprisingly) similar conclusions.

may have negative connotations in relation to the central shrine of the Jerusalem Temple, for that is also called a *naos*, and the tearing of the curtain in front of it may denote that God has departed (Luke 23:45).[3]

When Luke is narrating, he commonly writes simply of 'the Temple' (*to hieron*, e.g. 2:46; 3:1). Similarly, his Christian characters speak of the Temple this way (e.g. 22:17; 24:12, 18; 25:8; 26:21) or occasionally as a 'house' (7:47).[4] Both of these terms appear to be neutral and descriptive, rather than carrying a lot of theological freight. The final description 'this [holy] place' is found only on the lips of non-Christian Jews in Acts (6:13ff.; 21:28) and always in an accusation against Christians – in 6:13ff. against Stephen and in 21:28 against Paul.[5] The fact that no Christian speaker ever uses this phrase rather suggests that Luke does not believe in the holiness of the Temple thus asserted.

2. POSITIVE VIEWS OF THE TEMPLE

A number of features point to a positive view of the Temple on Luke's part.

First, *the early Christians go there to pray*. This is habitual, for they do it 'daily' (*kath' hēmeran*, 2:46). It can be at the time of sacrifice: 3:1 specifies that Peter and John were going into the Temple 'at the hour of prayer, the ninth [hour]' (*hōran tēs proseuchēs tēn enatēn*), which was the time of the prayers associated with the afternoon sacrifice.[6] While Luke does not specify explicitly that they go to pray, it does look as though he presents the apostles acting as devout Jews who live near enough to the Temple to take part in its services.[7]

---

[3] See the careful discussion in R. E. Brown, *The Death of the Messiah* (2 vols, ABRL; London: Geoffrey Chapman, 1994), vol. 2, pp. 1098–118, especially pp. 1101ff.

[4] This appellation gives rise to discussion whether the Pentecost event took place in the Temple courts, since the location is called 'the *house* where they were sitting' (*ton oikon hou ēsan kathēmenoi*, 2:2); cf. 7:47; Josephus, *Ant.* VIII:65 (VIII:3:2), both using *oikos* for the Temple. C. K. Barrett, *A Critical and Exegetical Commentary on the Acts of the Apostles* (2 vols, ICC; Edinburgh: T&T Clark, 1994, 1998), vol. 1, p. 114 is open to that possibility, contra E. Haenchen, *The Acts of the Apostles* (Oxford: Blackwell, 1971), p. 168, n. 1. However, the posture of sitting is unlikely in the Temple courts, and it is hard to believe that Luke, who is in many respects very focused on the Temple, would miss the opportunity to highlight the coming of the Spirit being in the Temple if he understood that to be the case.

[5] 7:6ff. has Stephen quote Genesis 15:13ff., adding the words 'and they will serve me in this place' (*kai latreusousin moi en tō topō toutō*), but the 'place' is the promised land in general, not the Temple.

[6] Daniel 9:21; Judith 9:1; Josephus, *Ant.* XIV:65 (XIV:4:3); also cited by J. Jervell, *Die Apostelgeschichte* (MeyerK; Göttingen: Vandenhoeck & Ruprecht, 1998[17]), p. 159 n. 311; F. F. Bruce, *The Book of Acts* (NICNT; Grand Rapids: Eerdmans, 1988 revised edn), p. 77; H. Conzelmann, *Acts of the Apostles* (Hermeneia: Fortress Press, 1987), p. 25.

[7] In agreement with C. K. Barrett, 'Attitudes to the Temple in the Acts of the Apostles' in W. Horbury (ed.), *Templum Amicitiae: Essays on the Second Temple Presented to Ernst Bammel* (JSNTS 48; Sheffield: Sheffield Academic Press, 1991), pp. 345–67, citing 347ff.

At a later date Paul also goes to the Temple to pray in order to rebut the charge that he teaches Jewish people to disregard the Mosaic Law (21:21) – a charge that was a (perhaps understandable) misunderstanding of Paul's insistence that Gentiles need not keep Torah. The rite in which he takes part involves offering sacrifice – indeed, the provision of a sin offering (Num. 6:13–20, especially vv. 14, 16) – and Paul agrees both to take part himself and to cover the hairdressing expenses of the others involved (21:24), thus demonstrating that he is an observant Jew. In response to charges that he has profaned the Temple by bringing in Greeks (21:28; 24:6), Paul is anxious to make clear that he has acted entirely properly in the Temple (24:12, 18; 25:8). Rather, he asserts, the reason he was arrested was because of his declaration that Gentiles could enter the people of God (26:19–21) – the real issue is following the lead of Jesus, not the Temple in itself.

Secondly, *the early Christians preach in the Temple courts*. Following the healing of the man with a congenital disability[8] (3:2) at the Beautiful Gate of the Temple, Peter preaches in Solomon's Portico (3:11ff.), which Luke presents as an habitual meeting place of the earliest Christians (5:12) – in line with the common practice in the ancient world of meeting in the open air (cf. 17:17).[9] Not only this, but the apostles are specifically commanded by an angel to preach in the Temple courts on their release from prison by the angel (5:20). The use of the imperfect tense 'they were teaching' (*edidaskon*, 5:21) suggests an ongoing activity, especially if it is seen as ingressive, marking the start of an activity which continued for some time (= 'they began teaching').[10] 5:42 goes on to make it clear that this public preaching in the Temple courts took place daily, in combination with daily meetings in the homes of the Jerusalem-based believers.

Thirdly, *God acts to reveal himself in the Temple*. This is evident in the healing of the man at the Beautiful Gate (3:1–10) and also in Paul's later account of his vision, while praying in the Temple, of Jesus calling him to ministry and mission among the Gentiles (22:17–21). Whilst (as we shall see) God is not limited to the Temple as a locus of revelation, neither does he regard the Temple as an exclusion zone for revelatory activity. More, it is precisely at the heart of the Jewish faith that

---

R. Stronstad, *The Prophethood of All Believers: A Study in Luke's Charismatic Theology* (JPTSup 16; Sheffield: Sheffield Academic Press, 1999), pp. 73ff. speculates that in 4:23 the phrase *pros tous idious* means Peter and John returned to a group of disciples numbering thousands on the Temple Mount, contra J. A. Fitzmyer, *The Acts of the Apostles: A New Translation and Commentary* (AB 31; New York: Doubleday, 1998), p. 307 (and many others).

[8] This terminology is used in agreement with K. H. Wynn, 'Disability in Biblical Translation', *Bible Translator* 52 (2001), pp. 402–14, especially p. 406.

[9] So also Barrett, 'Attitudes to the Temple in the Acts of the Apostles', p. 349.

[10] D. B. Wallace, *Greek Grammar beyond the Basics: An Exegetical Syntax of the New Testament* (Grand Rapids: Zondervan, 1996), pp. 544ff.

Paul receives his call to include the Gentiles in the renewed people of God.[11]

3. CRITICAL VIEWS OF THE TEMPLE?

There is wide scholarly agreement on the positive material about the Temple in Acts, but considerable disagreement on the apparently more critical passages, and two in particular: Stephen's speech (especially 7:48–50) and Paul's comments in Athens (especially 17:24).

3.1 Stephen's speech

Stephen's speech results from an accusation that he speaks against the Temple and the Torah and claims that Jesus will destroy the Temple and replace the Torah (6:13ff.). Luke makes it clear that he considers these accusations mischievous, for members of the hellenistic Synagogue of the Freedmen have stirred people up to make these accusations (6:11), but nevertheless there is a charge to be answered.

Within the speech itself Stephen does not criticize the Torah; his main thrust is to parallel the ancient people's rejection of Moses with the contemporary people's rejection of Jesus, the prophet-like-Moses (note 7:35, 37).[12] The crucial question from our perspective is how he regards the Temple, and there are broadly two streams within scholarship on this question: one sees Stephen as attacking the Temple, even regarding building it having been a mistake; the other sees Stephen's focus as on God's transcendence over the Temple and all earthly 'shrines'.[13]

Those who believe that Stephen sees the Temple negatively focus on five main points within the Stephen stories.

First, they note the criticisms of Stephen (6:11, 13ff.) and observe that Luke has not included in his Gospel the claims which Mark records, that Jesus will destroy/replace the Temple (Mark 14:57ff.; 15:29). Thus Stephen is the one, within Luke's narrative, who presents the Temple as bound for destruction.[14]

However, it is clear that Luke presents these accusations as scurrilous. Luke calls what they say 'false testimony' (6:13) and presents the synagogue members instigating some to accuse Stephen in this

---

[11] D. Peterson, *Engaging with God: A Biblical Theology of Worship* (Leicester: Apollos, 1992), p. 138 sees the preaching of the earliest Christians as part of God's activity of revelation.

[12] See the insightful discussion of L. T. Johnson, *The Acts of the Apostles* (Sacra Pagina 5; Collegeville: Liturgical Press, 1992), pp. 135–8.

[13] D. D. Sylva, 'The Meaning and Function of Acts 7:46–50', *JBL* 106 (1987), pp. 261–75, citing p. 261 n. 4 identifies three groups and provides useful documentation of sources.

[14] See Barrett, 'Attitudes to the Temple in the Acts of the Apostles', pp. 350ff.; H. W. Turner, *From Temple to Meeting House: The Phenomenology and Theology of Places of Worship* (Religion and Society 16; The Hague/Paris/New York: Mouton, 1979), pp. 116ff.

way (6:11).[15] The charges presented are in fact charges about Stephen's teaching about Jesus, and Stephen answers them not by a careful defence speech – for the charges are manifestly false[16] – but by going on the offensive and presenting his own positive testimony to Jesus. Careful reading of Luke also reveals that Jesus predicts the destruction of the Temple there as clearly as in Mark's account (e.g. Luke 21:5ff.).

Secondly, while verse 44 notes God's initiative in beginning the tent of meeting, and verse 46 sees David's desire to find a 'tent' (*skēnōma*) for God positively, verse 47 has no such note of divine approval for Solomon's building of the Temple.[17] More than that, David's actions, according to Simon and Haenchen,[18] are in relation to finding a proper place in Jerusalem for the tent of meeting, since verse 46 alludes to Psalm 131:5 LXX (MT 132:5),[19] and the Psalm itself refers to the taking of the ark to Jerusalem (2 Sam. 6:17).

On the latter point, however, Sylva notes[20] that this is Luke's only use of 'tent' (*skēnōma*), and it is used in the LXX with reference to both Temple[21] and tent.[22] This observation means that it is not possible to draw the clear conclusion that Stephen speaks of David locating the tent, rather than seeking a place for a Temple. More than that, Psalm 132 contains positive reference to God's choice of Zion (vv. 13ff.) and is linked to the dedication of the Temple by the use of verses 8–10 in the conclusion of the prayer at the Temple's dedication in 2 Chronicles 6:41ff.,[23] so that this link cannot be used to claim that verse 46 is implicitly anti-Temple.

---

[15] So F. D. Weinert, 'Luke, Stephen and the Temple in Luke–Acts', *BTB* 17 (1987), pp. 88–90, citing p. 89.

[16] B. Witherington III, *The Acts of the Apostles: A Socio-Rhetorical Commentary* (Carlisle/Grand Rapids: Paternoster Press/Eerdmans, 1998), pp. 256ff.

[17] J. Kilgallen, SJ, *The Stephen Speech: A Literary and Redactional Study of Acts 7, 2–53* (AnBib 67; Rome: Biblical Institute Press, 1976), p. 89.

[18] M. Simon, *St Stephen and the Hellenists in the Primitive Church: The Haskell Lectures 1956* (London/New York/Toronto: Longmans, Green, 1958), p. 51; Haenchen, *The Acts of the Apostles*, p. 285.

[19] Verse 46 has a difficult textual variant; some manuscripts read 'a tent for the *house* of Jacob' (*skēnōma tō oikō Iakōb*) and others 'a tent for the *God* of Jacob' (*skēnōma tō theō Iakōb*). The manuscripts are fairly evenly divided, although 'house' is supported by a combination of Alexandrian and Western manuscripts. Decisive is the fact that 'house' is the more difficult reading and that 'God' appears to betray the influence of Palms 131: 5 LXX; thus, 'house' is more likely original. See B. M. Metzger (ed.), *A Textual Commentary on the Greek New Testament* (Stuttgart: Deutsche Bibelgesellschaft/United Bible Societies, 1994[2]), pp. 308ff.

[20] Sylva, 'The Meaning and Function of Acts 7:46–50', p. 264.

[21] Psalm 14:1 (MT 15:1); 45:5 (MT 46:5); 73:7 (MT 74:7).

[22] 1 Kings 2:28; 8:4.

[23] A. Weiser, *The Psalms: A Commentary* (OT Library; London: SCM Press, 1962), p. 779, contra L. C. Allen, *Psalms 101–150* (WBC 21; Waco: Word, 1983), p. 207, although Allen concedes that 'The psalm … demands … a temple setting.'

Thirdly, the use of adversatives often translated 'but' in verses 47 (*de*) and 48 (*alla*) is held to suggest a contrast is being drawn which in each case presents Solomon's action in building the Temple negatively. Solomon is being presented as bad and David, who 'finds favour' with God, as good. Barrett argues that the only alternative is to take Luke as meaning that Solomon having built a house for God must be understood in the light of the principle found in verses 48–50.[24]

However, *de* (verse 47) is hardly a strong adversative: it frequently has the sense of a consecutive connective, meaning 'and'.[25] Further, the use of *alla* (v. 48), whilst certainly suggesting a contrast, need not suggest the contrast which Barrett proposes, nor his rejected alternative. Rather, it is more likely to have a concessive sense, 'though' or 'yet': 'Solomon built a house for him, *though* the Most High does not dwell in hand-made things' (vv. 47–48a, my rendering).[26] The statement about Solomon cannot be assumed to be negative, for it is a simple statement which contains nothing explicitly critical.

Fourthly, verses 49ff. indicate the divine displeasure with the Temple, for the Temple 'betrays the real meaning of God'[27] by suggesting that he can inhabit a temple. The use of 'hand-made' (*cheiropoiētois*, v. 48) suggests a number of contrasts, all negative. Simon observes that the word order in verse 48 might suggest a translation: 'It is not the Most High who dwells in temples made with hands', thus highlighting that it is *idols* who dwell in such temples.[28] Further, 'hand-made' in LXX usage standardly connotes idolatry,[29] and is here (v. 50) contrasted with God's hand, which makes all things.[30] Scharlemann also claims that being 'hand-made' is a feature of the golden calf of Exodus 32 (v. 41).[31]

However, it is clear that being 'hand-made' is not in itself a weakness, for the tent of meeting was (presumably) made by human hands – a fact which strongly suggests that the contrast being drawn is not between the tent and the Temple.[32] Rather, as we shall go on to argue, the issue is where God may be considered to dwell.

---

[24] Barrett, 'Attitudes to the Temple in the Acts of the Apostles', p. 352, n. 21.
[25] BAGD, p. 213; Sylva, 'The Meaning and Function of Acts 7:46–50', pp. 264ff.
[26] Weinert, 'Luke, Stephen and the Temple in Luke–Acts', p. 90; Witherington, *The Acts of the Apostles*, p. 273.
[27] Kilgallen, *The Stephen Speech*, p. 91; R. A. Cole, *The New Temple* (Tyndale Monograph series; London: Tyndale Press, 1950), p. 44.
[28] Simon, *St Stephen and the Hellenists in the Primitive Church*, p. 54.
[29] Leviticus 26:1, 30; Judith 8:18; Wisdom 14:8; Isaiah 2:18; 10:11; 16:12; 19:1; 21:9; 31:7; 46:6; Daniel 5:4, 23.
[30] Kilgallen, *The Stephen Speech*, p. 90; Barrett, *A Critical and Exegetical Commentary on the Acts of the Apostles*, vol. 1, p. 373.
[31] M. H. Scharlemann, *Stephen: A Singular Saint* (AnBib 34; Rome: Pontifical Biblical Institute, 1968), pp. 106, 119.
[32] Witherington, *The Acts of the Apostles*, p. 262; C. C. Hill, *Hellenists and Hebrews: Reappraising Division within the Earliest Church* (Minneapolis: Fortress Press, 1992), p. 79.

Finally, it is agreed that there is an allusion to the story of 2 Samuel 7, where David seeks Nathan's counsel over building a house for the LORD (vv. 1ff.). In both Hebrew and LXX texts there is considerable play on the words for 'house' (Hebrew *byt*; Greek *oikos*) throughout this chapter. After initially advising him to pursue the idea (v. 3), Nathan is then told by God that David must not do this (vv. 4ff.). Rather, God will build a house – that is, a dynasty – for David (vv. 11–16). A son from David's house will be the one to build a house for God (v. 13). Simon sees the allusion to this story as suggesting that God is declining to have a house built for him, and that, in Stephen's view, Solomon is therefore transgressing God's will in building a house for him.[33]

This need not follow, of course: the building of the Temple in 2 Samuel 7 has about it the same kind of ambivalence as the development of kingship within Israel,[34] and reflects a wider Old Testament caution about seeing Yahweh as localized in a particular place. This caution is reflected in other Jewish critiques of the Temple, such as Jeremiah's repeated 'Temple sermon' (Jer. 7; 26), or the view of the Qumran community that they themselves formed the true temple, replacing the polluted and discredited Herodian Temple.[35] And, what is more, God does say that David's heir will build the Temple (2 Sam. 7:13), which suggests that it is at least not a wholly bad idea.

The alternative, more persuasive, view sees the key emphasis in relation to the Temple as on God's transcendence and presence. A number of arguments show that this reading of the text makes most sense in context; for the sake of brevity, we confine ourselves to two major and two minor observations.[36]

First, Solomon's prayer at the dedication of the Temple (1 Kgs. 8:15–53, especially v. 27) recognizes the transcendence of God in very similar terms to Acts 7:48–50 and Isaiah 66:1ff. (quoted in Acts 7:49ff.).[37] Stephen is critical of the view that God may be confined to a temple, that he 'dwells' (*katoikei*) there,[38] but this does not mean that he believes

---

[33] Simon, *St Stephen and the Hellenists in the Primitive Church*, pp. 52ff.

[34] G. McConville, 'Jerusalem in the Old Testament' in P. W. L. Walker (ed.), *Jerusalem Past and Present in the Purposes of God* (Cambridge: Tyndale House, 1992), pp. 21–51, citing pp. 28ff.

[35] A. F. J. Klijn, 'Stephen's Speech – Acts VII. 2–53', *NTS* 4 (1957), pp. 25–31, citing pp. 28–31; W. Horbury, 'New Wine in Old Wine-Skins: IX. The Temple', *ExpTim* 86 (1974–5), pp. 36–42, citing p. 38; B. Gärtner, *The Temple and the Community in Qumran and the New Testament: A Comparative Study in the Temple Symbolism of the Qumran Texts and the New Testament* (SNTSMS 1; Cambridge: Cambridge University Press, 1965), pp. 22–30.

[36] 1QS 5:4–7; 8:4–7, 8–10; 9:3–6. See more fully Sylva, 'The Meaning and Function of Acts 7:46–50'.

[37] Weinert, 'Luke, Stephen and the Temple in Luke–Acts', p. 89; E. Franklin, *Christ the Lord: A Study in the Purpose and Theology of Luke–Acts* (London: SPCK, 1975), p. 106; J. B. Chance, *Jerusalem, the Temple, and the New Age in Luke–Acts* (Macon: Mercer University Press, 1978), p. 40.

[38] I. H. Marshall, 'Church and Temple in the New Testament', *Tyndale Bulletin* 40 (1989), pp. 203–22, citing p. 209.

that God cannot be encountered in a temple: 'the issue is not "tent" versus "house" but rather true and false thinking about God's presence'.[39] A careful reading of 7:48 underlines this point, for neither 'tent' (*skēnōma*) nor 'house' (*oikon*) are mentioned in this verse: it is simply that the Most High does not dwell in hand-made *things* – a principle with which any right-thinking first-century Jew would agree. At most this verse resists the idea that God is to be localized.[40] The quotation from Isaiah 66:1ff. in vv. 49ff. strengthens this point further, for the context in Isaiah is positive about the Temple (notice Isa. 66:6, which presents God as speaking from the Temple);[41] it simply resists the idea that God is limited to that location – it is not his 'resting place' (Isa. 66:1). If, as is very frequently the case in the New Testament, an Old Testament quotation or allusion brings with it the whole context in the Old Testament, this quotation in Stephen's speech should not be seen as criticizing the Temple.

Secondly, Sylva observes four elements which are found in both 1 Kings 8:14–30 and Acts 7:46–50 in the same sequence,[42] a parallelism which strongly suggests that similar theological points are in view. In each case the elements are:

(i) David's desire to find a place for God, 1 Kings 8:17; Acts 7:46;

(ii) an immediately following statement that Solomon will build the Temple, 1 Kings 8:17–21; Acts 7:47;

(iii) the question whether God will dwell with humans on earth, 1 Kings 8:27a; Acts 7:48;

(iv) an assertion of God's transcendence of the Temple by reference to God's relation to the heavens, the earth and a house, 1 Kings 8:27b; Acts 7:49ff. (quoting Isa. 66:1ff.).

This close parallel invites us to see the same theological perspective in both passages, a perspective that combines belief in God's transcendence and the appropriateness for Solomon's day of a Temple.

The first minor observation is that, throughout Stephen's speech, Yahweh is referred to as 'God' (*ho theos*),[43] except in verse 48, where God is 'the Most High' (*ho hupsistos*), a title that stresses precisely his transcendence, and thus underlines the thrust of the sentence as

---

[39] Witherington, *The Acts of the Apostles*, p. 263; so also Peterson, *Engaging with God*, p. 141.
[40] Hill, *Hellenists and Hebrews*, p. 74.
[41] T. C. G. Thornton, 'Stephen's Use of Isaiah LXVI, 1', *JTS* 25 (1974), pp. 432–4 notes a midrash on Isaiah 66:1, which may have roots in the first century, in which the author interprets Isaiah 66:1 to mean that the Temple is not to be seen as a guarantee of safety, for God can send someone to destroy it.
[42] Sylva, 'The Meaning and Function of Acts 7:46–50', pp. 266ff.
[43] 7:2, 6, 7, 9, 17, 20, 25, 32, 35, 37, 42, 45, 46, 56.

denying that God can be localized. The emphatic forward position of this title in its clause highlights the point further.[44]

The second minor observation is that there may be a polemical edge to the use of 'hand-made' (*cheiropoiētois*) in Stephen's speech, for by its use Stephen may be claiming that the Temple has in fact become an idol for the Jewish people,[45] in similar manner to Jeremiah's dire warnings about leaning on the Temple for safety in the face of foreign military might (e.g. Jer. 7:1–15).

Overall, then, the material in Stephen's speech related to the Temple should be seen as highlighting the transcendence of God over against the universal human temptation to localize the deity, and specifically against the common Jewish belief that Yahweh was locally present in the Temple in a way that was not regularly or predictably true of other locations on earth.[46]

3.2 Paul's Athens Speech

To listen to Luke's report of Paul speaking in Athens is to hear much of Stephen's theology, as we have understood it, transposed into a pagan key in order to communicate with Paul's hearers there. 17:24 certainly echoes the sentiments, and some of the precise words, of 7:48–50,[47] but in relation to pagan shrines, for Paul uses 'shrines' (*naous*), a word never used of the Jerusalem Temple in Acts, but used for the 'shrines' of Artemis in 19:24. Much of the Athens speech is standard Jewish polemic against pagan idolatry, using ideas (but not usually language) from the Old Testament critique of idols,[48] and the differences in emphasis and presentation relate to the different target audience.

---

[44] Barrett, *A Critical and Exegetical Commentary on the Acts of the Apostles*, vol. 1, p. 373; Barrett, 'Attitudes to the Temple in the Acts of the Apostles', p. 352.

[45] So P. W. L. Walker, *Jesus and the Holy City: New Testament Perspectives on Jerusalem* (Cambridge/Grand Rapids: Eerdmans, 1996), pp. 66ff.

[46] Cf. Matthew 23:21; Sir 36:18ff.; Josephus, *Ant.* III:215–218 (III:8:9), the latter speaking of God 'assisting' at the sacred ceremonies in the Temple. See further E. P. Sanders, *Judaism: Practice and Belief 63 BCE–66 CE* (London: SCM Press, 1992), pp. 70ff. Certainly Jews believed that Yahweh could manifest himself outside the Temple, but they strongly believed that he resided there and could be encountered there in particular, whereas appearances elsewhere could not be counted on.

[47] 'He does not dwell in hand-made things' is echoed precisely, but in 17:24 'shrines' (*naois*) is added; the subject of the verb is 'the Most High' (*ho hupsistos*) in 7:48 and 'he who is Lord over heaven and earth' (*houtos ouranou kai gēs huparchōn kurios*) in 17:24.

[48] J. D. G. Dunn, *The Acts of the Apostles* (Epworth Commentaries; Peterborough: Epworth Press, 1996), pp. 230ff; M. L. Soards, *The Speeches in Acts: Their Content, Context, and Concerns* (Louisville: Westminster Press/John Knox Press, 1994), pp. 97ff; C. H. Gempf, 'Athens, Paul at' in G. F. Hawthorne, R. P. Martin, and D. G. Reid (eds), *Dictionary of Paul and his Letters* (Downers Grove/Leicester: IVP, 1993), pp. 51–4; B. Gärtner, *The Areopagus Speech and Natural Revelation* (Uppsala: Gleerup, 1955); contra M. Dibelius, *Studies in the Acts of the Apostles* (London: SCM Press, 1956), pp. 36–77.

4. WHERE ARE WE NOW?

Thus far, then, we have seen much in Acts which seems at least not against the Temple *per se*, but rather critiques a view of the Temple as the primary locus of Yahweh's presence. We have also seen positive signs of the earliest Christians' use of the Temple for prayer and preaching, and God's use of the Temple as a venue for his activity. In what follows we shall attempt to put the specific references to the Temple into a wider framework in order to seek Luke's own perspective. Two key elements are important: seeing Jesus as performing the functions which the Temple was designed to perform; and noticing the locations where God acts in the apostolic mission.

5. JESUS AS THE TRUE TEMPLE?

In his fascinating study *From Temple to Meeting House* H. W. Turner proposes a fourfold phenomenological characterization of the functions of a sacred place.[49] First, a sacred place functions as a *centre* which provides orientation and focus to the society which it serves, offering a dependable anchor amidst the changes and vagaries of life. Thus, for example, the Jerusalem Temple was described as the navel of the earth.

Secondly, a sacred place functions as a *meeting point*, where God (or the gods) and humanity engage with each other. It is a place where God reveals himself and communicates with people, and where people go to commune with God. In the case of the Jerusalem Temple, the sacrificial system was centred on the Temple and provided daily atonement for sin, as well as being a focus for teaching which would enable faithful Jews to engage with Yahweh.

Thirdly, a sacred place is a *microcosm of the heavenly world*, a place which shares most fully on earth the characteristics of the other realm. It mirrors or models the heavenly regions. This finds expression in the shape and design of the building(s), as in the perfect cubical symmetry of the holy of holies, as well as in the design for the Temple being seen as God's handiwork.

Fourthly, a sacred place is a place of *immanent-transcendent presence*, both the location of the presence of the gods on earth, and at the same time a sign of their presence throughout the world. Hence the Jerusalem Temple was seen as the 'house of God', where God was specially thought to dwell.[50] The gradations of holiness within the Temple complex – which permitted only certain persons to progress into certain areas, climaxing in the high priest alone being allowed into the holy of holies, and that only on one day each year – highlighted the particular

---

[49] Turner, *From Temple to Meeting House*, pp. 18–42; he applies it to the Jerusalem Temple on pp. 54–67.
[50] See n. 47 above.

presence of God in that inner shrine. More than that, the absence of images in the Jerusalem Temple showed the transcendence of Yahweh who dwelt there,[51] and the remote nature of Temple worship, being in the main conducted by the priests and Levites on behalf of the people, emphasized further Yahweh's inaccessibility and transcendence.[52]

When we examine the Acts accounts of the life of the earliest Christians, it is striking that each of Turner's four functions of sacred places is actually performed by God, and in particular by Jesus and/or the Spirit.[53]

First, rather than the Temple being the focus of their prayers, providing a centre and point of orientation, the earliest Christians pray in many different locations,[54] but always focused on Jesus. More, his 'name' is the authority and power of their work.[55] *He* provides the 'centre' which they lean upon.

Secondly, rather than the Temple being the meeting point of heaven and earth, it is the person of Jesus who provides the means by which God and humanity are brought together:[56] through him forgiveness of sins is available (2:38; 3:19); by his work 'times of refreshing' come from the Lord (3:20); his is the only effective saving name among humanity (4:12) – and hence water baptism is in his name (2:38; 8:16; 19:5; 22:16); as Lord of all he brings peace between God and humankind (10:38); and through his grace Jews and Gentiles alike are saved (15:11; 16:31). He takes over this function of the Temple and extends it to Gentiles, who were not permitted into the majority of the Temple complex, as well as to women and Jewish laymen, who were not allowed into the places of sacrifice within the Temple.

Thirdly, rather than the Temple being a microcosm of the heavenly realm, Christians now experience the life of the heavenly realm – at least in part – because of Jesus. Hence they experience 'times of refreshing' (3:20) and healing (e.g. 4:10; 9:34), and they experience the Spirit's

---

[51] Turner, *From Temple to Meeting House*, p. 41.

[52] Ibid., p. 42.

[53] This approach, via Turner's four functions, avoids the criticisms of Chance, *Jerusalem, the Temple, and the New Age in Luke–Acts*, pp. 41–5 that, in order to demonstrate that Jesus supersedes the Temple, there need to be specific Acts texts transferring technical Temple *language* to Jesus.

[54] E.g. 1:13ff; 4:24–30; 7:59.

[55] S. Walton, 'Where Does the Beginning of Acts End?' in J. Verheyden (ed.), *The Unity of Luke–Acts* (BETL 142; Leuven: Leuven University Press and Peeters, 1999), pp. 448–67, citing p. 459; cf. J. A. Ziesler, 'The Name of Jesus in the Acts of the Apostles', *JSNT* 4 (1974), pp. 28–41; J. Jervell, *The Theology of the Acts of the Apostles* (NT Theology; Cambridge: Cambridge University Press, 1996), pp. 33ff; Franklin, *Christ the Lord*, p. 102.

[56] Cf. J. Calvin, *Commentaries on the Minor Prophets. Vol. 3: Jonah, Micah, Nahum* (Edinburgh: Calvin Translation Society, 1847), pp. 277ff. (on Mic. 4:7): 'Mount Zion then is now different from what is was formerly; for wherever the doctrine of the Gospel is preached, there is God really worshipped, there sacrifices are offered; in a word, there the spiritual temple exists.'

transforming work, making them into the people they are called to
be. For example: 1:8 has them experiencing 'power' by the Spirit to do
God's will; 2:16ff. interprets the Pentecostal gift as fulfilling the eschatological promise of Joel; 7:55ff. has Stephen by the Spirit seeing into
heaven, where Jesus stands at God's right hand; and 20:22 presents Paul
as ready to face suffering because he is 'captive to the Spirit'.[57]

Further, angels, the inhabitants of the heavenly realm, appear in the
story of the church in Acts (e.g. 5:19; 8:26; 10:7, 22; 11:13; 12:7–11; 27:23).
Not only that, but 6:15 shows Stephen's face shining like an angel's as
a result of his being filled with the Spirit, grace and faith (6:3, 5, 8, 10)[58]
– and this is a preparation for his entry into heaven itself (7:59ff.).

Fourthly, Jesus and the Spirit convey the immanent-transcendent
presence of God, which is not understood as localized. Transcendence
is clear from the departure of Jesus in the cloud (1:9), echoing the presentation of the Son of Man figure to the Ancient of Days (Daniel 7:13).
The martyr Stephen sees Jesus as this son of man at the right hand of
God, in a position of power and authority (7:55ff.).

Immediate presence is experienced by the Spirit, who comes upon
the early church and indwells them, both collectively (e.g. 2:4, 16ff., 38;
4:31) and individually (e.g. 4:8; 6:3, 5; 8:15, 17). The Spirit directs the
mission of the church, providing guidance to individuals and groups
(e.g. 8:29, 39; 10:19; 11:12, 28; 13:2, 4; 16:6ff.; 19:21;[59] 20:22). And this
presence is found, as we shall see, in a wide variety of locations.

6. WHERE GOD ACTS[60]

Throughout the book of Acts God acts outside the Temple and, indeed,
outside the land of which the Temple is the focus. 1:8 sets the agenda,
echoing Isaiah 32:15[61] and 49:6, seeing the apostolic mission as beginning with the renewal of Israel and extending to the whole world;[62] the

---

[57] See further M. Turner, *Power from on High: The Spirit in Israel's Restoration and Witness
in Luke–Acts* (JPTSup 9; Sheffield: Sheffield Academic Press, 1996), pp. 404–27, especially
pp. 415–18.

[58] C. H. T. Fletcher-Louis, *Luke–Acts: Angels, Christology and Soteriology* (WUNT 2:94;
Tübingen: Mohr Siebeck, 1997), pp. 96–8.

[59] See discussion in S. Walton, *Leadership and Lifestyle: The Portrait of Paul in the Miletus
Speech and 1 Thessalonians* (SNTSMS 108; Cambridge: Cambridge University Press, 2000),
p. 88, arguing that the reference of *en tō pneumati* is to the Holy Spirit.

[60] What follows draws extensively on the work of my student, Dr Dee Dyas, in D. Dyas,
'Where is God in Luke–Acts?' (unpublished paper: St John's College, Nottingham,
1999).

[61] See Turner, *Power from on High*, pp. 301ff., 345.

[62] This is the likeliest meaning of the phrase 'to the end of the earth' (*heōs eschatou tēs
gēs*, 1:8, echoed in 13:47) in the light of LXX usage (see Isa. 8:9; 14:22; 48:20; 49:6; 62:11; Jer.
10:13; 35:16 [MT]; 39:32 [MT 32:32]; 45:8 [MT 38:8]; 1 Macc. 3:9). See brief discussion in
D. Wenham and S. Walton, *Exploring the New Testament. Vol. 1: A Guide to the Gospels and
Acts* (London/Downers Grove: SPCK/IVP, 2001), p. 271.

remainder of the book charts the progress of that mission in Jerusalem (1:1–5:42), Judea and Samaria (6:1–11:18), and to the end of the earth (11:19–28:31).

Throughout the book the Spirit breaks barriers in order to enable people to come to God. Linguistic barriers are overcome in the miracle of Pentecost (2:5–11). Ethnic barriers begin to be overcome in Philip's mission to Samaria and the apostles' visit to pray for the Spirit to come upon the converts (8:4–25),[63] and of course continue in the gradual and increasing inclusion of Gentiles in the church. The Ethiopian eunuch, who has been to worship in Jerusalem (8:27) – although he would be excluded from full participation in Temple worship because of his castration (Deut. 23:1) – finds admission to full membership in the people of God through Philip's ministry (8:26–39).

God, often acting by the agency of the Spirit, brings people to himself in a variety of settings, whether the eunuch in the desert (8:26–39), an unclean Gentile household in Joppa (10:1–48), Saul of Tarsus well outside Jerusalem (9:1–19),[64] or many areas outside the land (as Paul's mission makes clear).

In the latter case, God directs the mission to these new areas: Barnabas and Saul are sent from Antioch in response to the Spirit's call (13:1–3), and Paul is called by God to Macedonia (16:9, 13) – both passages contain rare examples of 'call' language used for God's call to specific tasks,[65] which thus underlines that they are doing this not at their own behest but at the impulse of God. Further, Paul's arrival in Rome does not represent the arrival of the gospel message there, for Christians come from the city to meet him (28:14ff.) – God has got there before Paul!

A further dimension of this expansion is that God acts in homes and on the streets, and not simply in 'sacred places'. Certainly healing can come at the Temple gate (3:1–10), but it can also come on the streets of the city (5:15) or in a home (9:39–41; 20:9–12) – God's presence and activity is not tied to the Temple. Similarly, the believers meet in homes to pray (e.g. 2:46; 12:12; 20:7ff.), or on the beach (20:36–38), and the Spirit comes in homes (e.g. 10:44).

We can expand this point by noticing that the vocabulary of 'worship' is used by Luke, in common with other New Testament

---

[63] R. J. McKelvey, *The New Temple: The Church in the New Testament* (Oxford Theological Monographs; London: Oxford University Press, 1969), p. 88 notes that the admission of Samaritans to the believing community without mention of their worshipping at the Jerusalem Temple immediately downgrades the importance of the Temple, for Samaritans worshipped at a different temple, at Gerizim.

[64] Note 22:3, which shows that Luke understands Saul to have spent most of his life in the city.

[65] The only other clear New Testament examples are Romans 1:1 and 1 Corinthians 1:1, which both refer to Paul's call to be an apostle. See further S. Walton, *A Call to Live: Vocation for Everyone* (London: Triangle, 1994), especially ch. 2.

writers, for what Christians do with their whole lives, rather than being confined to what they do when they meet together.[66] For example, Paul can describe his apostolic mission and ministry using *latreuō* (24:14; 27:23).

Thus there is a clear stream of evidence in Acts that God's activities are not confined to the Temple, the land or any other form of sacred place.[67] Because of the death, resurrection and exaltation of Jesus, the world itself is now being repossessed by God. The Old Testament texts which saw the nations coming to Zion (e.g. Zech. 8:20–23) are now being redirected, as the apostolic gospel goes out from Zion to the nations.[68]

7. IS ACTS CONSISTENT?

Barrett's conclusion from the evidence of Acts is that Luke is not consistent, although he concedes that the same apparent inconsistency is there in Luke's treatment of the Jewish people (and wants to treat Luke's view of the Temple as part of this wider question).[69] But is Luke so inconsistent? We have seen reason to argue that the view (which Barrett holds) that Stephen is opposed to the Temple *per se* is mistaken, and have argued that Luke presents a wider understanding of God's transcendence within which the Temple fits – a view with which few first-century Jews would have argued, at least in principle. We have also seen that the broader work of God which Luke narrates deconstructs any notion of sacred space that is narrower than the world, for that world is the arena of God's saving activity. But Luke's presentation is not so explicit or clear-cut as the way in which other New Testament writers use 'Temple' language for the Christian community, even if it is accepted that James' quotation from Amos 9:11ff. in Acts 15:16ff. hints in this direction.[70]

---

[66] See the seminal article, I. H. Marshall, 'How Far did the Early Christians Worship God?', *Churchman* 99 (1985), pp. 216–29.

[67] For a similar conclusion based on Luke and Acts, see N. H. Taylor, 'Luke–Acts and the Temple' in J. Verheyden (ed.), *The Unity of Luke–Acts*, pp. 709–21, citing pp. 719ff.

[68] Cf. Paul's adaptation of Isaiah 59:20ff. in Romans 11:26ff., changing the coming deliverer's role from 'for the sake of Zion' to 'out of Zion'.

[69] Barrett, 'Attitudes to the Temple in the Acts of the Apostles', pp. 366ff.

[70] Cf. the valuable discussion of M. L. Strauss, *The Davidic Messiah in Luke–Acts: The Promise and its Fulfilment in Lukan Christology* (JSNTSup 110; Sheffield: Sheffield Academic Press, 1995), pp. 185–92, surveying four views and concluding that the rebuilt tent of David is about the restoration of the Davidic *dynasty* through Jesus' life, death and resurrection, rather than a reference to a people, whether Jewish or mixed Jewish and Gentile. The parallel with 4QFlor 1:12, which also quotes Amos 9:11, is significant; there 'the fallen tent of David is he who shall arise to save Israel' – that is, an individual messianic figure is seen as the fulfilment of Amos 9:11, thus showing that such a view was current in first-century Judaism.

This collection of conclusions suggests that in Acts we are seeing the process of change going on before our eyes.[71] The stories in Acts represent, as it were, the cusp of the change from a localized view of God dwelling in the Temple to what we might call a universalized view, in which God is available, and reveals himself, anywhere and everywhere. Luke says implicitly what Paul or Hebrews or 1 Peter or John or Revelation say explicitly, but does not express their view outright because he is concerned to describe faithfully the historical process of development. Luke is not imposing his own, later, view on the material, but is presenting the period as carefully as he can in order to enable his readers to see where the Christian faith has come from (Luke 1:1–4) and how a Jew-plus-Gentile church has come into being from the followers of a Jewish Messiah.

Thus Luke's presentation runs alongside the view of the other New Testament writers we mentioned, showing how the implications of the resurrection and exaltation of Jesus were gradually worked out and understood. Luke belongs with a salvation-historical development scheme in the sense that he engages us, his readers, in the process of development, and lets us in on the moments when new insights begin to take hold. He thus invites Christian readers not to buy into every perspective on the Temple which he offers, for some of them are 'works in progress' rather than the end of the development process.[72]

Luke's own perspective seems to be expressed most clearly by the insistence on the transcendence of God (7:48–50; 17:24), for this characteristic of God enables the church to be the church, crossing barriers and moving into new territory at the prompting of the Spirit – often, it must be said, after the believers' initial resistance to or hesitation about what God is doing. Within such an overarching view the early Christians' readiness to continue to pray, or even offer sacrifice, in the Temple should give no cause to accuse Luke of inconsistency – they are learning what it means to live in the light of the coming of the Messiah, who fulfils all that the Temple pointed towards, and who sees the whole of creation as his Temple in which he is to be worshipped and served.

---

[71] Cf. McKelvey, *The New Temple*, p. 85: 'One may say, therefore, that the apparent devotion of the first Christians to the temple of Jerusalem was a transitional phenomenon' [by 'the first Christians' he refers to the period described in Acts 2].

[72] This parallels the debate about how far Acts is descriptive and how far it is prescriptive in its material; for valuable introductory discussions, see I. H. Marshall, *The Acts of the Apostles* (NT Guides; Sheffield: JSOT Press, 1992), ch. 6; G. D. Fee and D. Stuart, *How to Read the Bible for all its Worth: A Guide to Understanding the Bible* (London: Scripture Union, 1982), ch. 6.

11

NEW TEMPLES IN CORINTH

Paul's Use of Temple Imagery
in the Ethics of the Corinthian Correspondence

MARK BONNINGTON

1. INTRODUCTION

The three references to the Temple (*naos*) in the Corinthian letters (at
1 Cor. 3:16–17; 6:19 and 2 Cor. 6:16) are only three of the prominent
uses of sacral language in the undisputed Paulines. Paul also mentions
the Jerusalem Temple explicitly (2 Thess. 2:4; 1 Cor. 9:13; cf. Rom. 9:4)
as well as making rich use of sacrificial imagery and other language
associated with the Temple (2 Cor. 2:15; 9:11; Rom. 12:1; Phil. 2:17;
4:18; Col. 1:22, etc.). Most commentators agree that these allusions are
precisely that – a drawing of richly suggestive theological patterns
drawing on the imagery and associations of Temple-related language.
Attempts to draw Paul's sacral language into a larger more coherent
scheme have proved as unconvincing as they have interesting.

It is possible that Paul alludes, rather indirectly, to the idea of
the church as the eschatological Temple in Galatians 2:9. Here Paul
describes the Jerusalem apostles as 'pillars' – terminology which is
linked to the heavenly (eschatological?) Temple in Revelation 3:12. But
we cannot be sure either that this is what Paul meant by 'pillars' or
even that he really meant it. Paul's account of the 'apostolic council' in
Galatians 2:1–10 demonstrates a notoriously ambiguous attitude to the
status of the Jerusalem apostles. His reference to them as 'pillars' may
not be approving.

The idea of the church growing into a holy Temple in Ephesians
2:21 is not far from the description of the Corinthian assembly as 'God's
field, God's building' and as 'God's temple' within a few verses in
1 Corinthians 3:5–17. Both are ecclesiological in emphasis and both
combine the idea of foundations with that of growth. But on closer
inspection similarities begin to fade – the Ephesians text is dominated
by its interest in the inclusion of the Gentiles and suffused with the
more universal, developed and developmental ecclesiology characteristic of Ephesians. 1 Corinthians 3:16–17 by contrast shares with
1 Corinthians 6 and 2 Corinthians 6 a concern for ethics – in this case the
unity of the local church as a holy people.

In determining the source and meaning of Paul's Temple theology, brief consideration of his practice is important, especially in the light of attempts to argue for a consistent Temple-replacement schema in Paul. That Paul avoided the temples of pagan gods is clear from 1 Corinthians 8:10. Paul's attitude to the Jerusalem Temple in practice is not easy to determine. He clearly expected it to be standing for the man of lawlessness to desecrate at the eschatological denouement (2 Thess. 2:4). According to Acts he worshipped in the Temple and the story of his final arrest indicates that he went beyond the Temple courts into the shrine itself. But the parallel of circumcision should give us pause before we conclude too quickly that Paul advocated a Temple-replacement theology, or the converse that he continued to participate in Temple worship. The parallel case of circumcision shows how complex such issues can be and give us reason to resist simple conclusions. In Galatians Paul gives no quarter in dismissing the demands of those who claim that righteousness involves accepting circumcision, and he can identify a new Christian congregation as simply 'the circumcision' (Phil. 3:3) whilst also exercising a considerable degree of missiological pragmatism in the case of Timothy (Acts 16:3). Given the complexity of his attitude to circumcision, Paul's Temple theology could easily stand in as complex a relationship to his practical relationship to the Temple and its worship.

2. THREE TEMPLE THEMES

The central thesis of this essay is simple. It is that Paul's use of Temple language is neither determined by a carefully articulated Temple-replacement theology, nor is it primarily a reflection on the experience of the Holy Spirit (as indicative of divine presence) in the individual or the community. Rather, Paul's use of Temple language draws on three major theological themes associated with Temple in Jewish tradition. Moreover, these three themes each contribute to the consequent placing of a demand for holiness and ritual purity on both the individual and the people of God collectively. The themes are:

(i) the Temple as a place of God's presence and therefore of his ownership;

(ii) the Temple as a place of God's holy separateness;

(iii) the Temple as a central, focused and bounded sacred space with spatial and sacral integrity.

I shall take it that these Temple themes were well established and therefore self-evident within both the Old Testament text and the religious life of Second Temple Judaism, and thus the New Testament period. Placing the Temple of God (or a temple of a pagan god for that matter) at the centre of a symbolic universe created not just a focus of divine presence but also a demarcated locus for sacred space with boundaries and thresholds of ritual purity. In Jerusalem these were marked out by the palisade that kept the Gentiles out of the shrine of the Temple and the various doors and other limits that marked the successive courts within. The consequence of this demarcation and stratification of sacred space was twofold. First, it corresponded to social distinctions and stratification (successively into Gentiles, women, men, priests and high priest). Secondly, it focused the concern for ritual purity both through the requirement of ritual integrity and through the barring or expulsion of impurity from sacred space.[1]

In due course I will show that these themes are present in Paul's use of Temple imagery and I will argue this point to a new conclusion: that Paul's Temple language is essentially ethical rather than ecclesiastical in its character and import. This conclusion is in contrast to the dominant tendency of scholarly interpretation in recent decades. Paul's first use of Temple language, 1 Corinthians 3:16–17, was the subject of a significant study by Lanci, published in 1997. He noted two different but compatible interpretative tendencies: those which see the Temple imagery as a vehicle for Paul's teaching that the church is a community indwelt by God's Spirit; and those which focus on the theme as a particular species of (inaugurated) expectation of an eschatological Temple. These are not so much logically inconsistent as divergent in their identification of the theological roots of Paul's theology of the Temple. The pneumatological interpretation points to the religious experience of believers as the fundamental datum for Paul's theological construction and therefore locates the basic rationale within the distinctive spiritual dynamics of the life of the earliest Christian communities. The eschatological Temple strand sees the theological roots of Paul's teaching in the Temple tradition and thus relies more heavily on parallels with Jewish texts.

Lanci notes that the overwhelming majority of twentieth-century scholars go beyond the Pauline text to draw the conclusion that Paul is advocating a Temple-replacement theology.[2] He argues that this is misguided on four counts:

---

[1] Most temples in the ancient world, like the Jerusalem Temple, consisted of temple grounds (*temenos*) and a shrine (*naos* from *naein* to dwell) so that roughly *temenos* + *naos* = *hieron*. Of course the language of shrine and temple are used in imprecise overlapping ways (cf. e.g. Josephus, *War* II:93 and *Ag. Ap.* II:119). What exactly Paul thought of as the *naos* is a point that can be bypassed here. It is the centred and bounded nature of sacred space that concerns us. The same would hold true if Paul had in mind the pagan temples of temples in first-century Corinth, to Octavia, Venus and most prominent of all high on the Acrocorinth, that to Aphrodite. Though the monotheistic claim 'one temple for the one God' (Josephus, *Ag. Ap.* II:193) heightened the symbolic significance of the Jerusalem sanctuary.

[2] J. R. Lanci, *A New Temple for Corinth: Rhetorical and Archaelogical Approaches to Pauline Imagery* (New York: Peter Lang, 1997).

(i) that the idea of the spiritualization of the cult and the rejection of a literal cult involves an anachronistic appeal to modern anti-cultic prejudices;

(ii) that it assumes a Jewish background (i.e. a reference to *the* Temple) that sits poorly with the Gentile context of the Corinthian church. Analysis of the *naos/hieron* language led Lanci to the conclusion that Paul's use of Temple imagery is more multivalent in reference;

(iii) that Paul cannot be said from his letters or Acts to have rejected the Temple cultus. Attempts to show, on the basis of 1 Corinthians 9:13 and 10:18 and Romans 15:16 (though compare Rom. 15:20 with 1 Cor. 3:10–15), that Paul saw himself as a new priest of a new cultus are misplaced; and

(iv) they rest too heavily on supposed parallels with the Qumran materials. The Temple theology of Qumran was discussed in relation to Paul in Gärtner's influential 1965 study, although his argument for a close parallel with a Pauline Temple-replacement theology has been superseded by recent discoveries and the more ambiguous picture that is revealed in texts such as 4QFlor 1:2–3 and 11QTemple 29:7–10. [3] These appear to contain a rejection of the Temple cultus in practice rather than in principle. They indicate that the community would have been happy with Temple worship if it were organized in line with its own teaching and that they held an expectation of a restored and everlasting Temple. In other words, they saw the existing Temple as an interim measure before a final restoration.

None of Lanci's arguments is especially convincing. Anti-cultic attitudes go much further back than the post-Reformation period, let alone modern times. Paul is constantly applying biblical material to his Gentile congregations. Formation in the Scriptures was part of his community-building programme and in any case the church in Corinth probably contained some if not many Jewish believers. Lanci's arguments about the parallel significance of pagan shrines to the Jerusalem shrine tend to undermine his own arguments for distancing Paul's language from a reference to the Jerusalem Temple. In comparing the Pauline use of Temple imagery with that of Qumran, the issue is not one of dependence. Qumran texts merely show what types of responses were possible within Second Temple Judaism. Walker points out that whatever the similarities Qumran has no parallels to the inclusion of the Gentiles or the application of Temple imagery to the individual. [4]

---

[3] B. Gärtner, *The Temple and the Community in Qumran and the New Testament: A Comparative Study in the Temple Symbolism of the Qumran Texts and the New Testament* (SNTSMS 1; Cambridge: Cambridge University Press, 1965).

[4] P. W. L. Walker, *Jesus and the Holy City: New Testament Perspectives on Jerusalem* (Cambridge/Grand Rapids: Eerdmans, 1996).

In my view, continuing either to choose (or perhaps mediate) between Temple-replacement theology on the one hand and pneumatological ecclesiology on the other is to miss the point. Paul's language does draw on Jewish Temple traditions but the principal concern is not to articulate a Temple-replacement theme. Rather Paul's Temple language articulates the idea of purity, understood in Paul as ethical purity, both personal and corporate. It is rooted in the Jewish tradition of the Temple as the dwelling place of the holy God and thus as the locus of purity. To justify this claim we now turn to the crucial Pauline texts in the Corinthian letters.

3. 1 CORINTHIANS 3:16–17

This brief mention of the church as Temple follows hot on the heels of Paul's exposition of his ministry in Corinth as planting and building (cf. Jer. 1:10). Through a neatly balanced pair of metaphors (cf. 3:9b as the hinge sentence) there is clear progression of thought as Paul's argument shows its teeth. The exemplary complementarity of the ministries of Paul and Apollos is expounded in the agricultural imagery (3:5–9). Paul's work was chronologically prior to that of Apollos in Corinth but their efforts were co-ordinated and both were subordinate to the divine contribution: 'God gives the growth' (3:7). By contrast, the construction metaphor in 3:10–15 is a warning. Paul is confident of God's grace working through him and of his foundation – none other than Christ himself. His own work is not destined for testing, for as Paul subtly makes clear in 3:14, only that which is built on the sound foundation is to be tested.

The third metaphor, that of the divine *naos*, is also a warning, this time a more direct one. It is only loosely linked to the preceding building image. The building materials of 3:12 (gold, silver, precious stones, wood, hay and straw) are no more realistic building materials for a temple than are the materials for the houses in the story of the three little pigs. The point of the different materials is their differing degrees of combustibility. Paul also separates the Temple imagery and the first building metaphor by mixing (or muddling?) his metaphors about fire in 3:15.

Paul's Temple language rather obviously demonstrates two of the three categories of Temple association set out above – the corporate temple–divine presence/ownership theme: 'Do you not know you are God's temple and that God's spirit dwells in you?' (3:16; and the holiness theme: 'For God's temple is holy and that temple you are' (3:17b). The plural address indicates that Paul is speaking of the Corinthian church corporately as God's shrine. The assertion of the indwelling Spirit is bold in the light of 1 Corinthians 2:6–16. In chapter 2 Paul challenged the Corinthian 'pneumatics' with the question of what constitutes true spirituality and casts doubts on their claims to be wise and spiritual on the basis of pneumatic inspiration. In 3:16–17 Paul's rhetorical strategy is different – he tells them that the Spirit is indeed within them and so calls the whole community to corporate responsibility for the integrity of the edifice. This time the pneumatics are fingered with the warning of 3:17a: 'If anyone destroys God's temple God will destroy them.' Paul clearly has in mind the destructive potential of the divisions caused by the pneumatics' claims to wisdom.

In 3:17a our third Temple association, the Temple as a centred and bounded entity, emerges more subtly, first through the idea of divine ownership and jealously or protectiveness for his possession and secondly in the concern for the integrity of the structure. Possession expresses the centred-ness of the whole on God and reorientates the church to divine concerns and priorities. Owned by God, the community is to reflect God's holiness and be different from the world. The concern for boundaries is concern not for ritual limits but for the structural integrity of the whole, a metaphor for pedagogical and relational integrity in the Corinthian congregation.

4. 1 CORINTHIANS 6:19

1 Corinthians 6 is a bold outline of a theological anthropology appropriate to deal with the ethical crises within the Corinthian congregation. This is part of a series of problems over sexual behaviour centred on the problem of *porneia*. Scholars agree that Paul is responding to a form of Hellenistic deprecation of the body that issued in libertinism on the one hand and asceticism on the other. Paul's theological response is part of his wider theological and anthropological interest, expressed throughout the letter, in the integrity of embodied existence.

Immediately preceding our text Paul has dealt with the problem of the incestuous brother and lawsuits amongst believers. Both demonstrate Paul's concern for the integrity of the Christian community and articulate solutions based on the idea that the church is a self-regulating community with boundaries within which problems are resolved and integrities maintained. This inside/outside polarity and Paul's emphasis on the Corinthian community as a transformed and transforming community protect Paul's instructions here from the accusations of exclusivism, harsh judgementalism or moralizing.[5] Immorality is the way of the world but not the church. When people come to Christ their habitual antisocial behaviours are left behind – the believers were washed, sanctified and justified in Christ and the Spirit (6:11).

The immediate problem of 6:12ff. arises out of a moral crisis grounded in a philosophical conviction: 'since all things are lawful for me', some(one?) in the church has been going to prostitutes (6:12, 15).

---

[5] So R. B. Hays, *1 Corinthians* (Louisville: Westminster/John Knox, 1997), s.v.

Rosner[6] has argued that the problem was Temple prostitution, and this would certainly explain the Temple reference. But if this were the case we would expect a clearer reference to idolatry and it is better to conclude that Paul's use of Temple imagery emerges from his own theologizing.

Paul's response relates a series of fundamental gospel verities to the ethics of embodied existence. Teleologically the purpose of embodied existence is to serve Christ: 'the body is for the Lord' (6:13b). Eschatologically, food and the stomach will come to nothing (6:13a), but the believers' bodies are due for resurrection (6:14). Mystically, believers are incorporated into Christ – joined with him in (the) Spirit. Soteriologically, believers have been redeemed – bought with a price and under divine ownership, they are bound to act for the sake of his good reputation: 'glorify God in your body' (6:20).

As part of this 'kerygmatic ethics' Paul declares the body of the individual believer to be a Temple of the Holy Spirit: 'Do you not know that your body is a temple of the Holy Spirit within you, which you have from God, and that you are not your own?' (6:19). A number of points are worthy of emphasis. First, it is clearly the individual not the community that is in view as a Temple. Secondly, the focus is soteriological: it is the donation of the Spirit in redemption (not the donation of the body in creation) that makes the body a Temple. The appeal is not to a universal anthropology but to a distinctively Christian anthropology grounded in pneumatology. Thirdly, the immediately preceding concern is with the special character of sexual sin. This Paul argues is different from other sin since in this case people sin against their own bodies.[7] This is precisely the concern with the sacral integrity of the bounded entity (in this case the human body not the believing community) that Temple language evokes and articulates. Fourthly, it should be noted that the 'god' of the somatic Temple is actually the Holy Spirit – it is his 'image' that is to be honoured in the Temple of the human body. In the next clause comes the principal *topos* of divine ownership through the redemption price paid by Christ (6:19c–20). The idea of the Holy Spirit is next-door-neighbour to the idea of the body as a bounded sacred space within which holy integrity is to be maintained. And it is next-door-but-one to the idea of the divine presence in the individual since the Spirit is never directly identified with the presence of God in the Temple, but is rather linked through a mediating idea, such as *doxa* or holiness.[8] The believer is placed under obligation to holiness because the body is the locus of honour for the Holy Spirit.

---

[6] B. S. Rosner, 'Temple Prostitution in 1 Corinthians 6:12–20', *NovT* 40 (1998), pp. 336–51.

[7] Attempts to argue that Paul quotes the Corinthians in 6:18 founder because it seems unlikely that the Corinthians recognized the presence of any sin.

[8] Some commentators have shown themselves uncomfortable with Paul's rather bald statement about the body as Temple of the Holy Spirit, without reference to Christ. Walker, for example, introduces two links to Christology. He claims that *katoikein* links

Whilst in the case of 1 Corinthians 6:19 it is the believer, not the church, that is a 'temple of the Holy Spirit', Paul's main concern in using Temple language is, once again, ethical. We should be less impressed with the progression or distinction between Paul's use of Temple imagery to refer to the community in 1 Corinthians 3 and the individual in 1 Corinthians 6 as by the common concern with ethics.

5. 2 CORINTHIANS 6:16

Our final reference to the Temple is located a stand-alone unit (2 Cor. 6:11–7.1) which gives us little internal clue as to its object. The final exhortation is to holiness and although idolatry is mentioned (6:16) it could simply be illustrative of the more general point. Other suggestions for the problem in view are sexual sin (Ambrosiaster, Chrysostom), consorting with demons, too much contact with unbelievers, or evil in general (Augustine, Jerome).

Each of Paul's rhetorical questions proposes a radical opposition in the form of a question. The last of Paul's five rhetorical questions – 'What does the temple of God has to do with idols?' – is followed by an explanatory comment: 'For we are the temple of the living God.'[9] The collection of quotes from Leviticus 26:12 and Ezekiel 37:27 expounds the implications of this imagery. Once again the appeal to Temple imagery includes the ideas of holy integrity and bounded separateness implicit in Temple language.

Two other points are noteworthy. First, there is clear use in the section of all three of our Temple themes: God's presence with them – 'I will live in them and walk amongst them' (6:16); the concern for holiness (7:1); and the protection of the integrity of sacred boundaries – 'come out from among them' … 'touch nothing unclean' … 'let us cleanse ourselves from every defilement'. Secondly, unlike the other texts we have considered there is crossover between the corporate and the individual: a pure corporate Temple requires holy individuals. It is hard to escape the rather self-evident conclusion: Temple language finds its place in this exhortatory section because of its ability to evoke important ethical themes.

6. CONCLUSION

Lanci argued that 'the temple image is an engine, a source of imaginative power, which Paul uses to articulate and propel his ecclesiology'.[10]

God's fullness indwelling of Christ in Colossians 2:9–10 and the idea of God dwelling in his Temple. He further argues that a link is made through the equivalence of 'in Christ' language to having the Spirit. It remains an open question whether there is any evidence for the interposition of Christ in 1 Corinthians 6:19.

[9] The textual variant 'you' is an import from 1 Corinthians 3:16–17.

[10] Lanci, *A New Temple for Corinth*, p. 5.

He also argues that 'With this image he asserts the idea that the community, not individuals or subgroups, is the basis of the indwelling Spirit.'[11] For most commentators who have followed McKelvey, the corporate use of the Temple imagery is primary and the more individualized use in 1 Corinthians 6 is secondary. This has usually been argued on the basis of a rather weak appeal to 'order', though for McKelvey this was because 2 Corinthians 6:14–7.1 was a letter fragment that antedated 1 Corinthians, whilst for others it is simply because 1 Corinthians 3 comes before 1 Corinthians 6.

Lanci and McKelvey represent in different ways a long tradition in scholarship that prefers the corporate over the individual and the ecclesiological over the ethical in its analysis of Pauline Temple imagery. I wish to argue that these are both wrong because they set the problem wrongly in the first place. We should be more impressed with what binds together Paul's Temple imagery than the different ways in which he uses it. It is Paul's concern for ethics – the ethical integrity of the community and the holiness of the believing individual – that is the common factor in his use of Temple language in Corinthians. Consequently it is neither a case of the individual or corporate being primary or the individual or corporate experience of the Spirit being prior to the other. Rather, both draw on a common stock of interrelated notions associated with the Temple in Jewish tradition and carrying common resonance even for pagans. The Temple is about divine presence and ownership, divine holiness and the existence of centred-bounded sacred space all of which demand of God's people individually and collectively holy purity. Temple imagery suited Paul's theological and pastoral purpose precisely because he conceived of both the believer and the church in somatic terms – bounded, bodily entities whose integrity in Christ and in the Spirit demanded ethical purity. Both in the life of the early believers and in the communities they formed, Paul taught that God had created by the work of the Spirit a new sacred space – a sacred space that the Gentiles could enter into, but more radically a sacred space which God had created within each believer. In practice this turned out to be no cosy doctrine of cheap grace based on religious experience or spiritual encounter for either believer or community. To know the divine presence in the Spirit was to face the demand to reflect his holy otherness by maintaining the sacral integrity of the sacred internal and social space that God himself has created and owns for his glory.

---

[11] Ibid., p. 130.

12

THE NEW TEMPLE

Christology and Ecclesiology in Ephesians and 1 Peter

DAVID PETERSON

Whereas in the gospels there are indications that Jesus himself fulfils the new Temple expectations of the Old Testament and various Jewish writings, in Ephesians and 1 Peter *Christians in union with Christ are that Temple*. This ecclesiology arises from profound statements about the centrality of Christ and his work to the divine plan of salvation. Paul also highlights the work of the Holy Spirit in bringing people to Christ and thus forming the new Temple community. The heavenly locus of this community is obvious from both passages, but both are part of a developing argument about the sanctity of the church and its calling to be faithful to Christ in a hostile and unbelieving world. I begin with a brief examination of Temple theology applied to the local church in 1 Corinthians 3:16–17 and 2 Corinthians 6:16–18 before turning to the larger picture presented in Ephesians and 1 Peter. In each of the passages examined, there is an ethical implication to this new Temple ecclesiology.

1. THE LOCAL CHURCH AS THE DIVINE SANCTUARY (1 COR. 3:16–17; 2 COR. 6:16–18)

The image of the *local church* as 'the temple of God' (*naos theou*) is introduced in 1 Corinthians 3:16–17 to deal with a problem of strained relationships and division in that congregation. Jealousy and quarrelling had arisen from different evaluations of particular leaders and their ministries (1:10–3:4). The apostle responds by first employing an agricultural metaphor to explain how the Corinthians are the 'field' which God is cultivating through his servants (3:5–9). Paul planted, Apollos watered, 'but God gave the growth'. This metaphor highlights the role which human beings play in the foundation and development of the church, while giving due emphasis to the sovereign operation of God throughout the process.

The apostle then develops the idea that they are God's 'building' (*oikodomē*), in which Jesus Christ is the 'foundation' (*themelion*, cf. Isa.

28:16) and Paul the 'skilled master of works' (*architektōn*),[1] who laid the foundation through his evangelistic ministry (3:9–11; cf. Rom. 15:20). The warning which follows in 1 Corinthians 3:12–15 is about the way to build a structure on that foundation that will survive the test of God's judgement. In effect, the Corinthians are challenged to go on applying to their corporate life and relationships nothing more nor less than the gospel truths and the traditions which they received from Paul. The building metaphor thus highlights the importance of *Christ as the foundation* and prepares for the apostle's elaboration of the concept of 'edification' (*oikodomē*) later in the letter.[2]

With the words 'Do you not know that you are God's temple and that God's Spirit dwells in you?' (v. 16, NRSV) the apostle develops the building metaphor in a specific way. The building that God is erecting in Corinth, on the foundation of Paul's preaching about Jesus, is actually a sacred community of people indwelt by the Spirit of God. As the Spirit creates one body (1 Cor. 12:13), so he has formed one 'temple' at Corinth. This metaphor qualifies the building image by adding *the dynamic of the Holy Spirit*. As with the agricultural metaphor, this ensures a proper recognition of the sovereign grace of God in forming, maintaining and advancing the church. But the metaphor also highlights the sacredness of the fellowship of believers and gives Paul ground for warning about the danger of sacrilege: 'If anyone destroys God's temple, God will destroy that person. For God's temple is holy, and you are that temple' (v. 17). Reading 1 Corinthians as a whole, we discern that the Temple can be destroyed by false teaching, by divisions based on worldly values, or by giving way to ungodliness in any form.

The expression *naos theou* marks out the Corinthian church as the divine sanctuary where God's Spirit dwells.[3] This is especially manifested when they gather to minister to one another, and thus to meet with God (cf. 14:24–25). The image reflects the Old Testament idea that God was specially present in the midst of his people (e.g. Exod. 29:44–46; 33:14–16; Ps. 114:2). Prophecies about the restoration of Israel after the Babylonian exile included the promise of the gift of God's Spirit, as the means by which he would dwell in or among his people and

---

[1] Translation of C. K. Barrett (*A Commentary on the First Epistle to the Corinthians*, BNTC [London: Black, 1971²], p. 86), based on the observation that in Plato (*Statesman*, 259E, 260A) an *architektōn* contributes knowledge and assigns tasks to workers on a building site.

[2] I have explored the concept of edification in *Engaging with God: A Biblical Theology of Worship* (Leicester: Apollos, 1992), pp. 206–18. I define edification as founding, maintaining and advancing the church God's way.

[3] In the LXX, but not necessarily in Greek usage more generally, *naos* refers to the sanctuary as the place where God dwells, whereas *hieron* refers to the whole Temple complex (including the sanctuary). Cf. O. Michel, *TDNT*, IV:880–90. *naos* is the word used in key New Testament passages concerning the fulfilment of Old Testament Temple typology (e.g. Mark 15:29; John 2:19–21; 2 Cor. 6:16; Eph. 2:21; Rev. 7:15).

bless them in a new way (e.g. Joel 2:28–32; Isa. 44:3–5; Ezek. 36:27–28; 37:14). The hope of a new Temple (e.g. Ezek. 40–48; *Jub.* 1:17; 1 Enoch 91:13; 4QFlor.), which was another way of speaking about the ultimate renewal of God's people, finds expression in the reality of the Christian congregation. The imagery for Paul thus has eschatological overtones. Under the New Covenant, God's dwelling on earth is no special building or sanctuary within a building, neither is it exclusively renewed Israel. 1 Corinthians 3:16–17 identifies the new Temple with a congregation of those who trust in Christ and are indwelt by his Spirit.[4]

The hortatory significance of Paul's Temple theology in 1 Corinthians 3:16–17 is that believers must zealously guard the unity created by the Spirit, for 'to cause disunity in the church is to desecrate the temple of God and desecration of a holy place leads to its destruction'.[5] God's special presence amongst his people is to be acknowledged, not by ritual or ceremony, but by the preservation of the integrity and vitality of the congregation. In 1 Corinthians 12–14 we see how this involves an appropriate use of the gifts and ministries that the Spirit enables in the fellowship of believers.

If the danger to the church is internal in 1 Corinthians 3, it is *external* when Paul applies the imagery of the Temple again in 2 Corinthians 6:16–18. It is possible that the affirmation 'for we are the temple of the living God' (*hēmeis gar naos theou esmen zōntos*) is a distributive image here ('people of God'), rather than strictly congregational, because of the supportive texts in verses 16–18 and because of the first person plural (*hēmeis*).[6] However, there is no doubt from the context (6:14–16; 7:1) that the application is local. The cultic regulations of the Mosaic Law, which were intended to secure the holiness of God's people by isolating them from contact with the heathen, have been abolished in Christ (cf. Mark 7:14–19; Acts 10:9–15; Eph. 2:14–16). Yet the *separation in belief and lifestyle* which those regulations sought to achieve is still required of Christians. They are not free to engage in relationships with

---

[4] G. D. Fee, *The First Epistle to the Corinthians* (NICNT; Grand Rapids: Eerdmans, 1987), p. 147, ignores Paul's emphasis on Christ as 'foundation' in the context, when he asserts: 'The presence of the Spirit, and that *alone*, marks them off as God's new people, his temple, in Corinth.' Cf. G. D. Fee, *God's Empowering Presence: The Holy Spirit in the Letters of Paul* (Peabody: Hendrickson, 1994), p. 115.
[5] R. J. McKelvey, *The New Temple: The Church in the New Testament* (London/New York: Oxford University Press, 1969), p. 101. Cf. R. Y. K. Fung, 'Some Pauline Pictures of the Church', *EQ* 53 (1981), p. 101, and the conclusion of Fee, *The First Epistle to the Corinthians*, pp. 149–50.
[6] The reading '*you* are the temple of God' (*humeis gar naos theou este*) appears to be secondary, and is an assimilation to 1 Corinthians 3:16, influenced by the context (2 Cor. 6:14, 17). The plural reading 'we are *temples* of God' (*hēmeis gar naoi theou esmen*) appears to be an entirely inappropriate assimilation to 1 Corinthians 6:19. Cf. B. M. Metzger (ed.), *A Textual Commentary on the Greek New Testament* (Stuttgart: Deutsche Bibelgesellschaft/United Bible Societies, 1994[2]), p. 512.

unbelievers that compromise their holy fellowship with the living God (2 Cor. 6:14–16).[7]

Leviticus 26:12 is combined with Ezekiel 37:27 in this passage to make the point that the new Temple expectations of the Old Testament are fulfilled in the church. Even more so than the Tabernacle of old, the Christian congregation is God's 'dwelling', and should therefore be 'set apart for its sacred purpose'.[8] The separation motif is continued in verse 17 with a quote from Isaiah 52:11 ('Therefore come out from them, and be separate from them, says the Lord, and touch nothing unclean; then I will welcome you'). Once again, a text which originally had a cultic meaning, being directed to the priests and Levites at the time of the Babylonian exile, finds an ethical application in the flow of Paul's argument. To this is attached the promise of God to be the Father of those who obey his call to holiness (cf. Ezek. 20:34, 41).

The passage concludes as it began, with a challenge to live a holy and separated life: 'since we have these promises, beloved, let us cleanse ourselves from every defilement of body and spirit, making holiness perfect in the fear of God' (7:1). Paul uses transformed cultic language to indicate that a sanctified lifestyle is the worship appropriate to the new Temple (cf. Rom. 12:1). Reverence for God is to be expressed by living differently from those outside the fellowship of believers. Paul does not mean that Christians are to withdraw from effective contact with unbelievers (cf. 1 Cor. 5:9–10), but they are to avoid any compromise with paganism (cf. 2 Cor. 6:16, 'what agreement has the temple of God with idols?'). Specifically, in the context, 'the Corinthian believers must not be joined with Corinthian "unbelievers" in the cultic life of the city, but rather "come out" from among them'.[9]

2. THE HEAVENLY CHURCH AS THE DIVINE SANCTUARY (EPH. 2:19–22)

In Ephesians 2 the central importance of Christ and his atoning work in establishing the new Temple of biblical expectation is developed. The

---

[7] Critical issues, such as the origin of this passage and its relation to the surrounding context in 2 Corinthians, are helpfully analysed by V. P. Furnish, *II Corinthians* (AB 32A; Garden City: Doubleday, 1984), pp. 367–83. The warning against being 'yoked together with unbelievers' cannot refer to involvement with Paul's opponents. Against Furnish, there is some support in the immediate context for the view that Paul is warning against involvement in pagan idolatries (vv. 15–16). Cf. C. K. Barrett, *A Commentary on the Second Epistle to the Corinthians* (BNTC; London: Black, 1973), pp. 195–9; P. Barnett, *The Second Epistle to the Corinthians* (NICNT; Grand Rapids/Cambridge: Eerdmans, 1997), pp. 337–58.

[8] McKelvey, *The New Temple*, p. 94. He observes that the addition of the words *enoikēsō en autois* means that 'God no longer dwells *with* his people in a sanctuary which they make for him; he dwells *in* them, and *they* are his temple' (p. 95).

[9] Barnett, *The Second Epistle to the Corinthians*, p. 345. Cf. Fee, *God's Empowering Presence*, pp. 336–8.

church appears to be more than a local entity here and there is a clear enunciation of the role of the Holy Spirit in forming this Temple, as in 1 Corinthians 3:16–17. But most importantly, Paul affirms in Ephesians that *Christians in union with Christ* fulfil the Temple ideal.

2.1 The Christological focus

Rather than being the foundation stone (*themelion*, 1 Cor. 3:11), Christ himself is portrayed as 'the cornerstone' (NRSV) or 'chief cornerstone' (NIV, Eph. 2:20; cf. 1 Pet. 2:6, citing Isa. 28:16). Some have argued that *akrogōniaios* means the top or final stone which holds the building together. This suits the emphasis of Ephesians on the role of the exalted Christ in relation to the church (cf. 1:22–23; 2:6; 4:7–16).[10] However, it is more likely that *akrogōniaios* refers to the cornerstone, meaning the primary stone of the foundation in relation to 'the foundation of the apostles and prophets' (*tō themeliō tōn apostolōn kai prophētōn*). This is more consistent with the picture of the church in Ephesians 2 as 'a growing and unfinished building'.[11] It is also consistent with Isaiah 28:16 (the sole example of the term in the LXX), where the sequence is, 'I am laying in Zion a foundation stone [*eis ta themelia*], a tested stone, a precious cornerstone [*akrogōniaion entimon*], a sure foundation [*eis ta themelia*].' This sequence of terms implies that the building work commences with the *akrogōniaios*, which then determines the 'lie' or line of the building.

This unusual term is employed in Ephesians 2:20 to give pre-eminence to Christ in relation to the divine building plan. 'In him the whole structure is joined together and grows into a holy temple in the Lord' (2:21). 'All is built on Christ, supported by Christ, and the lie or shape of the continuing building is determined by Christ, the cornerstone.'[12] The Christological dimension to the new Temple is even more obvious in Ephesians than it is in 1 Corinthians 3:11–17. At the same time, the terminology in Ephesians 2:20 allows Paul to highlight the importance of the apostles and prophets as foundational to the new Temple. The order of the words *tōn apostolōn kai prophētōn* and the use of the same phrase in Ephesians 3:5 suggest that New Testament prophets are in view. Together with the apostles, these prophets were 'the first authoritative recipients and proclaimers of God's revelation

---

[10] Cf. J. Jeremias, *TDNT*, I:792; IV:275 and A. T. Lincoln, *Paradise Now and Not Yet* (SNTSMS 43; Cambridge: Cambridge University Press, 1981), pp. 152–4.

[11] P. T. O'Brien, *The Letter to the Ephesians* (Grand Rapids/Cambridge: Eerdmans, 1999), p. 217. Cf. McKelvey, *The New Temple*, pp. 195–204 and W. A. Grudem, *The Gift of Prophecy in 1 Corinthians* (Lanham/New York/London: University Press of America, 1982), pp. 85–7.

[12] M. Turner, 'Ephesians' in D. A. Carson, R. T. France, J. A. Motyer and G. J. Wenham (eds), *New Bible Commentary: 21st Century Edition* (Downers Grove/Leicester: IVP, 1994), pp. 1232–3.

in Christ'.[13] So the point is being made that membership in God's new community depends on a faithful reception of, and continuance in, the normative teaching given to Christ's 'holy apostles and prophets by the Spirit' (3:5).

1 Corinthians 3:12–15 showed the need to build a structure on the foundation of Christ that would survive the test of God's judgement. It was noted above that this means applying to corporate life and relationships nothing more nor less than the gospel truths and the traditions received from Paul. The building metaphor in Ephesians 2:20 similarly highlights the importance of *Christ and the divine revelation given to his apostles and prophets* as the means by which God founds, maintains and advances his eschatological people. The implications of this are particularly explored in Ephesians 3:1–4:16.

More will be said below about the Christological focus to the message in Ephesians 2:11–22. Here it is important to note the link that this provides with the teaching of Jesus himself about the new Temple. In various ways he made it clear that Israel and the Jerusalem Temple had not functioned according to God's plan and that he would become the centre of salvation and blessing for the nations (e.g. Matt. 28:18–20; Luke 24:46–49; John 12:20–33). According to false witnesses at his trial, Jesus had said 'I will destroy this temple that is made with hands, and in three days will build another, not made with hands' (Mark 14:58; cf. Matt. 26:61).[14] Only the utterance of Jesus recorded in John 2:19 can account for the development of this confused testimony.

As in the Synoptic accounts, Jesus' cleansing of the Temple in John 2 is a prophetic-type protest against the profanation of God's house. At another level, the narrative suggests that Jesus was taking action to bring about the fulfilment of eschatological prophecies, in which God is to be glorified by the pure worship of his people. The immediate context in the Fourth Gospel also suggests that the action was a specifically messianic sign, pointing to the replacement of the Temple by Jesus.[15]

---

[13] O'Brien, *The Letter to the Ephesians*, p. 216. Note his critique of Grudem (*The Gift of Prophecy in 1 Corinthians*, pp. 93–101), who argues that the reference is to 'the apostles who are also prophets'. Against this view see also F. F. Bruce, *The Epistles to the Colossians, to Philemon and to the Ephesians* (NICNT; Grand Rapids: Eerdmans, 1984), pp. 304, 315, n. 29.

[14] The accusation of the crowds at the scene of the crucifixion reflects again the supposed claim of Jesus to destroy the Temple and rebuild it in three days (Matt. 27:39–40; Mark 15:29–30) and adds further weight to the suggestion that this charge may have been based on some genuine claim by Jesus.

[15] At the wedding in Cana of Galilee (2:1–12), Jesus changed the water in the six stone jars used by the Jews for ceremonial washing into wine and thus 'revealed his glory' to his disciples. This is the first of a series of signs indicating that Jesus is the one sent by the Father to replace the customs and feasts of Judaism. Jesus does this by bringing in the blessings of the messianic era, here signified by the abundance of choice wine. By cleansing the Temple, he further revealed himself as the one sent to replace the institutions of the Mosaic covenant.

Although the witnesses at Jesus' trial and the bystanders at the crucifixion charged Jesus with saying 'I will destroy this temple', John records that he actually said 'Destroy this temple' (*lusate ton naon touton*), using the imperative in an ironical way. Apart from other minor differences, the Synoptic reports use the verb 'to build' (*oikodomein*), which is applicable only to another edifice such as the existing Temple, whereas John's report uses 'to raise up' (*egeirein*), which may refer to a building or to the resurrection of Jesus' body. On the surface, this pronouncement refers simply to the Jerusalem Temple and could have been taken as a claim by Jesus to be *the builder of the eschatological Temple* ('Destroy the existing temple and I will raise it again in three days'). The insight that this saying referred to his resurrection body came only after he had been raised and the disciples 'believed the Scripture and the words that Jesus had spoken' (2:22).

The Scripture that the disciples 'believed' was probably Psalm 69: 9 (cited in John 2:17). John emphasizes the typological or predictive aspect of this psalm about a righteous sufferer by substituting the future tense ('Zeal for your house *will consume* me') for the past tense. As a prophecy of Jesus' death, it suggests that Jesus' concern to establish the purpose of God for Israel, Jerusalem and the Temple would destroy him! Because of this zeal, the Jewish leaders would bring about his death, but Jesus would take up his life again. John indicates that the glory of God is ultimately manifested in the death of Jesus on behalf of God's flock, so that he might raise them up to share the new life of the kingdom with him (cf. 10:14–30). The incarnation makes possible a manifestation of the glory of God surpassing anything experienced in the Tabernacle or Temple (1:14–18). But the hour of the Son's death is the hour of his ultimate glory and the moment when he completes the task of glorifying the Father, opening the way for believers from every nation to enjoy eternal life (cf. 2:4; 12:23–26; 17:1–5).

The Temple stood for revelation and purification: it was both the meeting place of heaven and earth and the place of sacrifice for purification from sin. Thus, it found fulfilment in the incarnation *and* the death and resurrection of Christ. The coming of the 'Greeks' to Jerusalem marked the beginning of the predicted pilgrimage of the nations to Zion and was the signal to Jesus that the hour of his glorification through death had come (12:20–33). His 'lifting up' from the earth would be the means by which he drew the nations to himself. The Temple of the new age in John's Gospel is not the church but *the crucified and resurrected Son of God*.[16] However, the link between Jesus' exaltation, the pouring out of the Holy Spirit and the establishment of the new people of God is clear

---

[16] R. Bultmann, *The Gospel of John: A Commentary* (ET; Oxford: Blackwell, 1971), pp. 127–8, n. 6, rightly argues that it is impossible that the body of Christ here should refer to the community of believers in a Pauline sense, since the object of *lusate* and *egerō* in John 2:19 must be one and the same.

in this Gospel. The apostle Paul explores and develops this linkage in Ephesians 2:11–22.

2.2 The heavenly or eschatological nature of the church

The church that is described as God's Temple in Ephesians 2:19–22 is a heavenly, rather than a local, assembly. Earlier in the chapter, the readers are numbered amongst those whom God has, even now, 'raised up with Christ and seated ... with him in the heavenly places in Christ Jesus' (2:6; cf. Col. 3:1–4; Heb. 12:22–24). This is a vivid way of speaking about the realization of eschatological realities for those who are in Christ. Christian believers have experienced God's power and salvation 'in the heavenly realms in Christ' (1:3) and are *already assembled with him there*.[17] The focus in 2:11–22 is on all who have been brought near to God by the sacrifice of the Messiah and the pouring out of the Holy Spirit. However, 2:6 suggests that they constitute a heavenly reality: a community with its locus 'in the heavenly places in Christ Jesus'.

This new people of God includes Gentiles, who were previously excluded from citizenship in Israel and were 'strangers to the covenants of the promise, having no hope and without God in the world' (2:11). The terms 'far off' (*makran*) and 'near' (*engus*), which are used to describe the status of Gentiles (vv. 13, 17), were Old Testament designations for Jews in their relationship to the Jerusalem Temple (Isa. 57:19; Dan. 9:7). Jews and Gentiles now have common access to God through the sacrificial death of the Messiah (2:13; cf. 1:7). They are on an equal footing because of Christ's reconciling work, which removed the 'dividing wall' of the Mosaic Law and 'abolished the law with its commandments and ordinances' (2:14–15).[18] Christ is thus 'the bringer of cosmic peace, the reconciler of heaven and earth as the two parts of the divided universe',[19] and within that framework the reconciler of Jew and Gentile.

A new humanity (*hena kainon anthrōpon*, 2:15) has been created in Christ, by his reconciling work. Jews and Gentiles have been united in him, 'the inclusive representative of the new order, as members of his body'.[20] Indeed, *both* Jews and Gentiles needed reconciling to God 'in

---

[17] Cf. M. Barth, *Ephesians 1–3* (AB 34; Garden City: Doubleday, 1974), p. 238. His extended note on this verse is very helpful (pp. 236–8).

[18] Cf. O'Brien, *The Letter to the Ephesians*, pp. 197–9 for a helpful discussion of what it means for the law-covenant to be abolished by Christ and replaced by a new means of access to God.

[19] Lincoln, *Paradise Now and Not Yet*, p. 150. He goes on to argue that *sumpolitai tōn hagiōn* means 'fellow-citizens of the angels' (rather than fellow citizens with Jewish Christians). If this is correct, the notion of the church as a heavenly assembly is further strengthened.

[20] O'Brien, *The Letter to the Ephesians*, p. 200. He rightly observes that, 'Nothing less than a new creation, an entirely new entity, was needed to transcend the deep rift between the two. It was effected through Christ's death, and the result is not an amalgam of the best elements of the two, but a "new person" who transcends them both.'

one body through the cross' (2:16), and by this to be reconciled to each other. But this does not mean that the whole human race has been automatically united and reconciled. The one who is 'our peace' and who made peace through his cross has come and 'proclaimed peace' to those who were 'far off' and to those who were 'near'. The reference here is most likely to 'the proclamation of the exalted Christ speaking by his Spirit in his messengers, the apostles'.[21]

In 2:18 it is affirmed that 'through him both of us have access in one Spirit to the Father'. In Christ, Jews and Gentiles together can relate to God as Father, because of the gift of his Spirit (cf. Gal. 4:6; Rom. 8:15–16). The parallel between 2:16 (*en heni sōmati*) and 2:18 (*en heni pneumati*) suggests that the Spirit, who enables people to be reconciled to the Father through trusting in the work of the Son, forms believers into that one body which is the heavenly church.

Most importantly, throughout this passage we see the primacy of *Christology*. Ecclesiology is a function of Christology in Ephesians.[22] The one new humanity is created 'in himself' (*en autō*, v. 15). Jews and Gentiles are reconciled to God 'in one body through the cross' (v. 16), which suggests that the church as that 'new humanity' is created by the crucifixion and resurrection of the Messiah. Proclamation of his reconciling work enables those who are destined for adoption as God's children through Christ (1:5) to be brought near and to become the community of those who have 'access in one Spirit to the Father' (vv. 17–18). In this new community, Gentile believers are now 'citizens with the saints and also members of the household of God', forming a spiritual edifice (vv. 19–20), which is growing into a holy Temple in the Lord (v. 21).

The metaphor of citizenship implies membership of a city (cf. Gal. 4:26) or commonwealth (cf. Phil. 3:20). This is another way of speaking about participation in the heavenly realm (2:6), which is ruled by God in Christ. Paul then changes from a socio-political metaphor to that of an intimate family: Jews and Gentiles are children together in God's own family (*oikeioi tou theou*). Membership of a household in Roman culture meant identity, refuge and protection, giving 'the security that comes with a sense of belonging'.[23] This would appear to be the assurance that Paul gives his Gentile readers with the application of the household metaphor here. Since 'house' (*oikos*) can mean either 'household' or 'temple' in biblical thought (e.g. 2 Sam. 7:5–11), the transition to new Temple theology is easy. This adds the dimension of divine

---

[21] Ibid., p. 207. He reviews the alternative interpretations and concludes that this is the most likely.

[22] Ibid., p. 202.

[23] P. H. Towner, 'Households and Household Codes' in G. F. Hawthorne, R. P. Martin and D. G. Reid (eds), *Dictionary of Paul and his Letters* (Downers Grove/Leicester: IVP, 1993), p. 418.

presence and sanctified status to the notions of security and belonging implied by the household image.

The preceding context shows how much Paul related the fulfilment of the Temple ideal to Old Testament promises that 'in the eschatological age the nations would be graciously accepted by Yahweh in his house'.[24] However, the assumption of Ephesians 2:16 is that Jews need to be reconciled to God through the cross as much as Gentiles and 2:18 indicates that Jews and Gentiles have access to God in Christ together, through the promised gift of the Spirit. In other words, new Temple imagery implies the renewal of worship for Israel as well as the inclusion of Gentiles in God's 'house'.

In Ephesians 2:20 it is *people* who are 'built upon the foundation of the apostles and prophets, with Christ Jesus himself as the cornerstone'. This is closer to 1 Peter 2:5, where believers are being built into a spiritual house 'like living stones', than to 1 Corinthians 3:10–15, where the focus is on the kind of *materials* used in the ongoing work of 'building' the church. The central role played by Christ in the construction of this eschatological Temple is stressed by the use of 'in whom' (*en hō*) at the beginning of verses 21, 22, and by the description of it as 'a holy temple in the Lord' (*naon hagion en kuriō*).

There is a mixture of building and organic images in the claim that 'in him the whole structure is joined together (*sunarmologoumenē*) and grows (*auxei*) into a holy temple in the Lord'. To speak of the building being 'joined together' refers not simply to the union of one stone with another, but also to the union of the whole construction with the cornerstone: 'the cornerstone unites the building because it is organically as well as structurally bound to it'.[25] Metaphors are mixed to affirm the personal union of believers with Christ, as well as the notion of a building under construction. The building grows as further stones are added to it, but growth in 4:15–16 also has to do with the body being strengthened through truth and love to reach God's final goal for his people (4:13).[26]

Jews and Gentiles have an equal place in this new community, being 'built together' (*sunoikodoeisthe*) into 'a dwelling-place of God in the Spirit' (*katoikētērion tou theou en pneumati*, v. 22). The last expression parallels 'a holy temple in the Lord' (*naon hagion en kuriō*, v. 21). The Old Testament can speak of the dwelling place of God as being in heaven (e.g. 1 Kgs. 8:39, 43, 49) but also in the Temple at Jerusalem (e.g. 1 Kgs. 8:13). According to Ephesians 2:6, believers have already been

---

[24] McKelvey, *The New Temple*, pp. 111–12. Cf. I. H. Marshall, 'Church and Temple in the New Testament', *Tyndale Bulletin* 40 (1989), pp. 203–22.

[25] McKelvey, *The New Temple*, p. 116. Both verbs occur together again in 4:15–16, where growth 'towards' Christ (*eis auton*) is facilitated by the whole body being 'joined and knit together by every ligament with which it is supplied' 'from him' (*ex hou*).

[26] Cf. Peterson, *Engaging with God*, pp. 209–11.

raised up and are seated with Christ 'in the heavenly places'. They are part of the heavenly Temple, where Christ is. Yet believers are still on earth, the people united with Christ and the heavenly realm through the indwelling Spirit. The notion of *growth* is not specifically linked to that of the Temple in the Corinthian texts, though the agricultural and building metaphors in 1 Corinthians 3:6–15 allow for this. There the Temple appears to be consecrated once and for all by the presence of the living God (2 Cor. 6:16) or the Spirit (1 Cor. 3:17; 6:19). When the figures of the building *(oikodomē)* and the Temple *(naon)* merge again in Ephesians 2:19–22, the distinct contribution of each image to the total picture must be carefully considered. 'Viewed as the building the church is still under construction; viewed as the temple, however, it is an inhabited dwelling.'[27]

McKelvey argues that although Ephesians attributes a heavenly existence to the church (1:3; 2:6):

> the temple described at 2.20–2 can hardly be regarded as heavenly in the same sense as the heavenly temple of the Jewish apocalypses, Hebrews and Revelation. The temple conception of 2.20–2 is directly connected with the discussion of the preceding verses (vv. 11–18) which, as we have noted, is concerned with the historical reconciliation of the races. It is the church as an historical actuality, the cult in which ex-Gentiles and ex-Jews here and now realize their oneness and enjoy common access to God the Father, which witnesses to this reconciliation.[28]

O'Brien, on the other hand, denies that the 'holy temple in the Lord' is 'the universal church', as many claim, arguing that this dwelling place of God is a *heavenly* entity.[29] This is so because believers have been raised with Christ (2:6), they have access to the Father in heaven through the reconciling work of Christ (2:18), and they are already citizens of the heavenly Temple-city (2:19). To this might be added the perspective that the 'new humanity' in Christ, which is the church, is in heaven where Christ is (2:15). We are only the new Temple of biblical expectation because we are 'in the Lord', who is the new Temple (cf. John 2:19–22). Of course it is necessary for believers on earth to 'realize their oneness and enjoy common access to God the Father', but the locus and focus of their unity and access to God is Christ in heaven. *The Spirit makes this new life a reality for believers vertically and horizontally.* Paul's way of speaking about the church here does not simply

---

[27] McKelvey, *The New Temple*, p. 117. He argues that the source of inspiration is 'no longer the closely knit and highly exclusive temple community of Ezekiel and the priestly writers, as in the Corinthians epistles, but the world-shrine of Isaiah and the inter-testamental writers' (p. 118).

[28] Ibid., p. 119.

[29] O'Brien, *The Letter to the Ephesians*, pp. 219–20; cf. P. T. O'Brien, 'The Church as a Heavenly and Eschatological Entity' in D. A. Carson (ed.), *The Church in the Bible and the World* (Exeter: Paternoster Press, 1987), pp. 101–3.

encourage a traditional visible–invisible distinction. Rather, the church is to be viewed eschatologically, as already existing in Christ but moving towards the final revelation and enjoyment of what is now true through faith in him.

What is the implication of all this for the local congregation? Every Christian gathering may be regarded as *an earthly expression of the heavenly church*.[30] Even now the members of the Messiah's community find the reality of God in their midst, in their holy fellowship. But this is only an anticipation of the ultimate reality, the fellowship of the heavenly city or 'the new Jerusalem', which will one day come down 'out of heaven from God' (Rev. 21:1–4). In that city the ideal of the Temple is fulfilled and God's people live in his presence forever, experiencing the blessings of 'a new heaven and a new earth' (Rev. 21:22 – 22:5). In the new creation, the Old Testament hope of the nations being united in the worship of God is realized (cf. Isa. 56:6–7; Rev. 7). That too should be anticipated in the gathering of God's people on earth. The task of the church is to keep on looking 'up' or 'forward', rather than merely looking inward at itself or even outward at the world and its needs (cf. Col. 3:1–4).

3. THE NEW TEMPLE AND THE NEW PEOPLE OF GOD (1 PET. 2:4–10)

As in Ephesians, the church in 1 Peter is more than a local entity (the word *ekklēsia* is not actually used). It is the community of all who have come to Christ and fulfil the role of eschatological Israel. However, this new people of God is not simply an earthly entity, with its locus in Jerusalem or Rome or anywhere else. Its locus is in heaven because it consists of those who have been brought by faith to the resurrected and exalted Christ (2:4–5; cf. 3:21–22), acknowledging him as the 'living stone', chosen by God to be the cornerstone and ongoing source of life for the 'spiritual house' he is constructing.

3.1 *The Christological focus*

Like Paul, Peter comes to express his doctrine of the church by way of Christology. Although verses 4–5 can be read in an imperatival way (so NRSV), it is more logical to read a series of assertions about believers (so NIV, 'As you come to him … you are being built'), following on from 'you have tasted that the Lord is good' (v. 3). It would be strange

---

[30] Cf. O'Brien, 'The Church as a Heavenly and Eschatological Entity', p. 116. He rightly argues that the New Testament rules out the view of the local church as simply a 'part' of some universal or heavenly reality. Cf. also R. J. Banks, *Paul's Idea of Community: The Early House Churches in their Historical Setting* (Exeter: Paternoster Press, 1979), pp. 51–60.

indeed to command believers to 'come' and 'be built into a spiritual house'.[31] This would obscure the point that membership of the church is an immediate consequence of believing in the gospel and being 'born anew' (1:22–25). Peter is going on to explain the corporate and ethical implications of coming to Christ for salvation.

Michaels rightly suggests that Peter's ecclesiology may have derived to some extent from his creative reflection on Isaiah 28:16 and the other 'stone' texts cited in 2:6–8 (Ps. 118:22; Isa. 8:14). But the apostle's emphasis on the process of 'building' (*oikodomeisthe*, 2:5), with its outcome being 'a spiritual house' (*oikos pneumatikos*), does not arise naturally out of any of the texts cited. 'It appears likely that 1 Peter is drawing here on tradition common to Paul and the Gospel tradition, rooted in Judaism (e.g. Qumran) but especially important to the earliest Christians because of its presence in their traditions of the words of Jesus.'[32] Jesus' use of Psalm 118:22 to imply that the process of divine 'building' is underway, despite the opposition of unbelieving Israel (Mark 12:10–11; Matt. 21:42–44; Luke 20:17–18), must surely have played a special role in Peter's thinking.

In 2:4 Peter begins to use terminology from the texts he will cite in verses 6–9. In so doing, however, he adds his own interpretative indicators. Thus, Jesus is 'a *living* stone' because of his resurrection, bringing new life to those who believe in him (cf. 1:3–9, 21–25). Though rejected by people generally, but especially by 'the builders' of historic, national Israel (cf. Ps. 118:22 in the light of Mark 12:1–12 and parallels),[33] in God's sight he is 'chosen and precious'. The intimate link between Jesus and his people outlined in this passage suggests that they too, though rejected by their contemporaries, are chosen and precious to God (2:9). Thus, as Davids suggests, the metaphor shifts from nourishment in 2:2–3 to 'security and honor' in 2:4–10.[34] Peter's ecclesiology is designed to assure his readers of God's initiative, power and presence in bringing them to Christ and forming them into 'a spiritual house'. At the same time, he wishes to stress the responsibilities that go with this privilege.

In Ephesians 2:20 the church is 'built upon the foundation of the apostles and prophets, with Christ Jesus himself as the cornerstone'. In 1 Peter 2:5 believers are 'living stones' because of *their personal link to*

---

[31] 'Even within a metaphor, stones cannot be commanded to "be built up" (passive) or to "build themselves up" (middle), for the initiative rests with the builder' (J. Ramsey Michaels, *1 Peter* [WBC 49; Waco: Word, 1988], p. 100).

[32] Ibid., p. 97. E.g. Matthew 16:18; 26:61 (= Mark 14:58); John 2:19.

[33] Peter's interpretative comment at the end of 2:8 suggests that he is using these texts with a special reference to the stumbling of disobedient Israelites, as suggested by the original contexts of the texts quoted.

[34] P. H. Davids, *The First Epistle of Peter* (NICNT; Grand Rapids: Eerdmans, 1990), p. 85. He later suggests that the church is pictured as 'impregnable, unlike physical temples and meeting places, a certain comfort to an oppressed Christian group' (p. 87).

Christ and their experience of new life in him. Christ's role as 'cornerstone' is mentioned in the quotation from Isaiah 28:16 in 2:6 (*akrogōniaios* as in Eph. 2:20). His critical importance for the establishment of God's 'house' is further emphasized by the quote from Psalm 118:22 in 2:7 ('the very head of the corner', *eis kephalēn gōnias*). The apostles and prophets are not mentioned as foundational to the new Temple but *the word of gospel* is clearly the means by which people are brought to the living Christ and made part of his 'spiritual house' (note the theology of the word in 1:22–25 and compare 2:8, *tō logō apeithountes*).

The role of the Holy Spirit in forming and indwelling this Temple is not articulated as it is in the Pauline texts. However, Peter's use of the phrase 'spiritual house' (*oikos pneumatikos*), following his programmatic statement about the work of the Holy Spirit in 1:2, allows us to affirm the Spirit's participation in the whole process. 'Sanctified by the Spirit' (1:2, *en hagiasmō pneumatos*) refers to a consecration 'wrought by the Spirit of God'.[35] It is emphatically a divine act and an aspect of Christian initiation. Attaching believers to the Father by faith, the Spirit makes them 'aliens and exiles' (1:2; 2:11), not really at home in the world where they live. Their true home is the inheritance that is 'imperishable, undefiled, and unfading', made possible by the resurrection of Jesus Christ from the dead (1:3–4). Israel was consecrated to God as a holy nation by the Exodus redemption from slavery in Egypt (Exod. 19:1–6). That status is now given to people of any race (1 Pet. 2:4–10), who are ransomed from a futile way of life 'with the precious blood of Christ' and have their faith and hope set on God because of the resurrection of his Son (1:18–21).

3.2 The priestly vocation of the people of God

Against Elliott and those who argue that *oikos pneumatikos* is simply a familial image here ('household'),[36] syntactically it appears to be defined by *hierateuma hagion*. It is a house 'for a holy priesthood' and is thus envisaged as a spiritual Temple. The purpose and function of that holy priesthood is 'to offer spiritual sacrifices acceptable to God through Jesus Christ'. The implied theology is that people need to be ransomed from sin and brought to new life in Christ before they can

---

[35] Michaels, *1 Peter*, p. 11. The genitive is subjective, as in 2 Thessalonians 2:13, rather than objective, which would make it a reference to 'the sanctification of (our) spirit'. Since the Gospel was brought to Peter's readers in association with or 'by the Holy Spirit' (1:12), the implication is that the consecration of people to God in Christ is brought about by the Spirit-empowered proclamation of the Gospel.

[36] Cf. J. H. Elliott, *The Elect and the Holy: An Exegetical Examination of 1 Peter 2:4–10 and the Phrase βασίλειον ἱεράτευμα* (Brill: Leiden, 1966), pp. 157–9. Note the literature cited in this connection by Davids, *The First Epistle of Peter*, p. 86, n. 21, and the critique by Michaels, *1 Peter*, pp. 100–1.

offer to God the 'worship' or service that pleases him (cf. Rom. 12:1; Heb. 9:13–14; 12:28–29; 13:15–16). With the 'spiritual house' imagery, Peter indicates that there is a corporate dimension to being a Christian and a corporate responsibility to offer the spiritual sacrifices that please God.

The notion of a 'holy priesthood' recalls Peter's foundational statement about sanctification by the Spirit, 'to be obedient to Jesus Christ and to be sprinkled by his blood' (1:2, *eis hupakoēn kai rhantismon haimatos Iēsou Christou*). It also recalls the use of Leviticus 19:2 in 1:15–16, where a relationship with the Holy One is said to demand holiness 'in all your conduct' (*en pasē anastrophē*). The 'spiritual sacrifices' offered by this 'holy priesthood' must include the whole pattern of obedient lifestyle set out in the central section of the letter (2:11–4:19). However, when the priesthood of this 'holy nation' is mentioned again in 2:9, its function is to 'proclaim the mighty acts of him who called you out of darkness into his marvellous light'. This could refer to praise offered to God corporately or to evangelistic proclamation in one form or another (cf. 3:15–16). Spiritual sacrifices must include all of the above, social conduct, praise and evangelism.

As in the Pauline letters, Temple imagery is used with related terminology in 1 Peter to emphasize the *holiness of the Christian community*. The focus is less on the divine indwelling in 1 Peter and more on the practical implications of that holy status. Holiness or sanctification is made possible by God's initiative, calling and enabling a people to come to Christ as the 'cornerstone', by the preaching of the gospel in the power of the Holy Spirit. The image of 'a spiritual house for a holy priesthood' is used as part of the challenge to realize holiness in the relationships and responsibilities of everyday life.

Ephesians makes much of the fact that Jews and Gentiles together constitute the new Temple, with the associated theology of a new humanity created in Christ. Peter lacks this emphasis, though 2:9–10 applies the covenantal language of Exodus 19:6, Isaiah 43:20–21 and Hosea 1:6, 9–10 and 2:23 to people who may well have been predominantly Gentile in background. As the 'spiritual house' of the eschatological era, they are now the race chosen and redeemed by God, a holy nation because of their relationship with the Holy One of Israel, and a priesthood belonging to God the King.

4. CONCLUSION

Ephesians and 1 Peter are significant contributors to the New Testament development of Temple theology from Old Testament roots. These documents show similarities with other passages highlighting the eschatological significance of new Temple imagery. Ecclesiologically, however, they present a heavenly and universal perspective, rather than a local, congregational focus. Christology is clearly central to both passages, providing a link with the teaching of Jesus about the new Temple. Ethically, the Temple imagery has force via the holiness motif, though 1 Peter is more outward looking than Ephesians in drawing out the lifestyle implications of this teaching.

13

THE TEMPLE IN HEBREWS

Is It There?

STEVE MOTYER

The presence or absence of the Temple in Hebrews is one of the most intriguing and significant exegetical and historical puzzles posed by the letter. As in the book of Revelation (with which Hebrews has much in common) there is great interest in the *furnishings and ceremonies* of both Temple and Tabernacle: in both books we meet the altar of incense (Heb. 9:4; Rev. 8:3), the ark of the covenant (Heb. 9:4; Rev. 11:19), the menorah (Heb. 9:2; Rev. 1:20, etc.), the sprinkling with blood (Heb. 9:19; 12:24; Rev. 19:13), the altar of sacrifice (Heb. 7:13; Rev. 14:18), the daily sacrifice (Heb. 10:11; Rev. 8:3) and possibly the Levitical orders (Heb. 7:11; Rev. 4:4 – if the number twenty-four, applied to the elders, refers to the number of the priestly orders). In addition, Revelation refers to the bronze Sea (Rev. 4:6), the pillars (3:12) and the Temple doors (4:1; 11:19), while Hebrews refers also to the veil (Heb. 6:19, etc.), the cherubim and the mercy seat (9:5), the red heifer (9:13) and of course the high priest and Day of Atonement. In both books the reality of the *heavenly* Temple, matching the earthly one, is crucial to their understanding of God and of atonement. Both books reach a climax in which 'Temple Mount' and Zion symbolism is vividly developed in a 'new creation' context (Heb. 12:22–29; Rev. 21:1 – 22:5). Both books refer of course to the 'Tabernacle' (*skēnē* – nine times in Hebrews, three in Revelation), a term which is used in Hebrews both of the earthly sanctuary and its heavenly counterpart (in Revelation, only of the heavenly: e.g. Heb. 8:2, 5; Rev. 15:5).

But whereas the word *naos* (temple, sanctuary) is used sixteen times in Revelation, it does not appear at all in Hebrews. This remarkable statistic must be carefully weighed. There is substantial semantic overlap between *naos* (temple) and *skēnē* (tabernacle), as illustrated by Revelation 15:5: 'the temple of the tabernacle of witness (*ho naos tes skēnēs …*) was opened in heaven'. When this is added to the interest in furniture, it is hard to avoid the conclusion that the avoidance of the word temple (*naos*) is deliberate in Hebrews:

which of course leads us to ask why this avoidance was deemed important by the author.[1]

It makes no sense to suggest, with Ellingworth, that the author uses
skēnē rather than *naos* because he has no 'interest in the later permanent temple'.[2] So widespread was the belief in the type–antitype relationship between the heavenly and earthly sanctuaries – as Attridge
shows in his excursus on the subject[3] – that it is quite impossible that
Hebrews could write about the heavenly sanctuary without connoting
the earthly, even if the Jerusalem Temple had been destroyed by the
time of writing. In this sense, therefore, the Temple certainly *is* there
in Hebrews. Any Jewish or Jewish Christian readers familiar with this
traditional Temple ideology would recognize its use in Hebrews and
would therefore hear a reference to the sanctuary in Jerusalem. Unless
we can believe that the author was indifferent to this inevitable reading,
we must allow that he had 'an interest' in the Temple.

Nor will it do to suggest, with Lindars, that the author avoids reference to the Temple and Temple practice because he wants to prove
from the Law (rather than from contemporary Jewish practice) that Jesus
passes the test of what constitutes true atonement.[4] This is, of course,
true. In particular the author wants to maintain that Jesus realizes the
prophetic expectation of the New Covenant. But *polemical implications*
are clearly drawn from this argument, for instance in Hebrews 8:13.
For the author, this exercise in the rereading of Scripture is undertaken
for *contemporary* reasons, not just as an exercise in abstract biblical
theology. Since the Temple was the primary 'sacred space' for Jews in
the first century, both before and after AD 70, why does Hebrews avoid
specific reference to it?[5]

So let us ask again: why is the Temple *not* explicitly present in
Hebrews, not even through use of the term *naos*, let alone through
direct reference to Jerusalem or to the pilgrim festivals? Lindars, I

---

[1] The alternative term *hieron* – the usual term for the Temple in the Gospels and Acts
– also does not appear in Hebrews. This term more naturally refers to the whole Temple
complex, whereas *naos* denotes the central sanctuary (cf. Luke 1:8–10). Hebrews, however, typically uses 'the holy places' (*ta hagia*) for the central sanctuary, and 'the tent' (
skēnē) for the whole thing.

[2] P. Ellingworth, *The Epistle to the Hebrews* (Grand Rapids/Carlisle: Eerdmans/Paternoster,
1993), p. 401; cf. p. 710, 'The author shows little interest in the contemporary Jerusalem
cultus.'

[3] H. Attridge, *The Epistle to the Hebrews* (Philadelphia: Fortress Press, 1989), pp. 222–4.

[4] B. Lindars, 'The Rhetorical Structure of Hebrews', *NTS* 35 (1989), pp. 382–406 (see pp.
395, 403).

[5] Close to the view of Lindars is Marie Isaacs, *Sacred Space: An Approach to the Theology of
the Epistle to the Hebrews* (JSNTSupp 73; Sheffield: Sheffield Academic Press, 1992). She
suggests that the author writes after the destruction of the Temple, in order to assure
Christian Jews that they have not lost their 'sacred space': it has been relocated in Jesus.
So they 'should not hanker after the lost Jerusalem' (p. 67). But this makes it all the more
puzzling, that there is no specific reference to the Temple or to its loss. It also sidelines the
significance of the paraenetic sections.

believe, suggests the right line of approach by underlining the *rhetoric* of the letter. Though the details of his reconstruction may be questioned,[6] his overall contention that the author of Hebrews engages in a ticklish task of persuasion, attempting to *influence* the readers to undertake an unpopular course of action, is widely accepted.[7] But the implications of this for the (non-)use of Temple language in Hebrews have not been realized or explored, so far as I am aware.[8]

We can begin to develop our argument by asking: What would have been the rhetorical impact if Hebrews had actually employed direct references to the Temple and Temple practices in the places where we can see clear allusions hidden under *indirect* language? Interestingly such places largely appear in the later chapters of the letter, a fact to which we will give some attention later. We can mention:

(i) 8:13. Rather than calling the *Old Covenant* 'obsolete' the author could have applied this term to the *earthly sanctuary* to which he referred in 8:5.[9]

(ii) 9:1–10:18. Throughout this passage, the author could have referred to the Jerusalem Temple (rather than to the Tabernacle), making it clear that its rituals cannot cleanse the conscience (9:9; 10:1–2), and that God is not pleased with its sacrifices (10:6) which are fundamentally ineffective (10:11).

(iii) 12:18–24. Here the author could have made clear the connections of the two mountains respectively with Old Covenant worship (Sinai) and with New Covenant worship (Zion): towards the former God is a fearful Judge, but the latter gives immediate access to him and to all the festal joy of heaven.

---

[6] Both in 'The Rhetorical Structure of Hebrews' (pp. 385–90) and in his *The Theology of the Letter to the Hebrews* (Cambridge: Cambridge University Press, 1991), pp. 6–15, he bases his reconstruction on a reading of Hebrews 13 which finds implications there about the readers' situation which few others have found.

[7] Guthrie's view that the *paraenetic* sections of Hebrews are central to its thrust and structure is now generally agreed: George H. Guthrie, *The Structure of Hebrews: A Text-Linguistic Analysis* (NovTSupp 73; Leiden: Brill, 1994).

[8] Lindars himself treats the lack of allusion to the cultus as an uncomplicated 'fact' from which historical-critical conclusions can be drawn: namely, that Hebrews should probably be dated before the destruction of the Temple ('The Rhetorical Structure of Hebrews', p. 402), and the readers should probably be located somewhere in the diaspora (ibid., p. 403). Rissi makes the opposite deductions from the same fact: Temple and cult are not mentioned because they have long since ceased to exist: M. Rissi, *Die Theologie des Hebräerbriefs* (WUNT 41; Tübingen: Mohr, 1987), p. 12.

[9] Though 'obsolete' is a usual translation in 8:13 (NIV, REB, NRSV; Lane; Koester), I suggest that it is too strong. In biblical Greek the verb used here, *palaioun*, has a strong connection with the 'wearing out' of garments (illustrated in Heb. 1:11). Linked to *gēraskein*, 'grow old', it is the notion of *ageing*, rather than of *obsolescence*, which is uppermost in the author's mind. I suggest: 'In speaking of a new covenant, God treated the first as worn out; and that which is wearing out and ageing is close to extinction.'

(iv) 13:10–16. Here the author could have said *directly* that those who seek to gain access to God through the Jerusalem Temple and through the festivals get nowhere near him, and then could have directly urged his readers to leave the synagogue and replace literal sacrifices with the 'good works' which really *do* please God. Instead he refers allusively to 'an altar' and to 'foods' and to following Jesus 'outside the camp'.

If we rewrote these passages in the ways suggested, the effect would be clear. Hebrews would mount a massive ideological assault on the Jerusalem Temple and cultus. It would become a *fierce* attack, going beyond anything else in the New Testament, severing the link between the heavenly and earthly temples, denying the effectiveness and even the divine origin of the earthly cult, and replacing it wholesale with the worship of Jesus who alone atones for sin and gives access to God.

When Stephen was *perceived* to attack the Temple and cult in this way (Acts 6:13–14), a violent reaction resulted. Stephen's speech is then a model of allusiveness containing, as William Manson maintained, many contacts with ideas in Hebrews[10] until he bursts out in vivid accusation at the end (Acts 7:51–53). Obviously Stephen's situation, as reflected in Acts, was very different from that of the author to the Hebrews. But Stephen's *obvious* (or so it seemed) hostility to the Temple and the cult evoked a very violent response. The argument of this paper is that the author of Hebrews, facing the same ticklish nexus of issues, avoids deliberate reference to the Temple and proceeds cautiously and slowly, basing his argument solidly on Scripture, and allowing the implications to appear gradually and unobtrusively, but yet clearly. A full-frontal assault on Temple and cult would be wholly counter-productive.

It is beyond the scope of this paper to engage with the debate about the precise situation of the addressees. However, I believe that a careful analysis of the author's *rhetoric* in dealing with this issue of the Temple will further support the traditional view that the letter is addressed to a group of Jewish Christians, perhaps including Gentile proselytes, who are being tempted to relapse into Judaism. The recent new favour bestowed on the view that the letter was addressed to *Gentile* Christians or to 'Christians generally' irrespective of ethnic background[11] leaves us with no answer to the question with which we concern ourselves

---

[10] W. Manson, *The Epistle to the Hebrews: An Historical and Theological Reconsideration* (London: Hodder, 1951).

[11] So, e.g., H. F. Weiß, *Der Brief an die Hebräer* (Göttingen: Vandenhoeck & Ruprecht, 1991), pp. 71–2; E. Gräßer, *An die Hebräer* (EKK XVII/1; Braunschweig/Neukirchen: Benziger/Neukirchener Verlag, 1990), pp. 24–6; David A. deSilva, *Perseverance in Gratitude: A Socio-Rhetorical Commentary on the Epistle 'to the Hebrews'* (Grand Rapids: Eerdmans, 2000), pp. 2–7.

here. Why should the author avoid direct reference to the Temple, for such an audience?

Elsewhere I have argued that the target readership is a messianic group who have not left their synagogue and have simply added messianic faith to their Judaism (probably through the experience of 'signs and wonders' and other 'powers of the coming age').[12] In addition to the Sabbath synagogue meetings, they have been meeting as a messianic group, probably on the first day of the week (cf. 10:25). But now – like the Jewish Christians in Jerusalem in Acts 21, forced to take sides over Paul – the position of these messianists has for some reason become very uncomfortable, and some of them are being tempted to abandon their Jesus-messianism and to rest content (as before) with being 'just' Jews.

This is the situation tackled by the author of Hebrews, I suggest. Lindars' version of the 'relapse' theory, now also held by Robert Gordon and Richard Nelson,[13] requires only that the author should bolster the readers' fidelity to the beliefs which took them *out of* the synagogue – and so the *focus* of the letter's argument, on this view, lies in chapters 10–12, the exhortation to 'faith'.[14] However, the revised version of the 'relapse' theory, which I presuppose in this paper, allows the focus of the argument to rest in the letter's Christology and soteriology, and makes its rhetorical aim *not* just the bolstering of 'faith' but more particularly *the creation of the conviction, not already held by the readers, that salvation is only to be found in Jesus Christ and can no longer be found in the synagogue.* So the 'difficult and delicate' rhetorical task[15] is actually to present a view of Jesus Christ in far 'higher' terms than those which the readers currently hold, and to present also a series of implications which will be most uncongenial to the readership. We can well imagine the task if – for the sake of argument – we picture the author in Jerusalem, trying to convince the 'thousands of believers among the Jews ... all zealots for the law' (Acts 21:20) that the Temple is now redundant, the sacrifices useless, the Old Covenant senescent, and Jesus the *only* high priest appointed by God.[16]

In tackling this difficult task, the author's strategy is to avoid spelling out directly the implications of his Christology, and instead to conduct the argument wholly in *scriptural* terms, using language which

---

[12] Paper to the Research Seminar at London Bible College, November 2000, currently under revision for publication.
[13] Robert P. Gordon, *Hebrews* (Sheffield: Sheffield Academic Press, 2000), pp. 20–1; Richard D. Nelson, *Raising Up a Faithful Priest: Community and Priesthood in Biblical Theology* (Louisville: Westminster/John Knox, 1993), p. 142.
[14] So explicitly Lindars, 'The Rhetorical Structure of Hebrews', p. 406.
[15] Lindars' description, ibid., p. 390.
[16] Although offered here for the sake of argument, I am increasingly drawn to the view that Jerusalem offers the 'best bet' for the readers' location.

distances his argument from the precise situation he addresses, while making his meaning clear for all who follow his presentation carefully, and sometimes using imagery which *imaginatively evokes* the response he wants to see in his readers. We must now look more closely at the letter, to observe this strategy in operation. Our technique will be to look for places where the Temple appears in disguise, lurking under the surface as an implicit referent within the wider argument – as in the four places listed above. A study of the author's whole rhetorical strategy lies beyond our scope, but the implied reference to the Temple is an important element within it, and well illustrates his allusive technique. We will pick out seven passages where our thesis can be illustrated.

(i) 3:1–6

The term 'house' here clearly has multiple meanings, and in investigating its rhetoric we need to be alert to the 'intertextual echoes' which it evokes, as well as to the direct quotation of Numbers 12:7 from which it is drawn. It is a 'heavily laden symbol', as Attridge observes.[17] In Numbers the 'house' within which Moses is a 'servant' is already ambiguous: 'he is entrusted with all my house' employs a household analogy, imagining Moses as the senior plenipotentiary in the 'household' of God himself. Is *Israel* God's household? The link with the parallel expression 'house of Israel' would suggest so.[18] This 'people' focus of the term is drawn out in verse 6, 'we are his house, if we hold fast ...' But other groups could also be called 'house of ...', and Peter Leithart suggests that the notion of the *priestly* house is uppermost in the author's mind here, along the lines of 1 Samuel 2:35.[19] He presses his case for the prominence of this 'priestly' house too far, I believe, but at the level of intertextual echo we must surely bear in mind that 'the house of Levi'[20] was the one to which Moses (and Aaron) belonged.[21]

But supremely the parenthetical verse 4, with its reference to God as 'the builder of all things', connotes the idea of the whole universe as God's 'house'. 'Here the author exploits the cosmic metaphorical value

---

[17] Attridge, *The Epistle to the Hebrews*, p. 109.

[18] Leviticus 10:6; Numbers 20:29, etc. The expression 'house of Israel' occurs 125 times in LXX.

[19] Peter J. Leithart, 'Womb of the World: Baptism and the Priesthood of the New Covenant in Hebrews 10.19–22,' *JSNT* 78 (2000), pp. 49–65 (here p. 60).

[20] Numbers 17:8 (LXX 17:23).

[21] Cf. Wisdom 18:20–25, where significance is found in the fact that Aaron's robes, when he stood between the living and the dead (Num. 16:48; LXX 17:13), had 'the whole world' engraved on them (18:24). Aaron is able to make atonement because he represents the creatorial power of God himself.

of the term "house" in extending his analogy,' comments Attridge.[22] We cannot but be reminded of the prologue (1:1–4), with its presentation of the Son as the 'heir of all things, through whom he also created the worlds' (1:2, NRSV). This is the biggest sense in which Jesus is 'over God's house as a son' (3:6) – as the agent through whom God made his 'house', who now sustains it by his powerful word (1:3).

So here, in a very subtle way, the notion of *the position of Jesus in the heavenly Temple* is introduced, and our membership of God's 'house' is implicitly linked to perseverance *with him*. The exhortation to perseverance which follows, arising out of Psalm 95, carries forward that association of membership in God's 'house' (people, Temple, heavenly dwelling) with faith in Jesus. *He* is the means of entering God's 'rest'.[23]

(ii) 4:14; 6:19–20

Hebrews frequently introduces key ideas in an off-the-cuff, low-key manner ahead of their main treatment in the argument. Jesus' high priesthood first appears in 2:17, 3:1, then disappears. It 'pops up' again in 4:14, where the full treatment of this theme begins. In turn the idea of Jesus' *entry as 'high priest' into the heavenly Temple* is mentioned first in 4:14 and 6:19ff., anticipating 9:11 – 10:18, and likewise the 'veil' first appears in 6:19, anticipating the fuller treatment in 9:3ff.

This is an 'advance warning' technique aimed at familiarizing the readers with ideas which could become a source of objection later. It is highly significant that the first appearances of the Temple in Hebrews are in the guise of the *heavenly* Temple, in which Jesus is cast as high priest. But even more significant is the subtle involvement of 'the veil' in 6:19. The term used here, *katapetasma*, is the usual word for the inner veil of the Temple or Tabernacle.[24] It is thus a thoroughly *earthly* curtain. Although in some texts the heavenly sanctuary is represented as having two parts, like the earthly,[25] there is no reference to a veil between the two parts. Almost certainly, Hebrews 6:19–20 is drawing on a tradition in which the inner sanctuary of the earthly Temple, the 'most holy place', was taken to represent heaven – a natural inference from belief

---

[22] Attridge, *The Epistle to the Hebrews*, p. 110. Philo is particularly fond of this metaphor: e.g. *De Sobr.* 63, *De Post.* 5, *De Plant.* 50. In this last place Philo himself plays on the overlap in meaning between 'house' and 'temple,' calling the world a 'sanctuary' (*hagiasma*), an 'outshining of holiness' (*hagion apaugasma*).

[23] The author handles the idea of 'the rest' in a similar way: Jesus subtly moves to the centre. Some readers might be familiar with the use of this metaphor which we encounter in *Joseph & Aseneth* 8:9, 15:7 and 22:13, where 'rest' signals 'a place in heaven prepared for the saved' (C. Burchard in J. H. Charlesworth [ed.], *The Old Testament Pseudepigrapha* [vol. 2; London: Darton, Longman & Todd, 1985], pp. 213ff.

[24] E.g. Exodus 26:31–35; Leviticus 16:2; 2 Chronicles 3:14; Mark 15:38; Josephus, *War* V:219; *Ant.* VIII:75; Philo, *Moses* II:101; cf. *Gig.* 53–54.

[25] E.g. 1 Enoch 14:9–25; *T. Levi* 3:4–8.

in the presence of God within that space. Rephrasing 'pass through the heavens' (4:14) as 'enter within the veil' (6:19), therefore, brings Jesus by association into close relationship with the *earthly* Temple. He has *truly* done what the high priest, on the Day of Atonement, only does symbolically: he has entered the heavenly sanctuary itself.

Gordon points out how extraordinary, in this context, is the description of Jesus as 'our forerunner' (6:20). The high priest was not the first of a crowd to enter. Nothing in the Old Testament cult prepares us for this idea – adumbrated here, to be developed in 10:19ff. – that the entry of *this* high priest paves the way for others.[26]

The author's argument here clearly rests upon the conviction of the ascension of Jesus into heaven, shared by him and his readers. But he gives that belief a 'Temple' spin, connecting it with their belief in heaven as a Temple; and by using the very earthly word *katapetasma* he anticipates his later polemic against Temple and cult.

(iii) 7:13

The punchline of the author's 'Melchizedek' argument has just appeared, in 7:11. As he draws out the implications of the extraordinary presence, within the Old Testament, of an *alternative* priesthood, the author points out that this means a priesthood from a tribe 'from which no one has ever approached the altar'.[27] The reference here, of course, is to the altar of sacrifice in the main court of the Temple, and this is what the readers would hear. So the author is presenting them with a priesthood which operates *without involvement with* the Jerusalem Temple, resting upon a scriptural text (Ps. 110) which Christians generally and readily applied to Jesus.

We do not know what the term 'Melchizedek priesthood' might have meant to the readers. We can only speculate, prompted by texts like 11QMelch and 2 Enoch 71–72, in which Melchizedek is an eschatological figure bringing final salvation and judgement. It is natural to connect these texts with those in which an expectation of an eschatological priest is developed, though without reference to 'Melchizedek'.[28] In none of these priestly or Melchizedek texts is any specific link made with the Jerusalem Temple or cult, although it would be reasonable

---

[26] Gordon, *Hebrews*, p. 79.

[27] The use of the perfect tense here – *proseschēken* – is a subtle indication that the Temple is still standing at the time of writing. If the Temple were no more, we would certainly expect the aorist. So far as I am aware, the significance of this for the date of Hebrews has not been explored. Unfortunately, the aorist (*proseschen*) is quite a strong variant here (P46 A C 33 81 1739), though firmly rejected by Metzger: B. M. Metzger, *A Textual Commentary on the Greek New Testament* (London/New York: United Bible Societies, 1971), p. 667.

[28] E.g. *T. Levi* 18:1–14; and the Qumran texts expecting the 'Messiah of Aaron' or the eschatological priestly instructor or war leader: 1QS 9:11; CD 6:11; 1QM 15:4; 16:14.

to suppose that the expectation was that this eschatological priest–messiah would exercise his rule from Jerusalem.

Hebrews 7:13, on the other hand, specifically distances the Melchizedek-priest from the Jerusalem cult, because he has 'passed into the heavens'. He is 'unlike the other high priests' (7:26), because he has offered a single, unrepeatable sacrifice: 'this he did once for all when he offered himself' (7:27). The author rests his argument very firmly on the words of Psalm 110:4, in order to give scriptural support to this idea of a non-Jerusalem, 'Melchizedek' high priesthood.[29]

If the readers shared this expectation of a priestly messiah, then in Hebrews 7 the author subtly decouples this expectation from Jerusalem.

(iv) 8:1–6; 8:11

8:1–6 can claim to contain the heart of the letter's message, beginning as it does: 'Now the main point in what we are saying is this ...' (NRSV). 'Main point' (*kephalaion*) is a literary or rhetorical term, denoting the essence or chief point(s) of a whole speech or work. Here, in a nutshell, the author spells out his contention about Jesus – a contention which he will then unpack in 8:7 – 10:18.

Having decoupled Jesus' priesthood from Jerusalem, the author now decouples the heavenly from the earthly sanctuary. By deliberately using the word 'tabernacle' (*skēnē*), and by quoting Exodus 25:40, he distances the *impact* of his contention from the present. But its *relevance* for the present is clear, for he continues to focus his argument on Jesus. If Jesus is a high priest, he says, he must have somewhere to minister. He cannot minister in the earthly Tabernacle, because that is already fully stocked with priests. In any case the earthly Tabernacle is only 'a sketch and shadow' of the heavenly one: and *that* is where Jesus ministers, seated at God's right hand as Son and priest, as Psalm 110 says.

So here is one huge respect in which the earthly sanctuary is *unlike* the heavenly: *bypassing* the earthly, this high priest has entered heaven, there to exercise 'a massively different ministry' (*diaphorōtera leitourgia*, 8:6). His ministry has no counterpart on earth, because he mediates and 'enacts' a 'greater' covenant and promises.[30]

To underline this difference, the author quotes Jeremiah 31:31–34, a text which then forms the basis of the discussion as far as 10:18. For

---

[29] Both Lindars ('The Rhetorical Structure of Hebrews', pp. 395ff.) and Isaacs (*Sacred Space*, p. 150) suggest that Psalm 110:4 is the source of the author's presentation of Jesus as high priest. It was our author who made the 'brilliant and original observation' (Lindars) that verse 4, as well as verse 1, could be treated messianically.

[30] The Greek *kreittōn* is better represented by English 'greater' than 'better': the focus of the idea falls on the *power* and *effectiveness* of the ministry and covenant instituted by Jesus. The author will illustrate his point from Jeremiah 31: the covenant promised there is *greater than* the Mosaic, because it will be *effective*.

our purposes, the vital thing is to note the missing priesthood in 8:11. The absence of *teachers* under the 'New' Covenant – because people of all types 'know me' through the implantation of the Law (8:10) – points to the absence of *priests*, who were the appointed teachers of Israel under the 'Old' Covenant. New 'legal arrangements' are now in place – the New Covenant 'has been enacted' (*nenomothetētai*) through Jesus (8:6): this word points not just to a new *establishment*, but also to the instruction or propagation which the new arrangement requires – as we can see in 7:11. Such instruction is to be *implanted*, apparently: Jeremiah (and certainly the author of Hebrews!) envisages no continuing teaching role for priests.[31]

We see what this means for the author in 10:15–18, where he returns to Jeremiah 31 and repeats his quotation of verses 33–34. The exegetical problem posed here is discussed in the footnote below, where a case is made for the view that, for our author, the testimony of the Holy Spirit *is* the tangible experience of inner renewal and forgiveness of sin. 10:18 appeals to the experience of the readers: if you have experienced the forgiveness of sins through Jesus Christ, what further need for sacrifice is there?[32]

Progressively, therefore, the Temple and its 'service' are more and more downgraded, without a direct *assault* being mounted.

---

[31] This implication is recognized by some commentators on Jeremiah (e.g. J. A. Thompson, *The Book of Jeremiah* [Grand Rapids: Eerdmans, 1980], p. 581), but not by any of the current major commentaries on Hebrews.

[32] The exegetical puzzle in 10:15 is to determine exactly what is the 'testimony' of the Holy Spirit. For the phrase with which the author introduces the re-quotation of Jeremiah 31:33–34, 'for after saying …', turns at least part of the quotation into a subordinate clause and makes us expect a main verb which, at first sight, never appears. Most translations follow (in effect, if not actually) the ancient scribe who inserted a gloss at the beginning of verse 17, 'he later says' (*husteron legei*, with variants), thus providing a main verb and placing the accent on the last part of the quotation ('I will remember their sins and their lawless deeds no more'), so that the Holy Spirit becomes the speaker throughout. On this view, therefore, the Spirit's testimony is identified with the quotation. However, the *Jerusalem Bible* follows the more sensible route of finding the main verb and subject in 'says the Lord' within the quotation (also Weiß, *Der Brief an die Hebräer*, pp. 515ff.; H. Hegermann, *Der Brief an die Hebräer* (THKNT 16; Berlin: Evangelische Verlagsanstalt, 1988), pp. 200ff.). This produces a translation like the following: 'For after saying, "This is the covenant I will make with them after those days", the Lord then says, "I will put my laws in their hearts … and will remember their sins … no more."' This has the effect of *not* identifying the testimony of the Spirit (10:15a) with the words of the quotation (contra Weiß and Hegermann, ibid.), because the subject of the sentence is actually 'the Lord'. Rather, these scriptural words *identify as prophesied* the testimony of the Spirit which is actually the *two-part experience* here described: the writing of the law on the heart, and the forgiveness of sin. So the testimony of the Spirit *is* the cleansing of the conscience, impossible under the old sacrificial system (9:9; 10:1–4), but achieved by the blood of Christ (9:14). So, for our author, the cleansing of the conscience is clearly a tangible experience of renewal, thus constituting an argument to which he can appeal to prove that *Jesus*, and not the cult, 'perfects those who are being sanctified' (10:14).

(v) 9:1–14

This is one of the passages where the author seems to be so taken up with the Tabernacle, its furnishings and ceremonies that it is easy to conclude (as many do) that he has no interest in the Temple. But once again, we must be sensitive to the *rhetoric* of the passage. The author deliberately (I believe) *highlights* the differences between the Tabernacle and the Jerusalem Temple. First, he relocates the altar of incense *inside* the holy of holies (behind the second curtain). In the Jerusalem Temple, of course, the altar of incense stood in the holy place, outside the veil. In placing it behind the veil, the author is probably influenced by a ground plan derived from Leviticus 16, where the incense is brought into the holy of holies by the high priest on the Day of Atonement, and is placed 'on the fire before the LORD, that the cloud of the incense may cover the mercy-seat' (Lev. 16:13). If this is so, then it underlines the author's deliberate desire to *distance* his description from the arrangements in the Jerusalem Temple.

Secondly, he emphasizes the furnishings within the holy of holies, picking out those things which were specific to the *original* Tabernacle: the ark, the urn containing the manna, Aaron's rod, the tablets of the Law, the mercy-seat and the cherubim. Both he and his readers will certainly have known that the holy of holies in the Jerusalem sanctuary contained nothing (cf. Josephus, *War* V:219). Rhetorically, this implicitly underlines for the readers the reality of change. Though divinely ordained and prescribed, all these things are no longer there. Now, the author wants the readers to embrace a much bigger change, inspired by Jeremiah's vision of a *New* Covenant which transcends the earthly sanctuary altogether.

In order to make this point the author does two things. First, in 9:8–10 he *appeals to the Holy Spirit* as his authority for an interpretation of the Tabernacle. This appeal is significant, in view of the evidence which points to the 'charismatic' nature of the readers' messianism. The references to 'signs and wonders, various powers and distributions of the Holy Spirit' in 2:4, and to being 'partakers of the Holy Spirit, tasting the good word of God and the powers of the age to come' in 6:4–5, suggest that *experience of the Spirit* was what convinced these Jews to believe in Jesus. They will have been used to revelations through the Spirit. This may be implied by the author's reference to their first leaders 'who spoke the word of God to you' (13:7). The readers are likely to take seriously any claim to speak with the voice of the Spirit.

And so, on the authority of the Spirit, the author suggests that the Tabernacle was a 'parable for the present time' (9:9) symbolizing *lack of* access to God (9:8) and surrounded by regulations that underline our *fleshly* nature and our need of 'a time of restoration' (9:10). This dramatic rereading of the Tabernacle follows from Jeremiah 31, which could easily be read as a prophecy of the 'time of restoration' indicated by the Spirit.[33] The fact that the high priest enters the holy of holies only once a year, on the Day of Atonement, is *the* factor in common between Tabernacle and Temple. The readers know this. The 'parable for the present time', therefore, is suggested to them as a way of understanding the Jerusalem Temple in which this limitation of access is still the case.

Secondly, in 9:11–14 the author presents *Jesus* as having broken the barrier symbolized by the Tabernacle/Temple, 'entering once for all into the Holy Place' through the offering of his own blood. Here it is not so much a matter of *bypassing* the earthly sanctuary (as in 8:1–6) as of *removing the obstacle* posed by it. It no longer forms a barrier, reminding us of our fleshliness, because Jesus has won an 'eternal redemption' which can truly 'purify our conscience'.

By thus avoiding direct reference to the Temple, the author is able not only to 'sweeten the pill', but also to use the Tabernacle as a parable, following the process, doubtless familiar to the readers, in which the Holy Spirit suggests a new reading of an old passage in the light of Christ.

(vi) 10:11–14, 19–25

10:11 is the closest the author comes to a direct attack on the Temple. But he is very careful to link this to Psalm 40:7–9, just quoted (10:5–7). Psalm 40 represents a string of texts, generally prophetic, in which the sacrificial system is questioned (cf. Isa. 1:12–15; Amos 5:21–25; Mic. 6:6–8). There are no similar scriptural passages in which the *status of the Temple* is challenged – although interestingly we meet in 2 Baruch 4:2–6 the view that the *heavenly* Temple was the one that God was really talking about when he promised inviolability to Zion. However, texts which question the atoning efficacy of the sacrifices have clear implications for the system of ministry within which they take place. 10:11 certainly makes more sense if the Temple is still standing at the time of writing. If it had been destroyed, we might expect an argument like that in 2 Baruch, which of course was prompted by the destruction of the Temple. Robert Gordon suggests that the author imposes an extraordinary 'self-denying ordinance' upon himself if the destruction of the Temple has indeed taken place, for a mention of it would be so germane to his argument.[34]

But whether the Temple is still standing or not, the author clearly wants his readers to look *at* the sacrificial system through the spectacles of Psalm 40:7–9, finding reference there to a *new* will of God,

---

[33] The word 'restoration' (*diorthōsis*) is a *hapax legomenon* here in the Greek Bible, but the cognate verb *diorthoun* is used in several prophetic and other contexts describing eschatological restoration: Isaiah 16:5; 62:7; Jeremiah 7:3–7; 2 Samuel 7:13, 16; 1 Chronicles 17:12, 14, 24; 22:10; 2 Maccabees 2:22; 5:20; Wisdom 9:17–18.

[34] Gordon, *Hebrews*, pp. 32–3.

not for sacrifices but for the full-orbed obedience of the Son who *truly* sanctifies us through the offering of the 'body' God prepared for him (10:10).

This leads into the exhortation in 10:19–25, in which Temple imagery abounds but once again is relocated on to Jesus and is thus stretched to breaking point. *His flesh* is the 'veil' through which *we* may enter the holy place. The high priest is no longer the only entrant. The privilege thus opened to 'us' is reflected in the dramatic use of *ordination language* in 10:14 and 10:22, drawn from Exodus 29:4 and Leviticus 16:4: 'we' have been appointed to the priesthood ourselves, and stand on the threshold of the holy place, awaiting our turn to enter. The power of this imagery is very considerable, and doubtless the author hoped that the readers would be gripped by it! – and inspired to maintain the *messianic* worship (10:25) in which this sense of standing on the threshold of heaven, experiencing its powers, is realized.

(vii) 13:13–14

Finally we glance at two verses in the concluding paragraph of the letter. The wider paragraph faces us with some tricky exegesis, but for our purposes it is sufficient to note the way in which the author's imagery at a subliminal level reinforces the rhetorical thrust of the letter. He urges the readers to 'go out to him, outside the camp, bearing his reproach' (13:13). The imagery, once again, is drawn from the Day of Atonement, imaginatively connected to the location of the crucifixion outside Jerusalem. So at one level the exhortation to 'go out to him' is simply a summons to discipleship and to embrace suffering for Jesus. But at another level it is a summons to *leave the synagogue* and indeed to abandon all attachment to Judaism. This *second* summons is where the author's real interest lies, I suggest. This is the thought picked up in the following explanation: 'for here we have no lasting city, but we seek the one which is to come' (13:14). The *synagogue* (Jerusalem, the Temple) provides no secure home, and the readers need to *leave* it, in order to find security in the 'coming' city – the kingdom which will appear when the world is shaken (12:26–28).

This last exhortation indexes nicely for us the author's whole approach. He has not told his readers directly that the Temple is *not* ordained by God and that they must leave Judaism wholly behind. But that is his message, wrapped so wholly and deeply in scriptural language that, if the readers drew this conclusion, they could only do so because they became convinced that *Scripture* was teaching it.

These seven passages, I believe, sufficiently illustrate my contention that the Temple does *not* appear in Hebrews precisely so that the profound message of the letter *about the Temple* may actually be heard in its scriptural depth, and not be rejected out of hand.

14

THE FINAL VISION OF THE APOCALYPSE AND ITS IMPLICATIONS FOR A BIBLICAL THEOLOGY OF THE TEMPLE[1]

GREGORY BEALE

Anyone who claims to have said the last word about anything in the last book of the Bible should repent. As I have continued to reflect on the Apocalypse, and especially the references to the Temple, since the writing of my commentary (published in 1999, but submitted for publication in 1995!), I have noticed even more connections between the various Temple texts in the book than I had observed previously. My purpose in this essay is to explore in more depth the significance of the Temple in John's Apocalypse. My beginning point is a revised analysis of an excursus on the vision of the Temple in Revelation 21:1–22:5 that I gave in my Revelation commentary a few years ago.[2] In this article I will attempt to amplify the evidence adduced in support of the thesis in order to enhance its plausibility. The thesis is that the Old Testament Tabernacle and Temples were symbolically designed to point to the cosmic eschatological reality that God's cultic presence, formerly limited to the holy of holies, was to be extended throughout the whole earth. If correct, the thesis provides crucial insight into an understanding of the biblical theology of the Temple in both testaments.

After summarizing my earlier conclusion about the world-wide scope of the Temple in Revelation 21:1–22:5, I will survey the evidence for the cosmic symbolism of ancient Near Eastern and Old Testament temples. Then I will argue that the Garden of Eden was the first archetypal Temple, which was the model for all subsequent Temples. Such an understanding of Eden will enhance the notion that the Old Testament Tabernacle and Temples were symbolic microcosms of the whole creation that were designed to point to a world-wide eschatological

---

[1] This essay is a radical abridgement of a paper delivered at the conference of the Biblical Theology Study Group of the Tyndale Fellowship, 4–6 July 2001. This paper has now been expanded into a book with the tentative title *Eden, the Temple and the Mission of the Church: A Biblical Theology of the Temple* (Leicester: IVP, forthcoming).

[2] G. K. Beale, *The Book of Revelation* (NIGTC; Grand Rapids/Cambridge/Carlisle: Eerdmans/Paternoster Press, 1999), pp. 1109–11.

Temple. It is this universally expanded eschatological Temple that is pictured in Revelation's last vision. Other relevant passages about the Temple in Revelation and the New Testament will be adduced in further support of this contention.

1. THE WORLD-WIDE EXTENT OF THE PARADISAL CITY-TEMPLE IN REVELATION 21–22

That the paradisal city-Temple of Revelation 21–22 encompasses the entirety of the newly created earth is apparent from drawing together some of the strands of earlier observations made on Revelation 21 (in my commentary) together with other considerations:

(i) Isaiah 54:2–3 together with several Jewish references support the notion of an expanded New Jerusalem or end-time Temple on an escalated scale in comparison to the former Jerusalem and Temple;

(ii) in the Old Testament, uncleanness was to be kept out of the Temple precincts; that the perimeters of the new Temple will finally encompass the whole of the new creation is suggested by the fact that Revelation 21:27 says that no uncleanness was allowed into the city-Temple, which probably indicates that no uncleanness will be allowed into the new world (especially since 22:15 says that the unclean will be excluded from the city, which means there they will also be excluded from dwelling in the new creation, since they will be in the lake of fire forever);[3]

(iii) John says in Revelation 21:1 that he saw 'a new heaven and new earth', and then in 21:2 and 21:9–22:5 he, in fact, sees only a paradisal city-Temple.

It is possible that John first saw the whole heavens and earth in 21:1 and then subsequently sees the city-Temple as a part of that new cosmos. It is, however, plausible, given the preceding points (i) and (ii), and the following points considered below, that the 'new heaven and new earth' of 21:1 is defined by and equated with the paradisal city-Temple of 21:2 and 21:9–22:5. This is further supported by J. D. Levenson's observation that 'heaven and earth' in the Old Testament may sometimes be a way of referring to Jerusalem or its Temple, for which 'Jerusalem' is a metonymy. He quotes Isaiah 65:17–18 as one of the texts most illustrative of this:[4] '*For behold, I create new heavens and a*

---

[3] See ibid., in loc. on 21:22, 27; 22:15.
[4] J. D. Levenson, *Creation and the Persistence of Evil: The Jewish Drama of Divine Omnipotence* (San Francisco: Harper & Row, 1988), pp. 89–90; J. D. Levenson, 'The Temple and the World', *Journal of Religion* 64 (1984), pp. 294–5.

new earth; and the former things shall not be remembered or come to mind. But be glad and rejoice forever in what I create; *for behold, I create Jerusalem* for rejoicing.' Since Isaiah 65:17 is alluded to in Revelation 21:1, it would appear that the New Jerusalem of 21:2 is equated with the 'new heaven and earth' of 21:1. That the new creation in verse 1 and new Jerusalem in verse 2 is interpreted in verse 3 to be 'the tabernacle of God' among all humanity would be a natural equation.

2. ISRAEL'S EARTHLY TEMPLE AS A REFLECTION OF THE HEAVENLY OR COSMIC TEMPLE

The rationale for the world-wide encompassing nature of the paradisal Temple in Revelation 21 lies in the ancient notion that the Old Testament Temple was a microcosm of the entire heaven and earth.[5] One of the most explicit texts affirming this is Psalm 78:69: 'And he built the sanctuary like the heights, like the earth which he founded *forever* [or from eternity].'[6] Similarly, the earlier 'pattern of the tabernacle and the pattern of all its furniture' was made 'after the pattern ... which was shown ... on the mountain' (Exod. 25:9, 40; cf. Num. 8:4; Heb. 8:5). The following study will assume that the symbolism of the Tabernacle is essentially the same as that of Israel's later Temple, an equivalence implied by their many similarities and by comparing Exodus 25:9, 40 with 1 Chronicles 28:19.[7]

Josephus understood the tripartite structure of the Tabernacle to signify 'the earth [= outer court] and the sea [= inner court], since these

---

[5] See R. Patai, *Man and Temple* (New York: KTAV, 1967), pp. 54–139; M. Barker, *The Gate of Heaven: The History and Symbolism of the Temple in Jerusalem* (London: SPCK, 1991), pp. 104–32; Levenson, 'The Temple and the World', pp. 283–98; J. D. Levenson, *Sinai and Zion* (San Francisco: Harper & Row, 1985), pp. 111–84; C. T. R. Hayward, *The Jewish Temple: A Non-biblical Sourcebook* (London: Routledge, 1996); C. R. Koester, *The Dwelling of God: The Tabernacle in the Old Testament, Intertestamental Jewish Literature, and the New Testament* (CBQMS 22; Washington: Catholic Biblical Association of America, 1989), pp. 59–63; C. H. T. Fletcher-Louis, 'The Destruction of the Temple and Relativization of the Old Covenant: Mark 13:31 and Matthew 5:18' in K. E. Brower and M. W. Elliot (eds), *'The Reader Must Understand': Eschatology in Bible and Theology* (Leicester: Apollos, 1997), pp. 156–62.
[6] On which see further Levenson, *Creation and the Persistence of Evil*, pp. 87–8 and V.(A). Hurowitz, *I Have Built You an Exalted House: Temple Building in the Bible in Light of Mesopotamian and Northwest Semitic Writings* (JSOTSS 115; Sheffield: Sheffield Academic Press, 1992), pp. 335–7. Psalm 78:69 has striking parallel to the Enuma Elish VI, 113, where it is said concerning the building of Marduk's temple: 'May he ... make a likeness on earth of what he has wrought in heaven.'
[7] The equivalence was also made by early Judaism (so Wisdom 9:8: the Temple was 'an imitation of the holy tabernacle which you prepared from the beginning'); see M. Haran, *Temples and Temple-Service in Ancient Israel: An Inquiry into the Character of Cult Phenomena and the Historical Setting of the Priestly School* (Oxford: Clarendon Press, 1978), pp. 189–204, on the organic correspondences between the Tabernacle and Temple; cf. also R. J. Clifford, 'The Temple and the Holy Mountain' in T. G. Madsen (ed.), *The Temple in Antiquity* (Provo: Brigham Young University Press, 1984), pp. 112–15.

... are accessible to all, but the third portion [= holy of holies] he reserved for God alone, because heaven also is inaccessible to men' (*Ant*. III:181; cf. *Ant*. III:123). Likewise, M. Haran has observed an increasing gradation in holiness beginning with the outer court and proceeding to the holy place and then into the holy of holies. Furthermore, he notes that this corresponds to a gradation in dress and furnishings dependent on the position of the person in the Temple (respectively worshipper, priest or high priest) or the location of the furnishings (curtains, furniture, etc.).[8] This may not be inconsistent with A. A. de Silva's view that the Old Testament Temple building narratives reflect a three-tiered structure with God at the top, kings (and, I would add, priests) in the middle, and Israel and the rest of the cosmos at the bottom.[9]

The cosmic identification of the outer court is suggested further by the Old Testament itself where the large molten wash basin and altar, both in the Temple courtyard, are called respectively the 'sea' (1 Kgs. 7:23–26) and the 'bosom of the earth' and the 'mountain of God' (Ezek. 43:13–17).[10] Thus both are cosmic symbols that would have been associated in the mind of the Israelite respectively with the seas and the earth.[11]

In the light of the above evidence, R. E. Clements' conclusion about similar evidence is cautious and judicious:

> Not all of these supposed symbolic references of features of the temple are convincing, but the essential claim that the temple and its furnishings did possess cosmic, or naturalistic, symbolism must be upheld. Such features were designed to stress the divine power over the created order, and to establish the temple as a source of blessing for the land and people of Israel. The underlying idea was that the temple was a microcosm of the macrocosm, so that the building gave visual expression to the belief in Yahweh's dominion over the world ... We need not suppose that every Israelite worshipper was conscious of this ... Thus the temple building ... signified the cosmic rule of God who was worshipped there ...[12]

---

[8] Haran, *Temples and Temple Service in Ancient Israel*, pp. 158–88, 205–221, 226–7, followed by W. J. Dumbrell, *The End of the Beginning: Revelation 21–22 and the Old Testament* (Homebush West, New South Wales: Lancer, 1985), p. 43.

[9] A. A. de Silva, 'A Comparison between the Three-Levelled World of the Old Testament Temple Building Narratives and the Three-Levelled World of the House Building Motif in the Ugaritic Tests KTU 1.3 and 1.4' in G. J. Brooke, A. H. W. Curites and J. F. Healey (eds), *Ugarit and the Bible* (Münster: Ugarit-Verlag, 1994), pp. 11–23.

[10] See further Levenson, *Creation and the Persistence of Evil*, pp. 92–3, who also suggests that the arrangement of the twelve bulls supporting the wash basin into groups of three facing to the four points of the compass may reflect the four quadrants of the earth. See likewise Levenson, *Sinai and Zion*, pp. 139, 162.

[11] On which see S. Terrien, 'The Omphalos Myth and Hebrew Religion', *Vetus Testamentum* 20 (1970), p. 323 for additional bibliography in support.

[12] R. E. Clements, *God and Temple* (Philadelphia: Fortress Press, 1965), p. 67; see also his larger discussion (pp. 64–75), where especially he cites texts from the Psalms underscoring God's rule from the Temple, e.g. Psalm 11:4: 'The Lord is in his holy temple, the Lord's

2.1 Ancient Near Eastern evidence

Some like de Vaux[13] allege that early Judaism's explicit cosmic understanding of the Temple was a late eisegetical development. A good response to this is not only the above-cited, though limited, evidence from the Old Testament itself, but also the observation that ancient Near Eastern archaeology and texts portray ancient temples as microcosms of heavenly temples or of the universe.[14] One of the best examples of this is the connection of the arboreal lampstand of Israel's Temple with 'cosmic trees' in ancient temples.[15] That the bronze 'sea' basin in the courtyard represented the cosmic seas is borne out by ancient New Eastern temples that also have artificial replicas of seas symbolizing either the chaotic forces stilled by the god or the waters of life at the cosmic centre.[16]

In other respects ancient temples reflected cosmic symbolism.[17] For instance, temples were symbolically the 'embodiment of the cosmic mountain' representing the original hillock first emerging from the primordial waters at the beginning of creation; such waters themselves were symbolized in temples together with fertile trees receiving life from the waters.[18] The names of various Mesopotamian temples also

---

throne is in heaven.' Levenson gives the same qualified assessment as Clements that the Temple was conceived as an institution representing the cosmos ('The Temple and the World', p. 286). The assessments of Clements and Levenson are partly a response to R. de Vaux, *Ancient Israel* (New York: McGraw-Hill, 1965), p. 328, who concludes that in the Bible there is 'feeble support for these theories' about the cosmological significance of the Temple (see Levenson, *Creation and the Persistence of Evil*, p. 82 for further response to de Vaux).

[13] De Vaux, *Ancient Israel*, pp. 328–9.

[14] See, e.g., Hurowitz, *I Have Built You an Exalted House*, pp. 335–7; C. Meyers, 'Temple, Jerusalem' in D. N. Freedman (ed.), *Anchor Bible Dictionary* (vol. 6; New York: Doubleday, 1992), pp. 359–60; O. Keel, *The Symbolism of the Biblical World: Ancient Near Eastern Iconography and the Book of Psalms* (New York: Seabury Press, 1978), pp. 171–6 (cf. also pp. 113–15); Levenson, 'The Temple and the World', pp. 285–6; J. J. Niehaus, *No Other Gods* (Grand Rapids: Baker Book House, forthcoming), ch. 5; and Fletcher-Louis, 'The Destruction of the Temple and Relativization of the Old Covenant', p. 159, n. 47.

[15] C. L. Meyers, *The Tabernacle Menorah: A Synthetic Study of a Symbol from the Biblical Cult* (ASOR Dissertation Series 2; Missoula: Scholars Press, 1976), e.g. pp. 169–72, 177, 180; see Terrien, 'The Omphalos Myth and Hebrew Religion', p. 318 for additional sources supporting this idea.

[16] C. L. Meyers, 'Sea, Molten' in Freedman (ed.), *Anchor Bible Dictionary* vol. 5, pp. 1060–1.

[17] E.g. see J. M. Lundquist, 'What is a Temple?' in H. B. Huffmon, F. A. Spina and A. R. W. Green (eds), *The Quest for the Kingdom of God: Studies in Honor of George E. Mendenhall* (Winona Lake: Eisenbrauns, 1983), pp. 205–19; *idem*, 'Temple Symbolism in Isaiah' in M. S. Nyman (ed.), *Isaiah and the Prophets* (Religious Studies Monograph Series 10; Salt Lake City: Brigham Young University, 1984), pp. 33–55, the latter showing how the ANE notion is reflected in Isaiah's description of Israel's Temple.

[18] So J. M. Lundquist, 'The Common Temple Ideology of the Ancient Near East' in T. G. Madsen (ed.), *The Temple in Antiquity* (Religious Studies Monograph Series 9; Salt Lake City: Brigham Young University, 1984), pp. 53–76, on which see other relevant secondary sources cited.

express notions about their 'cosmological place and function' and hence symbolic significance.[19] There are many examples of temples being repeatedly called such names as 'House like Heaven', 'House of Heaven and Underworld', 'House, Bond of the Land', 'Apsu ("fresh water or sea")-House', 'House of the Mountains', 'House of the Pure New Moon', etc.[20] In Ebla the explicit reference to 'Temple of the Creator' also occurs.[21]

Indeed, Levenson summarizes previous research on the Pentateuch that observes that the creation of the cosmos, the making of the Tabernacle and the building of the Temple 'are all described in similar, and at times identical language'. The reason for the similarity is to indicate 'that the temple and the world were considered congeneric'.[22] Levenson even notes that the similarity is a distillation 'of a long tradition in the ancient Near East, which binds Temple building and world building'.[23] Levenson also suggests that the same cosmic significance is to be seen from the fact that Solomon took seven years to build the Temple (1 Kgs. 6:38), that he dedicated it on the seventh month, during the Feast of Booths (a festival of seven days [1 Kgs. 8]), and that his dedicatory speech was structured around seven petitions (1 Kgs. 8:31–55). Hence, the building of the Temple was modelled on the seven-day creation of the world, which also is in line with the building of temples in seven days elsewhere in the ancient Near East.[24]

Among other biblical passages supporting the cosmic temple thesis,[25] Levenson offers Isaiah 6:3: 'Holy, Holy, Holy, is the LORD of hosts, the whole earth is full of his glory.' He contends persuasively that this 'glory' is the divine radiance by which God manifests his presence in the Temple. The significance of Isaiah's vision of the luminescent smoke filling the Temple (6:4) is explained by the seraphim to mean that the whole world manifests Yahweh's cultic heavenly glory that

---

[19] A. R. George, *House Most High* (Winona Lake: Eisenbrauns, 1993), p. 59.

[20] Ibid., pp. 63–161, where a profusion of examples are listed. See also W. Horowitz, *Mesopotamian Cosmic Geography* (Winona Lake: Eisenbrauns, 1998), pp. 122–3, for a similar reference in the Enuma Elish VI, pp. 55–68.

[21] M. J. Dahood, 'The Temple and Other Sacred Places in the Ebla Tablets', in *The Temple in Antiquity*, p. 85.

[22] Levenson, 'The Temple and the World', pp. 286–7.

[23] Ibid., pp. 287–8; so also M. Weinfeld, 'Sabbath and the Enthronement of the Lord: The Problem of the Sitz im Leben of Genesis 1:1–2:3' in A. Caquot and M. Delcor (eds), *Melanges bibliques et orientaux en l'honneur de M. Henri Cazelles* (AOAT 212; Kevelaer/ Neukirchen-Vluyn: Butzon & Bercker/Neukirchener Verlag, 1981), pp. 501–12. Cf. also B. Janowski, 'Tempel und Schöpfung. Schöpfungstheologische Aspekte der priesterschriftlichen Heiligtumskonzeption' in *Schöpfung und Neuschöpfung* (Jahrbuch für Biblische Theologie 5; Neukirchen-Vluyn: Neukirchener, 1990), pp. 37–69, especially with respect to a depiction of the establishment of the tabernacle according to the thematic lines of the creation narrative in Genesis 1:1–2:4.

[24] So Levenson, *Creation and the Persistence of Evil*, pp. 78–9.

[25] Ibid., pp. 289–98.

has unique correspondence in the earthly Temple. Isaiah 6:3b could well be rendered 'The fullness of the whole earth is his glory' (an alternative rendering proposed by Levenson and the NASB), that is, the entire world reflects God's glory in the Temple (though later Levenson interprets this a bit more speculatively: 'The world in its fullness is the temple').[26] While Levenson grants that the biblical evidence is 'muted and implicit', the Old Testament 'evidence is not quite so lacking as one would think at first glance'.[27]

3. ISRAEL'S EARTHLY TABERNACLE AND TEMPLE AS REFLECTIONS AND RECAPITULATIONS OF THE FIRST TEMPLE IN THE GARDEN OF EDEN

In addition to the notion that the earthly Temple reflected the heavenly, cosmic Temple, Revelation 22:1ff. appears to be aware of an earlier cultic interpretation of Eden. In this respect there are hints that the Garden of Eden was the archetypal Temple in which the first man worshipped God.[28]

First, Israel's Temple was the place where the priest experienced God's unique presence, and Eden was the place where Adam walked and talked with God. The same Hebrew verbal form (hithpael), *hithallek*, used for God's 'walking back and forth' in the Garden (Gen. 3:38), describes God's presence in the Tabernacle (Lev. 26:12; Deut. 23:14 [15]; 2 Sam. 7:6–7).

Secondly, Genesis 2:15 says God placed Adam in the Garden 'to cultivate [work] it and to keep it'. The two Hebrew words for 'cultivate and keep' are usually translated 'serve and guard' elsewhere in the Old Testament.[29] When these two words (verbal ['abad and shamar] and nominal forms) occur together in the Old Testament (within an approximately fifteen-word range), they sometimes have this meaning and refer either to Israelites 'serving' God and 'guarding [keeping]' God's word (approximately ten times) or to priests who 'keep' the

---

[26] Ibid., p. 296.
[27] Ibid., p. 286.
[28] Following for the most part M. G. Kline, *Kingdom Prologue* (South Hamilton: Gordon-Conwell Theological Seminary, 1989), pp. 31–2, 54–6 and *idem, Images of the Spirit* (Grand Rapids: Baker, 1980), pp. 35–42, as well as G. J. Wenham, 'Sanctuary Symbolism in the Garden of Eden Story', *Proceedings of the World Congress of Jewish Studies* 9 (1986), pp. 19–25, M. Barker, *The Gate of Heaven: The History and Symbolism of the Temple in Jerusalem* (London: SPCK, 1991), pp. 68–103, and, to lesser degree, Vern Poythress, *The Shadow of Christ in the Law of Moses* (Phillipsburg: Prebytery & Reformed, 1991), pp. 19, 31, 35; see further R. M. Davidson, 'Cosmic Metanarrative for the Coming Millennium', *Journal of the Adventist Theological Society* 11 (2000), pp. 109–11.
[29] Cf. U. Cassuto, *Commentary on the Book of Genesis* (Jerusalem: Magnes, 1989), pp. 122–3, who prefers these meanings in Genesis 2:15.

'service' (or 'charge') of the Tabernacle (see Num. 3:7–8; 8:25–26; 18:5–6; 1 Chr. 23:32; Ezek. 44:14).[30]

Thirdly, when Adam failed to guard the Temple by sinning and letting in an unclean serpent to defile the sanctuary, Adam lost his priestly role, and the two cherubim took over the responsibility of 'guarding' the Garden Temple: God 'stationed the cherubim ... *to guard* the way to the tree of life' (so Gen. 3:24). Likely, their role became memorialized in Israel's later Temple when God commanded Moses to make two statues of cherubim and stationed them on either side of the 'ark of the covenant' in the 'holy of holies'.

Fourthly, the 'tree of life' itself was probably the model for the lampstand placed directly outside the 'holy of holies'.[31] The lampstand looked like a small, flowering tree with seven protruding branches from a central trunk, three on one side and three on the other, and one branch going straight up from the trunk in the middle. Exodus 25:31–36 pictures the lampstand having a flowering and fructifying appearance of a tree with 'bulbs and flowers', 'branches' and 'almond blossoms' (see Exod. 25:31–36; likewise, see Josephus, *Ant.* III:145).

Fifthly, that the Garden of Eden was the first Temple is also suggested by observing that Israel's later Temple had wood carvings which gave it a garden-like atmosphere: 1 Kings 6:18, 29 says there was 'cedar ... carved in the shape of gourds and open flowers' (v. 18); 'on the walls of the temple round about' and on the wood doors of the inner sanctuary were 'carvings of cherubim, palm trees, and open flowers' (vv. 29, 32, 35); beneath the heads of the two pillars placed at the entrance of the holy place were 'carved pomegranates' (1 Kgs. 7:18–20).[32]

Sixthly, Eden was on a mountain (Ezek. 28:14, 16); Israel's Temple was on Mount Zion (e.g. Exod. 15:17); and the eschatological Temple was to be located on a mountain (Ezek. 40:2; 43:12; Rev. 21:10).

Seventhly, just as a river flowed out from Eden (Gen. 2:10), so the eschatological Temple in both Ezekiel 47:1–12 and Revelation 21:1–2 has a river flowing out from its centre (and likewise Rev. 7:15–17 and

---

[30] See likewise G. J. Wenham, *Genesis 1–15* (WBC; Waco: Word, 1987), p. 67; cf. also Isaiah 56:6; cf. M. G. Kline, *Kingdom Prologue*, p. 54, who sees this only with respect to the priestly 'guarding' of the Temple from the profane (e.g., Kline cites Num. 1:53; 3:8, 10, 32; 8:26, 18:3ff.; 1 Sam. 7:1; 2 Kgs. 12:9; 1 Chr. 23:32; 2 Chr. 34:9; Ezek. 44:15ff.; 48:11); so similarly Wenham, *Genesis 1–15*, p. 67.

[31] On which see further the references and discussion in Beale, *The Book of Revelation*, pp. 234–6.

[32] See L. E. Stager, 'Jerusalem as Eden', *Biblical Archaeology Review* 26 (May/June, 2000), pp. 36–47, 66 for Solomon's Temple as an intentional replication of the Garden of Eden; he also notes likenesses with other ANE temples containing gardens or garden depictions on their walls that also reflect the essential characteristics of the Garden of Eden (on which likewise see Keel, *The Symbolism of the Biblical World*, pp. 124–50 and L. Yarden, *The Tree of Light: A Study of the Menorah, the Seven-Branched Lampstand* [Ithaca: Cornell University Press, 1971], p. 38, where iconographic examples are found).

probably Zech. 14:8–9). Later Judaism understood that from 'the tree of life' streams flowed (Midr. Rab. Gen. 15:6; 2 Enoch [J] 8:3, 5). Indeed, Ezekiel generally depicts eschatological Mount Zion (and its Temple) in the colours of Eden in an attempt to show that the promises originally inherent in Eden would be realized in the fulfilment of his vision.[33]

Eighthly, Genesis 2:12 says that 'good gold' and 'bdellium and onyx stone' were in 'the land of Havilah', apparently where Eden was. Of course, various items of Tabernacle furniture were made of gold, as were the walls, ceiling, and floor of the holy of holies in Solomon's Temple (1 Kgs. 6:20–22). Furthermore, the onyx stones decorated both the Tabernacle and Temple, as well as the high priestly garments (Exod. 25:7; 28:9–12, 20; 1 Chr. 29:2). Gold and onyx are also found together on the priest's clothing (Exod. 28:6–27) and are mentioned together as composing parts of the Temple (1 Chr. 29:2).[34]

Ninethly, the ark in the holy of holies, which contained the Law (that led to wisdom), echoes the tree of the knowledge of good and evil (that also led to wisdom). The touching of both the ark and this tree resulted in death.

Tenthly, the entrance to Eden was from the east (Gen. 3:24), which was also the direction from which one entered the Tabernacle and later Temples of Israel and would be the same direction from which the latter-day Temple would be entered (Ezek. 40:6).

Judaism in various ways understood the Garden to be the first sanctuary. Perhaps the earliest (160 BC) and clearest expression of this is Jubilees 8:19: 'And he [Noah] knew that the Garden of Eden is the holy of holies and the dwelling of the LORD, and Mount Sinai the centre of the desert, and Mount Zion the centre of the navel of the earth: these three were created as a holy place facing each other.' This is quite interesting because it links the Garden as a Temple with not only that at Sinai, but especially the Temple in Jerusalem. 1 Enoch 24–27 and Testament of Levi 18:6, 10 also closely associate God's Temple with imagery of the Garden of Eden.[35]

---

[33] J. D. Levenson, *Theology of the Program of Restoration of Ezekiel 40–48* (Harvard Semitic Monograph Series 10; Missoula: Scholars Press, 1976), pp. 25–53.

[34] Pseudo-Philo, *LAB* 25–26, asserts that twelve precious stones almost identical to those composing the vestments of the high priest (see Exod. 28) were originally taken by the Amorites 'from the land of Havilah', and used for idolatry until they were taken by Israel and placed in the ark of the Temple. At the time of Israel's latter-day redemption one will come and 'build a house for my [God's] name' (26:12) and then the stones will be restored to all of the righteous.

[35] So see J. T. A. G. M. van Ruiten, 'Visions of the Temple in the Book of Jubilees' in B. Ego, A. Lange and P. Pilhofer (eds), *Gemeinde ohne Tempel/Community without Temple* (WUNT 118; Tübingen: Mohr, 1999), pp. 215–27 (p. 223); see also J. M. Baumgarten, '4Q500 and the Ancient Conception of the Lord's Vineyard', *JJS* 40 (1989), pp. 1–6, who discusses some early and later Jewish sources identifying Israel's Temple with Eden; see also M. Himmelfarb, 'The Temple and the Garden of Eden in Ezekiel, the Book of Watchers,

Similarly striking is the Qumran community's identification of itself as the 'sanctuary of Adam' (*miqdash adam*) in 4QFlorilegium and 'an Eden of glory [bearing] fruits [of life]' (1QH 8:20, though cf. all of 8:4–23).[36] Similarly, 1QS 8:5 identifies the community as 'the House of holiness for Israel' and 'an everlasting planting', the latter a reference to the Garden of Eden![37]

4. CONCLUSION: THE PURPOSE OF THE TEMPLE IN REVELATION 21 AS A REFLECTION, RECAPITULATION AND ESCALATION OF EDEN'S AND ISRAEL'S TEMPLE

Those who acknowledge the cosmic symbolism of the Temple understand its meaning in a variety of ways. As we have seen, some believe the symbolism indicates God's sovereignty over and sustenance or blessings for Israel and the creation. Levenson concludes his studies by affirming that the purpose of Israel's Temple, in addition to conveying God's presence in Israel and in the heavenly Temple, was to provide a kind of Platonic ideal in which the worshipper was caught up from a fallen world into a perfect created, Edenic reality of God's unthreatened reign and justice, and the worshipper's peaceful and unblemished life (through the sacrificial system).[38] 'In this theology, the Temple was a piece of primal perfection available within the broken world of ordinary experience – heaven on earth.'[39] He refers to this as an ideal 'spatial model of spiritual fulfillment'.[40] For Levenson, the Old Testament prophecies (e.g. of Isaiah) that there would be a new eschatological Temple in a new creation offer a 'temporal model' of fulfilment[41] but were also merely part of Judaism's mythic utopian expressions.[42]

---

and the Wisdom of ben Sira' in J. Scott and P. Simpson-Housley (eds), *Sacred Places and Profane Spaces* (Contributions to the Study of Religion 30; Westport, Connecticut: Greenwood, 1991), pp. 72–5, for Ben Sira's identification of the Temple with Eden. For the notion of Sinai as a Temple, see Lundquist, 'What is a Temple?' and, especially, D. W. Parry, 'Sinai as Sanctuary and Mountain of God' in J. M. Lundquist and S. D. Ricks (eds), *By Study and Also by Faith: Essays in Honor of H.W. Nibley* (Salt Lake City: Deseret, 1990), vol. 1, pp. 482–500.

[36] On the debated translation of 8:20, see G. J. Brooke, 'Miqdash Adam, Eden, and the Qumran Community' in B. Ego, A. Lange and P. Pilhofer (eds), *Gemeinde ohne Tempel/ Community Without Temple* (WUNT 118; Tübingen: Mohr Siebeck, 1999), p. 292.

[37] Similarly, see CD 3:19–20, on which see Brooke, 'Miqdash Adam, Eden, and the Qumran Community', pp. 292–3.

[38] So Levenson, 'The Jerusalem Temple in Devotional and Visionary Experience' in A. Green (ed.), *Jewish Spirituality* (New York: Crossroad, 1986), pp. 32–61; Levenson, 'The Temple and the World', pp. 297–8.

[39] Levenson, 'The Jerusalem Temple in Devotional and Visionary Experience', p. 53.

[40] Levenson, 'The Temple and the World', p. 298.

[41] Ibid.

[42] Levenson, 'The Jerusalem Temple in Devotional and Visionary Experience', p. 57.

As far as I am aware, few have come close to developing the following redemptive-historical significance to the cosmic symbolism of the Temple either in the Old or New Testament.[43] Nor has anyone in any significant way attempted to relate the cosmic symbolism of the Old Testament Temple to the notion of the Temple in the New Testament (Fletcher-Louis' article on the idea in Matthew and Mark being the only apparent exception).[44] We conclude this section by reflecting on the question raised in the introductory paragraph: Why does John see 'a new heaven and a new earth' in Revelation 21:1 and then in the rest of the vision he sees only a city in the form of a Temple that is garden-like? The final vision of Revelation 21 does not in all likelihood describe first the new heavens and earth in 21:1 and then a garden-like Temple-city as one localized geographical spot on the new earth. Instead, our study shows that it is natural that John sees the new heavens and earth as the urban Edenic Temple, because the Temple – which is God's glorious presence – encompasses the whole earth on account of the consummate work of Christ.

Not only was Adam to 'guard' the initial stage of this sanctuary, but he was also to subdue the earth, according to Genesis 1:28: 'And God blessed them ... Be fruitful and multiply, and fill the earth, and subdue it; and rule over the fish of the sea and over the birds of the sky, and over every living thing that creeps on the surface.' Genesis 1:27 provides the means by which the commission and goal of verse 28 was to be accomplished: humanity will fulfil the commission by means of being in God's image.[45] As Adam and Eve were to begin to rule over and subdue the earth, it is plausible to suggest that they were to extend the geographical boundaries of the Garden until Eden extended throughout and covered the whole earth.[46] In line with the ancient Near East, in which images of the god were in a garden-like Temple, so Adam is presumably that 'image' in Genesis 2. Just as ancient kings would set up images of themselves in distant lands over which they ruled in order to represent their sovereign presence, so Adam was created as the image of the divine king to indicate that earth was ruled over by Yahweh. In the light of Genesis 1:26–28, this meant that the presence of God, which was initially to be limited to Eden, was to be extended throughout the whole earth by his image bearers as they themselves represented and reflected his presence and his attributes.

---

[43] Though see n. 64 below on the contributions of Levenson, Kline, and Dumbrell.

[44] Fletcher-Louis, 'The Destruction of the Temple and Relativization of the Old Covenant', pp. 156–62.

[45] The same relationship exists between 1:26a and 1:26b; see also, in this respect, W. J. Dumbrell, *The Search for Order: Biblical Eschatology in Focus* (Grand Rapids: Baker Book House, 1994), p. 18–20.

[46] See Kline, *Kingdom Prologue*, pp. 55–6.

Hence, Genesis 2:15 continues the theme of subduing and filling the earth by humanity created in the divine image.[47] Adam's commission to 'cultivate' and 'keep' in Genesis 2:15 is most probably part of the commission given in 1:26–28. Similarly, that Adam and Eve were to become 'one flesh' in 2:24 is certainly part of the beginning of the commission to be 'fruitful and multiply, and fill the earth'. Adam, however, failed in the task with which he was commissioned. Rather than extending the divine presence of the garden sanctuary, Adam and Eve were expelled from it.

Adam's commission was passed on to Noah (so Gen. 9:1, 6–7) who also failed. The patriarchs and Israel were then given the commission (so Gen. 12:2; 17:2, 6, 8; 22:16ff.; 26:3ff., 24; 28:3; 35:11ff.; 47:27; 48:3ff.).[48] Commentators apparently have not noticed, however, something very interesting: that the Adamic commission is often repeated in direct connection with what looks to be the building of small sanctuaries. Just as the Genesis 1:28 commission was initially to be carried out by Adam in a localized place, enlarging the borders of the arboreal sanctuary, so it appears to be not accidental that the restatement of the commission to Israel's patriarchs results in the following:

(i) God appearing to them (except in Gen. 12:8; 13:3–4);

(ii) they 'pitch a *tent*' (literally a 'tabernacle' in LXX);

(iii) on a mountain;

(iv) they build 'altars' and worship God (i.e. 'calling on the name of the LORD', which probably included sacrificial offerings and prayer)[49] at the place of the restatement;

(v) the place where these activities occur is often located at 'Bethel' – the 'House of God' (the only case of altar building not containing these elements nor linked to the Genesis 1 commission is Gen. 33:20).

The combination of these five elements occurs only elsewhere in the Old Testament in describing Israel's Tabernacle or Temple![50]

---

[47] So also Dumbrell, *The Search for Order*, pp. 24–6.

[48] So N. T. Wright, *The Climax of the Covenant* (Minneapolis: Fortress Press, 1992), pp. 21–6, who sees that the command to Adam in Genesis 1:26–28 has been applied to the patriarchs and Israel primarily in the form of promises; see also Dumbrell, *The Search for Order*, pp. 29–30, 37, 72–3, 143 for the notion that the blessings conditionally promised to Adam are given to Israel.

[49] A. Pagolu, *The Religion of the Patriarchs* (JSOTSupp 277; Sheffield: Sheffield Academic Press, 1998), p. 62.

[50] See chapter 3 of my forthcoming book *Eden, the Temple, and the Mission of the Church* (on which see n. 1 above), which will present much fuller exegetical demonstration of the unique thesis offered in this and the next paragraph. The combination of 'tent' (*'ohel*) and 'altar' (*mizbeach*) occurs in Exodus and Leviticus only with respect to the tabernacle and associated altar (e.g. Lev. 4:7, 18). 'Altar' (*mizbeach*) and 'house' (*bayith*) occur twenty-

Therefore, though 'occasions for their sacrifices were usually a theophany and moving to a new place',[51] there seems to be more significance to the construction of these sacrificial sites. The patriarchs appear also to have built these worship areas as impermanent, miniature forms of sanctuaries that symbolically represented the notion that their progeny were to spread out to subdue the earth from a divine sanctuary in fulfilment of the commission in Genesis 1:26–28.[52] Though they built no buildings, these patriarchal sacred spaces can be considered 'sanctuaries' along the lines comparable to the first non-architectural sanctuary in the Garden of Eden. These informal sanctuaries in Genesis pointed then to Israel's later Tabernacle and Temple from which Israel was to branch out over all the earth, though not many commentators hold this view. G. Vos agrees that the theophanies at these altar sites prepared for the more permanent theophany at the Jerusalem Temple. He makes the astounding, and as far as I can tell, unique claim that these episodes do not merely point to a future and greater Temple but represent 'the renewal of the paradise-condition and as such presages a full future paradise. It points to the new world.'[53]

Certainly, just as Adam's obedience within the garden sanctuary was the key to carrying out his mandate, so Israel's obedience within their 'Garden of Eden' to the laws regulating the Temple were part of carrying out their renewed corporate Adamic commission (for the comparison of Israel's land to the Garden of Eden, see Gen. 13:10; Isa. 51:3; Ezek. 36:25; 47:12; Joel 2:3). The Genesis 1:26–28 commission to have dominion, first expressed through Adam's role in Eden, is expressed in Israel's Temple that also represented God's cosmic rule.[54]

---

eight times in the Old Testament with reference to the Temple and its altar. Rarely do any of the words in these two combinations ever refer to anything else other than the Tabernacle or Temple. The building of these worship sites on a mountain may represent part of a pattern finding its climax in Israel's later Temple that was built on Mount Zion (the traditional site of Mount Moriah), which itself becomes a synecdoche of the whole for the part in referring to the Temple. We do not mean to say that 'tent' in the patriarchal episodes is equivalent to the later tabernacle, only that it resonates with tabernacle-like associations because of its proximity to the worship site.

[51] Pagolu, *The Religion of the Patriarchs*, p. 85.

[52] Later midrashic exegesis on the Temple may have been partly inspired by Genesis 1:26–28 in its understanding that the Temple brought the blessing of fertility, even of children. While some of these references are speculative and fanciful, they show, nevertheless, an awareness of some kind of a relationship between Genesis 1:28 and the Temple (see Patai, *Man and Temple*, p. 90, 122–8).

[53] G. Vos, *The Eschatology of the Old Testament* (Phillipsburg: Presbyterian & Reformed, 2001), pp. 85–6; though he gives no exegetical evidence, I have subsequently found that his approach is almost identical to the one being forged in this section.

[54] So Clements, *God and Temple*, pp. 67–73. Later midrashic exegesis on the Temple may have been partly inspired by Genesis 1:26–28 in its understanding that the emple brought the blessing of fertility, even, for example, of children (S. Buber [ed.], *Midrash Tanhuma: Numbers* [Vilna: Rom, 1885], p. 33, and y. Yeb. 6b, cited from Patai, *Man and Temple*, p.

This commission is expressed well through Exodus 19:6, which says of the whole nation 'you shall be to me a kingdom of priests and a holy nation'. They were to be mediators in spreading the light of God's cultic presence to the rest of the dark world. Israel, as God's true humanity, also failed to carry out the commission. In contrast, Revelation pictures Christ as finally having done what Adam, Noah[55] and Israel had failed to do. Likewise, Luke 2:32 and Acts 26:23 picture Christ as fulfilling this commission to be a 'light' to the end of the earth (in allusion to the Servant Israel's commission in Isa. 49:6).

The Edenic imagery beginning in Revelation 22:1 reflects an intention to show that the building of the Temple that began in Genesis 2 will be completed in Christ and his people and will encompass the whole new creation. The cosmic reflection of the broad tripartite structure of the Temple implicitly suggested that its purpose was to point to a future time when it would encompass the whole world (much like an architect's model of a newly planned building is but a small replica of what is to be built on a much larger scale). Since the Old Testament Temple was the localized dwelling of God's special revelatory presence on earth, the Temple's correspondence with the cosmos pointed to an eschatological goal of God's presence tabernacling throughout the earth, an eschatological goal which Revelation 21:1–22:5 appears to be developing (cf. Rev. 21:3).

Christ is the Temple toward which all earlier temples looked and which they anticipated, as Revelation 21:22 comes close to saying explicitly. He is the epitome of God's presence on earth as God incarnate, thus replacing the Temple, which actually was a foreshadowing of Christ's presence all along. Christ repeatedly refers to himself in the Synoptic gospels as the 'cornerstone of the temple' (Mark 12:10; Matt. 21:42; Luke 20:17), and in John 2:18–21 Jesus says to the Jewish leaders 'Destroy this temple, and in three days I will raise it up. The Jews said, "it took 46 years to build this temple and you will raise it up in three days". But he was speaking of the temple of his body.'

Paul affirms that when people believe in Jesus and identify with him they become a part of Jesus and the Temple: 1 Corinthians 3:16, 'do you not know that you are a temple of God, and that the Spirit of

---

90; cf. b. Ber. 63b–64a; Midr. Rab. Num. 4, 20; Midr. Rab. Song of Songs 2,5; Midr. Rab. Num. 11,3; b. Yoma 39b, to which I was alerted by Patai). Likewise, the existence of the Temple and the rites performed therein procured blessing and fruitfulness for Israel (and implicitly the earth in general; so Patai, *Man and Temple*, pp. 122–8, who cites, e.g., The Fathers According to Rabbi Nathan 4).

[55] For the idea, intriguingly, that Noah's Ark was a Temple, see S. W. Holloway, 'What Ship Goes There: the Flood Narratives in the Gilgamesh Epic and Genesis Considered in Light of Ancient Near Eastern Temple Ideology', *ZAW* 103 (1991), pp. 328–54; see C. T. R. Hayward, 'Sirach and Wisdom's Dwelling Place' in S. C. Barton (ed.), *Where Shall Wisdom be Found?* (Edinburgh: T&T Clark, 1999), p. 37, for the LXX's intention to present the ark in the Temple in the light of Noah's ark by translating both by *kibōtos*.

God dwells in you?'; 1 Corinthians 6:19, 'do you not know that your body is a temple of the Holy Spirit who dwells in you?'; 2 Corinthians 6:16, 'for we are the temple of the living God' (so likewise Eph. 2:21–22; 1 Pet. 2:5; Rev. 3:12; 11:1–2).

Christ perfectly obeyed God as the last Adam, and expanded the boundaries of the Temple from himself to others. As the Son of Man (i.e. Adam), Christ commissioned his followers to continue that task of sharing God's presence with others until the end of the age (Matt. 28:16–20, in partial allusion to Dan. 7:14), when God will complete the task and the whole earth will be under the roof of his Temple. This is another way of saying that God's presence will fill the earth in a way it never had before. The special Shekinah presence of Yahweh formerly limited to the holy of holies within the nation of Israel has burst forth to encompass not only Israel but the entire new earth.

Why is the city in Revelation 21:18, 21 described as pure gold? The reason is that the floor, ceiling and walls of the holy of holies in Solomon's Temple were also covered with gold. In addition, the inner room was cubic in structure and its measurements were analogous to those in Revelation 21:16a: the equal measurement of the 'length ... and the breadth ... and the height' of the holy of holies in Solomon's Temple (1 Kgs. 6:20), forms part of the background here.[56] Note the nearly identical language of the 1 Kings text describing that 'the length ... and the breadth ... and the height' of the holy of holies was equal in measurement. Revelation 21:16 also says that the city is laid out as a square, further enhancing its identification with the Temple's inner sanctuary. Jubilees 8:19 refers to the 'garden of Eden' as the 'holy of holies and the dwelling of the Lord', which is noteworthy since the vision of the New Jerusalem and Temple of 21:9–27 is also alluded to as a restored Eden in 22:1–3. Therefore, Revelation 21:27 says that 'nothing unclean ... shall ever come into' this eternally perfected temple.[57]

Thus, the outer two sections of the Temple representing the visible heavens (the holy place) and the visible earth and seas (the court-

---

[56] So G. B. Caird, *A Commentary on the Revelation of St. John the Divine* (New York: Harper & Row, 1966), pp. 272–3.

[57] Similar to Revelation 21–22, Jubilees 4:26, in conjunction with 8:19, says that there have been four 'sanctuaries' or 'holy places' in biblical history, the first being Eden and the last Israel's Temple in Zion which 'will be sanctified in the new creation for a sanctification of the earth; through it will the earth be sanctified from all its guilt and its uncleanness throughout the generations of the world'. I would add that the unspoken reason that Jubilees says that both the Temple and the earth 'will be sanctified' is because the earth will have become a universal Temple! 1QS 8:5–9 refers twice to the community at Qumran as 'the Holy of Holies of Aaron' in conjunction with calling it 'the tried wall, the precious corner-stone' with 'foundations', and 'the House of *perfection* and truth in Israel'. So also see 1QS 9:3–6. This shows that a branch of sectarian Judaism contemporary with the early Christian community also perceived themselves in figurative manner as the 'Holy of Holies'.

yard) have been shed like a cocoon to make room for the irrupting of the formerly invisible realm represented by the holy of holies, which has expanded over the entire new creation. This is consistent with Testament of Benjamin 9:4: 'And the veil of the temple shall be rent, and the Spirit of God shall pass on to the Gentiles as fire poured forth.' Here the 'veil' symbolizes God's limited dwelling with Israel that will be removed for the sake of the world at the eschaton.

Revelation's concept of an expanding Edenic holy of holies is also remarkably reflected in Qumran (4Q418 frag. 81 = 4Q423 8 + 24?). God is said to be 'your portion and your inheritance among the sons of Adam, [and over] his [in]heritance he has given them authority' (line 3). Thus, the members of the Qumran community are those who are the true 'sons of Adam' whom God has given authority over an 'inheritance'. Those who 'inherit the earth' will 'walk' in an 'eter[nal] plantation' (lines 13–14), likely referring to the whole earth as a large Eden. They 'shall fill [apparently the earth] and … and be satiated with the abundance of good' (line 19). So far, the description of the community echoes the commission of Genesis 1:26, 28. They are also to 'honour' God 'by consecrating yourself to him, in accordance to the fact that he has placed you as a holy of holies [over all][58] the earth, and over all the angels …' (line 4). Strikingly, the community is seen to be the eschatological 'holy of holies' extending over all the earth! As such, they are 'sons of Adam', finally doing what he should have done in his primeval garden sanctuary. Just as we have seen earlier that the commission of Genesis 1:26–28 was to have begun commencement in the garden sanctuary of Genesis 2, so this Qumran passage reflects the same kind of linkage between the first two chapters of Genesis. This Dead Sea Scroll passage also exhibits a fascinatingly similar picture to that of Revelation 21, showing that early Judaism interpreted Eden and Israel's Temple in a nearly identical manner as did John. Both even link the saints' participation in the new world to an 'inheritance' (cf. Rev. 21:7).

It is true in one sense that during Israel's history even the entire cosmos was a kind of divine Temple, reflecting God's attributes, though contaminated with the sin of humanity (this is possibly what Isa. 6:3 alludes to). Systematicians sometimes refer to this as God's 'common grace' omnipresence throughout the earth. On the other hand, God's Shekinah presence, his 'special revelatory presence' before which no human could stand, except the high priest, was limited to the holy of holies (and even the high priest could not directly gaze on Yahweh's glory because of the incense cloud in his midst). This 'presence' was

---

[58] The Martinez and Tigchelaar Hebrew–English DSS edition rightly supplies the lacunae with 'over all' because of the following parallelism with 'over all the angels [literally "gods"]', though in Martinez's earlier English edition he did not do so and gave an otherwise quite different translation, which does not reflect the Hebrew as well.

never intended to be secluded forever within the back room of the Temple but was eventually to burst forth and invade the old creation, climaxing in its destruction and in the creation of a sanctuary composed of the new heavens and earth. This is what Revelation 21:1–22:5 pictures. John sees that the inner sanctuary of God's presence will finally envelop the entire creation. The same was to be true in Eden, which was equivalent to the 'holy of holies'. The intent there, even before Adam's 'fall', was that God's special presence limited to Eden was to be extended throughout the earth, so that the outer earthly regions surrounding Eden still awaited a greater glorification than they possessed at the conclusion of Genesis 1.

The Lord's prayer has been fully answered: 'Our Father who art in the heavens, hallowed be Thy name. Thy kingdom come. Thy will be done, on earth as it is in heaven' (Matt. 6:9–10). John's closest visionary version of this prayer is Revelation 21:2: 'And I saw the holy city, the new Jerusalem, coming down out of heaven from God.' Throughout the Apocalypse what is seen is often directly interpreted by a voice, and the same pattern is true here. Revelation 21:3 interprets what is seen in verse 2: 'And I heard a great voice from heaven saying, "Behold, the tabernacle of God is with men, and he will tabernacle with them, and they will be his people, and God himself will be with them, and he will be their God."' The city of Jerusalem descending from heaven is interpreted to be God in his Tabernacle consummately descending to be with his true people throughout the earth. And verses 2–3 are the interpretation of 'the new heaven' and 'new earth' John sees in verse 1.

This analysis of verses 1–3 confirms our thesis that the portrayal of Revelation 21:1–22:5 is that of God's eschatological Temple enveloping the whole earth. This also is consistent with Levenson's contention that in the Old Testament Jerusalem is often an abbreviation for Jerusalem's Temple.[59]

J. D. Levenson concludes his germinal though at times complex article 'Temple and World' in strikingly similar manner to my directly preceding conclusion about the Temple in the Old Testament: '*Endzeit gleich Urzeit*, the canonical shape of these books [the prophets] seems to say, "eschatology is like protology." The future will see the ruins of primal perfection overwhelm the fallen world in which they lie, only ostensibly vanquished.'[60] He does not, however, elaborate, and his article up to this point, as far as I can tell, does not clearly lead up to nor support this surprising conclusion.

---

[59] Levenson, 'The Temple and the World', pp. 294–5; likewise M. Eliade, *Patterns in Comparative Religion* (Cleveland/New York: World, 1966), pp. 375–9; it remains for me to confirm a suspicion that the Psalms are replete with this synonymity or synecdoche of the whole for the part.

[60] Levenson, 'The Temple and the World', p. 298.

What precisely Levenson means by saying that 'eschatology is like protology' is not clear. For example, in summarizing an analysis of a series of texts in Isaiah prophesying restoration, new Temple and new creation (56:1–7; 61:1–2; 65:17–18; 66:1–2), Levenson says that, in contrast to other Old Testament data that views 'the sanctuary as a world', the Isaiah texts see 'the world as a sanctuary'.[61] If he had held here that these were only unfulfilled prophecies of the future, then the support for his conclusion would be a bit clearer. He affirms, however, that Isaiah conceives of the entire cosmos as a *present* Temple, for example:

> YHWH has already built his Temple, which is the world, 'heaven' and 'earth.' The endurance of the created order [as a Temple] renders its earthly replica, or antitype [i.e., the earthly Temple], superfluous ... The world in its fullness is the temple ... There is no place in the world for a Temple to stand ... The real Temple, which is the world, is protological and therefore admits of no historical duplication.[62]

I think it more appropriate to speak of the original, pre-fall creation as a pristine Temple of God (with the Garden of Eden perhaps as the holy of holies) and the post-fall creation and Israelite Tabernacle and Temples as contaminated with sin, thus needing judgement followed by eschatological recreation of the cosmos and Temple. It is this that Isaiah 65–66 is underscoring. While Levenson can affirm that there is a sense that Isaiah 2:2–4 (= Mic. 4:1–5) refers to the end-time 'invasion of the world by the Temple',[63] the upshot of Levenson's discussions is a lack of clarity about exactly how he understands the relationship of the present world as a divine Temple to the prophecies of the eschatological Temple in the new creation.

Nevertheless, Levenson's conclusion comes closer than anyone whom I have read in Old Testament studies to my own understanding of the symbolic eschatological significance of Israel's Temple, except for Meredith G. Kline and William Dumbrell.[64] Levenson's previous studies

---

61 Ibid., p. 296.
62 Ibid., p. 296.
63 Levenson, 'The Temple and the World', pp. 55–6; so likewise Isaiah 6:3b: 'His presence fills all the earth' (Levenson, 'The Jerusalem Temple in Devotional and Visionary Experience', pp. 54–5). Because of space constraints, I have had to delete further analysis of Levenson on this issue which is crucial in order to give him a fair hearing and evaluation (this will appear in the expanded form of the article in my forthcoming book *Eden, the Temple and the Mission of the Church*, cited in n. 1 above).
64 After writing an earlier draft of this article, I found W. Dumbrell's article that briefly drew some of the same conclusions as I have drawn, especially with regard to Adam being placed as a 'king-priest' in Eden as a sanctuary in order to expand the sanctuary world-wide ('Genesis 2:1–17: A Foreshadowing of the New Creation' in S. J. Hafemann (ed.), *Biblical Theology: Retrospect and Prospect* [Downers Grove: IVP, 2002], pp. 53–65). In so doing, he expresses dependence partly on my earlier commentary excursus (Beale,

have been very helpful to my own understanding of the Temple. It was not in Levenson's purview to include New Testament evidence about the Temple and its relation to the Old Testament, though the New Testament perspective, I think, gives an early Jewish-Christian insight into Isaiah's eschatological intention. Furthermore, while Levenson proposes that eschatology merely recapitulates protology, it is better to go further and say that eschatology also escalates the beginning.[65]

The Book of Revelation, pp. 1109–11), which was the 'seedbed' for this present article, as well as some of the sources upon which I was originally dependant (e.g. Cassuto and Wenham). Here Dumbrell actually develops similar thoughts from his earlier *The End of the Beginning*, pp. 37–8, 41–2. Likewise, I discovered recently that Kline, *Kingdom Prologue*, pp. 55–6, 62–3 briefly anticipated my thesis, and it is quite possible that years ago my reading of Kline and Dumbrell's earlier work planted the seed of this idea in my mind.
[65] On which see further Beale, 'The Eschatological Conception of New Testament Theology' in *'The Reader Must Understand'*, pp. 11–52.

15

A LITTLE DWELLING
ON THE DIVINE PRESENCE

Towards a 'Whereness' of the Triune God

DANIEL STRANGE

1. INTRODUCTION

My four-year-old son has an uncanny ability to prick my theological pride with innocent but persistent questioning that leaves his 'erudite' father somewhat tongue-tied to know how to reply in a manner that will satisfy his thirst for knowledge. One example of this was a bedtime conversation some time ago: 'Dad, you said God is everywhere, but why do we pray to God in heaven? Dad, where is God now? Dad, where does God live? Dad, where is God's home?' Later on, in the solace of my office, I reflected further on these questions: Where *exactly* is God? Where is his dwelling? In what precise ways is God present or absent to the world and his creation? Quickly I came to realize that if I was to answer these questions, and be faithful to the totality of the biblical revelation, these seemingly innocent and child-like questions had a complexity and nuance that required some hard theological graft and ultimately took me to the edge of the precipice of my finite understanding.

In Jeremiah 23:23–24 we hear God asking a series of rhetorical questions: '"Am I only a God nearby," declares the Lord, "and not a God far away? Can anyone hide in secret places so that I cannot see him?" declares the Lord. "Do I not fill heaven and earth?" declares the Lord.' However, Proverbs 15:29 declares that 'The Lord is far from the wicked, but hears the prayer of the righteous.' Scripture records God coming and going, ascending and descending (see Gen. 11:5; Isa. 64:1–2), and yet we also read that we live and move and have our being in God (Acts 17:28). We say confidently that God is 'in heaven', but what does that mean, and does this mean that God is not 'in hell'? Scripture tells us that God dwelt in the Tabernacle, and the Temple, how he dwelt in Christ by hypostatical union, how he now dwells with believers and how one day he will dwell in the new heaven and new earth. But how are we to understand these statements conceptually? In modern evangelical parlance there are also questions to be asked: Why do some Christians place a special emphasis on 'the sanctuary' in their church? What do worship leaders mean when they talk about 'coming into the presence of God'? Are there places where God is present in a special way? Are there places where God is absent?

My aims in this chapter are quite modest as I try to complement from the perspective of systematic theology the other essays in this collection. With some fear and trembling, I want to take a predominantly descriptive whistle-stop tour around the doctrines of God's immensity and omnipresence; doctrines usually located under God's incommunicable attributes in systematic theology. This will involve, first, a description of what I call God's 'generality of presence' and secondly (and more relevant to our theme of the Temple), God's 'speciality of presence'. The guides for this tour will be various famous friends from the 'Reformed' stable of the Christian church, including Henri Blocher, Louis Berkhof, Donald Macleod, Abraham Kuyper and above all the Reformed Scholastic Francis Turretin.

2. GOD'S GENERAL PRESENCE

First, let us define and distinguish between God's immensity and his omnipresence under what can be called *the essential universal generality of divine presence*. This may seem tangential to the overall theme on the presence of God in the Temple, but I believe it provides the background against which we can accurately place the Temple and the nature of God's dwelling in it.

God's immensity and omnipresence are those perfections of the Divine Being:

> by which he transcends all spatial limitations, and yet is present in every point of space with his whole being ... The last words are added in order to ward off the idea that God is diffused through space so that one part of his being is present in one place, and another part in some other place.[1]

There are a number of biblical statements that are the source for this doctrine: 1 Kings 8:27; Proverbs 15:3; Amos 9:2–4; Jeremiah 23:23–24; Ezekiel 8:12; Acts 17:27–28. It is perhaps Psalm 139:5–10 which is the most beautiful articulation of this truth:

> You hem me in – behind and before;
> you have laid your hand upon me.
> Such knowledge is too wonderful for me,
> too lofty for me to attain.
> Where can I go from your Spirit?
> Where can I flee from your presence?
> If I go up to the heavens, you are there;

---

[1] Louis Berkhof, *Systematic Theology* (Edinburgh: Banner of Truth, 1958), pp. 60ff.

> if I make my bed in the depths, you are there.
> If I rise on the wings of the dawn,
> if I settle on the far side of the sea,
> even there your right hand will guide me,
> your right hand will hold me fast.

Distinguishing between God's immensity and his omnipresence we can say the following:

> Immensity points to the fact that God transcends all space and is not subject to its limitations while 'omnipresence' denotes that He nevertheless fills every part of space with his entire being. The former emphasises the transcendence, and the latter the immanence of God. God is immanent in all His creatures, in His entire creation, but is in no way bounded by it.[2]

> Although the immensity and omnipresence of God are always connected together, yet they admit of distinction. The former indicates an absolute property belonging to him from eternity; the latter, based upon it, denoted a habitude to place existing in time. They are related to each other as a first and second act or a principle (*principii*) and a principiate (*principiate*). For out of immensity arises omnipresence, which supposes immensity as its foundation. God is therefore omnipresent because he is immense.[3]

There are certain trinitarian appropriations which accompany these two truths, remembering that the doctrine of appropriation does not mean an exclusive tie between attribute and person, but rather a belief that the Bible gives us warrant to speak of a 'special kinship, a privileged affinity and significant correspondence between *this* attribute and *that* Person'.[4] Immensity and transcendence are usually appropriated to the Father and omnipresence and immanence with the Spirit. As Blocher notes:

> The Spirit is the bearer of the divine presence ... The Spirit is the pervading presence as the sustaining power of life. He is so intimately united with created being that many passages remain ambiguous: do they speak of man's created breath or of God's own life-giving breath? We may never identify the two but how close they are![5]

By holding together both God's immensity and omnipresence we seek to avoid three deficient views of God and his relation to the world, views which still underlie much modern theological thought. First, pantheism that denies transcendence, fusing together God and creation. Secondly,

---

[2] Ibid., p. 61.

[3] Francis Turretin, *Institutes of Elenctic Theology, Vol. 1* (tr. G. M. Giger; ed. J. T. Dennison, Jr; Phillipsburg: Presbyterian & Reformed, 1992), p. 201.

[4] Henri Blocher, 'Immanence and Transcendence in Trinitarian Theology' in K. J. Vanhoozer (ed.), *The Trinity in a Pluralistic Age: Theological Essays on Culture and Religion* (Grand Rapids: Eerdmans, 1997), p. 121.

[5] Ibid., p. 122.

and at the opposite end of the spectrum, Deism that denies immanence, claiming God is only present in creation *per potentiam* (by power) and not *per essentiam* (by essence). Thirdly, and the most potent threat in our day, that of panentheism. Vanhoozer describes panentheism thus:

> Panentheism holds that the world is in some sense *in* God, though God exceeds the world. This is a novel solution to the problem of how to 'make room' in the material world for God – namely, by making room in God! To speak of God the Creator implies not a hard and fast distinction between God and the world but rather a recognition of 'the presence of God *in* the world and the presence of the world *in* God.'[6]

As with so much orthodox theology, we need to keep the biblical balance, overprivileging neither immensity nor omnipresence, neither transcendence nor immanence.

Having outlined immensity and omnipresence it is necessary to delve a little deeper into these doctrines. It is part of orthodoxy to maintain that God is not present physically anywhere in space although 'he can make his presence known in some physical way, but none of those physical manifestations are identical to his immaterial nature'.[7] Here, Feinberg makes a useful distinction:

> We must distinguish *physical presence* from what I shall call *ontological presence*. Ontological presence means that some entity or being is actually present at a given place in space. If the being is physical in nature, the being that is really there (ontological presence) will also be physically present. However, if the being is immaterial, then it can still be somewhere (ontological presence), but as immaterial it cannot be present physically. With this distinction, we can affirm that God is present *ontologically* in just one place. This is so not because as immaterial he is present nowhere physically, but rather because, as immense, he is not limited to being present in just one place at a time. He is simultaneously everywhere ontologically.[8]

At this point I want to follow the argument of Turretin. Turretin argues that God is said to be present in three modes: by power and operation, by knowledge and by essence:

> He is said to be everywhere by his power because he produces and governs all things and works all things in all ... He is present with all by his knowledge because he sees and beholds all things which are and become in every place as intimately present to and placed before him. Hence 'all things' are said 'to be naked and unto the eyes of him' and 'there is no creature that

---

[6] Kevin J. Vanhoozer, 'Effectual Call or Causal Effect? Summons, Sovereignty and Supervenient Grace' *Tyndale Bulletin* 49.2 (1998), p. 226.
[7] John S. Feinberg, *No One Like Him: The Doctrine of God* (Wheaton: Crossway, 2001), p. 250.
[8] Ibid.

is not manifest in his sight' (Heb. 4:13). Finally, he is everywhere by his essence because his essence penetrates all things and is wholly by itself intimately present with each and everything.[9]

This is summarized in the scholastic maxim *Enter praesenter est, et ubique potenter* ('meanwhile God is present and everywhere powerfully'). Commenting on this, Blocher relates this threefold division to Acts 17:28:

> We *live* by his sustaining power (power to live and love); in him we *move* – our every move is known, measured, determined, interpreted, of him; and we *have our being*. Do we perceive the semantic shade of immanence? Divine immanence is *pervasive* presence, granted to galaxies down to the last particle of matter. Divine immanence is inhabitation, *indwelling* presence: God is 'at home' in the world; he is not present as a visitor in a foreign territory – all these things which he has made are his; the earth is the Lord's greater temple, resounding in every corner with his praise (Ps. 29:9).[10]

If this statement is true, how can anyone say that God is localized to a particular building?

It is regarding God's presence of essence that Turretin's opponents, Socinius and Vorstius, object, arguing that God is contained in heaven in his essence and is only present on earth as to virtue and operation ('just as the sun is said to be present with us by the power of his rays although, very far distance in his body').[11] Turretin's response is to note the three modes of being in a place:

> circumscriptively – attributed to bodies because they are in place and space so as to be commensurate with parts of space; definitively – applicable to created spirits and incorporeal substances (which are defined by certain places, and are so here as to not be anywhere else; and repletively – which is ascribed to God because his immense essence is present with all and, as it were, completely fills all space ... Therefore God is so said to be repletively everywhere on account of the immensity of his essence, that this should be understood in a most different manner from the mode of being in place of bodies (i.e., beyond the occupation of space, and the multiplication, extension, division of itself, or its mingling with other things, but independently and divisibly). For wherever he is, he is wholly; wholly in all things, yet wholly beyond all; included in no place and excluded from none; and not so much in a place (because finite cannot comprehend infinite) as in himself.[12]

Here we are pushed to the limits of our language and understanding. As Blocher notes:

---

[9] Turretin, *Institutes of Elenctic Theology, Vol. 1*, p. 197.
[10] Blocher, 'Immanence and Transcendence in Trinitarian Theology', p. 111.
[11] Turretin, *Institutes of Elenctic Theology, Vol. 1*, p. 197.
[12] Ibid.

Both transcendence and immanence tell us of the divine *more*, and *beyond*, the true *akhbar*. St Augustine had his own unsurpassed way of confessing it: *... Thou wast more deeply within myself than my innermost part, and higher than the highest part of my being.*[13]

3. GOD'S GENERAL PRESENCE COMPARED WITH HIS SPECIAL PRESENCE

The description of God's essential presence now leads us into a further delineation in divine presence, for if God does not have spatial dimensions, if he cannot be contained by space and yet fills all space, then the biblical descriptions of God 'coming' and 'going', of him 'ascending' and 'descending', of him being 'far off' and 'near' and of him dwelling in certain places and not in others cannot be literal descriptions of God's essence because he is omnipresent and immense. Rather, these depictions must be seen to be metaphorical, indicating a special manifestation of God's presence in his operation and working. God is present in different ways, in different places and he acts differently in different places. This might be designated *the particular speciality of divine presence*. Both Berkhof and Turretin summarize this well, noting that God is not equally present and present in the same sense in all his creatures:

> He does not dwell on earth as He does in heaven, in animals as He does in man, in the inorganic as he does in the organic, in the wicked as he does in the pious, nor in the Church as He does in Christ. There is an endless variety in the manner in which He is immanent in His creatures, and in the measure in which they reveal God to those who have eyes to see.[14]

> The divine presence can either be symbolical, when under some visible form he manifests himself to believers (as to Moses in the bush, to the people in the cloudy pillar, to the patriarchs under the from of angels and men); or a sacramental and mystical presence, when under external signs and elements he exhibits and confirms his grace to us; or a spiritual and vivifying presence and when by his Spirit he dwells in the hearts of believers.[15]

Before plunging into some specific details over this speciality of presence, I wish to note some helpful observations made by John Frame that I hope will give some foundations to the rest of our discussion.[16] When speaking about God's presence, Frame insists that we must speak of God being *covenantally* present: 'he is with his creatures to bless and judge them in accordance with the terms of the covenant'.[17]

---

[13] Blocher, 'Immanence and Transcendence in Trinitarian Theology', p. 111.
[14] Berkhof, *Systematic Theology*, p. 61.
[15] Turretin, *Institutes of Elenctic Theology, Vol. 1*, p. 197.
[16] John Frame, *The Doctrine of God* (Phillipsburg: Presbyterian & Reformed, 2002).
[17] Ibid., p. 94.

He goes on to explore how God's covenant presence has a number of dimensions that take seriously God's immanence whilst not denying his transcendence. First, God's presence is temporal – he is present *now*. For Frame this is the significance of John 8:58, 'I AM here again indicates the continuity of the Lord's presence over time. Jesus was present to Abraham and present to all times. He is the I AM.'[18] Secondly, God is present in space and place – he is present 'here' (a point I wish to 'dwell' on in the second half of this chapter). Thirdly, God is not only present to his covenant people but is covenantally present universally because of creation, the covenant between God and Adam (which includes the entire human race even though we are breakers of this covenant), and the covenant between God and Noah's family which is made to 'every living creature on earth' (Gen. 9:10). Frame concludes: 'so the Lord is present everywhere and to everyone, as the one who blesses and curses according to his covenant. He is unavoidable, closer to us than anyone else. We cannot escape from him. As his control and authority are absolute, so is his presence.'[19]

Putting together God's general and special presence, I wish to define three ways in which God is present to his creation: (i) generally sustaining; (ii) specially but negatively judging, punishing and 'absenting'; (iii) specially and gloriously gracing and blessing. I will briefly comment on the first two before concentrating on the third.

God is universally present to sustain the creation or else the creation would not be. At this point let us remember that the living God of the Bible has not revealed himself ontologically and economically as a monadic philosophical concept but as triune: One God – Father, Son and Spirit. From the perspective of Son and Spirit, I wish to make a few observations with regards to divine presence.

First, Grudem, commenting on the sustaining providential presence of God, notes that 'in this sense the divine nature of Christ is everywhere present: "He is before all things and in him all things hold together" (Col. 1:17); Hebrews says of God the Son that he is continually "upholding the universe by his word of power" (Heb. 1:3).'[20] As a slight digression, and I realize a polemical one for some, I wish to note two diverse Christological implications of this.

Robert Reymond notes that the doctrines of omnipresence and immensity, as I have already indicated, mean that biblical language for example of God 'coming' and 'going' cannot be understood as literal descriptions but rather must be understood metaphorically, indicating a special manifestation of God's working. He continues:

---

[18] Ibid., p. 99.
[19] Ibid., p. 102.
[20] Wayne Grudem, *Systematic Theology* (Leicester: IVP, 1994), pp. 175ff.

Furthermore, since all that we say about God's nature *per se* is equally true of each of the persons of the Godhead, this conclusion has major implications with regard to the meaning of both the Incarnation and the Holy Spirit's 'coming' into the world at Pentecost. Being omnipresent himself, God the Son did not literally 'come' into the world in the sense that he came to a place where he was not before. The event of the incarnation should not be interpreted to mean that God the Son 'literally' 'left heaven' and 'came into the world' and 'confined' himself to the earthly body of Jesus. This would mean that he divested himself of his omnipresence. It intends rather to convey the fact that the Son, through the instrumentality of the virginal conception, took into union with himself our human nature in such a real and vital sense that we properly declare that Jesus of Nazareth was God manifest in flesh. But we do not for a moment intend to suggest that the Son of God somehow divested himself of his omnipresence when he became a man.[21]

This is the basis for the *extra Calvinisticum*, creedally formulated in Question 18 of the Heidelberg Catechism: 'Since [Christ's] Godhead is illimitable and omnipresent, it must necessarily follow that the same is beyond the limits of the human nature he assumed, and yet is nevertheless in his human nature, and remains personally united to it.'[22]

However, a further qualification is in order regarding the subject of the divine 'presence' in Christological formulation. This concerns part of the debate over the relationship between the two natures of Christ. The doctrine of the communion in attributes (*communicatio idiomatum*) with its constitutive parts (the communion of natures [*communio naturarum*], the communion of the natures in the work of Christ as Mediator [*communicatio apotelesmaton*] and the communion in grace [*communio gratiarum*]) attempts to understand this relationship.[23] While it is agreed that the attributes of both natures are attributed to the one Person, there is strong disagreement between Reformed and Lutheran believers over whether the attributes of the one nature are communicated to the other, the Reformed believing the communication to be only verbal, the Lutherans believing it to be literal.[24] Underlying and fuelling this seemingly abstruse debate is the manifest difference between the Reformed and Lutheran regarding the Lord's Supper. Macleod explains the issue as follows:

> The Reformed spoke of the presence of Christ in the sacrament as 'spiritual'. Lutherans, insisting on the literal acceptance of the words 'This is my body,' spoke of it as physical: the body of Christ is received in, with and under the

[21] Robert Reymond, *A New Systematic Theology of the Christian Faith* (Nashville: Thomas Nelson, 1998), p. 170.
[22] 'The Heidelberg Catechism (1563)' in *The Three Forms of Unity* (Protestant Reformed Churches in America, 1966).
[23] For a good summary of this doctrine, see Donald Macleod, *The Person of Christ* (Leicester: IVP, 1998), pp. 193–9.
[24] Ibid., p. 196.

elements (the doctrine which later came to be known as 'consubstantiation'). This had clear implications for Christology. If there were to be a physical presence in the sacrament, then his humanity must be in some sense omnipresent. This was secured in the peculiarly Lutheran doctrine of the *communicatio*, referred to as the *genus majesticum* because according to it the Son of God communicated his divine majesty to the flesh he assumed, with the result that even the human nature of Christ 'is in full possession, and capable of full use, and participant in the full glory of the divine.' In particular, according to Lutherans, the properties of omniscience, omnipotence and omnipresence were communicated to the Saviour's human nature. It was also, because of the participation in the divine glory, entitled to worship and adoration.[25]

For a number of reasons (perhaps most importantly the difficulties this raises for a true understanding of Christ's humanity), Reformed believers have strongly criticized the Lutheran understanding, Charles Hodge saying that the Christological construction 'forms no part of catholic Christianity'.[26]

Secondly, we can understand the doctrine of divine presence from the perspective of the Holy Spirit. We have already noted that it is appropriate in terms of trinitarian language to speak of the Spirit as the bearer of the divine presence. But what presence are we referring to? In his majestic and comprehensive book, *The Work of the Holy Spirit*, Abraham Kuyper comments on the relationship between the Spirit's generality and speciality of presence. He states that to say the Spirit ever moves from one place to another is an impossibility and directly opposes God's omnipresence, eternity and immutability. However, he does recognize the difference between David's song in Psalm 139 and the testimony of Luke, 'The Holy Spirit fell on all them which heard the Word.' His explanation is that David's description applies to 'local presence in space, but not to the world of spirits' and that both spirit and matter have different laws:

> We emphasise the word *law*. According to the analogy of faith, there must be laws that govern the spiritual world as there are in the natural; yet owing to our limitation we cannot know them. But in heaven we shall

---

[25] Ibid., pp. 196ff.

[26] Charles Hodge, *Systematic Theology*, Vol. 2 (Grand Rapids: Eerdmans, 1952 [1871]), p. 418. All of Hodge's criticisms can be found in *Vol. 2*, pp. 407–18. See also Macleod, *The Person of Christ*, pp. 197ff.; Berkhof, *Systematic Theology*, pp. 325ff. I should note that Reformed theologians do hold that Christ is present 'spiritually' in the Lord's Supper. Macleod notes that 'although [Christ's] human nature is neither omnipotent, omniscient or omnipresent, he himself is … [Christ's] personal presence is not limited to his bodily presence. His humanity is limited and localized, but it exists only in union and conjunction with his deity … It is as such, as the God-man, that he gives us the privilege of eating and drinking not merely in remembrance of him, but with him, at his table. Neither the divine nor the human is now excluded from anything he does.' Macleod, *The Person of Christ*, p. 199.

know them, and all the glories and particulars of the spiritual world, as
our physicians know the nerves and tissues of the body. This we know,
however, that that which applies to matter does not therefore apply to
spirit. God's omnipresence has reference to all space, but not to every
spirit. Since God is omnipresent, it does not follow that He dwells in the
Spirit of Satan, hence it is clear that the Holy Spirit can be omnipresent
without dwelling in every human soul; and that He can descend without
changing place, and yet enter a soul hitherto unoccupied by Him; and that
He was present among Israel and among the Gentiles and yet manifested
Himself among the former and not among the latter. From this it follows
that in the spiritual world He can come where he was not; that He came
among Israel, not having been among them before; and that He manifested
Himself among them less powerfully and in another way than on and
before the day of Pentecost.[27]

In terms of the Old Testament, the conclusion of Kuyper is that there
are three aspects concerning the presence of the Spirit: first, his omnipresence in space; secondly, his spiritual presence among Israel; and
thirdly (which is in fact a subset of his spiritual presence), his work
from without in imparting gifts and/or his work from within imparting
the 'unlosable gift of salvation'.[28]

It is important that we distinguish properly between God's general
presence and his special presence and do not confuse the two. Unfortunately, much modern thinking, including some evangelical thought,
has a tendency to see a fusing uniformity when it comes to speaking of
God's presence, grace and revelation, which must be resisted because of
the implication it has for the understanding of salvation. One example
of this is the salvific inclusivism of Clark Pinnock. In his desire to reject
the historical axiom *extra ecclesiam nulla salus* (outside the church there
is no salvation) and replace it with *extra gratia nulla salus* (outside of
grace there is no salvation), Pinnock equates all biblical references to
God's general presence (Ps. 139, etc.) with God's potentially salvific
prevenient grace, universally offering humanity a relationship with
God:

> The cosmic breadth of Spirit activities can help us conceptualise the univer-
> sality of God's grace. The creator's love for the world, central to the Chris-
> tian message, is implemented by the Spirit.[29]

> The Spirit is present in all human experience and beyond it. There is no
> special sacred realm, no sacred-secular split – practically anything in the
> created order can be sacramental of God's presence.[30]

---

[27] Abraham Kuyper, *The Work of the Holy Spirit* (Grand Rapids: Eerdmans, 1900), p. 119.
[28] Ibid., p. 120.
[29] Clark H. Pinnock, *Flame of Love: A Theology of the Holy Spirit* (Downers Grove: IVP, 1996), p. 187.
[30] Ibid., p. 62.

We refuse to allow the disjunction between nature and grace ... on the supposition that, if the triune God is present, grace must be present too.[31]

I would want to maintain that, unlike Pinnock's position, the Bible does not confuse and blur God's universal activity and presence in terms of providence and creation with God's particular activity in redemption. The fact that God is present does not necessarily mean a salvific presence. For Pinnock, this uniform understanding of presence is a building block towards his thesis that the unevangelized (those who never hear the gospel) can respond to the presence of the Spirit and be saved ontologically whilst being epistemologically unaware of Christ and his work.[32]

With the clear distinction between God's general presence and special presence in place, one can better explain God's relationship to unholy things:

It is not unworthy of the divine majesty to be everywhere on earth, even in the most filthy places, because he is not there by physical contact or by any mingling and composition, but as the efficient and conserving cause of things. If it was not unworthy of God to create all things, even the most mean, why should it be unworthy of him to be perpetually present with them? The sun by its rays permeates sordid places without being polluted by them, and how much less God? God is far off from the wicked (as to the special presence of his favour and grace), but is always present with them by his general presence of essence.[33]

If we were being pedantic we could say that Turretin is not quite right here because there is a sense in which God does present favour and blessing to the wicked: in his common grace. Interestingly this is a manifestation of grace that seems to sit quite comfortably within an explanation of God's general presence, as it sustains and restrains naturally rather than spiritually.[34] As a consequence it is not a redemptive presence to bless.

---

[31] Clark H. Pinnock, 'An Inclusivist View' in D. L. Okholm and T. R. Phillips (eds), *Four Views of Salvation in a Pluralistic World* (Grand Rapids: Zondervan, 1995), p. 98.

[32] Another example of this 'merging' is Karl Rahner's 'supernatural existential' which is the foundation for his 'anonymous Christian'. For further description and analysis of both Pinnock and Rahner's position, see Daniel Strange, 'Presence, Prevenience, or Providence? Deciphering the Conundrum of Pinnock's Pneumatological Inclusivism' in Tony Gray and Christopher Sinkinson (eds), *Reconstructing Theology: A Critical Assessment of the Theology of Clark Pinnock* (Carlisle: Paternoster Press, 2000), pp. 184–220; Daniel Strange, *The Possibility of Salvation Among the Unevangelised: An Analysis of Inclusivism in Recent Evangelical Theology* (Carlisle: Paternoster, 2002), pp. 85–108, 226–56; Bruce Demarest, 'General and Special Revelation' in Andrew Clarke and Bruce Winter (eds), *One Lord, One God: Christianity in a World of Religious Pluralism* (Carlisle: Paternoster, 1992), pp. 189–206.

[33] Turretin, *Institutes of Elenctic Theology, Vol. 1*, p. 200.

[34] On 'common grace', see Berkhof, *Systematic Theology*, pp. 432–44; John Murray, 'Common Grace' in *Collected Writings of John Murray, Vol. 2* (Edinburgh: Banner of Truth, 1977), pp. 93–123.

In terms of God's presence negatively to punish, judge and be absent we can cite passages like Amos 9:1–2:

> Strike the tops of the pillars so that the thresholds shake. Bring them down on the heads of all the people; those who are left I will kill with the sword. Not one will get away, none will escape. Though they dig down to the depths of the grave, from there my hand will take them. Though they climb up to the heavens, from there I will bring them down.

There is also the question of God's presence in hell that I would argue is not an absence of God in terms of essential presence but rather a complete absence of blessing and a complete presence of punishment:

> It is absurd to suppose God to be in the devils and the wicked as he is in believers (as a gracious God), but not to be in them as a Judge and the avenger of crimes; not as an approver of wickedness, but as the Creator and sustainer of nature. Although he is differently in heaven and in hell (here by grace, there by justice; here as blessing, there as punishing), yet he can be in both places as to the immensity of his essence.[35]

Commenting further on God's 'absence' in the present, Donald Macleod notes that although believers enjoy that presence of God that is essential to their perseverance and can truly trust in God's promise never to forsake us, the Bible does speak of God sovereignly withdrawing his gracious presence even for the believer.[36] He notes three ways we see this. First, there are times when 'God withholds all sense of His love and all ability to be patient and all understanding of His will, then, in a very real sense, we walk in darkness and have no light'.[37] Secondly, there are times when God withdraws the help we are used to due to our own iniquity (Isa. 59:1–2). Thirdly, God can withdraw his presence in the sense of withholding consolations: 'We may be both kept and helped and yet we ourselves, because we are unaware of it, derive no comfort from it.'[38]

Despite the believer sometimes experiencing a lack of God's presence, the lack of presence for the unbeliever is total and as such much more distressing:

> For the natural man this is his day-to-day situation. It is the only relation to God he has ever known. His Creator is always at a distance, remote, inaccessible and threatening. This graphically illustrated in Genesis 3:24 ... Communion can only be re-established by a specific act of reconciliation. This is precisely the significance of the atonement. Christ makes peace *through the blood of His cross* (Col. 1:20). The flaming sword is plunged into

---

[35] Turretin, *Institutes of Elenctic Theology, Vol. 1*, p. 200.
[36] Donald Macleod, *Behold your God* (Fearn, Ross-shire: Christian Focus, 1995), p. 85.
[37] Ibid., p. 86.
[38] Ibid.

the heart of the Last Adam (Zech. 13:7). Only through that vicarious curse-bearing can the problem of inaccessibility of God be overcome.[39]

With the cross of Christ in full view, finally and most importantly we come to God's glorious presence of blessing and grace which is most often the way Scripture talks about God's 'presence'. There are many ways I could approach and develop this idea, but I want to focus specifically on the concept of 'God dwelling' especially as this refers to heaven, the Temple and the new heaven and earth that has been the focus of the papers in this collection.

4. THE NATURE OF GOD'S DWELLING

I repeat the question I asked at the beginning of this paper: Where is God? I hope so far we have established that from the general perspective of essence, God's dwelling place is the whole universe. However, various passages throughout Scripture indicate that God's proper dwelling place is in heaven (1 Kgs. 8:30; Isa. 6:1–2; Ps. 89:7; Job 1:6; Rev. 4:1–11). What does this mean? Does this mean that God is more present in heaven than anywhere else? What it may mean is that in a special way God dwells in heaven in his undiluted and fully manifested grace, glory and holiness. Interestingly Turretin, after refuting his opponents, does note that we can legitimately maintain that God is in heaven:

> God is said to be in heaven, not exclusively of the earth, as if he is included in heaven as to essence; but because in heaven as a royal palace, he displays his glory in an eminent manner. Nor if worshippers raise their eyes to heaven, either by natural instinct or by command of the word, is this done not because God is included in heaven (which the apostle proves, Acts 17:24), but (1) in order that when we are about to approach unto God, we may elevate all our thoughts above these terrestrial and fleeting things and think nothing concerning God but what is great and lofty; (2) that we may know heaven to be the seat and throne of God, where there is a more illustrious display and a richer communication of glory and grace, whence all blessings are to be looked for and sought (as under the old dispensation the worshippers turned their faces towards the ark and temple and not because God was included in the ark or temple but on account of the remarkable manifestation of grace usually made there); (3) that we may also remember that heaven is the habitation prepared for us by God ... (4) to show that our prayers should no longer be directed to a certain fixed place on earth, but should be elevated to heaven, to be placed upon our altar (Christ in heaven) to be sanctified by him.[40]

Although heaven is the focus of this special presence of glory, grace and blessing, we do see many ways in which God dwells and appears

---

[39] Ibid., p. 87.
[40] Turretin, *Institutes of Elenctic Theology*, pp. 199ff.

in his glorious presence on earth, all of them organically related across the redemptive historical index. Here I briefly note some examples.

First, there are the texts where God appears as a theophany[41] in human form, the more explicit instances being Genesis 18:1–33; 32:24–32; Numbers 22:22–35; Joshua 5:13–6:5; Judges 6:11–23; 13:3–23. Although there is no consensus as to the exact interpretation of these passages (an appearance of God, a messenger from God, an angel or the pre-incarnate Christ?), one of the most recent studies is by Borland who, I think, persuasively argues them to be Christophanies, defining them as 'those unsought, intermittent and temporary, visible and audible manifestations of God the Son in human form, by which God communicated something to conscious human beings on earth prior to the birth of Jesus Christ'.[42]

Secondly, there are other theophanies or appearances of God, such as dreams and visions (e.g. Gen. 20:3; 28:12; 46:2), voices (Gen. 3:8), angels of the Lord and the burning bush (Exod. 3:2–6). The pillar of cloud (Exod. 13 – 14) was perhaps the foretaste of God's Shekinah glory that began to abide over the ark of the covenant (Exod. 40:34–35):

> Following Israel's sin in worshipping the golden calf, Moses erected a tent outside the camp and called it 'the tent of meeting' (Exod. 33:7). There God and Moses met. When the pillar of cloud descended to the tent, God spoke with Moses and all Israel worshipped. The tent was placed outside the camp to symbolize the removal of God's presence from the midst of the camp because of Israel's sin. Yet the significance of this tent is like that of the tabernacle erected in the midst of Israel since the tabernacle was called the 'tent of meeting' (40:2). Both tent and tabernacle symbolized the presence of God with Israel (33:14), the fact, that is, that God had chosen to dwell in the midst of Israel (25:8; 29:45).[43]

Interestingly, Meredith Kline links God's theophanic presence on earth to God's heavenly presence that we have already mentioned. He describes this glory-cloud in terms of a window to heaven and so a holy space:

> When the inner reality veiled within the theophanic cloud is revealed, we behold God is in heaven. The world of the Glory theophany is a dimensional realm normally invisible to man, where God reveals his presence as the King of glory enthroned in the midst of myriads of heavenly beings. It is the realm into which the glorified Christ, disappearing from human view, entered to assume his place on the throne of God. It is the invisible (or 'third') heaven brought into cloud-veiled visibility.[44]

---

[41] I am defining 'theophany' quite broadly as a visible or auditory manifestation of God.
[42] James A. Borland, *Christ in the Old Testament* (Fearn, Ross-shire: Mentor, 1999), p. 32.
[43] D. E. Holwerda, *Jesus and Israel: One Covenant or Two?* (Grand Rapids/Leicester: Eerdmans/Apollos, 1995), p. 62.
[44] Meredith Kline, *Images of the Spirit* (Grand Rapids: Baker Book House, 1980), p. 17, quoted in Frame, *The Doctrine of God*, p. 586.

Although God promises to David that he will build a house for God (2 Sam. 7:1–17), it is Solomon who finally turns the tent into the Temple that is destroyed by the Babylonians but then rebuilt after the exile.

Thirdly, we see Christ himself, the apex of God dwelling on earth, which everything before points to and which everything after flows from. He is Immanuel – God present with us. This is not just another Christophany but something completely different – incarnation: 'the same Son, our Lord Jesus Christ, the same perfect in Godhead and also perfect in manhood; truly God and truly man, of a reasonable soul and body; consubstantial with the Father according to Godhead, and consubstantial to us according to Manhood ...'[45] Macleod comments on the amazing significance of God dwelling with us in the incarnation:

> He is the glory of God, the very Shekinah itself, tabernacling among men. The tangible physicalness of this form of the divine presence should not be overlooked. During those years men could see His glory (John 1:14). They could witness with amazement His mighty acts. They could literally hear Him expound the ethics of His kingdom. God was on earth, experiencing the human condition at first hand and engaging the enemy at close quarters. He was present in our poverty, our suffering and our temptations until the last moment of supreme paradox when He dwelt in the anathema. Then the cross became his Tabernacle.[46]

Affirming Chalcedonian orthodoxy means we do not have necessarily to contradict what we stated earlier about God being physically absent from the universe. Note what Frame says:

> In Christ, God certainly perceives the world not only from his transcendent perspective, not only from all creaturely perspectives, but uniquely from one particular creaturely perspective ... But at the very same time, God (the Son, as well as the Father and the Spirit) has an experience that transcends all physical limitation. God is not, therefore, to be defined as a physical being. (Even as the incarnate Son of God had a divine sovereignty over space and time.) But as Lord of all things that are material and physical, he is supremely able to understand the world from the perspective of every physical being, to reveal himself in any physical form that he chooses, and even to take human flesh, so that he has his own body, without abandoning his transcendent existence ... This doctrine [God's incorporeality] does not exclude God from physical reality. Rather it teaches that he relates himself to physical reality as the Lord, transcending it and using it as he chooses.[47]

Fourthly, there is our union with Christ (and all the benefits this brings) by the indwelling of the Spirit in the believer. Though this union is spiritual and mystical 'this nonmaterial union with Christ is as real as though there were in fact a literal umbilical cord uniting them,

---

[45] The Chalcedonian Creed (451), printed in Grudem, *Systematic Theology*, p. 1169.
[46] Macleod, *Behold your God*, p. 89.
[47] Frame, *The Doctrine of God*, p. 587.

reaching "all the way" from Christ in heaven to the believer on earth'.[48] Commenting on the nature of God's presence/dwelling in the believer, Ferguson notes the following:

> The relationship is more intimate than that of mere divine influence, but the exact character of the Spirit's indwelling is nowhere explained or explored. In the nature of the case it parallels the mysteries of the divine-human engagement in providence, inspiration and incarnation. The analogy we are offered is that the mutual indwelling of Christ and the believer is shaped according to the pattern of inner-trinitarian relationships. Just as there is mutual indwelling of Father and Son revealed by the Spirit, so, by the indwelling of the same Spirit, Christ and the believer are united (Jn. 14:20).[49]

Fifthly, and an implication of the previous point, is that God by his Spirit dwells in the people of God corporately – the church which is the body of Christ. Believers are given one and the same Spirit to drink (1 Cor. 12:12–13) and this is what unites believers: 'God's presence makes us his people; the presence of Jesus constitutes the church as his temple, built of living stones, joined to him as God's elect Stone (1 Pet. 2:4–6). The church itself is a temple, the house of God, sanctified by the presence of the Spirit (1 Cor. 3:16)'[50] and 'a communion gathered by the Word and marked by the sacraments'.[51]

Sixthly, and finally, we have God's dwelling in the new heaven and new earth, the nature of which I will comment upon below. How do all these types of dwelling and divine presence fit together? What is relevance of this for the believer today? While there is more than enough material here for a whole book on a biblical theology of God's presence, here I limit myself to five brief observations primarily related to the focus of this study – the Temple.

First, we can say as the writer of Hebrews tells us, that the Tabernacle and Temple are not only both 'little replicas of heaven'[52] and little replicas of Eden,[53] but they are also types of the supreme archetype of dwelling: Christ. As Poythress notes:

---

[48] Reymond, *A New Systematic Theology of the Christian Faith*, p. 738.
[49] Sinclair Ferguson, *The Holy Spirit* (Leicester: IVP, 1996), p. 176.
[50] Edmund Clowney, *The Church* (Leicester: IVP, 1995), p. 46.
[51] Ibid., p. 58. I have already mentioned how Christ is specially present in the Lord's Supper. Many believers wish to speak in terms of 'presence' when discussing the preaching of the Word. Lloyd-Jones famously asks, 'What is the chief end of preaching? I like to think it is this. It is to give men and women a sense of God and His presence.' D. Martyn Lloyd-Jones, *Preaching and Preachers* (London: Hodder & Stoughton, 1985), p. 97.
[52] Vern Poythress, *The Shadow of Christ in the Law of Moses* (Phillipsburg: Prebyterian & Reformed, 1991), p. 34.
[53] See Greg Beale's essay above.

Christ Himself is the ultimate dwelling of God with human beings. Matthew 1:23 says that Christ is called 'Immanuel' which means 'God with us'. In John 2:19–22 Jesus says 'Destroy this temple, and I will raise it again in three days'. And John comments, 'But the temple he had spoken about was his body'. John 1:14 says that the 'Word was made flesh and dwelt among us', deliberately using a word for dwelling that alludes to the Old Testament tabernacle. Finally, John 14:11 says, 'I am in the Father and the Father is in me.' This and similar language in John about the mutual indwelling of the Father and Son presents us with the ultimate form of dwelling, namely, the original indwelling of the Persons of the Trinity. This original uncreated dwelling must be the model for all instances of God dwelling with human beings who are made in the image of God.[54]

Secondly, can we ask why and how in any sense can God dwell on earth. Like Poythress, I think the key here is holiness: 'in a supreme sense, God himself is holy. But other things can be called holy when they are dedicated to him and are associated with his presence'.[55] So all God's dwellings are holy and need to be thus if God is to dwell, and God cannot stand the presence of sin, it being a contradiction of his being. This, I think explains Berkhof's somewhat cryptic comment that the nature of God's indwelling is in harmony with that of his creatures. A holy God cannot but both recoil and react in wrath to anything that is unholy and sinful. Hence we see no wrath in heaven because heaven is pure and undefiled, but many instances of wrath throughout Scripture. How then is God by his Spirit able to dwell in our hearts? Only by the blood of Christ that cleanses the believer of sin, continues to reconstruct us in the image of Christ and produces fruit in our lives. However, we should note the stress in the Bible of holiness not only being a divine gift but a human task:

> Holiness is primarily a gift of the presence of God. The temple is holy because God dwells there. God's people are holy because they are the temple in which God lives. But holiness is also a requirement for retaining the presence of God. Therefore Paul quotes also from the commands given to the priests when the people of Judea departed from Babylon (Isa. 52:11; 2 Cor. 6:17). Just as the priests who bore the vessels of the Lord had to leave behind everything that was unclean and purify themselves because the Lord would be accompanying them on their journey, so now believers who are the temple, must separate themselves from iniquity, darkness, idolatry and belief ... They are like priests in the temple who must be holy because God is holy. Holiness is a gift, but it must become perfectly expressed in the lives of God's people. Holiness applies to people, no longer to a building, and temple services no longer refer to ritual acts but to life itself.[56]

---

[54] Poythress, *The Shadow of Christ in the Law of Moses*, pp. 32ff.
[55] Ibid., p. 33.
[56] Holwerda, *Jesus and Israel*, p. 82.

Thirdly, a correct systematic understanding of God's speciality of presence and the nature of his dwelling with his creation must be accompanied by a correct biblical-theological understanding of the same revelation. Only then will we understand, first, that the types of 'God dwelling' in redemptive-history are inextricably linked to one another, and, secondly, how the believer is to interpret and apply this revelation today. One small example of this will suffice. I would like to argue that a true grasp of the nature of God's presence and dwelling will prove a necessary antidote to two dangerous misunderstandings that plague the Christian church today, ironically one associated with an older generation of believers and the other with the younger. First, it is wrong to localize God's special presence, or an act of 'worship', to any one particular place or any one time. A special part of the church called a 'sanctuary' which is the only place where we can 'meet and worship God' and where we must dress in a particular way misunderstands that 'God is concerned with our hearts and not our architecture and wardrobe'.[57] Worship is in spirit and in truth, in the heart of every believer wherever they might be: 'This is an amazing thing to contemplate, that the almighty and most holy God, the creator of the universe, should lower himself to not only save us, but to come and make our hearts, the hearts of sinners, his home.'[58] The second misunderstanding is the phenomenon of the 'worship leader' who calls us into God's presence as if as believers we are not in his presence already and need to 'do something' to actualize the presence of God. The terrible logic of this is that the worship leader is being set up as a rival priest, forgetting that there is only one high priest and mediator who has brought us into God's presence once for all (Heb. 10:5–12).

Fourthly, I would like tentatively to suggest that wherever and however God is present whether generally or specially, there is an appropriate amount of revelation present. Where God is, God makes himself known. Therefore in tandem with God's general presence is God's general revelation of himself and God's common grace, and in tandem with God's special presence is his special revelation. This would seem to make sense of the Berkhof quotation that 'there is an endless variety in the manner in which he is immanent in his creatures, and in the measure in which they reveal God to those who have eyes to see'. So God tells us something of himself by being generally present in creation but God's archetypal dwelling in Christ is also God's fullest revelation of himself to us.

Finally, what can we say about the nature of God's presence in the new heavens and new earth? We have heard that with the coming of Christ there is a progression from the localization of God's special pres-

---

[57] D. L. James. 'What on Earth *is* Christian Worship?', *Foundations* 43 (Autumn 1999), p. 11.
[58] Ibid.

ence and dwelling symbolized in the Temple to a universalization of God's dwelling in the hearts of believers. Still, there is a distinction to be made between the God's special dwelling in believers and his general presence in the world. What the new heaven and new earth will bring is what might be called the 'specializing of the general' as there will be no distinction between God's general presence and special presence as he will be specially present to all in the holy city. As Clowney writes:

> Yes, the church now has a heavenly glory, tasting by the Spirit the saving realities of the world to come. But there is a world to come, and the fore-taste of the Spirit fills our hearts with the yearning of Christian hope … In hope the church waits for the final glory to be brought with the returning Lord. The Lord is One, and his presence in the Spirit is no mere sign; yet there is a final fullness when Christ will claim the possession that is sealed by the downpayment of the Spirit. Heaven offers no other Christ, and no temple beyond Christ, for the Lord God, the Almighty, and the Lamb are the temple of the New Jerusalem to come (Rev. 21:22).[59]

Not only will the church enjoy this special presence but we will see Christ as he is, and with this will be complete intimacy and with this understanding. Amazingly it seems that for the redeemed they will be *literally* in the presence of the Lamb, a physical nearness to God.[60]

---

[59] Edmund Clowney, 'The Final Temple', *WTJ* 35 (1973), p. 187.
[60] For more details on the paradisal city-Temple in Revelation, see Beale's essay above.

16

THE TEMPLE IN THE
THEOLOGY OF KARL BARTH

JONATHAN NORGATE

1. INTRODUCTION

It is often suggested that Karl Barth's theological project, including his
major (unfinished) work, *Church Dogmatics*, is shaped overwhelmingly
by his active recognition of the reality of God on whose action and
initiative everything depends. Once we recognize this, as Robin W.
Lovin comments, God's 'action becomes the starting point from which
to comprehend the world and our own lives'.[1]

Barth himself is even more precise than this, for we recognize the
reality of God only in his *particular* self-revelation in Jesus Christ: God
may be 'known only in the particular way in which he gives Himself to
be known'.[2] There must be no abstract speculation in theological investigation, for all thought must be tied to the positive and actual form and
content of God's revelation, the God–man Jesus Christ.

In turning our attention to the place of the Temple (and by exten-
sion, the Tabernacle and other divine dwelling places) in Christian
dogmatics we must therefore, according to Barth, see that our understanding of the Temple will be properly oriented only as and when we
hold it up against the light of the particular divine revelation of God in
Jesus Christ, much as an X-ray acetate must be held up against a strong
light in order for the hidden picture to become explicable. For Barth,
Jesus Christ is the light beaming through the acetate. Any attempt to
investigate the meaning and significance of the Temple without *primary
reference* to Jesus Christ would thus be pointless.

Thus, we must turn to the question of the Temple with Jesus Christ
as our light source. Significantly, however, in the process of turning we
also will *see more clearly* the light source, for the Temple, along with the
rest of the contents of the Bible, constitutes a 'single witness to God's

---

[1] Robin W. Lovin, 'Foreword', from K. Barth, *The Holy Spirit and the Christian Life* (New
York: Westminster John Knox Press, 1993), p. ix.
[2] K. Barth, *Church Dogmatics*, IV/2 §2 (Edinburgh: T&T Clark, 1958), p. 26 (hereafter cited
as IV/2).

revelation of grace'.[3] For Barth, the Temple is part of the witness of
the 'speaking and acting of God in the people and among the men of
the people of Israel' (II/1, p. 108). As such, it is a witness to God in his
revelation, and a reminder that God may not be known *in abstracto*,
independently of the special way in which he has revealed his grace
'in His covenant with Israel and in the fulfilment of the promise of the
Messiah of Israel establishing this covenant' (II/1, p. 109).

We may note at this stage, however, that while it forms a part of
his overall theological project Barth gives no extended treatment of the
Temple in the *Church Dogmatics* (from which we will draw the material
for this essay), although, as we shall see, in developing his doctrine of
the divine perfections he makes considerable reference to the concept
of divine *presence as dwelling*. Yet while there is not a single extended
consideration of the place, meaning and power of the Temple, we
suggest that Barth recognized its significance to the biblical theologian.
In addition to its place in the single witness of God's revelation of
grace, he argues that to fail to take note of the 'specially defined spheres
of God's presence' and the concomitant 'definite commanded activity
of man' would be to pursue a *theologia gloriae*. This is not Barth's aim.
Rather, the place of the Temple should have an assured place in a
Christian dogmatics because it speaks both of the presence of God and
the problems of humankind.[4]

We will pursue our investigation of Barth's theology of the Temple
using three contexts which Barth himself offered as the best way
to understand the place, meaning and power of the Chalcedonian
dogma of the two natures of Christ. In Volume IV, Part 2 of the *Church
Dogmatics*, Barth sets out three contexts which help him clarify this
historic Christological formulation: (i) its first and final basis in the
divine election of grace; (ii) its historical fulfilment in the event of
the incarnation; and (iii) its basis of revelation in the resurrection
and ascension of the man Jesus (IV/2, p. 31). We make use of these
'contexts' primarily because they provide an appropriately Christological structure to our enquiries. They allow us to consider how the
Tabernacle and Temples of Israel fit into the eternal divine election of
grace, how the Temple of Herod fits into the historical fulfilment of
the eternal divine election in the event of the incarnation (which for
Barth is a salvific act), and how the description of the Christian and the
Christian community as Temples of the Holy Spirit fits into the age of
eschatological expectation following the resurrection and ascension of
our Lord Jesus Christ.

---

[3] K. Barth, *Church Dogmatics*, II/1 §26 (Edinburgh: T&T Clark, 1957), p. 108 (hereafter
cited as II/1).
[4] K. Barth, *Church Dogmatics*, III/4 §53 (Edinburgh: T&T Clark, 1961), p. 49 (hereafter
cited as III/4).

2. THE DIVINE ELECTION OF GRACE: CREATURELY INTEGRITY AND DIVINE DWELLING IN SPACE AND TIME

We begin with the first 'context', the 'divine election of grace', which Barth posits as the key to explicating the two natures dogma so as to avoid the Scylla of divinizing the human nature and the Charybdis of humanizing the divine. Barth contends that Jesus Christ's 'human essence' is that 'determined wholly and utterly, from the very outset and in every part, by the electing grace of God' (IV/2, p. 88). (We should note here that Barth uses the term 'essence' as that which is 'given in the act of electing and is in fact, constituted by that eternal act'.[5] This 'essence' is not some matter which pre-existed independently of this divine act.) It is this very electing grace which upholds and sustains the creatureliness of the human essence. In discussing the *humanitas* of the Son of Man who was and is also the Son of God, Barth argues that while there is 'identification' of the human nature in the divine, and identification of the divine in the human, this identification is not a mingling of natures: it does not entail a mutual participation. The confrontation of the divine with the human and the human with the divine is determined in such a way that it preserves the distinctiveness of the natures and yet provides for a unique mutual identification. This determination by the electing grace of God means that 'the Son of Man exists only in His identity with the Son of God, and His human essence only in its confrontation with His divine' (IV/2, p. 88). We suggest that it is this theological context, of the divine election of grace, which lies at the heart of his understanding of the localized and particular divine dwelling places recorded in biblical history. The eternal election of grace is the key to understanding both *the way* in which the Godhead dwells bodily in Jesus Christ (Col. 2:9), and the way in which *it is possible* for an omnipresent God to make a dwelling in space and time. These states are possible because God determines they be possible. Let us turn to each in turn.

2.1 'Jesus Christ: in whom the fullness of the Godhead dwells bodily'

As we have noted, the human nature of Jesus Christ is determined exclusively and totally by the divine election of grace. It is because of the divine determination that the creaturely integrity of this dwelling place is upheld. Maintaining this theological context as the key to understanding the concepts used in the early Lutheran and Reformed

---

[5] Bruce McCormack, 'Grace and Being: The Role of God's Gracious Election in Karl Barth's Theological Ontology' in J. Webster (ed.), *Cambridge Companion to Karl Barth* (Cambridge: Cambridge University Press, 2000), p. 99.

Christologies – *communicatio idiomatum*,[6] *communio naturarum*,[7] and *unio hypostatica*[8] – it is the *communicatio gratiarum*, the total and exclusive determination of the human nature of Jesus Christ by the grace of God, which maintains the integrity of the created place in which God dwells, even when it is the 'fullness' of the Godhead which dwells (cf. Col. 2:9). Barth's exegesis of this *locus classicus* turns on his concern that we must not overlook the significance of the concept of *katoikei* (dwelling). Barth aligns himself at this point with Calvin, quoting approvingly Calvin's description of the place of Jesus' conception, the Virgin's womb, as a 'temple in which he might dwell'.[9] He describes himself puzzled why it should be thought necessary to deify the flesh taken up by the Son of God, or why a dwelling is not thought sufficient to describe the human essence of Jesus Christ. The *communicatio gratiarum* issues and maintains the human essence (albeit one which is exclusively claimed and sanctified by God), and a dwelling or a Temple is a sufficient way to describe this human essence. It is sufficient because of the eternal election of grace: Temple is a sufficient way to account for the 'two natures' doctrine *because it is determined by God to be sufficient*.[10]

Furthermore, there are for Barth, as for Calvin, soteriological reasons why the creaturely integrity of the Temple is upheld. It is crucial to Jesus Christ's work as mediator that the dwelling place remains human: 'If the human essence of Jesus Christ is deified, can he really be the Mediator between God and us?' (IV/2, p. 89). His human essence is the same as ours, and even as the exalted Son of Man, he is still our brother, and in this way accessible and recognizable and able to be the first-born among many brothers. At this point Barth takes one step beyond Calvin as he explicates his doctrine of predestination. For Barth, Jesus Christ, the God–man in his divine–human unity, is the subject (as well as object) of election: the *logos* was God *as the One who 'became flesh'* (John 1:14). This means that the divine dwelling place, the Temple of the human essence,

---

[6] Barth argues that the doctrine of the '*communicatio idiomatum*' referred originally to the doctrine developed by early Lutheran and Reformed theology to refer to the impartation in Jesus Christ of the distinctive features of the two natures of God and man, and the communion of the features in the person of Jesus Christ. Only later did Lutheran and Reformed theologies differ on the doctrine. Barth here refers to the early definition (IV/2, p. 75).

[7] '*Communio naturarum*, the communion of the divine and human essence in the one Jesus Christ without change or admixture, but also without cleavage and separation' (IV/2, p. 51).

[8] '"*Hypostatic*" union, i.e., the union (of natures) made by God in the *hypostasis* (the mode of existence) of the Son' (IV/2, p. 51).

[9] John Calvin, *Institutes of the Christian Religion*, (tr. Henry Beveridge; London: James Clarke, 1953), book II, chapter XIV, §1, p. 415.

[10] Barth goes on to maintain that when the Son of God became this man, Jesus of Nazareth, he ceased to all eternity to be God only, receiving and having and maintaining to all eternity human essence as well. The human essence of Jesus Christ is 'His *temple* which He does not leave' (IV/2, p. 101).

has a part in whom this God has determined himself to be, become, and to be always. The divine dwelling-places which precede the historical fulfilment of the eternal election of grace are witnesses to this *logos* who was God *as* the One who 'became flesh'. That there were divine dwelling places in Israel is determined by the eternal decision of the God who became flesh, Jesus Christ, to fully dwell in bodily form. That is what 'underlay Beth-El and Sinai, Jerusalem and Shiloh' (II/1, p. 481). We suggest that Barth would say that there were (and are) temples only because of the character of the *logos*. In electing himself to become flesh, he determined that he would be 'for' humankind in a way which is characterized by dwelling in a particular space and time. We turn now to the question of how Barth understood God's freedom to dwell.

2.2 God's Dwelling Place: 'God is certainly everywhere. But God is not only everywhere'

In the longest discussion of Israel's divine dwelling places in the *Church Dogmatics* (II/1, §31, I), Barth speaks of the God who is 'certainly everywhere (but) not only everywhere' (II/1, p. 478). He is setting out his understanding of the divine perfections,[11] and in the context of his discussion of the unity and omnipresence of God he responds to the question of *how the God who is everywhere may also be somewhere*.

As Colin Gunton has suggested, 'Because God is involved economically in time and space, he cannot be conceived to be merely timeless and non-spatial ... God is not simply shapeless ... but eternal interpersonal life.'[12] For this reason, Barth conducts his survey of the omnipresence of God in the context of his special presences in the world, rather than according to a philosophically pre-conceived concept of omnipresence. Theological investigation must not be carried out apart from the special concrete form of revelation, and for this reason he begins with the special, the particular (following the order of biblical thinking) as the basis for the general. God is free to be not only everywhere because he is the living God who has determined to reveal himself and reconcile the world to himself in a special way. God is free to be present in the way he has determined, and the way he has determined to be omnipresent is '*by way of* His special presence'[13] (my italics). This is so because 'it is *through God's Word* that the world is created, preserved

---

[11] Barth displays his actualistic divine ontology. 'Rather than addressing the attributes of God in metaphysical terms, Barth articulates them in the light of the way in which God determines himself to be in revelation.' Alan Torrance, 'The Trinity' in Webster (ed.), *Cambridge Companion to Karl Barth*, p. 87.

[12] C. Gunton, *The One, the Three and the Many* (Cambridge: Cambridge University Press, 1998), p. 164.

[13] Ibid.

and upheld'.[14] In other words, the path from the presence with which
the triune God is present to himself, to the world is via the word who
is the essence and mystery of God's revelation and reconciliation. The
way God is to the world is primarily special, and only then general. We
should not first confess God as the Lord, but the Lord as God. Barth
maintains that the way God determines himself to be everywhere is
bound up with the special nature of his presence in his revealing and
reconciling work, and this is ontologically and not merely noetically
true. ('Both noetically and ontologically the general presence is bound
to this special presence. For all things are created and preserved by
God's Word, by the Word which is nothing other than the Word of His
revelation and reconciliation' [II/1, p. 483].) It is on this basis that Barth
argues that the historical fulfilment of this is that the dwelling of the
God of Israel is in 'a definite place chosen and designated by Himself'
(II/1, p. 479). The definite is bound up with the special nature of his
revealing and reconciling presence to Israel, and this means that we
must not think of God dwelling in the midst of his people 'figuratively'
but rather 'literally' (II/1, p. 479). We must recognize that what is said
about the particular dwelling of God in particular places, at Sinai, in the
Tabernacle, and in Jerusalem is literal. Barth explains what he means by
'literal' dwelling in relation to the 'concrete' election of Israel. Just as it
is a literal people which has been chosen and called, so too is it a literal
'place' which has been chosen and sanctified to 'house' the presence of
God. Literal presence is bound up with election.

Barth argues, then, that it is the special presence that is the *basis* for
the general presence. Elected Israel looks out from the Tabernacle and
Temple at the world and sees God's general presence in the world (cf.
Ps. 19: II/1, p. 101).

Yet he makes a third distinction which underlies these two, namely
the *proper* presence of God in his creation. This proper presence is
the basis of his special presence, and therefore the meaning and pre-
supposition of his general presence. *This proper presence is Jesus Christ.*
All other attestations of God's dwellings stand only as expectations or
recollections. This dwelling of God in Jesus Christ is the 'origin and
the goal, the basis and the constituent centre of the whole series of the
special self-representations of God' (II/1, p. 484). It is because Jesus
Christ is the one unique and proper presence of God that the special
presence of God in the Temple stood fulfilled and its status transformed by the historical fulfilment of the eternal election of grace in the
event of the incarnation.

However, it is worth noting here that Barth refers to Sinai not, as is
usual among scholars, in terms of theophany but in terms of 'abiding'.
While he recognizes a difference between the kind of divine presence

---

14 Ibid.

on Sinai (Exod. 24:16) and among the people (Exod. 25:8), he sees the key issue to be the fact that in both cases God is revealing himself particularly to the particular nation of Israel. In this respect, it is not so much the *type* of revelation but the fact that it is rooted in election which is to the fore. It may be argued that Barth's lack of differentiation leads to a 'one-size-fits-all' approach to the different occurrences of God's presence, with the consequence that, for example, the distinctives of the Sinai revelation (as a place where God reveals himself to the whole nation of Israel, and as a place from which Israel is led by a divine warrior) are obscured by Barth's decision to make his point about election.

3. THE EVENT OF INCARNATION AS HISTORICAL FULFILMENT: JESUS DETERMINES AND LIMITS THE TEMPLE

We turn now to the second context, the event of incarnation as historical fulfilment. This event in time is 'grounded in God's eternal election of grace and actualised accordingly'; and when we ask what the content of this eternal election of grace is, Barth tells us it is the 'true humanity of Jesus Christ, as the humanity of the Son' (IV/2, p. 37). Jesus Christ is the object of election. All other divine decisions and actions (including the divine dwellings before and after the incarnation) follow on from this, and in the historical fulfilment of the eternal election of grace is the 'execution and revelation of not merely *a* but *the* will of God' (IV/2, p. 31). We saw how Jesus Christ is the basis for the special dwelling places. As the proper dwelling place, all special dwelling places find in him their basis and constituent centre. He is the origin and goal of the special presence. We will tie this ontological and teleological order into another aspect of Jesus Christ's identity: as the execution and revelation of God's will he is the one in whom all things find their *limitation* as well as foundation. The will of God is not 'limited or determined by any other, and therefore by any other happening in the creaturely sphere, but is itself the sum of all divine purposes, and therefore that which limits and determines all other occurrence' (IV/2, p. 31). It is this eternal election of grace in Jesus Christ which determines the meaning, power and significance of the Tabernacle and Temples of Israel, and in the historical fulfilment in the event of the incarnation, we see that Jesus will not be limited or determined by the Temple, but instead will limit and determine the Temple, fulfilling in history the eternal election of grace. We will suggest that for Barth it is in this predestinarian sense that Jesus is able to replace Herod's Temple, and provides the explanation of his confession that 'one greater than the temple is here' (Matt. 12:16). Jesus' act (or acts) of Temple 'cleansing' (Mark 11:15–17 and parallels) may then be seen as an act of purification, but one which functions as an apocalyptic act, preparing for its inevitable and necessary destruction. Since the proper Temple is now here, even the once special dwelling place must go.

We shall proceed by addressing three questions to this context of fulfilment: (a) What does fulfilment mean for the Temple?; (b) What does rejection of Messiah mean for the Temple?; and (c) What do Jesus' actions mean for the Temple?

3.1 What does fulfilment mean for the Temple?

It was noted that Barth held the view that the special divine dwellings should be taken literally. The reality of the divine presence is affirmed. Yet, he argues that it is with the New Testament that this special dwelling is clearly shown to be only a *relative* reality. The 'dignity and power' (II/1, p. 480) of the special presences lay only in their quality as indicators and shadows (as Heb. 9:23ff. argues). The non-relative real dwelling place was manifest in the Word become flesh (John 1:14), whose 'glory' resides in the fact that he is the 'dwelling' of God with humankind (rather than in any demonstrable quality of splendour or outward beauty). With regard to this Revelation 21:3 is the eschatological confession of this 'glory': 'Behold, the tabernacle of God is with men, and he will dwell with them and they shall be his people, and God himself shall be with them.' We take this to mean that the fulfilment of the eternal election of grace opens up the possibility for and, perhaps more than that, *instantiates* an intimate communion with God ('He may be seen and heard and tasted and believed by men with human faculties and senses') which may be experienced proleptically by all who live in light of the resurrection as they await the consummation of the age. What this means precisely for those living in the end-time we shall go on to see, yet what it means for the Temple is clear: 'Something greater than the temple is here' means that the Temple (and all that preceded it) has found its fulfilment in Jesus Christ, and not its annulment. Indeed, fulfilment means that all that the Old Testament said of the special nature of the divine dwelling places is finally *confirmed*, and the testimony to the special nature of God himself now corresponds to what is fulfilled in Jesus Christ. The Temple must go, but it will go as a witness to the fact that God may now be in his proper place for us.

3.2 What does Rejection of Messiah mean for the Temple?

The Temple must go because something greater is now here. Yet Barth also considers the rejection of Messiah by Israel as a key to the fact that 'the time has also passed of God's dwelling at those special places whose special nature was bound up with the conditions that have now lapsed ... Special places can no longer exist in this sense' (II/1, p. 480). To attempt to reinstate such holy places would be to relapse into Judaism. Since Israel's Messiah has come and been rejected by his people, and as a consequence been revealed as the Saviour of believers from both Jews and Gentiles, 'there does not exist any more a holy mountain or holy city or holy land which can be marked on a map' (II/1, p. 480); God's holiness in space is now called Jesus of Nazareth. The rejection of the Messiah means that the Temple belongs to a period of expectation and not fulfilment. Jesus Christ comes and fulfils what had been founded on his eternal election. We might even say that the Temple had participated in the eternal election as a special dwelling place of God; yet when Jesus Christ came, and the election of grace was fulfilled in time, the Temple participated in his death, indeed its destruction was determined by his death.

3.3 What do Jesus' actions mean for the Temple?

For Barth, Jesus' violent actions in the Temple are 'detailed signals (which) give warning to the real threat and revolution which the kingdom of God and the man Jesus signify and involve in relation to this sphere' (IV/1, p. 176). These signals are given further clarification when he issues his prophecies concerning the destruction of the Temple (Mark 13:1ff.), according to which he 'could not ascribe to it any permanent place or significance in the light of what He Himself brought and was. Unlike the Law in Matt. 5.17f., it was not to continue until heaven and earth passed away' (IV/1, p. 177). According to Barth, Jesus' actions and words represent a warning of the inbreaking of a new age within which the Temple order cannot exist. We suggested earlier that the acts of expulsion were acts of preparation for its inevitable and necessary destruction. In addition to this, we suggest that Barth sees its destruction not only in terms of the institution of a new age in which God will no longer be worshipped in Jerusalem (cf. John 4:21), but also in terms of its participation in the 'Messianic woes which not even the cosmos can evade'.[15] That is to say, the Temple is destroyed because it cannot co-exist with the proper presence of God, but in its destruction it also participates in the divine judgement, effected in the death of Jesus. This destruction is the 'great shadow of the cross falling on the cosmos' (III/2, p. 501). The Temple is destroyed because Jesus Christ was hung on a cross; and the Temple which is rebuilt is not Herod's but Christ's, and with this rebuilding comes the basis for the age of eschatological anticipation, in which the Christian and Christian community are addressed as Temples awaiting the day when there will be no Temple.

---

[15] K. Barth, *Church Dogmatics*, III/2 §47 (Edinburgh: T&T Clark, 1960), p. 501 (hereafter cited as III/2).

4. THE BASIS OF REVELATION IN THE RESURRECTION
AND ASCENSION OF THE MAN JESUS: THE CHRISTIAN
COMMUNITY AND THE TEMPLE OF THE HOLY SPIRIT

We continue by introducing the third and final 'context', the basis of revelation in the resurrection and ascension of the man Jesus. Here we encounter the site of the 'great verdict of God, the fulfilment and proclamation of God's decision concerning the event of the cross' (IV/1, p. 309). This is the end-time, and it is the gospel of the resurrected and ascended Christ which is preached to the world.

For Barth, the reality with which theology must deal is one rooted in the actuality of the resurrected Jesus who speaks today no less than yesterday. As Ingolf Dalferth has concluded, it is 'the reality of the resurrection in which the eschatological kingdom of God became manifest and which, in the proclamation of the gospel, continually represents itself by the power of the Spirit'.[16] With reference to the two-natures doctrine, it is the resurrection and ascension of Jesus Christ which is the basis for the revelation of this fact. We come now to a discussion of the place of the Christian and the Christian community within the concept of *present reality* awaiting a *future manifestation* as we survey Barth's references to the community as Temple in three sections: 'now', 'not yet', and 'consummation'.

4.1 'Now'

Barth's discussion of the church as a 'temple of the Holy Spirit' (1 Cor. 3:16; 6:19; 2 Cor. 6:16) brings him to a confirmation of the reality of the Spirit's work in the present age (what he calls the 'End-time'). Paul's description of the Christian as a 'temple of the Holy Spirit' is an expression of the fact that 'to be a Christian is *per definitionem* to be in the Spirit' (Rom. 8:9) (IV/2, p. 321). That is to say, this expression speaks primarily of the pneumatic status of the Christian. The reference to the building is a reference to the 'creative' Spirit's work in providing the 'security' and 'only foundation for the life of the individual Christian and Christian community' (IV/2, p. 320). Thus, being a Temple is about being that which has been constructed – thus for Barth the Christian is a Temple *by* the Holy Spirit. (This concept of upbuilding ties into the concept of ownership and thus to the ethical life of the believer; being a Temple implies, for Barth, belonging to the Lord [2 Cor. 6:13], with the consequences associated with being owned, indeed, joined to the master [III/4, p. 135].) Thus, the Christian and the Christian community are marked out as having been exposed to the sovereign and creative

---

[16] Ingolf U. Dalferth, 'Karl Barth's Eschatological Realism' in S. W. Sykes (ed.), *Karl Barth: Centenary Essays* (Cambridge: Cambridge University Press, 1989), p. 20.

activity of the Spirit, an activity which shows God declaring 'Himself in solidarity with [humankind] by constantly giving Him His Spirit' (III/2, p. 366). With this, the Spirit, in building and maintaining a 'Temple' continues the divine activity of condescension 'apparent in the sphere of creation' (III/2, p. 366) and fulfilled in the event of incarnation, and continued in his work of forming and continually renewing the Christian. Thus, the 'condescension' of God has a renewing purpose. But renewing for what and for whom? The believer is called, indeed commanded, to glorify God in his corporeality. The effectual call of Jesus Christ establishes the basis (as the Temple of the Holy Spirit) for the purpose of glorifying God. As a Temple, the believer is 'free for what is necessary for him in the light of the resurrection of Jesus Christ' (III/2, p. 306). However, while this is present freedom, it is a present freedom awaiting a future confirmation or consummation. We do well to recognize that Barth's is a highly realized eschatology, the reality is present, and yet it is as a reality of the future that it is present. We need now to set out the 'not yet' part of the present/future equation in order to see how being a Temple is part of this reality of the future.

4.2 'Not Yet'

Barth, as a theologian who spoke within and about the church, was uneasy using the term 'church', preferring instead to speak of the 'Christian community'. The reason for this unease is explained by his Christological focus. While he came to describe the church as the body of Christ, as 'the earthly-historical form of his own existence' (IV/2, p. 614), this form was and is merely *but actually* the 'provisional representation' of Jesus Christ (IV/2, p. 622). This is because Jesus Christ is the basis and fulfilment of the eternal election of grace, his is the body which is the complete and proper presence of God in his creation which means all else is subordinate to him, including the church. However, as we have noted, in God's condescension he shows himself to be in solidarity with believer and by the communion of the Spirit, he gives 'an indirect share in the primordial communion that obtains between the Father and Son'.[17] All things find their completion in Jesus Christ, yet the same Spirit who sustained and raised Jesus from the dead is at work presently in the believing community. However, while we have seen how Barth takes the description of this community of believers (and the believers who are a part of the community) as a Temple as an appropriate and meaningful description of a present reality, he does so only as he recognizes this as an *eschatological description*, which will find its consummation in Jesus

---

[17] George Hunsinger, 'Karl Barth's Doctrine of the Holy Spirit' in Webster (ed.), *Cambridge Companion to Karl Barth*, p. 179.

Christ. In perhaps his most important discussion of the believer as Temple in 1 Corinthians 3:16–17, he reads it in the light of 2 Corinthians 5: 1–5. Speaking of the New Testament references to upbuilding (*oikodomē*), he acknowledges that there are occasional references to the building as already present. However, the completion of the building is never understood as the 'supreme achievement of the community', but rather its completion is always considered in the light of 'another actuality in which the community is not merely future to itself, but transcendent. The holy city, New Jerusalem (Rev. 21:2), does not grow up from earth to heaven, but "comes down" from God out of heaven, "prepared as a bride adorned for her husband"' (IV/2, p. 628). This building is future and transcendent to the community: 'The community knows already that it is at home – but only in the there and one day, not in the here and now. "Our citizenship (and therefore our city) is in heaven" (Phil. 3:20)' (IV/2, p. 628). The 'present state is described as only a transitory abode' (IV/2, p. 629). Yet the 'house not made by human hands, eternal in heaven' is the 'new form of the community (identical with the citizenship of Phil. 3:20 and the heavenly Jerusalem of Rev. 21:2), which here and now is future and transcendent, but perfect and comes down from heaven' (IV/2, p. 629). Barth's point is that the building is, in his phrase, 'here and now absolutely future'. Relating this to 1 Corinthians 3:16–17, he speaks of the community to which the title of 'provisional representation' is given.[18] For Barth, this *must* be the case, since Paul could not be addressing the Corinthian community as the Temple of God 'already present'. Since they were presently dishonouring God, this expression of Paul's is 'exhortatory'. The references to the Temple here (as in the holy Temple of Ephesians 2:21, to which he gives a strictly eschatological reading) are to 'the community in its eternal form which is still hidden and awaits a future manifestation' (IV/2, p. 630). While Barth's is a realized eschatology when it comes to the absolute and present fulfilment of the eternal election of grace in Jesus Christ, we must recognize that all things finding their fulfilment in him has the consequence of limiting the sense in which that can be said to be fulfilled in the Christian community in the present, except in the sense of being the Temple here and now in the future.

4.3 'Consummation'

For Barth, the community of believers' time is the end-time, in which it exists for the sake of the world as a sign to bring light (as a provisional representation of the *justification* which *has* taken place in Jesus Christ). But this time will come to an end with the coming Jerusalem in which

---

[18] Barth's exegesis at this point is questionable. The weight of Paul's warning in verse 17 seems to imply that the eschatological community has a present, albeit incomplete, *spiritual* existence.

there will be no more Temples (Rev. 21:22), because God will himself be its Temple. Barth interprets this picture of the new age as one which sees an end to the Christian community's 'service'. The exhortation to be a 'Temple' in the present anticipation and expectation of the future is one which is set in the context of this community as a witness to the one who will be his own witness at the end. For Barth, Temple is a concept which can only properly be said to describe Jesus Christ.

However, an important caveat must be added to this exposition of Barth's theology of the church as Temple. We have noted the primacy of Christ, both ontologically and hermeneutically, to Barth's scheme. Yet his agenda brings with it considerable problems, characteristic of which is his reading of Paul's letters to the church in Corinth. Could it be that Barth, in commending (rightly) the primacy of Christ as the only proper space of God's dwelling, has limited the divine freedom to make himself present *now* among his people in a way which is literal, albeit provisional, and has thus misread Paul's strong ecclesial descriptions?

While Barth's theological agenda limits an overrealized eschatological ecclesiology, we suggest that with his questionable reading of 1 Corinthians 3:16, 17 and 2 Corinthians 6.16, with their simple indicatives ('you are'), he has also threatened the spiritual character of the church as it awaits the consummation: perhaps for Barth there is not enough *now* and too much *not yet*?

5. CONCLUSION

We began by noting that Barth's theological agenda is shaped by his recognition of the gracious initiative of God made known in the particular self-revelation of Jesus Christ. As we have surveyed Barth's discussions of Temple, Tabernacle and divine dwelling, we have seen that the concrete person of Jesus Christ, the subject and object of the eternal election of grace, functions as the key to properly understanding the Temple concept. Yet this schema brings with it certain difficulties, chief among them an endangering of the spiritual integrity of all non-Christ dwelling places; the relative dwelling places (Temple and church) are properly conceptualized as hanging, in a secondary way, on the proper dwelling place, but in his exploration of this relationship we suggest that Barth comes uncomfortably close to implying that all other sites of divine dwelling are in fact 'improper' since they are not 'proper'. (Is this not an implication of his reading of Paul's words to the Corinthians?) Yet in wanting to recognize Jesus Christ as the one proper dwelling place of God from eternity to eternity, Barth has made an important attempt to look out at the world from God's Tabernacle and consider what he has done, is doing, and will do.

17

THE TEMPLE IN CONTEMPORARY CHRISTIAN ZIONISM

STEPHEN SIZER

On the 8 January 2001 Carmi Gillon, the former Shin Bet secret service chief, and Assaf Hefetz, the former Israeli police commissioner, together with several leading Israeli academics, delivered a report to the Israeli Prime Minister Ehud Barak entitled 'Target Temple Mount'. Examining the threats posed by extreme militant and messianic groups committed to occupying the Temple Mount by force, the report claimed: 'The Temple Mount is like a smouldering volcano that is bubbling and threatening to erupt – a threat that is liable to endanger Israel's existence.'[1]

On the same day 500,000 secular, religious and ultra-orthodox Jews gathered near the Temple Mount at the Western Wall 'and swore faithfulness to the Temple Mount and Jerusalem'.[2] In July 2001 the Rabbinical Council of Judea, Samaria and Gaza called upon all rabbis to bring their communities to visit the Temple Mount. This was the first time the Council had ruled it permissible for Jews to ascend the Temple Mount. In a provocative move, the rabbis also called upon the Yesha Council of Jewish settlements to organize mass visits to the Temple Mount. The settlers illegally occupying the Palestinian territories represent the more right wing and politically active religious Jews.[3] During the same month, the Israeli Supreme Court made a significant decision, again for the first time, allowing the Temple Mount Faithful to hold a 'symbolic' cornerstone laying ceremony for the Third Temple near the Dung Gate adjacent to the Western Wall. Each year the Temple Mount Faithful attempts to place a three-ton cornerstone on the Temple Mount on Tisha b'Av (29 July), when the Jews mourn the destruction of the First and Second Temples, and then again during the Feast of Sukkoth, usually in early October.[4]

---

[1] <http://keshev.org.il/english/reports/harhabayit/index.shtml>.

[2] G. Salomon, *The Voice of the Temple Mount Faithful*, 5761/2001, pp. 15–17.

[3] N. Shragai, 'Rabbis call for Mass Visits to Temple Mount', *Ha'aretz*, 19 July 2001.

[4] 'Future Events of the Temple Mount Faithful', *The Voice of the Temple Mount Faithful*, 5761/2001, pp. 22–3.

This chapter will examine the reasons why Christian Zionists believe that the rebuilding of the Jewish Temple is imminent and why they actively support Jewish groups committed to achieving this.[5] Zionist Jews and Christians are united in the conviction that the Muslim Dome of the Rock must be destroyed, the Third Jewish Temple built, priests consecrated and sacrifices reinstituted in order to fulfil biblical prophecy and to hasten the coming, or return, of the Messiah.[6] Belief in a rebuilt Jewish Temple lies at the heart of the controversy concerning the claims to exclusive Jewish sovereignty over Jerusalem, the continued settlement of Occupied Palestine and the eventual expansion of the borders of Israel to include most of the Middle East from Egypt to the Euphrates.[7] Grace Halsell cites two Jewish Zionists as illustrative of this position. The first is Yisrael Meida, a member of the ultra right-wing Tehiya party, who has written: 'It is all a matter of sovereignty. He who controls the Temple Mount, controls Jerusalem. And he who controls Jerusalem, controls the land of Israel.'[8] Similarly, Rabbi Shlomo Chaim Hacohen Aviner states: 'We should not forget ... that the supreme purpose of the ingathering of exiles and the establishment of our state is the building of the temple. The temple is at the very top of the pyramid.'[9]

Christian Zionists see the founding of the State of Israel in 1948 and the capture of Jerusalem in 1967 as highly significant, signalling the end of 2,000 years' exile and the termination of the 'Times of the Gentiles' predicted by Jesus (Luke 21:24). Hal Lindsey, regarded as the 'Father of the Modern-Day Bible Prophecy movement'[10] claims the Temple Mount is 'the most disputed 35 acres on the Planet'[11] and that the fate of the earth will be determined by its contested ownership:[12]

> Obstacle or no obstacle, it is certain that the Temple will be rebuilt. Prophecy demands it ... the most important sign of Jesus Christ's soon coming is before us ... It is like the key piece of a jigsaw puzzle being found ... For all those who trust in Jesus Christ, it is a time of electrifying excitement.[13]

---

[5] For an introduction to Christian Zionism, see S. Sizer, 'Christian Zionism, A British Perspective' in N. Ateek and M. Prior (ed.), *Holy Land, Hollow Jubilee: God, Justice and the Palestinians* (London: Melisende, 1999), pp. 189–99.

[6] T. Ice and R. Price, *Ready to Rebuild: The Imminent Plan to Rebuild the Last Days Temple* (Eugene: Harvest House, 1992).

[7] D. Brickner, *Future Hope: A Jewish Christian Look at the End of the World* (San Francisco: Purple Pomegranate, 1999²), p. 90.

[8] Yisrael Meida, cited in G. Halsell, *Forcing God's Hand* (Washington: Crossroads International, 1999), p. 68.

[9] Rabbi Shlomo Chaim Hacohen Aviner, cited in G. Halsell, 'Eradicating Muslims and Christians from Jerusalem', *Washington Report*, November/December 1996, pp. 16–17.

[10] H. Lindsey, *The Final Battle* (Palos Verdes: Western Front, 1995), back cover.

[11] H. Lindsey, *Planet Earth 2000 AD* (Palos Verde: Western Front, 1994), p. 156.

[12] H. Lindsey, 'World's Fate Hangs on 35 Acres', FreeRepublic.com, 21 February 2001.

[13] H. Lindsey, *The Late Great Planet Earth* (London: Lakeland, 1970), pp. 56–8.

Zionism may be likened then to three concentric rings. The land represents the outer ring, Jerusalem the middle and the Temple the centre. The three rings comprise the Zionist expansionist agenda, of which the outer was claimed in part in 1948, the middle in 1967, the inner ring being now the focus of controversy.

1. INTRODUCTION: THE TEMPLE OF PRAYER – THE IMPORTANCE OF THE TEMPLE TO JEWS AND ZIONIST CHRISTIANS

Over the past nineteen centuries, many religious Jews have prayed three times a day: 'May it be Thy will that the Temple be speedily rebuilt in our days.' It is claimed that the Torah 'obligates the Jewish nation to rebuild the Temple whenever it becomes possible to do so (Exod. 25:8)'.[14] A Gallup poll conducted in 1996 found that 58 per cent of Israelis supported the Temple Mount Faithful and the rebuilding of the Jewish Temple. This was the largest show of support any organization in Israel had ever received on any subject. Significantly, the highest percentage of support came from young Israelis.[15]

Contemporary Christian Zionists who support the rebuilding of a Jewish Temple include Thomas Ice and Randall Price,[16] Grant Jeffrey,[17] Hal Lindsey,[18] Tim LaHaye[19] and Dave Hunt.[20] Their combined published book sales exceed 80 million in more than fifty languages. Their views are therefore influential and cannot be dismissed as marginal or esoteric. They are endorsed by some of the largest theological colleges and missionary institutions in the United States[21] as well as a significant proportion of evangelical, Charismatic, Pentecostal and fundamentalist Christians world-wide. It is estimated that 10 per cent of Americans support the movement.[22] Other Christian Zionist leaders

---

[14] R. Price, 'Time for a Temple? Jewish Plans to Rebuild the Temple', *Friends of Israel Gospel Ministry* {<www.foigm.org/img/timetemp.htm>}.

[15] R. Price, *The Coming Last Days Temple* (Eugene: Harvest House, 1999), p. 26.

[16] Ice and Price, *Ready to Rebuild*; R. Price, *Jerusalem in Prophecy* (Eugene: Harvest House, 1998); Price, *The Coming Last Days Temple*.

[17] G. Jeffrey, *Armageddon: Appointment with Destiny* (Toronto: Frontier Research, 1988); *Messiah: War in the Middle East & Road to Armageddon* (Toronto: Frontier Research, 1991); *Heaven the Mystery of Angels* (Toronto: Frontier Research, 1996).

[18] Lindsey, *Planet Earth 2000 AD*, pp. 153–67.

[19] T. LaHaye and J. B. Jenkins, *Are We Living in the End Times?* (Wheaton: Tyndale, 1999); *Apollyon: The Destroyer is Unleashed* (Wheaton: Tyndale, 1999).

[20] D. Hunt, *The Cup of Trembling: Jerusalem in Bible Prophecy* (Eugene, Oregon: Harvest House, 1995).

[21] For example, Dallas Theological Seminary and the Moody Bible Institute, Campus Crusade for Christ and Jews for Jesus.

[22] G. Halsell, 'Militant Fundamentalists Plot Destruction of Al Aqsa Mosque', Lexington Area Muslim Network, 18 March 2000 {<www.leb.net>}.

including James DeLoach, Paul Crouch, Terry Risenhoover and Doug Kreiger have also been influential in gathering significant American financial and political support, involving donations of millions of dollars for extreme Jewish organizations such as Gush Emunim and the Temple Mount Faithful.[23]

2. THE TEMPLE OF DISPENSATIONALISM: THE HISTORICAL ORIGINS OF THE CHRISTIAN ZIONIST TEMPLE MOVEMENT

2.1 *The pre-millennial presuppositions of a rebuilt Temple*

Of the three eschatological positions, amillennial, post-millennial and pre-millennial, it is the latter, with its belief in a literal and physical thousand-year messianic reign on earth, centred in Jerusalem, which has sustained belief in a future Jewish Temple. While this view was held prior to 1948,[24] it was the founding of the State of Israel, and more especially the Israeli capture of the Old City of Jerusalem in 1967, which became the catalyst for speculation on the imminent rebuilding of the Temple.[25]

2.2 *A futurist literal hermeneutic*

Speculation about the rebuilding of the Temple is largely the consequence of a futurist literal hermeneutic, popularized in the early nineteenth century by Edward Irving,[26] the Albury Circle meeting in Surrey,[27] later by John Nelson Darby and the Powerscourt Conferences in Ireland,[28] and then most effectively by Cyrus Scofield in the United States through his Scofield Reference Bible and the Bible Prophecy Conference movement.[29] It is based on the premise that prophecies made in the Old Testament which have not yet been fulfilled literally, word for word, must therefore await future fulfilment. Similarly, the

---

[23] G. Halsell, *Forcing God's Hand*, pp. 63–73.

[24] G. H. Pember, *The Great Prophecies of the Centuries Concerning Israel and the Church* (London: Hodder & Stoughton, 1902), p. 353.

[25] J. F. Walvoord, 'Will Israel Build a Temple in Jerusalem?', *Bibliotheca Sacra* 125 (1968), p. 100.

[26] E. Irving, Preliminary Discourse, *'On Ben Ezra': The Coming of Messiah in Glory and Majesty, by Juan Josafat Ben-Ezra a converted Jew, Translated from the Spanish, with a Preliminary Discourse* (London: L. B. Seeley & Sons, 1827).

[27] D. W. Bebbington, *Evangelicalism in Modern Britain: A History from the 1730s to the 1980s* (London: Unwin Hyman, 1989), p. 88; R. Coad, *A History of the Brethren Movement* (Exeter: Paternoster, 1968), p. 109.

[28] J. N. Darby, *Letters of John Nelson Darby, Volume 1, 1832–1868* (London: Stow Hill and Bible Tract Depot), p. 6.

[29] C. B. Bass, *Backgrounds to Dispensationalism* (Grand Rapids: Eerdmans, 1960), p. 18. See also L. Boettner, *The Millennium* (Grand Rapids: Baker Book House, 1958), pp. 369ff.

futurizing of passages such as the Olivet Discourse in Matthew 24 require a rebuilt Temple for their fulfilment.[30] So, Scofield insists, 'Not one instance exists of a "spiritual" or figurative fulfilment of prophecy ... Jerusalem is always Jerusalem, Israel is always Israel, Zion is always Zion ... Prophecies may never be spiritualised, but are always literal.'[31]

One of Scofield's disciples, Lewis Sperry Chafer, founder of Dallas Theological Seminary in 1924, became his most articulate and influential exponent producing the first and definitive eight-volume systematic theology of dispensationalism based on Scofield's scheme.[32] Chafer defines the literal hermeneutic upon which dispensationalism and Christian Zionism is based. 'The outstanding characteristic of the dispensationalist is ... that he believes every statement of the Bible and gives to it the plain, natural meaning its words imply.'[33]

John Walvoord, Chancellor of Dallas Theological Seminary, specifically applies this principle to belief in the rebuilding of the Temple:

> Orthodox Jews for many years have been praying daily for the rebuilding of the temple. In this expectation, they have had the support of premillennarians who interpret Scriptural prophecies as meaning what they say when they refer to a future temple in Jerusalem. The world as a whole, as well as the majority of the church, have tended to ignore this expectation as being too literal an interpretation of prophecy.[34]

Based on this futurist literal hermeneutic, Walvoord claims that the founding of the State of Israel and capture of Jerusalem has proved the pre-millennial dispensationalist correct.[35]

2.3 The dispensational distinction between the church and Israel

The logical outcome of a dispensational literalist hermeneutic is a distinguishing between God's continuing purposes for the Jewish people from those for the church.[36] The idea that the Jews are God's earthly people and the church God's heavenly people was first argued by John

---

[30] G. DeMar, *Last Days Madness* (Atlanta: American Vision, 1997), p. 80.
[31] C. I. Scofield, *Scofield Bible Correspondence Course* (Chicago: Moody Bible Institute), pp. 45–6.
[32] L. S. Chafer, *Systematic Theology* (8 vols; Dallas: Dallas Theological Seminary, 1975).
[33] L. S. Chafer, 'Dispensationalism', *Bibliotheca Sacra* 93 (October 1936), pp. 410, 417.
[34] Walvoord, 'Will Israel Build a Temple in Jerusalem?', p. 100.
[35] Ibid., p. 102. For alternative perspectives, see Robert Clouse (ed.), *The Meaning of the Millennium* (Downers Grove: IVP, 1977).
[36] For an introduction to Dispensationalism, see S. Sizer, 'Dispensational Approaches to the Land' in P. Johnston and P. W. L. Walker (eds), *The Land of Promise: Biblical, Theological and Contemporary Perspectives* (Leicester/Downers Grove: Apollos/IVP, 2000), pp. 142–71.

Nelson Darby.[37] Charles Ryrie insists the *sine qua non* of dispensationalism to be: '1. A dispensationalist keeps Israel and the Church distinct ... 2. This distinction between Israel and the church is born out of a system of hermeneutics that is usually called literal interpretation ...'[38]

Scofield taught that, as a consequence of this distinction, promises made to Israel may not be applied to the church. Instead it remains God's intention not only to restore the nation of Israel to Palestine but also to rebuild the Temple and reinstitute the priesthood and sacrificial system. 'According to the prophets, Israel, regathered from all nations, restored to her own land, and converted, is yet to have her greatest earthly exaltation and glory.'[39] Christian Zionists believe the Temple will be rebuilt therefore because of a pre-millennial eschatology, a futurist literal hermeneutic and the dispensational distinction between Israel and the church. These foundational presuppositions stand or fall together.[40]

3. THE TEMPLE OF PROPHECY: THE BIBLICAL BASIS FOR THE REBUILDING OF THE JEWISH TEMPLE

The conviction that the Temple must be rebuilt is based on the assumption that certain Old Testament prophecies referring to the Temple have not yet been fulfilled literally, and upon a few New Testament references which, when read using a futurist literal hermeneutic, also imply the existence of a Jewish Temple immediately prior to the return of Christ.

3.1 Unfulfilled Old Testament prophecies

The most important Old Testament passage used by Christian Zionists is Daniel 9:24–27. Read chronologically, the sanctuary appears to have already been destroyed by verse 26, yet sacrifices are brought to an end in verse 27 and then the '*abomination that causes desolation*' desecrates the Temple. Dispensationalists believe it is legitimate to place a gap of nearly 2,000 years between verses 26 and 27. In doing so they disregard the immediate fulfilment which occurred under Antiochus Epiphanes in 168 BC, recorded in the book of Maccabees (1 Macc. 1:10–64; 4:36–59; 2 Macc. 10:1–8). David Brickner, International Director of Jews for Jesus, argues:

---

[37] J. N. Darby, 'The Character of Office in the Present Dispensation' in W. Kelly (ed.), *The Collected Writings of J.N. Darby: Eccl. I: Vol. I* (Kingston-on-Thames: Stow Hill Bible and Trust Depot, 1962), p. 94.

[38] C. Ryrie, *Dispensationalism* (Chicago: Moody Press, 1995), pp. 39–40.

[39] Scofield, *Scofield Bible Correspondence Course*, p. 1206, n. 1.

[40] C. P. Venema, *The Promise of the Future* (Edinburgh: Banner of Truth, 2000), pp. 277ff.

Obviously the Temple has been rebuilt because Daniel tells us this ruler puts an end to sacrifice and sets up some kind of abomination (a loathsome horror that would be anathema to Jewish worship) right inside the Temple in Jerusalem. Ultimately this ruler is destroyed in a final conflagration of enormous proportion.[41]

Kenneth Barker also posits five rather questionable reasons for the gap or *'parenthesis'*[42] between Daniel's sixty-ninth and seventieth week. His two strongest arguments are based on literalist dispensational presuppositions which evaporate if they are themselves questioned.

The seventieth seven could not have been fulfilled because the results of the Messiah's work outlined in v. 24 have not yet been realized ... All the remaining unfulfilled prophecies become unintelligible unless the present church age is regarded as a distinct period of time of unknown duration in God's prophetic program.[43]

There is actually nothing in the text of Daniel 9 that requires a futurist scenario, or suggests a gap of 2,000 years between the sixty-ninth and seventieth weeks, or predicts the rebuilding of a Jewish Temple. 'The idea of separation and the placement of an indeterminable gap between the two sets of weeks is one of the most unnatural and nonliteral interpretations of Scripture found in any eschatological system.'[44]

Other commentators regard attempts to date Daniel's 'weeks' as essentially flawed.[45] They argue that these prophecies should be read symbolically, pointing to Jesus Christ, rather than date setting using an arbitrary literal chronology. So, for example, Goldingay claims Daniel is using chronography, 'a stylised scheme of history used to interpret historical data rather than arising from them, comparable to cosmology, arithmology, and genealogy'.[46] Nevertheless, the same futurist assumptions are used to interpret predictions of the destruction of the Temple found in the New Testament.

---

[41] Brickner, *Future Hope*, p. 18.

[42] J. N. Darby, 'The Hopes of the Church of God in Connection with the Destiny of the Jews and the Nations as Revealed in Prophecy' in W. Kelly (ed.), *The Collected Writings of J.N. Darby: Prophetic I: Vol. II* (Kingston-on-Thames: Stow Hill Bible and Trust Depot, 1962), p. 363.

[43] K. Barker, 'Premillennialism in the Book of Daniel', *The Master's Seminary Journal* 4.1 (1993), p. 36.

[44] DeMar, *Last Days Madness*, p. 81.

[45] E. W. Hengstenberg, *Christology of the Old Testament* (Florida: MacDonald, n.d.), pp. 792–930; E. J. Young, *The Prophecy of Daniel* (Grand Rapids: Eerdmans, 1949), pp. 203–4; J. E. Goldingay, *Daniel* (WBC; Milton Keynes: Word, 1991), p. 268.

[46] Goldingay, *Daniel*, p. 257. For a fuller critique see Young, *The Prophecy of Daniel*, pp. 201–21 and J. G. Baldwin, *Daniel: An Introduction and Commentary* (Leicester, IVP, 1978), pp. 172–8.

3.2 The New Testament fulfilment

The most important New Testament passage used to support the belief in the rebuilding of the Jewish Temple is Matthew 24:1–2 and 15. While dispensationalists agree that in the first two verses Jesus is warning of the imminent destruction of Jerusalem,[47] they claim that by verse 15 Jesus is describing the desecration of another future Temple. This futurist interpretation of Matthew 24, like that of Daniel 9:24–27, requires a gap of some 2,000 years to be placed between these verses. John Walvoord argues: 'This prediction obviously could not refer to AD 70 as it is an event immediately preceding the second advent of Christ described, in Matthew 24:27–31. The prediction, however, gives us the clue concerning the future Temple.'[48] Hal Lindsey takes a similar if rather more dogmatic view:

> Of course, for Temple rites to be stopped in the last days, we know they must be restarted. The words of Jesus Himself in Matthew 24:15 require that a new holy place be built and a complete sacrificial system re-instituted. And since only a consecrated temple can be defiled, this prophecy shows that the physical Temple must not only be rebuilt, but a functioning priesthood must begin practising once again.[49]

Lindsey is also not averse to adding words to the text of Scripture where they help to reinforce his interpretation: 'Therefore when you see the Abomination which was spoken of through Daniel the prophet, standing in the holy place [of the rebuilt Temple] (let the reader understand), then let those who are in Judea flee to the mountains …'[50] Dispensationalists such as Lindsey reject the weight of historical evidence substantiating a first-century context, preferring instead to interpret Matthew 24 as prophecy awaiting future fulfilment. So when Jesus promised that these events would be witnessed by 'this generation' (Matt. 24:34), Lindsey understands the word '*this*' to refer to his own generation who had witnessed the founding of the State of Israel in 1948 and capture of the Old City of Jerusalem in 1967.[51] A simple reading of the text, however, indicates that Jesus spoke with urgency intending his hearers to recognize the signs of the times and escape the imminent death and destruction about to befall Jerusalem. The other New Testament passages frequently used to justify the rebuilding of the Temple are 2 Thessalonians 2:1–4[52] and Revelation 11:1–2. Lindsey uses the following logic:

---

[47] Walvoord, 'Will Israel Build a Temple in Jerusalem?', p. 103.
[48] Ibid.
[49] Lindsey, *Planet Earth 2000 AD*, p. 158.
[50] H. Lindsey, *The Apocalypse Code* (Palos Verdes: Western Front, 1997), p. 78.
[51] Lindsey, *The Late Great Planet Earth*, p. 54. See also Lindsey, *Planet Earth 2000 AD*, p. 104.
[52] Walvoord, 'Will Israel Build a Temple in Jerusalem', pp. 104–5.

The Apostle John wrote the Book of Revelation about the year AD 95. This means that the Temple ... was non-existent for the twenty-five years preceding John's writing ... What Temple, then, was John referring to? There can be only one answer – a yet-to-be-built structure![53]

In fact such a claim cannot be substantiated from any of the references to 'Temple' in the New Testament. While Jesus repeatedly warned of the destruction of the Temple, he never promised that it would ever be rebuilt (John 2:19; Matt. 26:61; 27:40; Mark 14:58; 15:29). In Hebrews, the author describes the offering of sacrifices between the death of Christ and the destruction of the Temple as an 'illustration' of, and 'copies' of, heavenly realities, a 'reminder of sins' but unable, unlike the finished work of Christ, to take sin away (Heb. 9:9, 23; 10:1–3, 11). Peter uses the same terminology to describe the way Christians are being made into the new house of God (1 Pet. 2:5), in which Jesus is the 'precious cornerstone' (1 Pet. 2:7). Christian Zionists consistently ignore the way in which the Temple is invested with new meaning in the New Testament as a *'type'* for Jesus Christ and his church (Eph. 2:19–21). Instead they advocate a return to the very practices made redundant by the, once and for all, atoning work of the Son of God.

4. THE TEMPLE OF SACRIFICE: THE THEOLOGICAL PURPOSE FOR THE REBUILDING OF THE JEWISH TEMPLE

The reintroduction of the Mosaic sacrificial system is implicitly assumed by those who support the rebuilding of the Jewish Temple. Based on his reading of Daniel, Walvoord, for example, claims:

> Judging by Scriptures, this is precisely what they will do as it would be impossible to cause sacrifices to cease if they were not already in operation. The usual method of dismissing this as something which occurred in AD 70 does not provide a reasonable explanation of the text nor account for the fact that the second coming of Christ occurs immediately thereafter.[54]

Scofield in his Reference Bible claimed, however, that the sacrifices mentioned in Ezekiel 43:19, would only be a *'memorial'* offering. 'Doubtless these offerings will be memorial, looking back to the cross, as the offerings under the Old Covenant were anticipatory, looking forward to the cross. In neither case have animal sacrifices power to put away sin (Heb. 10.4; Rom. 3.25).'[55]

---

[53] H. Lindsey, *There's a New World Coming: A Prophetic Odyssey* (London, Coverdale, 1973), p. 160.

[54] Walvoord, 'Will Israel Build a Temple in Jerusalem', p. 104.

[55] C. I. Scofield, *Scofield Reference Bible* (New York: Oxford University Press, 1945), p. 890.

For one so committed to 'literalism', such an interpretation is un-convincing, for the verse explicitly refers to the sacrifice of a 'young bullock as a sin offering'. If Scofield appears to fudge the issue, the note on the same verse in the revised New Scofield Reference Bible goes even further, undermining the entire hermeneutical premise of dispensationalism:

> The reference to sacrifices is not to be taken literally, in view of the putting away of such offerings, but is rather to be regarded as a presentation of the worship of redeemed Israel, in her own land and in the millennial Temple, using the terms with which the Jews were familiar in Ezekiel's day.[56]

If this particular reference to sacrifice need not be taken literally, then the whole dispensationalist literalist edifice collapses, flawed by its own internal inconsistency.[57] It is impossible to confuse or equate the sacrifice of a young bullock with a memorial offering, which consisted of grain and oil (Lev. 2:2, 9, 16). The immediate context for Ezekiel's vision of a rebuilt Temple is the promised return of the Jews from Babylonian exile, not some long-distant eschatological event. This would have been utterly meaningless to the exiles longing to return to Israel. Furthermore, if Ezekiel was referring to some future millennial age, Jesus Christ could not serve in such a Temple anyway, because he was not of the tribe of Levi (Heb. 7:14).[58] However, even if he could do so, it would still be incongruous for Jesus to offer animal sacrifices when he had replaced them by the shedding his own blood.[59] Such an interpretation undermines the New Testament emphasis on the finished and sufficient work of Christ (Heb. 2:17; Rom. 3:25). Nevertheless, Zahava Glaser, of Jews for Jesus, describes how over the past 1900 years the liturgy used in the synagogue has kept the memory of the Temple alive in Jewish hearts and prayers. He therefore insists, 'when God instituted the sacrificial system, it was instituted for all time'.

> What flour is to bread, the sacrificial system is to the religion revealed in the Jewish Scriptures. It is not a garnish. It is not a flavoring. It is the very substance out of which the Jewish religion was constructed. We can forever design our own substitutes, but they cannot satisfy our yearnings the way God's own provision can. Though some rabbis might minimize the revealed system of worship and its requirements, can the individual Jew neglect what God says? Can there be a 'proper' Judaism without a priesthood, an altar, a sacrifice and a place on earth where God meets the individual?[60]

---

[56] *The New Scofield Reference Bible* (ed. E. S. English; New York: Oxford University Press, 1967), p. 864.
[57] Venema, *The Promise of the Future*, p. 285.
[58] Ibid., p. 286.
[59] DeMar, *Last Days Madness*, p. 85.
[60] Z. Glaser, 'Today's Rituals: Reminders or Replacements', *Issues*, 8, 3.

Glaser represents those who hold that the Temple will be rebuilt because the Jews have a separate covenant relationship with God, centred on the Temple and apart from the church. He therefore does not appear to see Jesus as having fulfilled or superseded the Jewish Temple sacrifices. By insisting on a continuing separation between God's purposes for the Jews and those of the church, Christian Zionists are promoting Old Testament 'shadows' alongside their New Testament 'substance' (Col. 2:16–17; Heb. 10:1, 5). In doing so they are seeking to revive what the New Testament says is now obsolete (Heb. 8:13). If religious Jews do indeed rebuild their Temple and reinstitute sacrifices, it will only confirm their rejection of the atoning work of Jesus Christ, 'The lamb of God who takes away the sin of the world' (John 1:29).

For Christians to support them in the belief that their future sacrifices may atone for sin is apostasy (Heb. 6:4–6). This is because the New Testament repeatedly sees such Old Testament concepts as the Temple, high priest and sacrifice as 'types' pointing to and fulfilled in Jesus Christ (John 1:14; 2:19–22; Col. 2:9). Typology in Scripture never typifies itself, nor is it ever greater than that which it typifies.[61] The movement in the progressive revelation of Scripture is always from the lesser to the greater. It is never reversed. Christians who therefore advocate the rebuilding of the Temple are regressing into a pre-Christian sacrificial system, superseded and annulled by the finished work of Jesus Christ. Turning the clock back in redemptive history[62] they are Judaizing the Christian faith (Gal. 3:1–5; 3:13–16). 'With the true lamb slain, the earthly temple could no longer operate as a place of sacrifice. The action of the high priest, "standing in the holy place" (24:15), continuing to offer sacrifices in the temple, was an abomination, a rejection of the work of Christ.'[63] The Temple was therefore a temporary edifice, 'a copy and a shadow of what is in heaven' (Heb. 8:5), anticipating the day when God would dwell with people of all nations.

In the mid nineteenth century, when J. N. Darby's dispensational 'end-time' speculations concerning an imminent Jewish restoration were gaining ground in both Britain and America, J. C. Ryle, the Anglican Bishop of Liverpool, challenged those who anticipated the rebuilding of the Temple. Based on passages such as Matthew 24, Ryle insisted:

> It surprises some to find so much importance attached to the taking of Jerusalem: they would rather regard the whole chapter as unfulfilled. Such persons forget that Jerusalem and the temple were the heart of the old Jewish dispensation: when they were destroyed, the old Mosaic system came to an end. The daily sacrifice, the yearly feasts, the altar, the holiest

---

[61] J. Noe, *The Israel Illusion* (Fishers: Prophecy Reformation Institute, 2000), p. 16.
[62] Venema, *The Promise of the Future*, p. 288.
[63] DeMar, *Last Days Madness*, p. 97.

of holies, the priesthood, were all essential parts of revealed religion, till Christ came, – but no longer. When he died upon the cross, their work was done: they were dead, and it only remained that they should be buried … The Lord Jesus specially predicts the desolation of 'the holy place'. The great High Priest describes the end of the dispensation which had been a schoolmaster to bring men to Himself.[64]

Nevertheless, the weight of argument in favour of a historical or preterist interpretation has not hindered Christian Zionists from supporting and indeed funding the work of rebuilding the Jewish Temple.

5. THE TEMPLE OF DESTINY: THE PRACTICAL ISSUES OF REBUILDING THE JEWISH TEMPLE

5.1 *When – the timing for the rebuilding*

Brickner believes the preparations for rebuilding the Temple began in 1967 with the capture of the Old City of Jerusalem.[65] Lindsey confidently asserts, 'Right now, as you read this, preparations are being made to rebuild the Third Temple.'[66] Jewish organizations such as the Temple Mount Faithful are actively engaged in achieving that end.

5.2 *Where – the location of the first and second Temples*

One of the unresolved difficulties is agreeing where to build the Temple. It is critical that any future Temple be built on the same site as the Temples of Solomon, Zerubbabel and Herod and centred on the holy of holies. With the complete destruction of Jerusalem nearly 2,000 years ago, there is no unanimity today among Jewish scholars as to where the Temple stood. There are three main options advocated by historians and archaeologists.

One theory suggested by Father Bellarmino Bagatti, a Franciscan scholar, and supported by Tel Aviv architect Tuvia Sagiv is based on early archaeological findings, Josephus and topographical elevations. They argue that the Temple was situated at the south-west corner of the platform near to where the Al Aqsa mosque is today.[67] Based on infrared thermographic imaging of the Temple Mount they claim that underground structures may be the remains of Hadrian's temple to

---

[64] J. C. Ryle, *Expository Thoughts on the Gospels: St. Matthew* (London: John Clarke, 1954), p. 317.
[65] Brickner, *Future Hope*, p. 137.
[66] Lindsey, *Planet Earth 2000 AD*, p. 156; Lindsey, *The Final Battle*, p. 103.
[67] Cited in Price, *The Coming Last Days Temple*, pp. 337–42; T. Sagiv, *The Hidden Secrets of the Temple Mount* (Tel Aviv: 1993). Accessible from <www.templemount.org/tem pmt.html>

Jupiter. If this is so, and if the Romans built their pagan temple over the destroyed Jewish Temple, as was often their custom, this may indicate that the Temple was originally at this location.

A more popular theory is advocated by Asher Kaufman, a physicist at the Hebrew University.[68] His research relies on details given in Mishnah *Middot* (*Measurements*) as well as calculations of the angles of line of sight between the Mount of Olives where the red heifer was allegedly sacrificed and the eastern court of the Temple where the Great Altar stood. Kaufman claims that based on these calculations the Temple was built on the north-western corner of the Temple platform, about 330 feet away from the Dome of the Rock. He believes that a small cupola at this site, known in Arabic as the Dome of the Tablets, was the Foundation Stone within the holy of holies.[69]

The most commonly held theory, however, and supported by the majority of Israeli archaeologists today, argues that the Temple stood on the site of the Dome of the Rock. Research by Benjamin Mazar, Leen Ritmeyer (who served as chief architect for the Western Wall excavations) and Dan Bahat, professor of archaeology at Bar Ilan University, conclude that the physical evidence indicates that both the First and Second Temples were situated under the Dome of the Rock.[70] Ritmeyer claims to have found within the Muslim Dome of the Rock the foundation trenches and the walls of the holy of holies, as well as the place where the ark of the covenant rested.[71] Nevertheless, it is Kaufman's northern site theory which is increasingly favoured by Christian Zionists such as Randall Price, Hal Lindsey and David Brickner,[72] since it does not require the destruction of the Dome of the Rock. Some have changed their views over time. In the 1970s, for example, Hal Lindsey insisted the Jewish Temple would have to be built in place of the Dome of the Rock.

> There remains but one more event to completely set the stage for Israel's part in the last great act of her historical drama. This is to rebuild the ancient Temple of worship upon its old site … There is one major problem barring the construction of a third Temple. That obstacle is the second holiest place of the Muslim faith, the Dome of the Rock. This is believed to be built squarely in the middle of the old temple site. Obstacle or no obstacle, it is certain that the Temple will be rebuilt. Prophecy demands it.[73]

---

[68] See A. Kaufman, 'Where the Ancient Temple of Jerusalem Stood', *Biblical Archaeology Review* 9.2 (1983), pp. 40–59; also 'Where was the Temple? The Debate Goes On', *Biblical Archaeology Review* 3 (2000).

[69] Price, *The Coming Last Days Temple*, pp. 342–4.

[70] L. Ritmeyer, *The Temple of Herod* (Harrogate: Ritmeyer Architectural Design, 1993); *The Temple and the Rock* (Harrogate: Ritmeyer Architectural Design, 1996), pp. 38–48.

[71] Price, *The Coming Last Days Temple*, pp. 345–54.

[72] Brickner, *Future Hope*, p. 61.

[73] Lindsey, *The Late Great Planet Earth*, pp. 56–8.

He even appeared to know the exact location of the former structure.[74] However, by 1983 Lindsey had changed his mind. Favouring Kaufman's position, he now claimed:

> I also believe that this discovery has accelerated the countdown to the events that will bring the Messiah Jesus back to earth. The reason for this belief is that the predicted Third Temple can now be built without disturbing the Dome of the Rock ... the Temple and its immediate guard wall could be rebuilt and still be twenty-six meters away from the Dome of the Rock.[75]

Having discovered the true site of the Herodian Temple, Lindsey proceeded to find scriptural verification for this new location in Revelation 11.[76] In 1994, Lindsey heightened speculation still further by insisting that, having measured the distances on the Temple platform, he realized that:

> God had left out the outer court because it allowed for the Gentile temple to remain alongside the rebuilt Jewish Temple during the Tribulation. Folks, the footsteps of our Lord and Savior, Jesus Christ, can already be heard as He approaches the doors of heaven to return. The Temple is the last sign that needs to fall into place before events irreversibly speed toward the return of Jesus.[77]

Most orthodox Jews, however, remain convinced that the Dome of the Rock must be removed before the Temple can be rebuilt.[78] Gershon Salomon even claims the Dome of the Rock was built by Caliph Abd el-Malik in AD 691 as a Jewish house of prayer.[79]

5.3 How – the means for rebuilding

Chaim Richman, a spokesman for the Temple Institute, claims detailed blueprints for the Third Temple have existed for several years. Other buildings associated with a future Temple are planned, or have already been built. Rabbi Shlomo Goren, for example, has supervised the construction of a replica of the seventy-seat Supreme Court building for the new Sanhedrin, adjacent to the Temple Mount in the Jewish Quarter. The legal stipulations which the Sanhedrin will use to supervise Temple practices are also being published. The first volume was printed in 1986 by the Research Center for Jewish Thought under the direction of Yoel Lerner.[80] A member of Meir Kahane's Kach movement, Lerner was

---

[74] Lindsey, *There's a New World Coming*, p. 163.
[75] H. Lindsey, *Israel and the Last Days* (Eugene: Harvest House, 1983), p. 29.
[76] Ibid., p. 30.
[77] Lindsey, *Planet Earth 2000 AD*, p. 160.
[78] Price, *The Coming Last Days Temple*, p. 346.
[79] G. Salomon, 'The Riddle of the Dome of the Rock: Was it Built as a Jewish Place of Prayer?', *The Voice of the Temple Mount Faithful*, Summer 5761/2001, p. 13.
[80] R. Price, 'Time for a Temple?'.

arrested and convicted in 1982 for attempting to sabotage the Dome of the Rock, for which he was sentenced to two and a half years in prison.[81]

5.3(i) Training the priests – the Temple Mount Yeshivas

According to rabbinic tradition, although the genealogical records of the Temple were lost in AD 70 when the Jews were dispersed, Levites were forbidden to change their family names when other Jews assimilated into the Roman Empire. The use of modern DNA tests has also been used to confirm the authenticity of men suitable to train as Temple priests. Rabbi Nachman Kahane, head of the Young Israel Synagogue together with the Institute for Talmudic Commentaries, maintains a computer database of all known priestly candidates in Israel. Other orthodox organizations in Israel are helping to educate them. The Yeshiva founded by Motti Dan Hacohen, known as *Ateret Cohanim*, for example, is preparing students to perform priestly service. Its sister organization *Atara Leyoshna* has aggressively acquired, or illegally occupied, many Arab properties in the Muslim Quarter near the Temple Mount in order to establish and consolidate a Jewish presence in preparation for rebuilding the Temple.[82] Brickner cites the following advert placed in Ha'aretz in March 1998.

> Children wanted for future Temple service. Ultra-orthodox Jewish sect is searching for parents willing to hand over newborn sons to be raised in isolation and purity in preparation for the rebuilding of the biblical temple in Jerusalem. Only members of the Jewish priestly caste, the Kohanim, need apply.[83]

Brickner is convinced that ultra-orthodox groups will fulfil the vision of a fully functioning Jewish Temple.

5.3(ii) Consecrating the priests – breeding the red heifers

The dilemma facing prospective Temple priests is how to gain ritual purity in order to begin serving in a future Temple once again. According to the book of Numbers, the ashes of a pure unblemished red heifer, itself previously offered by a ritually pure priest, must be mixed with water and sprinkled on both them and the Temple furniture. With the destruction of the Temple in AD 70 the ashes used in the ceremony were lost and the Jews of the diaspora have since therefore been perpetually unclean. The search for the ashes of the last red heifer have so far proved

---

81 L. Dolphin, 'Preparations for a Third Jewish Temple' <http://hope-of-israel.org/3rdjewt.htm>.
82 Price, 'Time for a Temple'.
83 *Ha'aretz*, 1 March 1998, cited in Brickner, *Future Hope*, p. 53.

unsuccessful. In 1998, however, Clyde Lott, a Christian and Mississippi rancher, formed Canaan Land Restoration of Israel, Inc. for the purpose of raising livestock suitable for Temple sacrifice.[84] According to *Newsweek*, in 1997 the first red heifer for 2000 years was born at the kibbutz Kfar Hassidim near Haifa, and named 'Melody'.[85] Doubts emerged when a few grey hairs were found on her tail. The quest for producing a pure red heifer continues.

The cost of the work of rebuilding the Temple, the training of its future priests, the supply of red heifers and Temple furnishings is being funded, in large measure, by Christian Zionists.

5.3(iii) Funding the work – the Temple Treasury

The International Christian Embassy as well as mega-churches such as Chuck Smith's Calvary Chapel in Costa Mesa, California, have contributed to the funding of the Jerusalem Temple Foundation (JTF) founded by a Jewish terrorist, Stanley Goldfoot, and several leading American evangelicals.[86] Pat Robertson's Christian Broadcasting Network has also assisted in fund raising for Gershon Salomon's Temple Mount Faithful.[87]

6. THE TEMPLE OF ARMAGEDDON: THE POLITICAL CONSEQUENCES OF REBUILDING THE JEWISH TEMPLE

The aspirations of Jewish and Christian Zionists who are committed to the rebuilding of the Jewish Temple clearly has political ramifications which threaten to destabilize the entire Middle East.[88] However, despite Muslim sensitivities, Lindsey suggests that a Jewish Temple could be

---

[84] Randall Price incorrectly attributes this story to *Time* when it actually appeared in *Newsweek*. He also misspells one of the contributors' names. *The Coming Last Days Temple*, p. 375. 'Red Heifers', *New York Times*, 27 December 1998. See also J. Atkins, 'Biblical Mystery of the Red Heifer affects Farmer in Mississippi', *The Daily Mississippian*, 23 July 1998; J. Shere, 'A Very Holy Cow', *Jerusalem Post*, 25 May 1997; C. Richman, 'The Mystery of the Red Heifer' <www.templemount.org/heifer.html>.
[85] K. Hamilton, J. Contreras and M. Dennis, 'The Strange Case of Israel's Red Heifer', *Newsweek* (May 19, 1997).
[86] L. Rapoport, 'Slouching towards Armageddon: Links with Evangelicals', *Jerusalem Post International Edition*, 17–24 June 1984; Halsell, *Forcing God's Hand*, p. 68. As a member of the Stern Gang and also Irgun, Goldfoot was responsible for planting the bomb at the King David Hotel in Jerusalem on 22 July 1946, which killed 100 British soldiers and officials. In 1948 he was also convicted and jailed by an Israeli court for the murder of UN envoy Count Bernadotte.
[87] J. Gary, 'The Temple Time Bomb', *Presence Magazine*, 2 July 2002. Available from <www.christianity.com/partner>
[88] R. Dunn, 'Israel holds Disciples of "Second Coming" Cult', *The Times*, 4 January 1999, p. 12.

built alongside the Muslim shrine and become *'the greatest tourist attraction in the world'*.[89] In his earlier writings, Lindsey was rather less optimistic, but probably more accurate:

The dispute to trigger the war of Armageddon will arise between the Arabs and Israelis over the Temple Mount and Old Jerusalem (Zech. 12:2–3), the most contested and strategic piece of real estate in the world. Even now we are witnessing the escalation of that conflict.[90]

Christian Zionists rarely elaborate on the political consequences of their activities, which find expression in their solidarity with the State of Israel generally and the Temple movement specifically, yet these invariably lead to an antipathy toward Arabs and Muslims, to a confrontational stance on the Middle East and a pessimistic view of the future.

6.1 Support for the Jewish state

Christian Zionists tend to show greatest solidarity toward the religious right wing of Israeli society. For example, the Israeli Prime Minister has spoken at every one of the International Christian Zionist Congresses held annually in Jerusalem since 1980. Brickner is typical of other Christian Zionists in lamenting the fact that, ten days after Moshe Dyan captured the Old City in 1967, he returned the Temple Mount area to the Islamic authorities.[91] In an open letter to Benjamin Netanyahu, then Israel's ambassador to the United Nations, the International Christian Embassy affirmed its commitment to Jews worshipping again on the Temple Mount.[92] Van der Hoeven, former director of the ICEJ (International Christian Embassy Jerusalem) quotes from the speech made by Teddy Kollek, then mayor of Jerusalem, at the 1985 Christian Zionist Feast of Tabernacles celebration. Behind him was a futuristic painting of Jerusalem showing a rebuilt Jewish Temple.

> Thank you for being here, for coming here faithfully, every year. Your faith gives us strength ... I am glad I am speaking here against the background of this beautiful painting of Jerusalem. It is not yet the Jerusalem of today. If you look properly, you will see that the Temple, the Holy of Holies, has been restored! ... Our return is the first sign that the city will be existing again as it is in this painting![93]

---

[89] Lindsey, *Planet Earth 2000 AD*, p. 163.
[90] Lindsey, *Israel and the Last Days*, p. 19.
[91] Brickner, *Future Hope*, p. 60.
[92] J. W. van der Hoeven, *Babylon or Jerusalem?* (Shippensburg: Destiny Image, 1993), p. 169.
[93] Ibid., p. 163.

Christian Zionists not only support but also defend Israel from international criticism and often equate anti-Zionism with anti-Semitism.[94]

6.2 Support for the Temple Mount movement

There is a clear and unambiguous symbiotic relationship between Christian and Jewish Zionist organizations committed to rebuilding the Jewish Temple. For example, Jews for Jesus provides information on, and offers direct Internet links to, eight extreme and militant Jewish organizations involved in attempts to destroy the Dome of the Rock, rebuild the Jewish Temple and reinstitute worship and sacrifices there. These include the Temple Institute and Temple Mount Faithful.[95] Randall Price also provides information on how to support eighteen different Temple organizations.[96] One of the most extreme is the Temple Mount Faithful founded by Gershon Salomon and claiming to have 9,000 Christian and Jewish supporters. Brickner points out, approvingly, that they are ready to commence building '*at any moment*'. We have noted already in the introduction above the twice-yearly attempts to set the cornerstone for the rebuilding of the Temple.

Zhava Glaser, also of Jews for Jesus, affirms Salomon's motives, describing him as a 'man of courage', whose credentials as an Israeli patriot, soldier, politician and Zionist are 'impeccable'.[97] Salomon is, however, quite explicit in asserting that the Dome of the Rock must be destroyed. Speaking at the Jerusalem Christian Zionist Congress in 1998, Salomon insisted:

> The mission of the present generation is to liberate the Temple Mount and to remove – I repeat, to remove – the defiling abomination there ... The Jewish people will not be stopped at the gates leading to the Temple Mount ... We will fly our Israeli flag over the Temple Mount, which will be minus its Dome of the Rock and its mosques and will have only our Israeli flag and our Temple. This is what our generation must accomplish.[98]

In a *Times* article, Sam Kiley described Salomon as the 'almost acceptable face of millennial cults'.[99] He quotes Salomon as saying:

---

[94] H. Lindsey, *The Road to Holocaust* (New York: Bantam, 1989). Lindsey accuses those who oppose dispensationalism of anti-Semitism: 'the same error that founded the legacy of contempt for the Jews and ultimately led to the Holocaust of Nazi Germany' (back cover).

[95] R. Robinson, 'Israeli Groups Involved in Third Temple Activities', *Jews for Jesus Newsletter* 10, Adar 5753, 1993. See also Brickner, *Future Hope*, p. 60.

[96] Price, *The Coming Last Days Temple*, pp. 616–20.

[97] Glaser, 'Today's Rituals'.

[98] N. Shragai, 'Dreaming of a Third Temple', *Ha'aretz*, 17 September 1998, p. 3.

[99] S. Kiley, 'The Righteous will Survive and the Rest will Perish', *The Times*, 13 December 1999, p. 39.

The Israeli Government must do it. We must have a war. There will be many nations against us but God will be our general. I am sure this is a test, that God is expecting us to move the Dome with no fear from other nations. The Messiah will not come by himself, we should bring Him by fighting.[100]

Salomon also believes Ariel Sharon's provocative visit to the Temple Mount, days before Barak and Arafat were about to sign a deal on joint sovereignty of Jerusalem with President Clinton, as well as Sharon's subsequent election as Israel's Prime Minister, were acts of God:

This was the judgment of G–d, leading to the election by such a majority of the man who visited, fought, and demonstrated for Him and His holy mountain. It was also a clear message that G–d ... showed everyone that – whether they want it or not – the Temple Mount will very soon be the site of His holy temple.[101]

Such provocative convictions reflect a deeper antipathy toward Muslims generally and Palestinians in particular, which can only be described as racism.

6.3 Antipathy toward Muslims

At the Third International Christian Zionist Congress, held in 1996 under the auspices of the ICEJ, the following affirmation was unanimously endorsed.

The Islamic claim to Jerusalem, including its exclusive claim to the Temple Mount, is in direct contradiction to the clear biblical and historical significance of the city and its holiest site, and this claim is of later religio-political origin rather than arising from any Qur'anic text or early Muslim tradition ...[102]

Similarly, in 1994, Lindsey predicted that Judaism and Islam were on a collision course which would have cosmic repercussions. 'The whole prophetic scenario is in place. We see the Islamic nations united in mutual hatred of Israel. The dispute has nothing to do with borders or territory. It has to do with the existence of Israel and its claim on Jerusalem.'[103] Such theological determinism not only undermines attempts to find a peaceful settlement of the Arab–Israeli conflict, but reinforces stereotypes and inflames racial hatred. The pessimistic eschatology of Christian Zionism is in danger of becoming a self-fulfilling prophecy.

---

[100] Ibid.
[101] G. Salomon, 'An Upheaval in the Israeli Government', *The Voice of the Temple Mount Faithful*, Summer 5761/2001, p. 6.
[102] *International Christian Zionist Congress Proclamation*, International Christian Embassy, Jerusalem, 25–29 February 1996.
[103] Lindsey, *Planet Earth 2000 AD*, pp. 155, 216.

6.4 The Battle of Armageddon

Brickner is not alone in his conviction that, based on a literalist reading of the Bible, the rebuilding of the Temple will be associated with the deaths of most Israelis. 'A full two-thirds of the population of Israel will perish in the ensuing conflict, according to Zechariah 13:8. The hope of the Jewish people in seeing the glorious Temple rebuilt will, in fact, lead to their greatest calamity and suffering.'[104]

Moishe Rosen also speculates on such a future scenario, suggesting the Dome might be destroyed by scuds fired by Israel to implicate Iraq and turn Muslim rage away from Israel and on to Saddam Hussein:

> In truth, the fusillade of missiles had not all come from Iraq – only the ones which hit Jewish neighbourhoods. The rest were Scud-class missiles launched by Israelis from mobile launchers deployed deep in the Judean wilderness, near the Israeli/Jordanian border. Yitshak Shamir had his revenge.[105]

Lindsey describes the centrality of the Temple Mount in this apocalyptic scenario:

> The Russian force will establish command headquarters on Mount Moriah or the Temple area in Jerusalem. Daniel pointed this out when he said: 'And he shall pitch his palatial tents between the seas [Dead Sea and Mediterranean Sea] and the glorious holy mount Zion; yet he shall come to his end with none to help him' (Daniel 11:45, Amplified).[106]

Gordon Welty, a sociologist and anthropologist, explains the apparent contradiction of evangelical Christians supporting Jewish terrorism, whose actions might precipitate a global war:

> Their power is to keep inconsistencies in airtight compartments, so that they themselves never recognize these inconsistencies ... If the money a muscular Christian donates to the Jewish terrorists buys the dynamite that destroys the mosque, the muscular Christian will say simply, 'It was an act of God.'[107]

Enthusiasm for the rebuilding of the Jewish Temple among Christian Zionists is therefore only part of a wider apocalyptic scenario involving great suffering and mass destruction. The prophets Daniel and Ezekiel as well as the book of Revelation are interpreted in such a way that they are seen as foretelling pre-written history of the end times.[108]

---

[104] Brickner, *Future Hope*, p. 62.
[105] M. Rosen, *Overture to Armageddon? Beyond the Gulf War* (San Bernardino: Here's Life, 1991), p. 140.
[106] Lindsey, *The Late Great Planet Earth*, p. 160.
[107] Cited in G. Halsell, *Prophecy and Politics: Militant Evangelists on the Road to Nuclear War* (Westport: Lawrence Hill, 1986).
[108] Lindsey, *Planet Earth 2000 AD*, p. xiii.

7. CONCLUSIONS

It has been shown that the Christian belief in, and support for, the rebuilding of the Jewish Temple arises generally from a pre-millennial eschatology and specifically from the novel dispensational distinction between Israel and the church combined with, and arising from, an ultra-literalist and futurist hermeneutic. On the basis of what are allegedly unfulfilled Old and New Testament prophecies, Christian Zionists are convinced that a Third Temple will be built in place of, or next to, the Dome of the Rock. They are convinced that a Jewish priesthood will once again offer sacrifices and offerings there. They also believe this yet-to-be-built Temple will be desecrated by the Antichrist and finally replaced by a fourth Millennial Temple, as described by Ezekiel.

Christian support for the rebuilding of the Jewish Temple is also invariably linked to the political claims of exclusive Jewish sovereignty over not only the Temple Mount and Jerusalem but over much of the Middle East as well. Whether intentionally or otherwise, therefore, Christian Zionists are complicit in perpetuating a form of apartheid as well as the ethnic cleansing of Palestinians from the Occupied Territories. Many regard this reading of history as questionable, coloured by a literal exegesis of highly selective biblical passages, profoundly misguided and essentially racist. Far from demonstrating a ministry of reconciliation to all nations, which is at the heart of the Christian faith, Zionism perpetuates religious intolerance and incites ethnic cleansing. Fuelled by a fatalistic conviction of an imminent apocalyptic war associated with the rebuilding of the Temple, Christian Zionists are indeed 'Anxious for Armageddon'.[109]

It has been demonstrated that this conviction, and the hermeneutic upon which it is based, is flawed because it fails to recognize how Jesus Christ interprets, completes and fulfils the role of the Temple and its sacrificial system. Jesus taught that he himself was greater than the Temple (Matt. 12:6) and, when his authority was questioned, described his body as the only Temple that mattered (John 2:19). The New Testament reveals how the Temple was only an illustration (Heb. 9:9), a copy (Heb. 9:23) and shadow (Heb. 8:5) for the atoning work of Jesus Christ who now dwells on earth by the Holy Spirit. The Temple therefore finds its ultimate significance and fulfilment not in another manmade sanctuary but in Jesus Christ (Heb. 9:24). The Christian Zionist preoccupation, therefore, with locating the site of the Temple, with training priests, breeding red heifers and funding the Temple Treasury is at best a distraction from the gospel imperative and at worst promoting apostasy (Heb. 10:29; Gal. 1:8–9).

By his death Jesus has opened a new way into the presence of God making the Jewish Temple redundant, a mere fading shadow of the

---

[109] D. Wagner, *Anxious for Armageddon* (Scottdale: Herald Press, 1995).

true reality in heaven (Eph. 2:14–22). The New Jerusalem which will one day come down from heaven needs no Temple, for we shall see God face to face (Rev. 21:22; 22:4). God's answer therefore to those who still seek him at the Western Wall or in a rebuilt Temple may be summarized in Jesus reply to the Samaritan woman:

> Believe me, woman, a time is coming when you will worship the Father neither on this mountain nor in Jerusalem ... Yet a time is coming and has now come when the true worshippers will worship the Father in spirit and truth, for they are the kind of worshippers the Father seeks. God is spirit, and his worshippers must worship in spirit and in truth (John 4:21–24).

Today the Western Wall is a vivid reminder that God no longer dwells in temples made by hands but in the heart of all who trust in Christ (Acts 17:24).

EPILOGUE
Heaven on Earth

1. INTRODUCTION

In popular Christian thought the concept of Temple evokes a wide range of responses. For some Christians, 'temple' conjures up images of pagan worship with idols set up in brightly coloured shrines. For others, the word 'temple' brings to mind the edifice associated with the Temple Mount in Jerusalem, which stood at the heart of Jewish worship in the time of Christ until it was destroyed by the Romans in AD 70 and which today still attracts considerable attention, especially among those who anticipate its restoration.[1] For still others, probably the majority, the concept of Temple plays no part in their daily religious experience or thought. When 'Temple' is mentioned, this latter group probably assume, mistakenly, that the concept of Temple is identical to that of church – a place where people come together to worship. Such views, which are in no way exhaustive, reveal that 'Temple' has a low profile among Christians.

The central aim of this book is to raise awareness about the concept of Temple by exploring its place and role within the Bible and explaining the implications of this for Christian theology. If, however, we start by focusing on a building, we are likely to be disappointed. While the Temple is of architectural interest, its function is what makes it especially important. It was God's dwelling place on earth. As such it was an important interface between God and humanity. It provided a location where human beings had the opportunity to come into regular and prolonged contact with the living God. Viewed in terms of this function, the Temple takes on greater significance. Yet, the question still remains, how does this relate to Christians who now attach so little weight to the idea of a Temple? To answer this question, it is necessary to understand how the concept of Temple develops within the Bible.

The essays presented in this volume highlight the changing role of the Temple as a divine–human interface. Explaining the nature of

---

[1] As discussed in more detail in Sizer's essay.

these changes, they draw out in differing ways their significance from various perspectives. This concluding essay seeks in very brief sketch form to pull some of these different strands together in order to give an overview of what has been set out in greater detail above.

2. OLD AND NEW CREATIONS

For Christians, the Bible is framed by two accounts that focus on God's creative activity. Whereas Genesis 1–3 recounts the divine creation of the earth, with particular emphasis being given to Adam and Eve within the Garden of Eden, Revelation 21–22 anticipates the creation of a 'new heaven and a new earth, for the first heaven and the first earth had passed away, and the sea was no more' (Rev. 21:1). With good reason, scholars have observed a rich variety of connections between these two passages, seeing the 'new earth' as bringing to fulfilment a process that started originally in Genesis 1–3.[2] Yet, although the biblical meta-narrative is framed by two similar accounts, the picture is not static. Major developments occur as the Garden of Eden is replaced by a resplendent city, and Adam and Eve are replaced by the nations.

In both passages God and humanity engage directly with each other, with people enjoying unrestricted access to God. The immediacy of this relationship contrasts sharply with what is revealed in the rest of Scripture, where God and human beings rarely encounter each other; when such meetings take place they are usually of short duration and limited intimacy.[3]

The initial change between these two levels of encounter comes after Adam and Eve rebel against God in Eden. As a result, they are expelled from God's presence and prohibited from returning (cf. Gen. 3:22–24). Significantly, the restoration of full and unrestricted intimacy between God and humanity forms the heart of the biblical meta-narrative. For this reason, the story comes almost full circle when the human inhabitants of the new Jerusalem once more encounter God face to face. Furthermore, having been prohibited in Genesis 3:22 from eating of the tree of life, Revelation 22 describes how the tree of life will yield fruit every month and constantly blossom 'for the healing of the nations' (v. 2).

---

[2] The relationship between Revelation 21–22 and the rest of the Bible is explored at length by W. J. Dumbrell, *The End of the Beginning: Revelation 21–22 and the Old Testament* (Grand Rapids: Baker Book House, 1985). While Eden is portrayed as a garden and the new Jerusalem of Revelation 21–22 is a holy city, there is good reason to see the latter as reflecting God's original design for Eden. Eden was the green-field site on which the city of God was to be created.

[3] Those not associated with the Tabernacle / Temple often take the form of a theophany. See J. J. Niehaus, *God at Sinai: Covenant and Theophany in the Bible and Ancient Near East* (Grand Rapids / Carlisle: Zondervan / Paternoster, 1995).

Remarkably, neither Eden nor the new Jerusalem contains a Temple, at least not a Temple as commonly understood in the rest of Scripture. This point is made explicitly in Revelation 21:22, where John states, 'And I saw no temple in the city.' Yet, he qualifies this immediately by saying, 'for its temple is the Lord God the Almighty and the Lamb' (ESV). The situation regarding Genesis 2–3 is also somewhat ambiguous. Wenham highlights close parallels between Eden and the later Old Testament Tabernacle/Temple.[4] Recently, Walton has suggested that the garden pictured in Genesis 2–3 was attached to a Temple.[5] While neither Genesis 2–3 nor Revelation 21–22 made explicit reference to a Temple building, the presence of God gives both locations a unique status.

3. THE DIVINE PLAN OF REDEMPTION

Between its beginning and end, the biblical meta-narrative moves from describing the human undoing of creation to recounting the slow and gradual process of divine redemption that eventually culminates in a new heaven and a new earth. While at the start and end of this story humanity has unhindered access to God, the intervening period is predominantly one of alienation. During this stage, the earthly Tabernacle/Temple plays a significant, but changing, role in the redemptive activity of God. In all of this its primary function is to form a major interface between God and humanity. Although God is primarily viewed as living in heaven, he is also present on earth in his Temple.

While the opening chapters of Genesis focus on the 'fall' of humanity and the dire consequences of being alienated from God, the possibility of reconciliation is linked directly to the family line that descends through Adam's third-born son, Seth, leading eventually to the patriarchs, Abraham, Isaac and Jacob. Over time God reveals to the members of this lineage the process by which he will eventually reconcile the world to himself.[6]

As part of this process God promises to make a great nation of Abraham's descendants (e.g. Gen. 12:2). While, according to Genesis 15:13–14, this nation will be oppressed for 400 years, it will eventually come to possess the territory divinely promised to Abraham. When in due course the Israelites are rescued by God from the tyranny of the Egyptian pharaoh, the divine promise of nationhood moves towards

---

[4] G. J. Wenham, 'Sanctuary Symbolism in the Garden of Eden Story', *Proceedings of the World Congress of Jewish Studies* 9 (1986), pp. 19–25.

[5] J. H. Walton, 'Eden, Garden of' in T. D. Alexander and D. W. Baker (eds), *Dictionary of the Old Testament: Pentateuch* (Downers Grove/Leicester: IVP, 2003), pp. 202–6.

[6] T. D. Alexander, *From Paradise to the Promised Land: An Introduction to the Pentateuch* (Carlisle/Grand Rapids: Paternoster Press/Baker Book House, 2002[2]), pp. 101–28.

fulfilment. However, before they take possession of the promised land, the Israelites are invited by God to enter into a special covenant relationship with him. At the heart of this is God's desire to make of them a 'holy nation' (Exod. 19:6).

To this end, instructions are given to Moses for the construction of a specially designed tent (or Tabernacle) that will become God's dwelling place among the Israelites. The importance of this structure for the covenant relationship being established between God and Israel is underlined not only by the number of chapters in Exodus devoted to describing firstly its design and furnishings (most of Exod. 25–30) and then its construction (most of Exod. 35–40), but also by the way in which this description is tied into the account of the golden calf incident.[7] While the Tabernacle is designed to be portable, in every other regard it functions like a Temple. This is where God, the Holy One, will dwell among the Israelites as they journey from Mount Sinai through the wilderness before entering the land of Canaan.[8] Significantly, it is God's presence among the people that makes Israel a holy nation, unique from all others.

The book of Exodus comes to a fitting climax when the 'glory of the LORD' fills the Tabernacle. This event brings to completion an important transformation that occurs between the start of Exodus and its end. Whereas Exodus begins with God appearing distant and apparently unconcerned by the plight of the Israelites, it concludes with God living in close proximity to his people. Indeed, this new situation calls for special arrangement to be made in order to sustain the presence of a holy God among a sinful populace. With good reason, the book of Leviticus gives particular attention to promoting the holiness of the Israelites.

Before outlining later developments, three observations ought to be made regarding the Tabernacle. Firstly, in the light of parallels that exist between the Tabernacle and the Garden of Eden, the impression is given that through God's coming to dwell among the Israelites a partial return to Eden is achieved. Secondly, although God comes to live among the Israelites, access into his divine presence remains very restricted. The tent, with its surrounding screen, forms a barrier between God and the people. Only on the Day of Atonement does the high priest enter the holy of holies, and even then a cloud of incense shields him from God. Both of these observations point to the temporary nature of the arrangements instituted at Mount Sinai. Thirdly, by modelling the Tabernacle on the heavenly Temple, a bond is forged between heaven and earth. In a limited way, the Tabernacle is heaven on earth.

---

[7] This is developed more fully in Palmer's essay above.
[8] This function is underlined by the title given to the tabernacle; it is frequently designated the 'tent of meeting' *'ōhel mô'ēd* (e.g. Exod. 27:21; 28:43; 29:4; 40:2; Lev. 1:1; 3:2; Num. 1:1; 2:2).

4. FROM TABERNACLE TO TEMPLE

When the Israelites eventually settle in the land of Canaan, the tent of meeting is set up by Joshua and the people at Shiloh (Josh. 18:1). While the books of Joshua and Judges provide limited information about the Tabernacle, the impression is given that it resides permanently at Shiloh, in the region of Ephraim.[9] However, as the early chapters of Samuel reveal, the spiral of moral and spiritual decline that has dominated the book of Judges comes to a climax when God permits the ark of the covenant, his earthly throne, to be captured by the Philistines. The full significance of this event is captured well by Eli's daughter-in-law, who names her son Ichabod, because 'The glory has departed from Israel!' (1 Sam. 4:21).

The negative impact of having the ark present among them is soon felt by the Philistines: it is moved from Ashdod to Gath and then Ekron before being returned to Israelite territory where it remains at Kiriath-jearim for twenty years (1 Sam. 5:1–11). Through these events God displays his disfavour with both the Israelites, especially the tribe of Ephraim, and their enemies, the Philistines. Under the wrong circumstances God's presence brings disaster rather than blessing.

At this stage two important developments take place. First, having rejected Shiloh as the location for the 'house of the LORD', God chooses Mount Zion as a replacement. This coincides with the rejection of the tribe of Ephraim and the divine choosing of David from the tribe of Judah to provide a royal line to lead the people of Israel.[10] The convergence of these events is highly significant (cf. Ps. 78:59–72).

In due course the appointment of David leads to the building of the Temple at Jerusalem by Solomon, David's son. The close connection between the 'house of God' (i.e. the Temple) and the 'house of David' (i.e. the dynasty) is underlined in 2 Samuel 7 (cf. 1 Chr. 17). In the light of this, it is hardly surprising that the futures of both monarchy and Temple are intimately connected. Moreover, the special 'Father–son' relationship established between God and David is reflected in the close proximity of the divine and human palaces.[11]

God's presence in Jerusalem holds out great potential for the Davidic dynasty and the people of Judah. However, the book of Kings reveals that this is jeopardized by the sins of David's descendants. While the presence of the LORD among the Israelites should have been a source

---

[9] Two factors point in this direction. Firstly, Judges 18:31 speaks of the 'house of God' (*bêt-hā'ĕlōhîm*) being located at Shiloh, and later 1 Samuel 1:9 refers to Eli sitting at the gate of the 'temple of the Lord' (*hêkal yhwh*) (cf. 1 Sam. 1:24). Secondly, Judges 21:19 and 1 Samuel 1:3 both suggest that Shiloh was the location to which Israelites travelled annually to celebrate a feast before the Lord.

[10] See the essay by Pitkänen.

[11] In Hebrew the same term, *hêkal*, is translated as 'temple' or 'palace'.

of blessing, bringing peace, prosperity and security, their rebellious nature produces the opposite effect.

5. THE DESTRUCTION OF THE TEMPLE

Eventually, as the final chapters of Kings describe, the city of Jerusalem is sacked by the Babylonians, the Temple is destroyed and the Davidic monarchy is removed from its position of authority. In all of this there are echoes of the time of Samuel, when God abandoned his people, handing them over to their enemies. Nevertheless, whereas God previously rejected Shiloh and the line of Ephraim (cf. Jer. 7:8–15; 26:4–9), he does not completely abandon Jerusalem and the royal line of Judah (cf. Jer. 33:14–26). Due to the divine commitment previously made to David, restoration will occur after a time of exile.

The destruction of the Temple, God's house, sends a dramatic theological message to the people of Jerusalem and Judah. Due to their sinful activities, many of which took place within the Temple area, their God is no longer willing to dwell among them. To a people indoctrinated into believing in the invincibility of Jerusalem, based on God's covenant promises, the Temple's demise raises profound questions. Has God revoked his commitment to the people? How do these events affect God's purposes regarding the blessing of the nations through a royal descendant of Abraham?

In the light of such questions, the book of Ezekiel conveys an important message. Although God's house has been destroyed, his commitment to the 'righteous remnant' of Israel remains steadfast. While God may have departed from his house, distancing himself from the guilty, he reveals himself in glorious splendour to the exiled Ezekiel in distant Babylon. Through this event, which plays a central role in summoning Ezekiel to prophetic office, God discloses that he is not confined to the Temple in Jerusalem. Moreover, Ezekiel's vision of the restored land and new Temple in chapters 40–48 emphasizes God's commitment to his redemptive purposes for the world. The transformation of the city from Jerusalem (*Yerushalayim*) to 'Yahweh is there' (*Yahweh-Shammah*) (Ezek. 48:35) is a powerful reminder that God is in control of all that happens. Although the sins of the people of Judah, and especially those of certain Davidic kings, cause God to punish the people, he remains firmly committed to fulfilling his previous undertakings. At the same time, the symbolic nature of the vision of the new Temple leaves open the issue of how things will develop in the future.

6. THE TEMPLE RECONSTRUCTED

When the Persian emperor Cyrus the Great conquers the Babylonians in 538 BC he issues an edict (see Ezra 1:1–4; 6:1–5) permitting Judean exiles to return home and rebuild the Temple. Eventually, it is completed and rededicated (in 516 or 515 BC), but not before the prophets Haggai and Zechariah have had to intervene in order to encourage the inhabitants of Jerusalem to complete the reconstruction. As the books of Haggai and Zechariah highlight, the restoration of the Temple was divinely sanctioned, underlining God's ongoing commitment to Judah and its population.

In the biblical writings of the post-exilic period, the building of the Temple forms an important step towards the restoration of the Davidic line. In the books of Haggai and Zechariah, this is reflected in the role played especially by Zerubbabel in overseeing the whole project. Although never designated 'king', Zerubbabel was a descendant of David. Similarly, the book of Chronicles recounts at length, and in more detail than in Samuel–Kings, the close connection between the Jerusalem Temple and the Davidic monarchy. Writing about 300 BC, from the perspective of the Temple having been restored, the Chronicler urges the people to see it as a place where prayers of repentance may be offered to God in order that the Davidic line may once more reign.

7. THE ADVENT OF JESUS

When Jesus comes on the scene, the Temple becomes a key locus of activity. In the Markan prologue the heavenly voice of God tells the Son that his path will be prepared. The context of the reference to Malachi 3:1 identifies the messenger as John and the Lord as Jesus of Nazareth. There is no explicit reference in the Markan context to the Lord coming to the Temple, since the Malachi quote is cut off to make way for the 'voice' of Isaiah 40:3. [12] However, it is noteworthy that the triumphal entry in the synoptic gospels is immediately followed by the cleansing of the Temple. Briefly after, when Jesus is in discussion with his opponents in Mark 12:35–37, it is in the Temple that he makes the boldest statement thus far in the Gospel about his identity as Lord (cf. Mal. 3:1); it could thus be said that the Temple becomes the location of the revelation of Jesus' lordship, as he expounds the meaning of the statement 'The LORD said to my Lord' in Psalm 110:1.

The Temple is also an instrument for Jesus' public revelation as Son of God in Mark. In Mark 1:11, the declaration of Jesus' divine Sonship takes place in a voice from heaven, following the division of the

---

[12] Malachi 3:1: 'See I will send my messenger who will prepare the way before me. Then suddenly, the Lord whom you are seeking will come to his temple; the messenger of the covenant, whom you desire, will come.' Cf. Mark 1:2–3: 'I will send my messenger ahead of you, who will prepare your way – a voice of one calling in the desert, "Prepare the way for the Lord, make straight paths for him."'

heavens and the descent of the dove. In Mark 15:37–39, Jesus breathes his last, and this is immediately followed, echoing that earlier 'division' of the heavens, by the division in two of the curtain in the Temple.[13] It seems to be the final exspiration of Jesus and the breaking of the Temple curtain which leads the centurion to cry out 'surely this man was the Son of God' (15:39), the first confession of its kind by a human person in the Gospel. Thus the Temple in Mark's narrative is co-opted into becoming a witness to the divine Sonship of Jesus, revealed in his death. Although there is not space here to deal with, or even summarize effectively, the picture in the other gospels, we can see a similar function for the Temple in Luke 2:49, where it serves as the context for a startling expression of Jesus' self-understanding as Son of God.

Although the two accounts should not be prematurely conflated, there is much in Mark's account of the passion that anticipates the more developed interpretation of the atoning death of Christ in Hebrews (as described in Motyer's essay above). The Temple concept is explored there as Jesus' death and exaltation is seen as his passing behind the curtain in the heavenly sanctuary (Heb. 6:19–20), or again as Jesus' own crucified body is seen as the curtain through which we can pass in order to approach God (Heb. 10:20). This latter element is probably implied in the Markan narrative, inasmuch as the juxtaposition of the rending of the curtain and the confession of the centurion strongly suggests a new access to God effected by the death of Jesus. Thus the atoning death of Christ is recounted in narrative form here, as well as being described elsewhere in propositional form (as in, for example, Mark 10:45).

One final aspect of the treatment of the gospels that should not go unnoticed is the light they shed on the destruction of the Temple in AD 70. The sacking of Jerusalem is seen by the evangelists as one of the initial signs preceding the end, before the coming of the Son of Man (Mark 13:1–23 and parallels). Further, it is particularly clear in Matthew that the destruction of the Temple is the consequence of the rejection of Jesus. In Matthew 23:13, Jesus begins a series of woes, pronounced from the Temple, which continues properly speaking to the end of the chapter. Towards the end of these woes, Jesus emphasizes the way in which the generation of his contemporaries had followed completely the sinful precedents set by their forefathers, in their decisive rejection of himself (Matt. 32:37). As a result, Jesus announces the desertion of the Temple by God (Matt. 23:28), a desertion which Jesus perhaps is then depicted as enacting two verses later: 'And Jesus left, and walked away from the temple ...' (Matt. 24:1). Immediately, then, in response to the question from the disciples, he tells them that the building will be

---

[13] See Peter Head's essay on the Temple in Luke for discussion of the different possibilities for the interpretation of this curtain.

utterly demolished: 'not one stone will be left upon another which will not be destroyed' (Matt. 24:2).

8. INTERPRETING THE TEMPLE

In the New Testament books placed after the gospels and Acts in the canon, the Temple is often interpreted in ways other than simply in reference to the physical building. These interpretations are a vital guide to us in the conclusions that we draw about the Temple for Christian theology. As noted above, for many Christians, the Temple is something of an irrelevance. On the other hand, in some periods in the history of the church, the Temple has attracted great interest, and this has led to a good deal of imaginative allegorizing along the way. When James Palmer first read his paper on Exodus in the conference that led to this collection of essays, he began by recounting an old example of a Christological interpretation of the Tabernacle from J. F. Cramer, who, on the basis of the square shape of the Tabernacle, asks the question 'in what sense can Christ be square?'[14] On the other hand, Stephen Sizer's essay documents a rather more sinister interest in the building. It may be helpful, then, to indicate some of the strategies which are a *sine qua non* for Christian interpretation of the Old Testament, and which this book aims, to some extent, to exemplify.

The first test which any Christian theology of such Old Testament institutions as Temple, Law or priesthood must pass is the test of Christology. Despite protests to the contrary, it is always insufficient to produce an account of (say) the Temple which does not see how it functions as a witness to Christ. (This, as Norgate's essay indicated, is a helpful emphasis in Barth's theology.) The attempt in this volume has consequently been to combine Old and New Testament papers together so that one cannot simply be left with the impression of a spurious theology of the Old Testament 'on its own terms'. In this respect, the above essays (especially the New Testament pieces) should challenge the assumption that we can simply import certain aspects of the Temple into Christian thinking, whether that means equating parts of church buildings with the parts of the Temple, or reading the Old Testament in other ways which simply bypass the New. Christological interpretation of the Temple is not simply an option, but a necessity.

Secondly, however, any Christian theology worth the name must pass the test of having dealt rigorously with the Old Testament text. There is a danger of a Marcionite ignoring of the Temple, or of an understanding of the Temple which only looks seriously at the New Testament texts.

---

[14] Noted in B. S. Childs, *The Book of Exodus* (OTL; Louisville: Westminster Press, 1974), p. 548.

There is also another Scylla and Charybdis to be avoided, however. New Testament study has historically been guilty at times of anti-Semitism, and this danger lurks in the background whenever we as Christian theologians examine aspects of the Old Testament. On this issue, the Temple has not been as much of a victim as the Law, for example, but because of the considerable overlap, the Temple service can often be caricatured as reliant upon multitudes of silly minutiae for the proper running of the ritual. This should be viewed as self-evidently false, since the Old Testament Law ought to be regarded by Christians as 'holy, righteous, and good' (Rom. 7:12).

On the other hand, however, there is also the danger in the opposite direction: it is possible in the attempt to safeguard interpreters against anti-Semitism to canonize certain theological principles which can at times lead to a distortion of the biblical evidence. One such dogma is the a priori rejection in some circles of any kind of supersessionism. While some theologians have articulated a supersession of the nation of Israel in ways which are certainly unhelpful, the ideas of the replacement of Israel or that the church is a third entity made from both Jew and Gentile are certainly not theological positions which should be removed from discussion at the outset. The Temple provides us with an interesting case study here, and we have seen varying positions put forward in the essays above.

Some of the contributors to this volume would strongly maintain the position that the physical Old Testament Temple was always part of the divine plan, both for Israel's worship and as a witness to Christ. Scholars have proposed differing interpretations of the controversial reference to God's refusal to 'dwell in temples made of human hands' in Acts 7. Walton, in his essay on Acts above, explains clearly the arguments on both sides and concludes that even here the Temple is not to be regarded as a mistake. Armerding, on the other hand, takes the position that an attentive reading of some Old Testament passages may point to a divine scepticism about the validity of the Temple-building enterprise (cf. the similar comments by Fyall). It is important that all these attempts to deal with the biblical data in its entirety should be given a hearing without prior commitments to what results should appear.

9. THE TEMPLE AND CHRISTIAN DOCTRINE

In our discourse about *God*, the Temple highlights very clearly the way in which God in salvation history elects to deal with people in special ways. If what we have said about Mark's Gospel above is true, then the Temple is God's chosen instrument implicated in the process of revelation, specifically the revelation of Jesus' lordship and divine Sonship. Similarly, Walton has highlighted the way in which in Acts, too, the Temple is a locus of revelation. On the other hand, already in Ezekiel we see the way in which God rejects his people's attempts to confine him to a specific sphere of action on account of his infinite 'mobility', and this critique finds its strongest expression in Stephen's speech in Acts 7. The critique of things 'made by human hands' in fact ties in with a general early Christian hermeneutic of the Old Testament, which is instructive for Christian theology's reflection on how the two testaments cohere. The critique of temples made by human hands in Acts 7:48 and 17:24 (cf. Heb. 9:11; 9:24) finds analogy in the criticism of circumcision done by human hands (Col. 2:11) and the transitory nature of our biologically generated bodies in contrast with our new bodies, to accompany our transformation, which are not made by human hands (2 Cor. 5:1). This fits in with a general pattern in New Testament (and especially Pauline) theology, whereby what belongs to the human realm has no capacity in itself for eternal duration or divine approval. It could further be paralleled with the category of 'the flesh' (*sarx*) which exhibits the same inability (Rom. 3:20; 8:3, 7).

In terms of the application of our understanding of the Temple to *Christology*, we have already noted briefly above the way in which the New Testament uses the sacrificial system to illuminate Christ's atoning death on the cross. We also need to consider the dimension of divine fellowship with humanity, since this is also a key aspect of the Temple's symbolism.[15] There is of course considerable debate over the extent to which the presence of God is to be taken 'literally' or 'metaphorically' in the statements about God's dwelling or about the location of his 'name'. Whatever is the case with regard to these, the presence of Christ among his people, which is the result of the incarnation, is to be taken as a kind of immediate presence: the Emmanuel is not the presence with us of someone very like or very close to God: he is in fact God with us. As Steve Walton noted in connection with the book of Acts, it is not the Temple which is ultimately 'heaven on earth', but Christ himself. Again, the whole tenor of John's Gospel is that 'we' have actually seen God in the manifestation of Christ. This applies further to those who, post-Pentecost, do not see Christ in the flesh, but who are in possession of the Spirit. Those of us who are Christians today are by no means disadvantaged in our experience of God, which is just as immediate and direct. It would probably be inappropriate to talk of the 'mediation' of God's (or Christ's) presence to us by the Spirit since the danger of such a formula (1 Tim. 2:5 notwithstanding) is that it would imply a degree of separation which is alleviated through something which is neither one thing nor the other.

---

[15] As the essays by Fyall and Norgate both note in different ways, the Temple and the contexts in which it is mentioned highlight both the transcendence and the immanent presence of God. Solomon observes in his prayer of dedication that even the heavens cannot hold God, and so how much less the Temple (1 Kgs. 8:27)! On the other hand, Barth notes neatly that God is everywhere, but not only everywhere: he also elects to dwell or reveal himself in specific localities.

Via Christology, the Temple becomes important for the articulation of Christian *ecclesiology*. It is here, then, that the challenge to Zionism and other forms of expectation for the rebuilding of a physical Temple in Jerusalem becomes most sharply focused, because the building of God's Temple is most frequently described in the New Testament as the growth of the church on the foundations of Christ, the prophets and the apostles. In fact Paul makes the principal criterion for deciding how to act within the Christian community as 'edification', or 'building' (1 Cor. 12 – 14). This is of course not without some difficulty; there remains the extremely puzzling reference to the man of lawlessness who 'will set himself up in God's temple' (2 Thess. 2:4).

The ecclesiological statements made in connection with the Temple are very often focused on the *ethics* required of the Christian community. In the Old Testament, the priesthood and the Temple belonged to the realm of perfect holiness, a point which Paul echoes in his requirement for Christians, as the Temple of God, also to be 'perfect in holiness':

> What agreement has the temple of God with idols? For we are the temple of the living God; as God said, 'I will make my dwelling among them and walk among them, and I will be their God, and they shall be my people. Therefore go out from their midst, and be separate from them, says the Lord, and touch no unclean thing; then I will welcome you, and I will be a father to you, and you shall be sons and daughters to me, says the Lord Almighty.' Since we have these promises, beloved, let us cleanse ourselves from every defilement of body and spirit, perfecting holiness in the fear of God (2 Cor. 6:16 – 7.1).

As we have seen in the essays above by Mark Bonnington and David Peterson, the Temple is also used by Paul not only to denote the church corporate, but also as an image of the physical body of the individual Christian. As such, it is to be kept scrupulously pure, and sexual sin becomes the ultimate defilement of these Temples which we possess.

The call to perfect holiness would seem to be an apt note to end on, since the goal of scholarship is not to solve puzzles but to consider how best to think about God and his action in Christ, and to live lives pleasing to him. This reflection looks not only back to God's action in the past, but also forward to the hope of the new Jerusalem in Revelation 21–22, where finally we will enjoy uninterrupted fellowship with God in Christ.[16] In appreciating the sweep of biblical revelation in both Old and New testaments, we see how the Temple, as the meeting place between God and humanity, teaches us vital lessons about how to understand his action in salvation history, how we are to understand Christ (square or otherwise!), and how we are to act in holiness. On this note, perhaps Habakkuk should be allowed to have the last word: 'The LORD is in his holy temple: let all the nations be silent before him' (Hab. 2:20).

---

[16] See Gregory Beale's essay above on this theme.

NAMES INDEX